CLOCKWORK PLANET

I

STORY BY YUU KAMIYA & TSUBAKI HIMANA
MANGA BY KURO
CHARACTER DESIGN BY SHINO

ClockWork Planet
CONTENTS

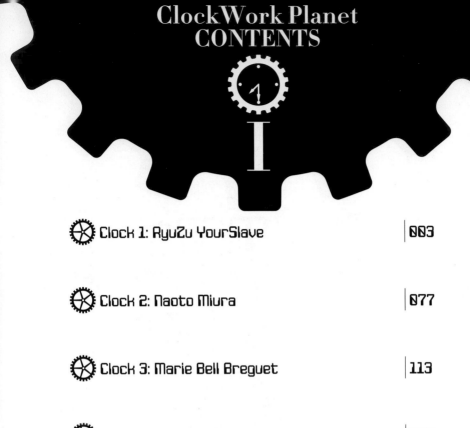

I

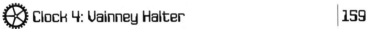

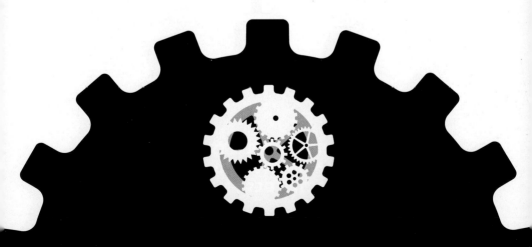

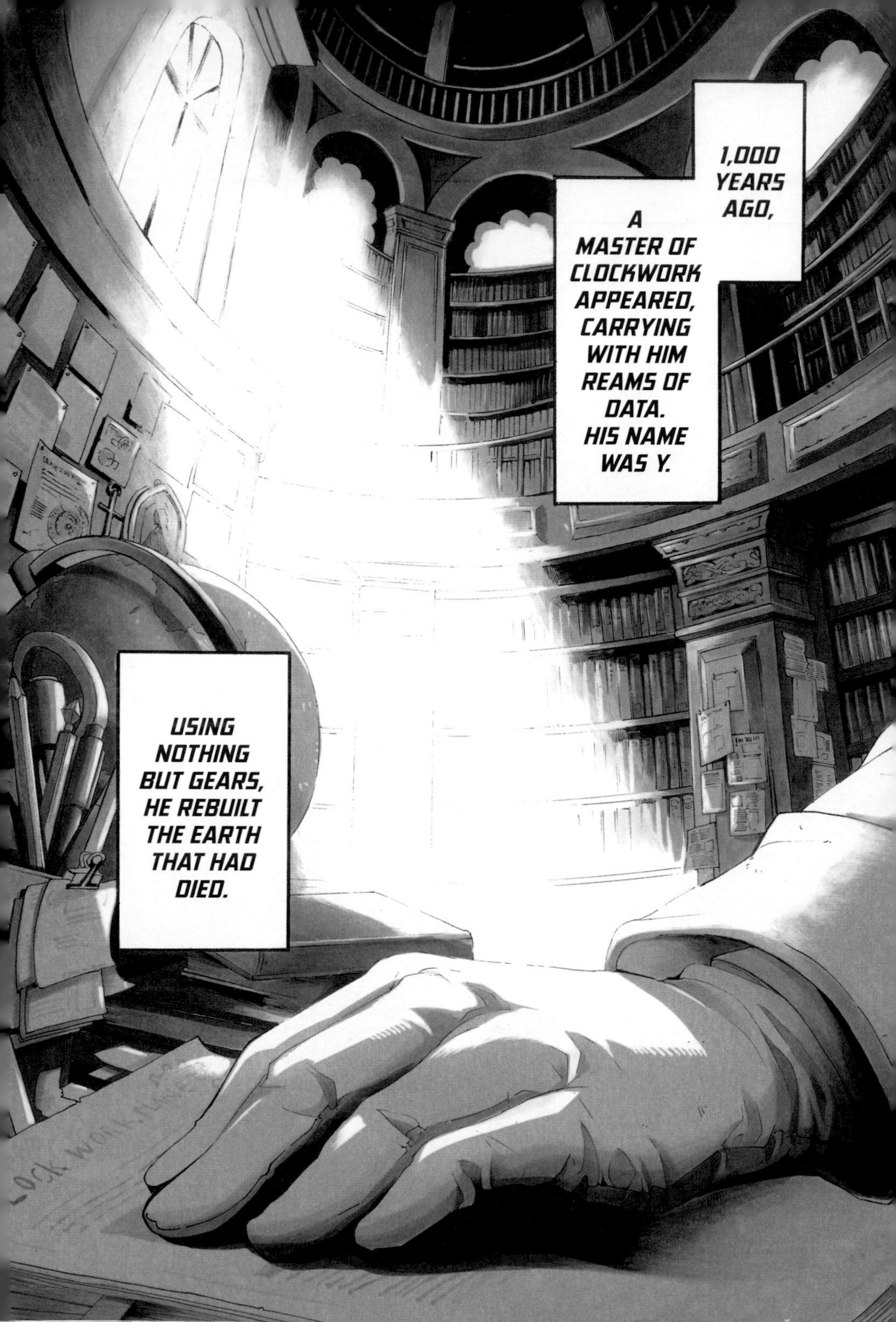
1,000 YEARS AGO,
A MASTER OF CLOCKWORK APPEARED, CARRYING WITH HIM REAMS OF DATA. HIS NAME WAS Y.
USING NOTHING BUT GEARS, HE REBUILT THE EARTH THAT HAD DIED.

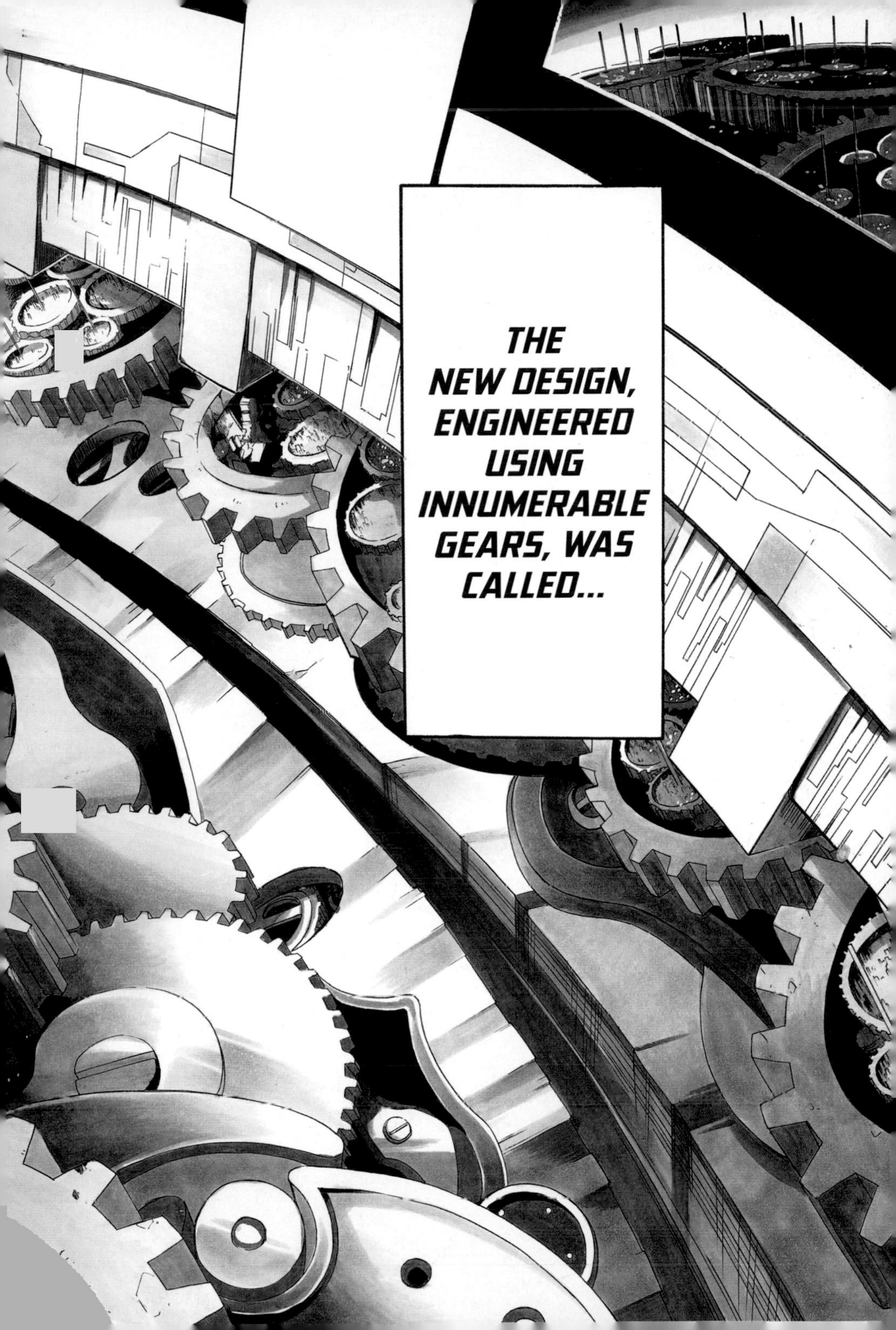
THE NEW DESIGN, ENGINEERED USING INNUMERABLE GEARS, WAS CALLED...

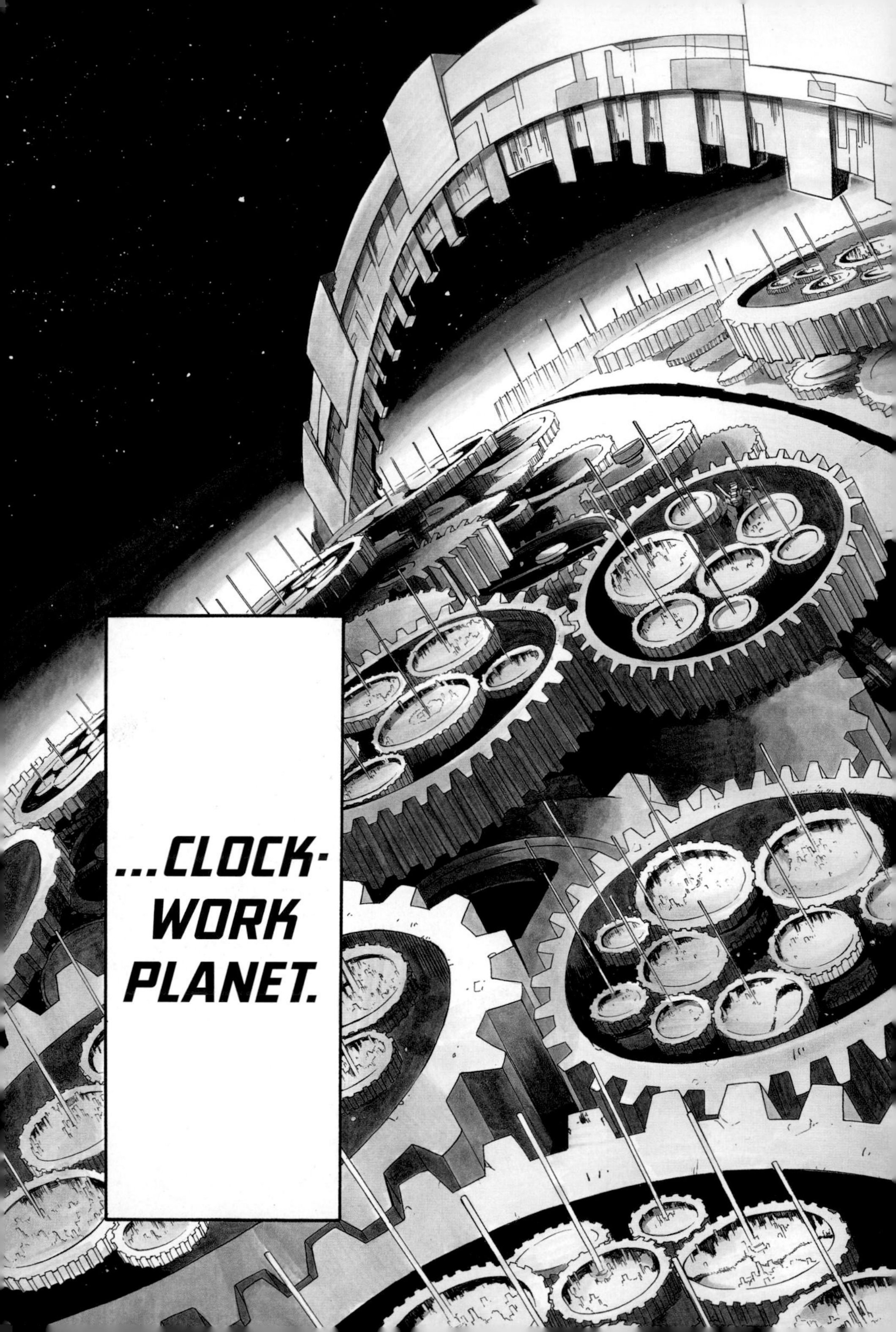
...CLOCK-WORK PLANET.

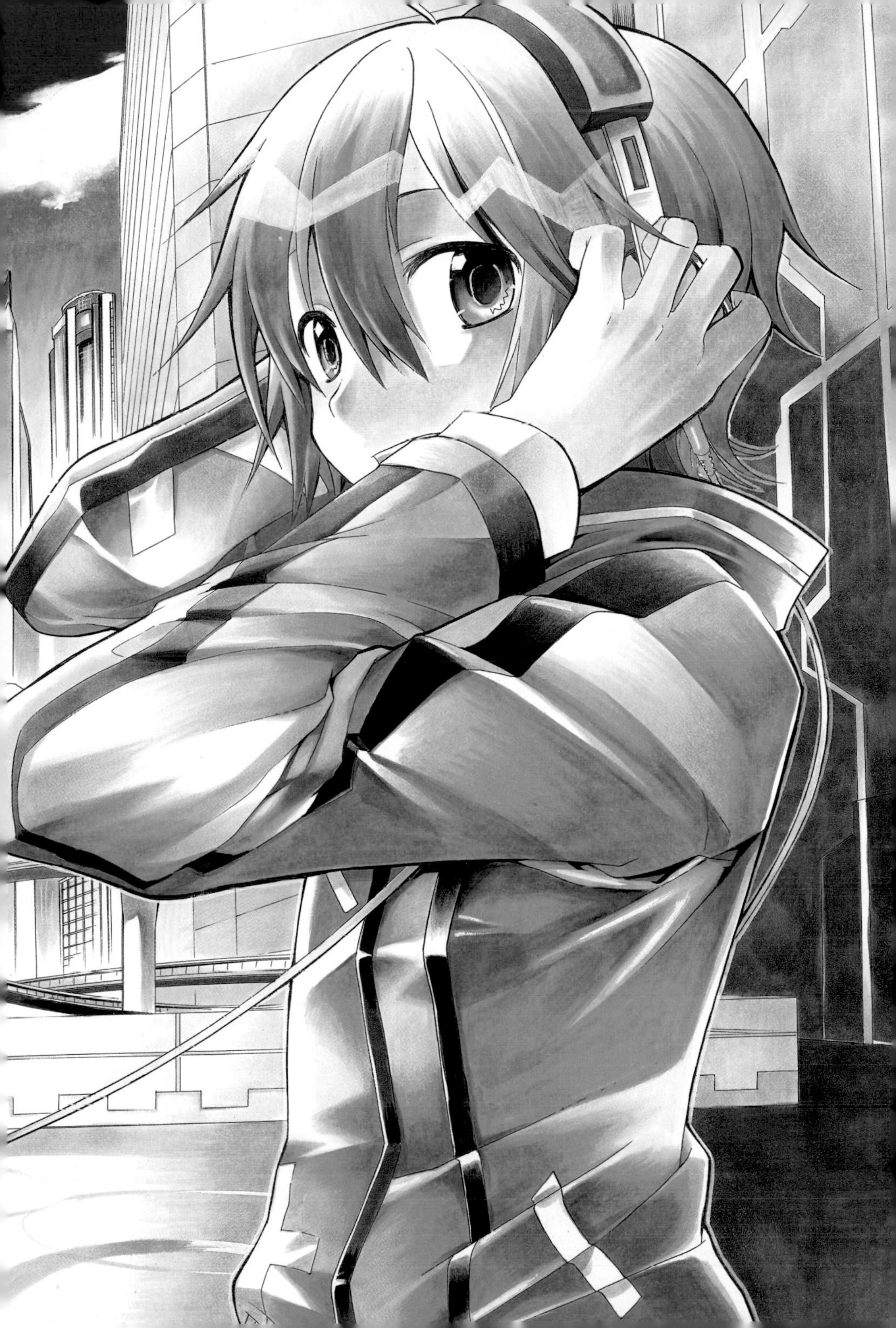

Clock 1: RyuZU YourSlave

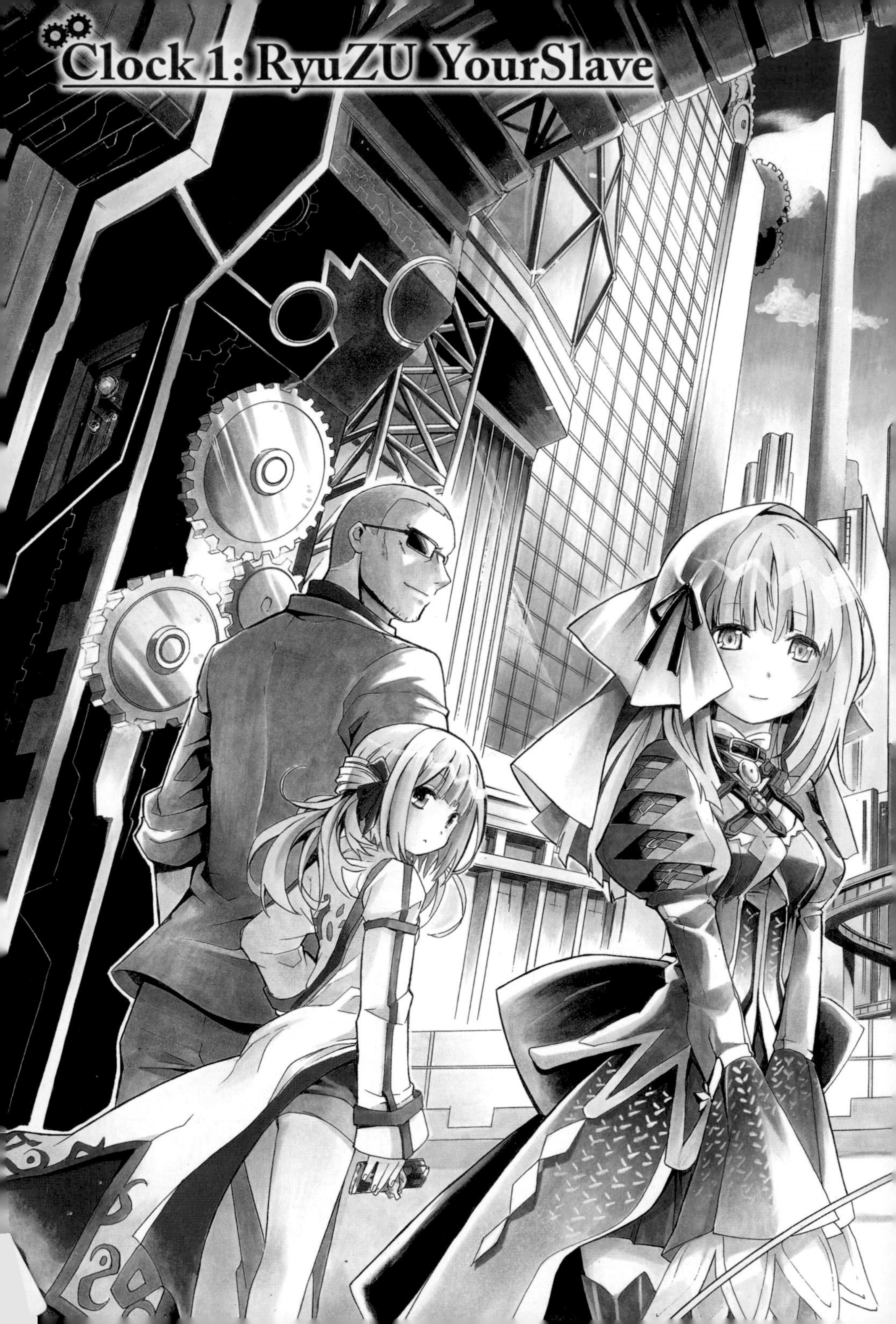

Clockwork Planet

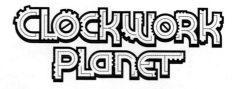

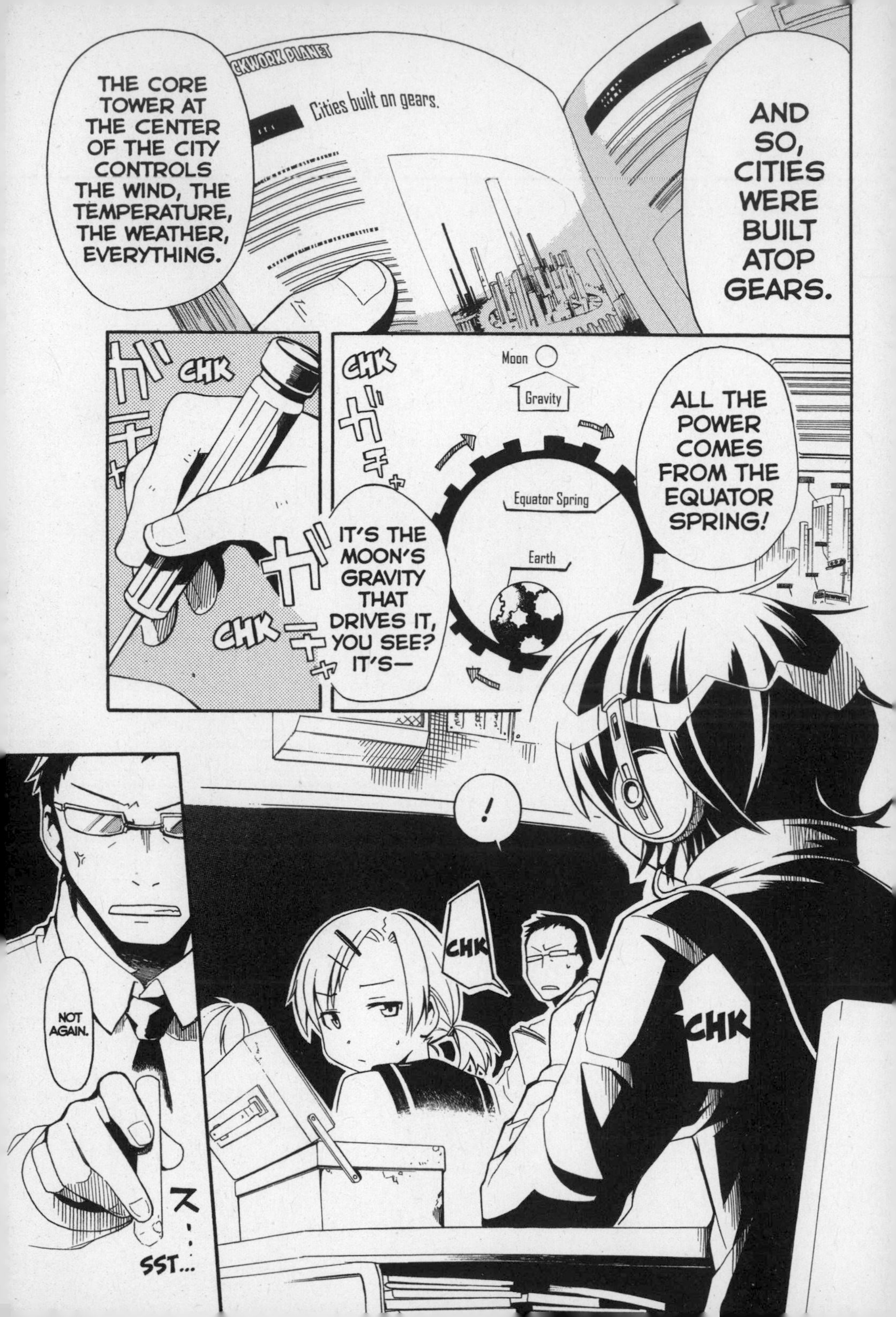
AND SO, CITIES WERE BUILT ATOP GEARS.
CKWORK PLANET
Cities built on gears.
THE CORE TOWER AT THE CENTER OF THE CITY CONTROLS THE WIND, THE TEMPERATURE, THE WEATHER, EVERYTHING.
ALL THE POWER COMES FROM THE EQUATOR SPRING!
Moon
Gravity
Equator Spring
Earth
CHK
ガチャ
IT'S THE MOON'S GRAVITY THAT DRIVES IT, YOU SEE? IT'S—
CHK
ガチャ
CHK
ガチャ
!
CHK
CHK
NOT AGAIN.
ス…
SST...

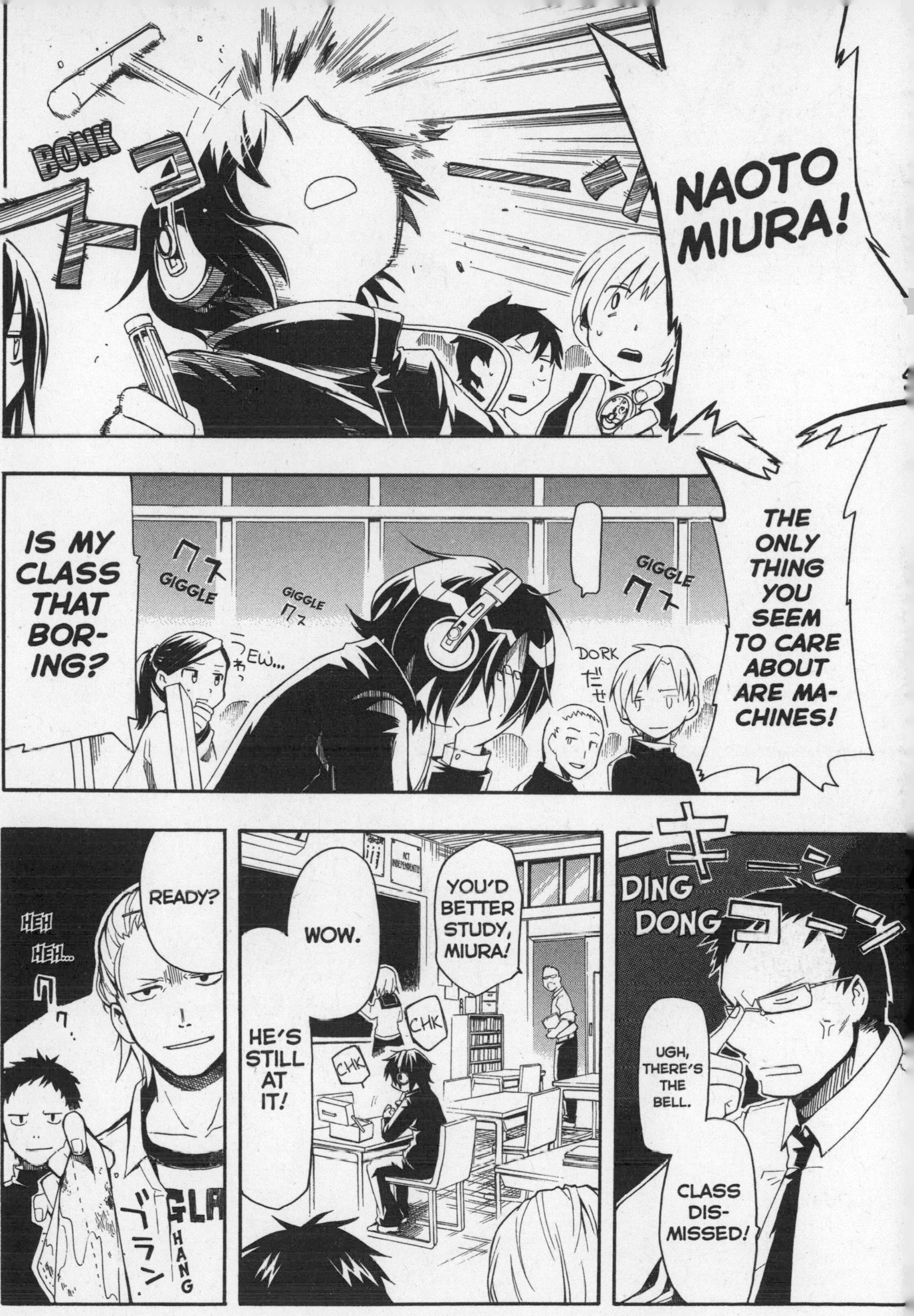
NAOTO MIURA!
BONK
THE ONLY THING YOU SEEM TO CARE ABOUT ARE MA-CHINES!
GIGGLE
DORK
GIGGLE
GIGGLE
EW...
IS MY CLASS THAT BOR-ING?
DING DONG
UGH, THERE'S THE BELL.
CLASS DIS-MISSED!
ACT INDEPENDENTLY!
YOU'D BETTER STUDY, MIURA!
WOW.
CHK
CHK
HE'S STILL AT IT!
READY?
HEH HEH...
HANG

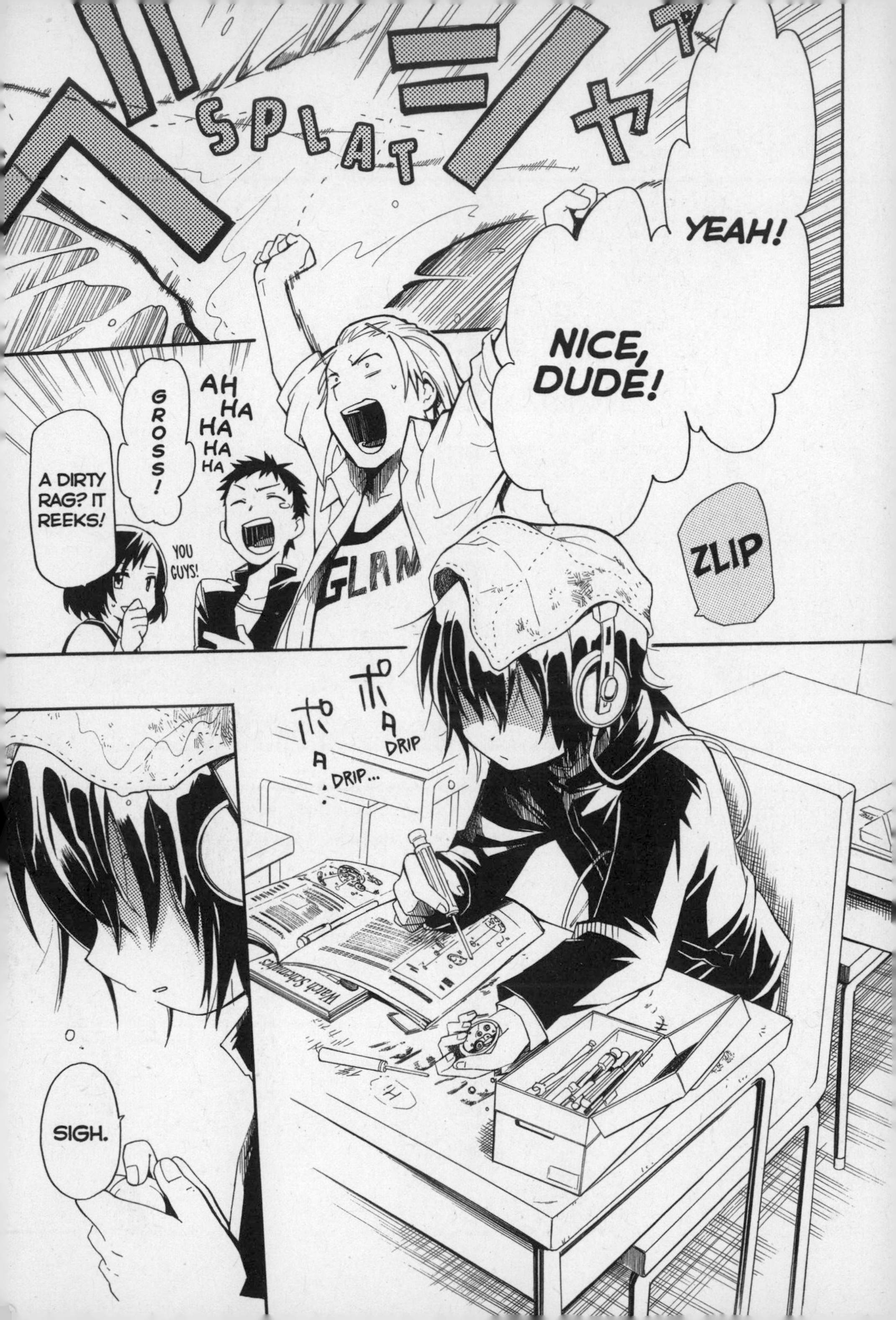
SPLAT
YEAH!
NICE, DUDE!
AH HA HA HA HA HA
GROSS!
A DIRTY RAG? IT REEKS!
YOU GUYS!
ZLIP
DRIP
DRIP...
Watch Schematics
SIGH.

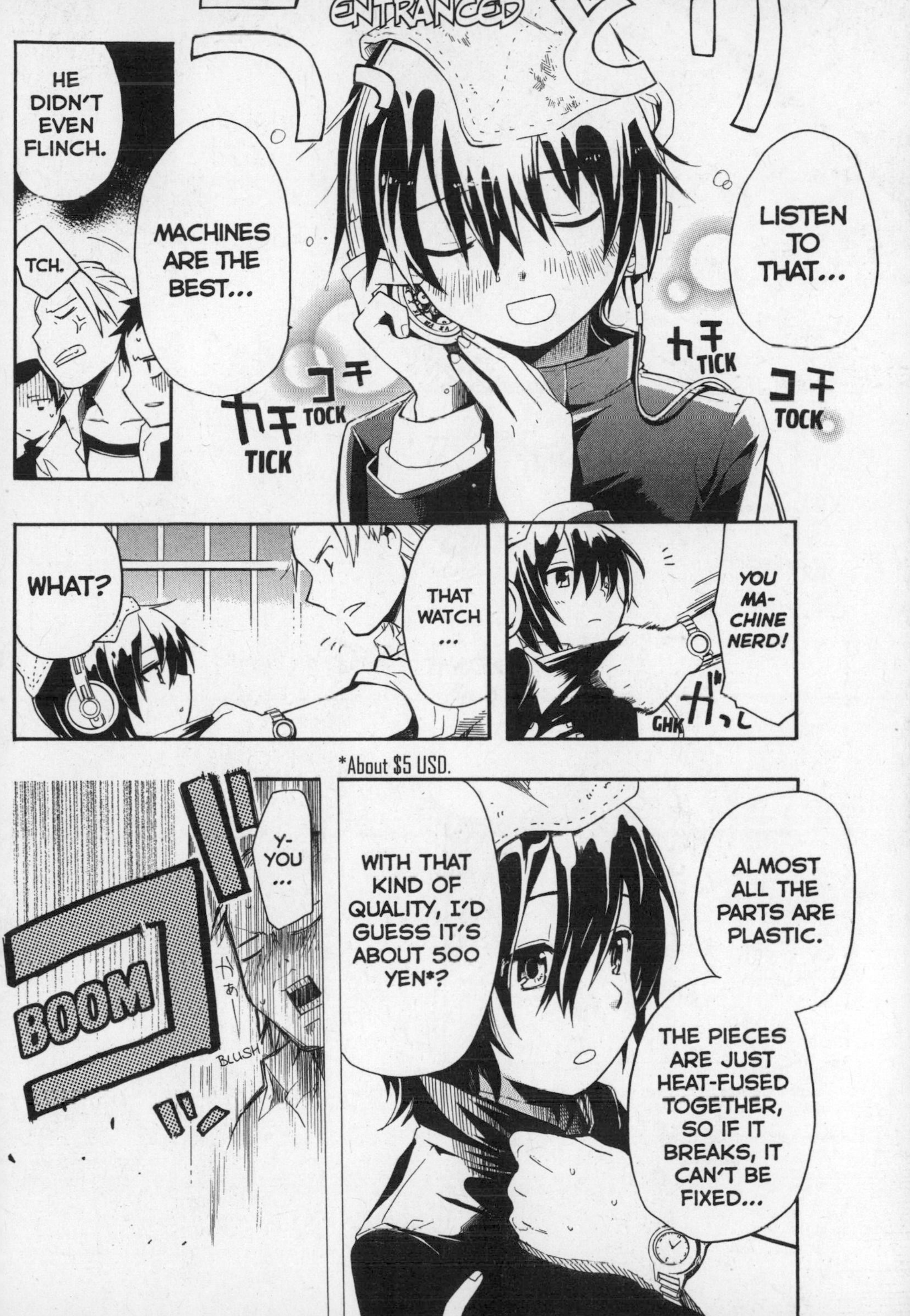
ENTRANCED
LISTEN TO THAT...
カチ TICK
コチ TOCK
コチ TOCK
カチ TICK
MACHINES ARE THE BEST...
HE DIDN'T EVEN FLINCH.
TCH.
YOU MA-CHINE NERD!
ガッし GHK
THAT WATCH ...
WHAT?
ALMOST ALL THE PARTS ARE PLASTIC.
WITH THAT KIND OF QUALITY, I'D GUESS IT'S ABOUT 500 YEN*?
THE PIECES ARE JUST HEAT-FUSED TOGETHER, SO IF IT BREAKS, IT CAN'T BE FIXED...
Y-YOU ...
BOOM
BLUSH

*About $5 USD.

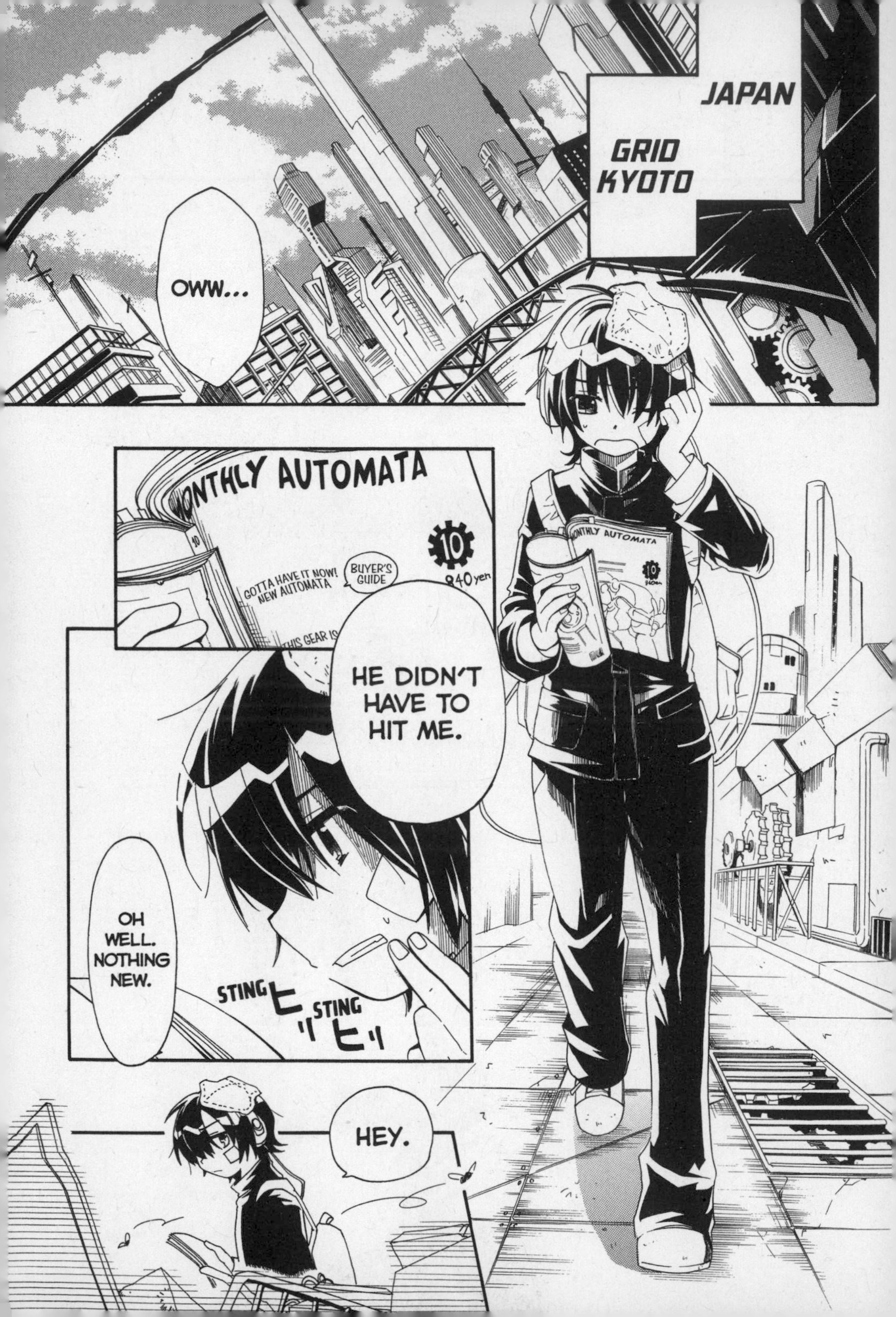

JAPAN
GRID KYOTO
OWW...
MONTHLY AUTOMATA
10
840 yen
GOTTA HAVE IT NOW! NEW AUTOMATA
BUYER'S GUIDE
THIS GEAR IS
HE DIDN'T HAVE TO HIT ME.
OH WELL. NOTHING NEW.
STING ヒリ STING ヒリ
HEY.

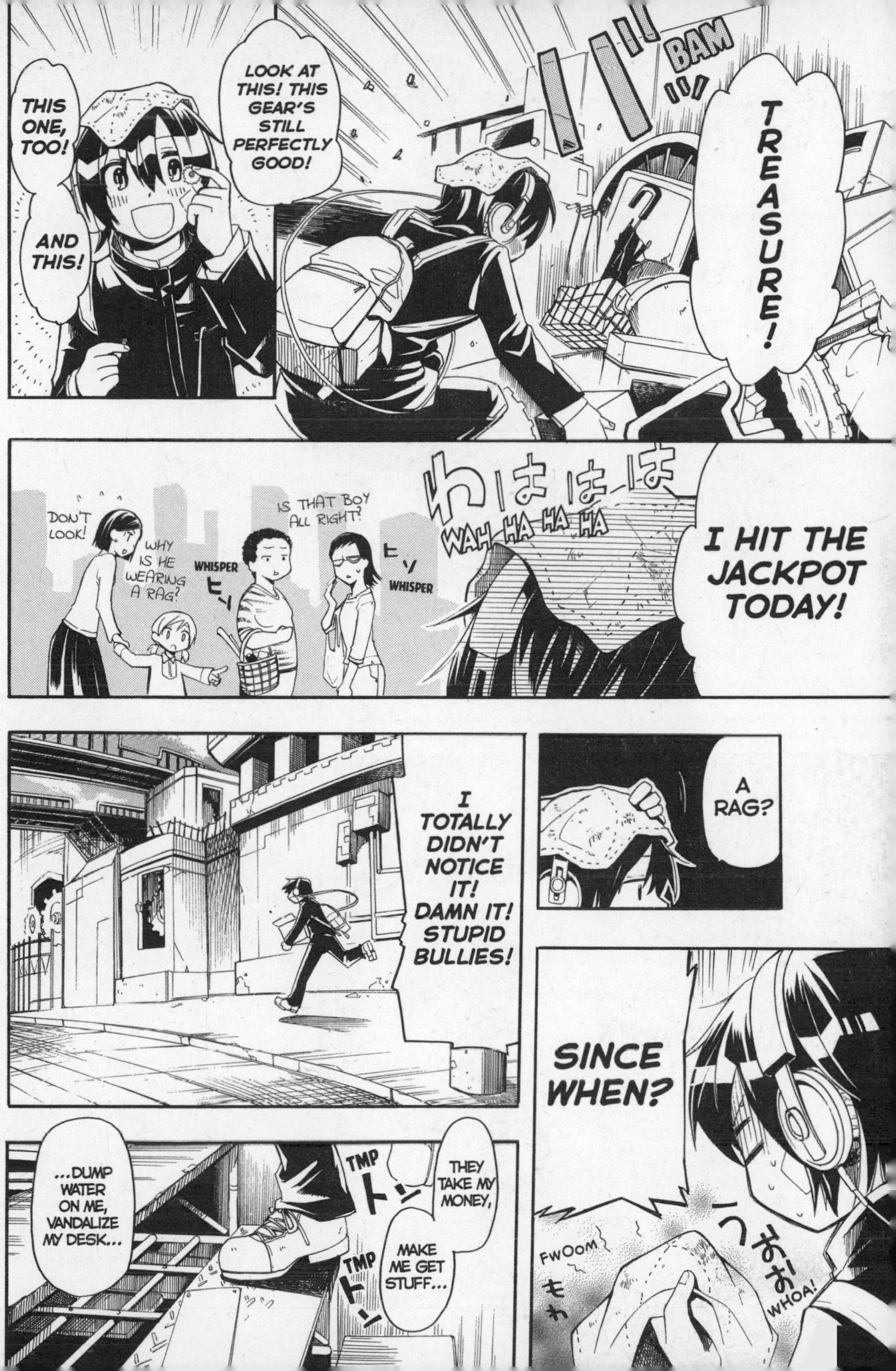
BAM
TREASURE!
LOOK AT THIS! THIS GEAR'S STILL PERFECTLY GOOD!
THIS ONE, TOO!
AND THIS!
I HIT THE JACKPOT TODAY!
わははは
WAH HA HA HA
IS THAT BOY ALL RIGHT?
ヒソ
WHISPER
DON'T LOOK!
WHY IS HE WEARING A RAG?
ヒソ
WHISPER
A RAG?
SINCE WHEN?
FWOOM
WHOA!
I TOTALLY DIDN'T NOTICE IT! DAMN IT! STUPID BULLIES!
TMP
THEY TAKE MY MONEY,
TMP
MAKE ME GET STUFF...
...DUMP WATER ON ME, VANDALIZE MY DESK...

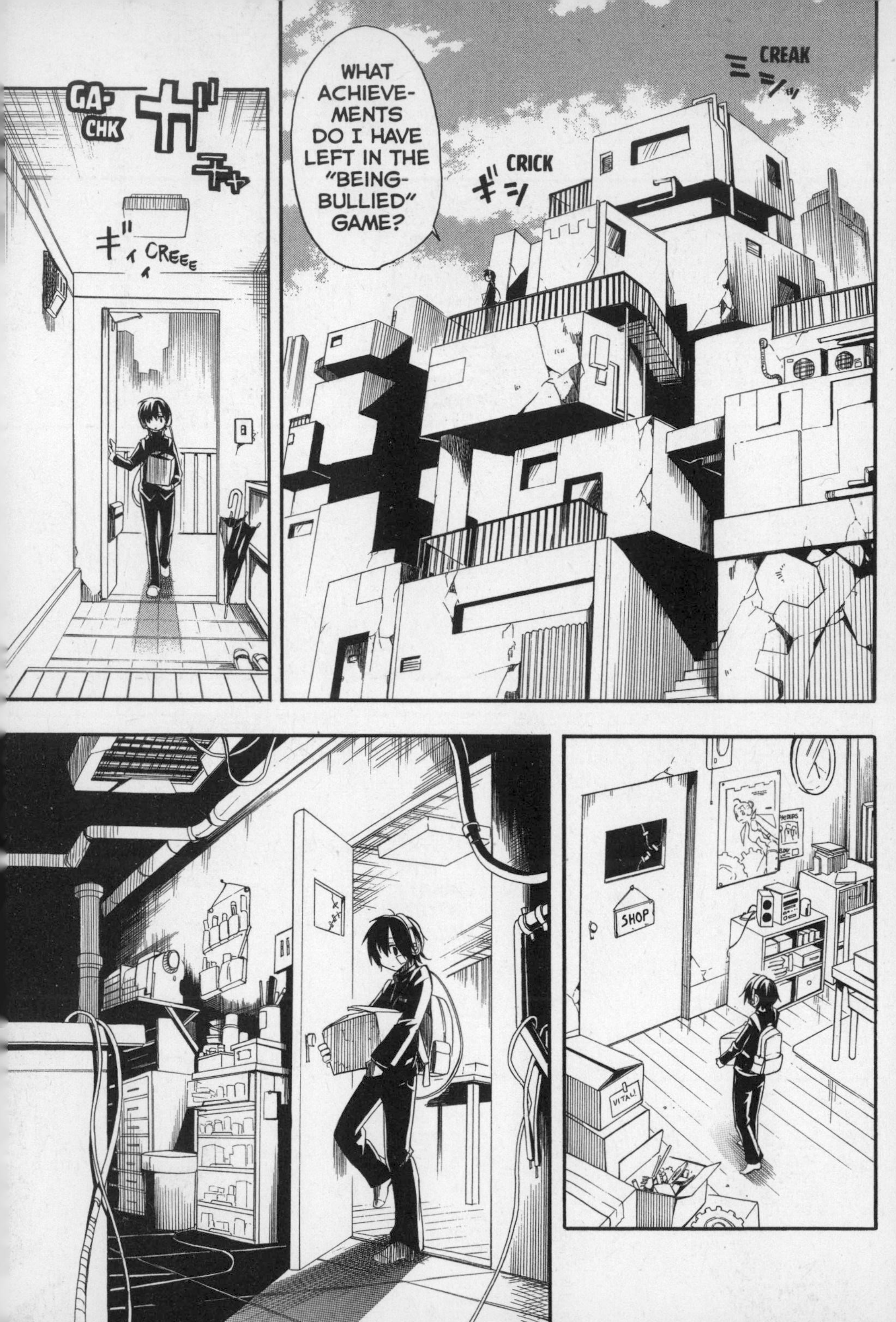

CREAK
WHAT ACHIEVEMENTS DO I HAVE LEFT IN THE "BEING-BULLIED" GAME?
CRICK
GA-CHK
CREEE
SHOP
VITAL!

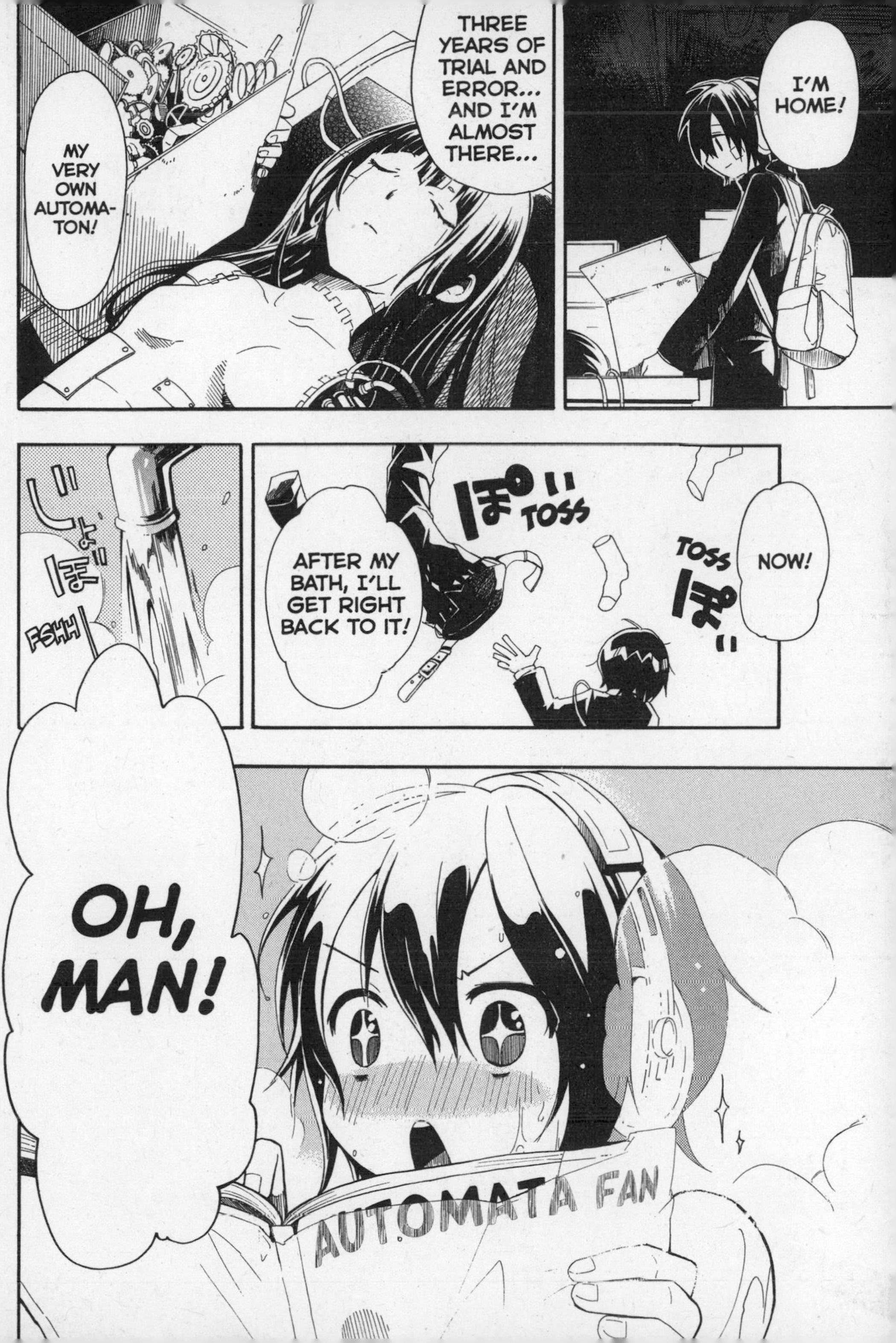
I'M HOME!
THREE YEARS OF TRIAL AND ERROR... AND I'M ALMOST THERE...
MY VERY OWN AUTOMA-TON!
NOW!
ぽい
TOSS
ぽい
TOSS
AFTER MY BATH, I'LL GET RIGHT BACK TO IT!
じょぼぼ
FSHH
OH, MAN!
AUTOMATA FAN

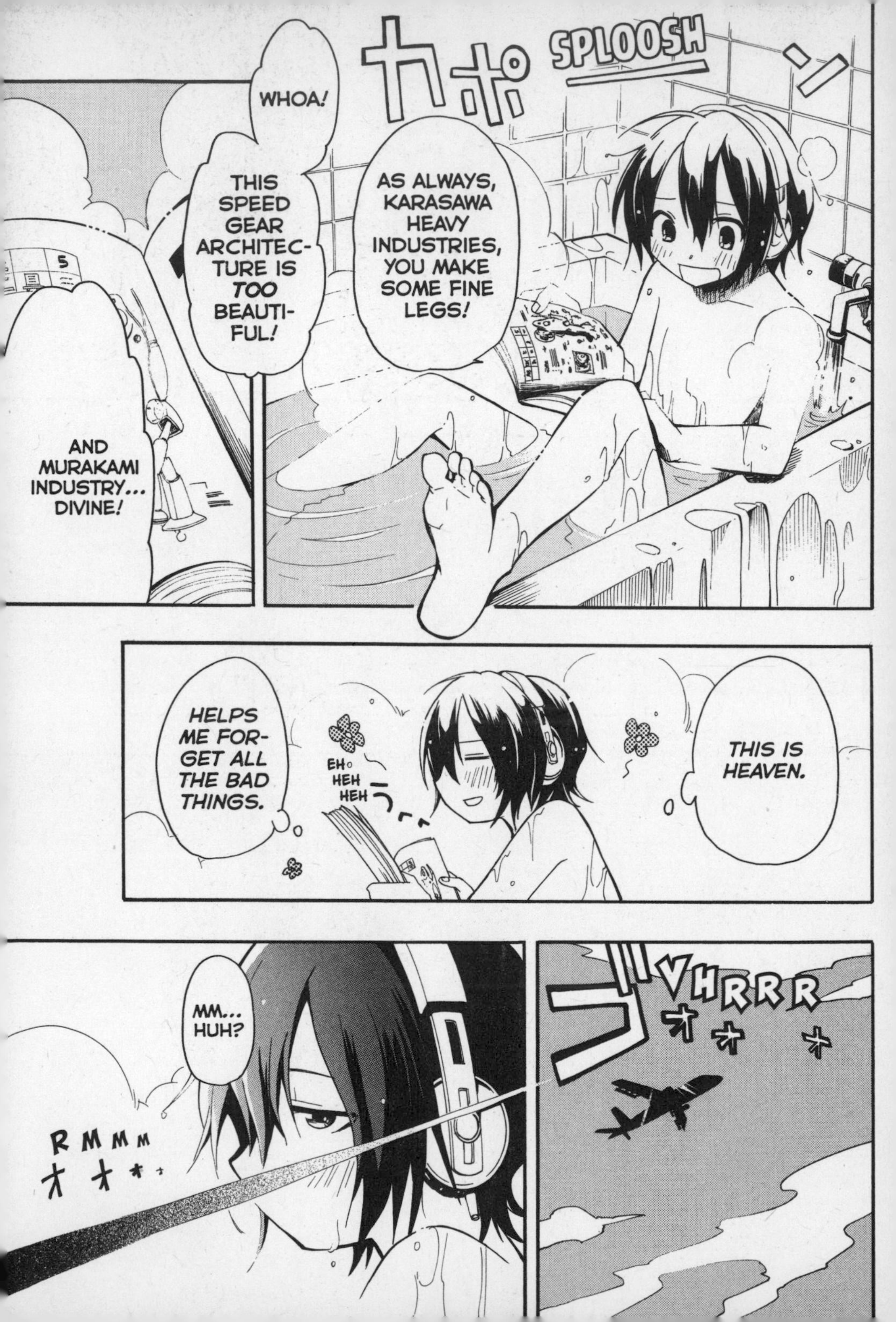
SPLOOSH
WHOA!
THIS SPEED GEAR ARCHITECTURE IS *TOO* BEAUTIFUL!
AS ALWAYS, KARASAWA HEAVY INDUSTRIES, YOU MAKE SOME FINE LEGS!
AND MURAKAMI INDUSTRY... DIVINE!
THIS IS HEAVEN.
EH HEH HEH
HELPS ME FORGET ALL THE BAD THINGS.
VHRRR
MM... HUH?
RMMM

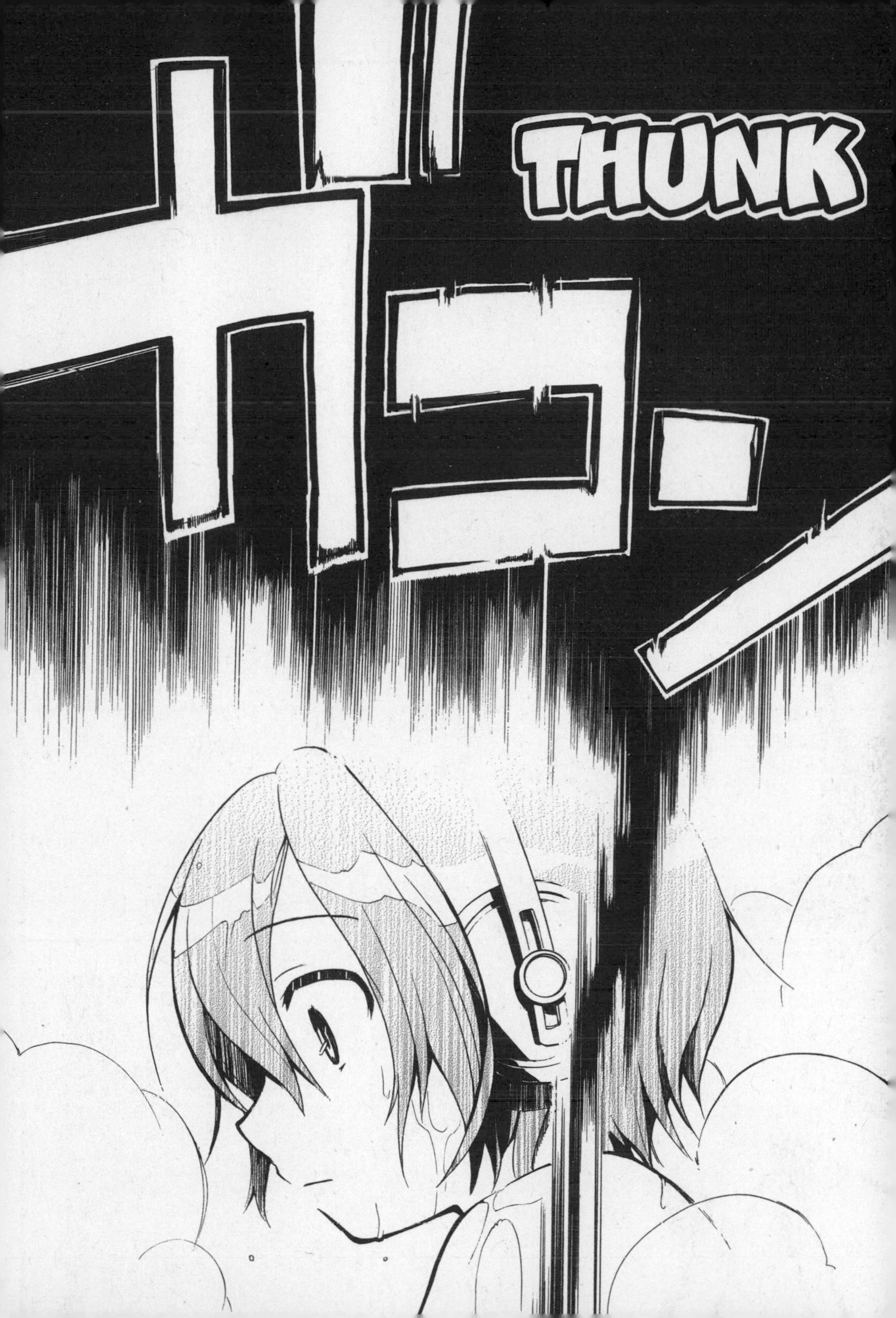
ナコ
THUNK

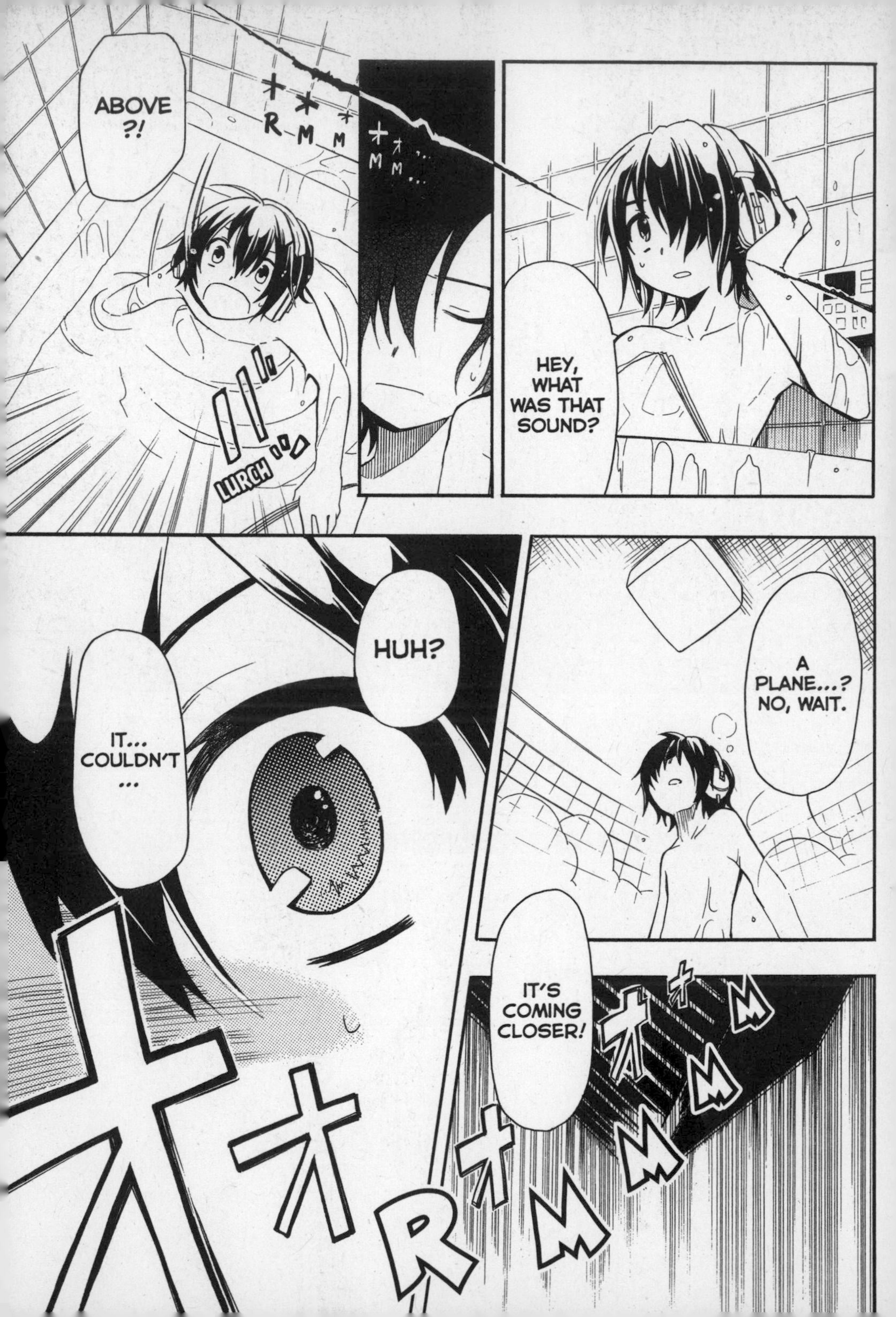
HEY, WHAT WAS THAT SOUND?
MM...
RMM
ABOVE?!
LURCH
A PLANE...? NO, WAIT.
IT'S COMING CLOSER!
HUH?
IT... COULDN'T ...
RMMMMMM

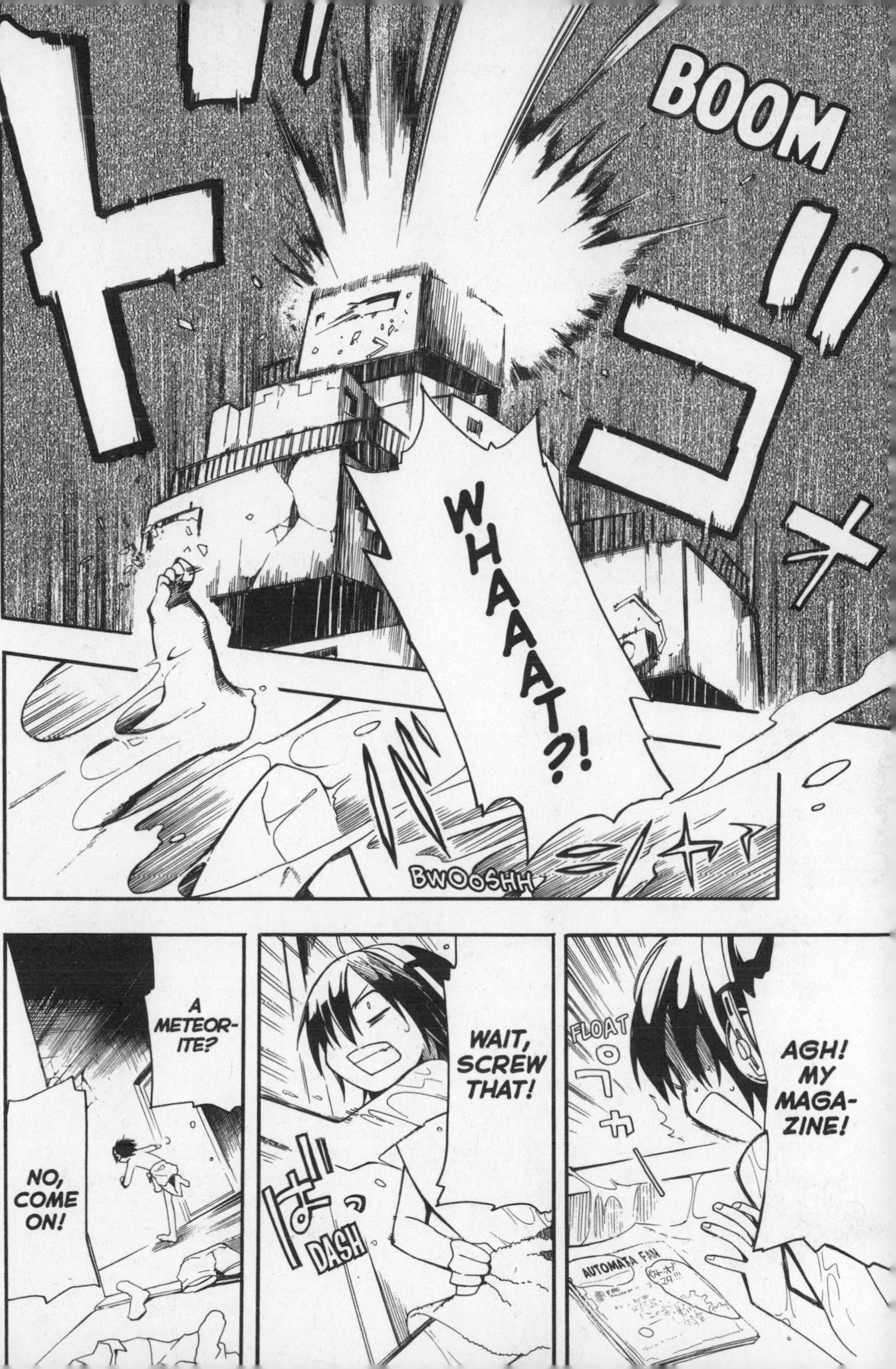
BOOM
WHAAAT?!
BWOOSHH
AGH! MY MAGA-ZINE!
FLOAT
AUTOMATA FAN
WAIT, SCREW THAT!
DASH
A METEOR-ITE?
NO, COME ON!

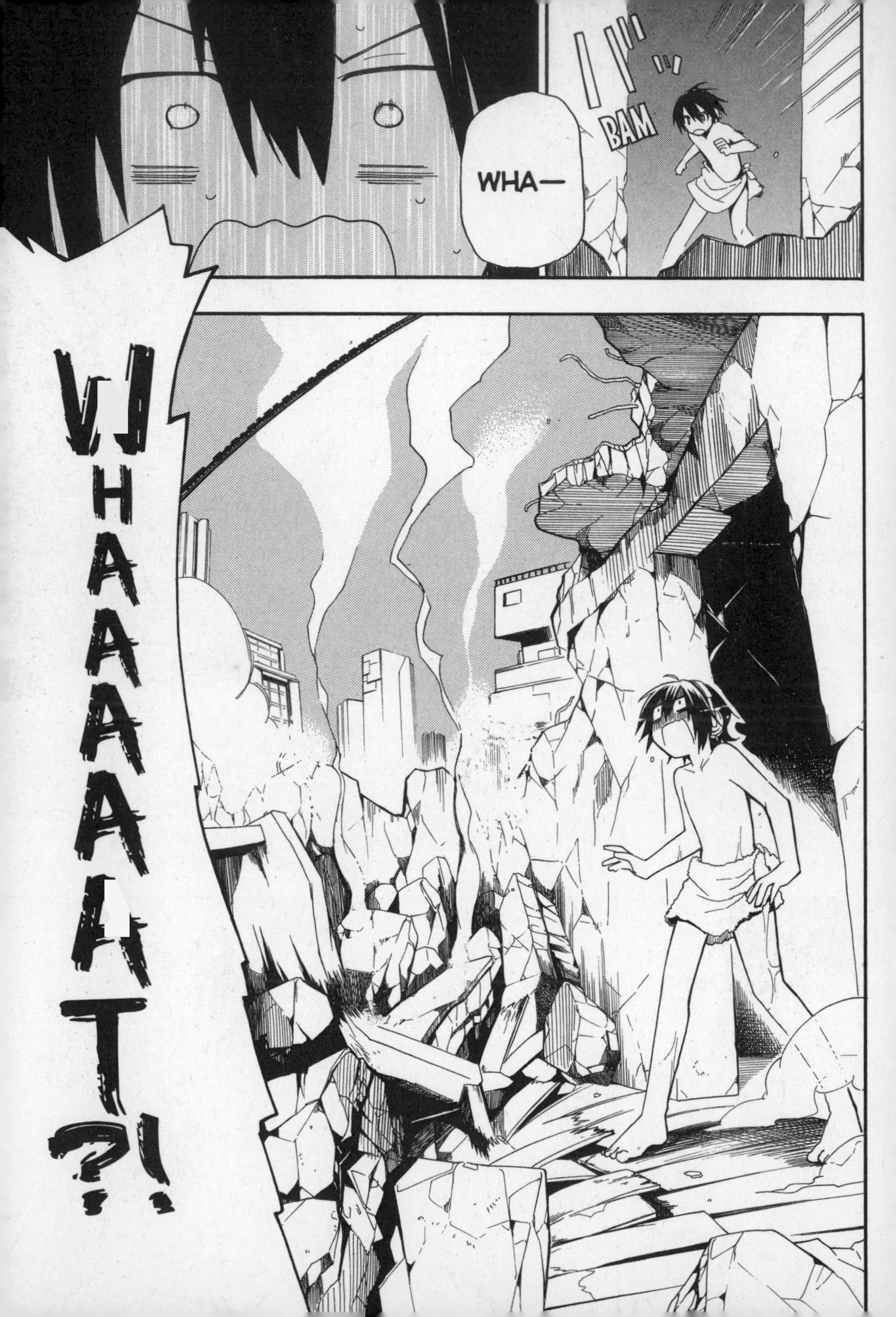
BAM
WHA—
WHAAAAAT?!

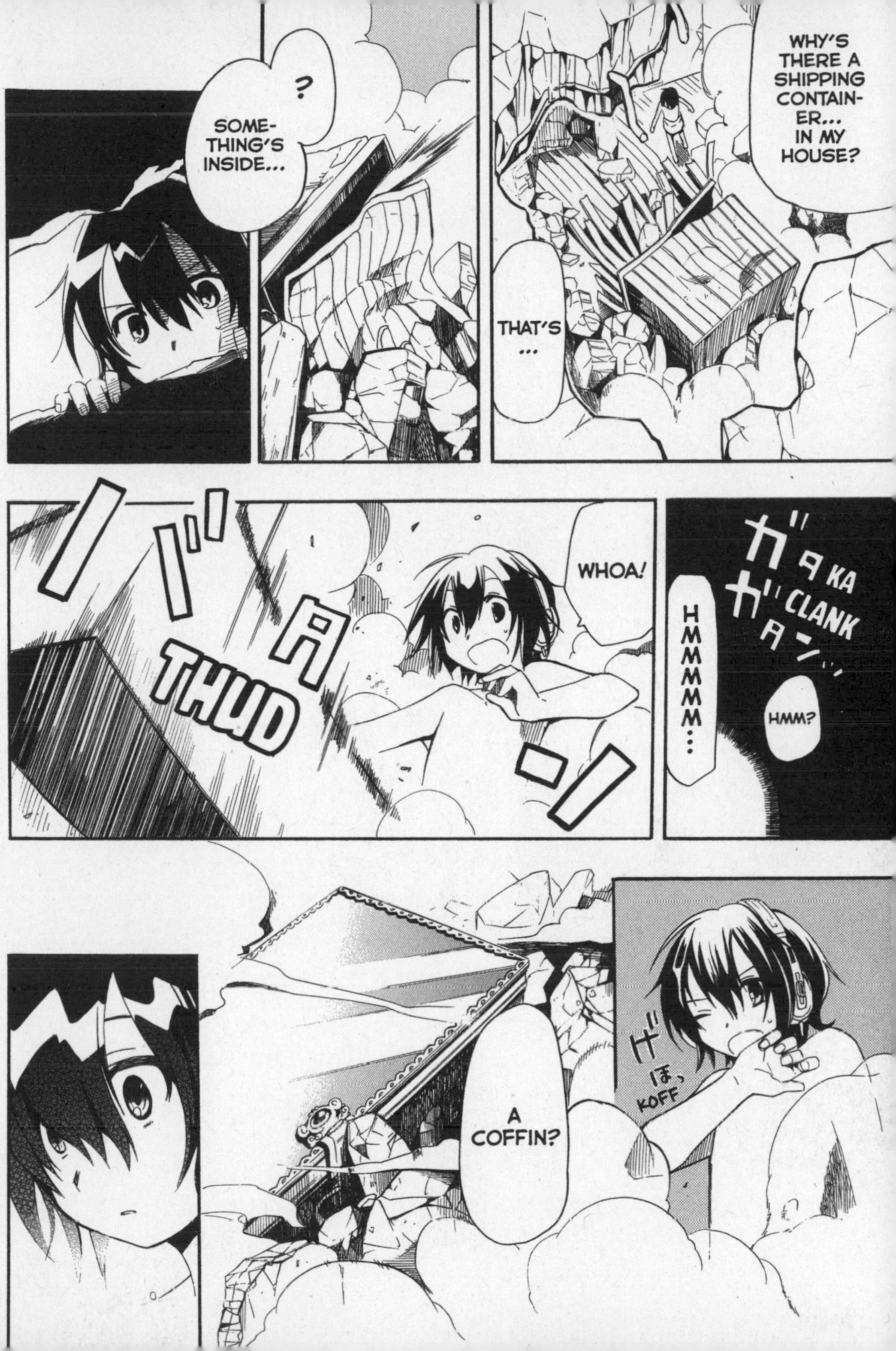
WHY'S THERE A SHIPPING CONTAINER... IN MY HOUSE?
THAT'S ...
?
SOME-THING'S INSIDE...
KA CLANK
HMMMMM...
HMM?
WHOA!
THUD
KOFF
A COFFIN?

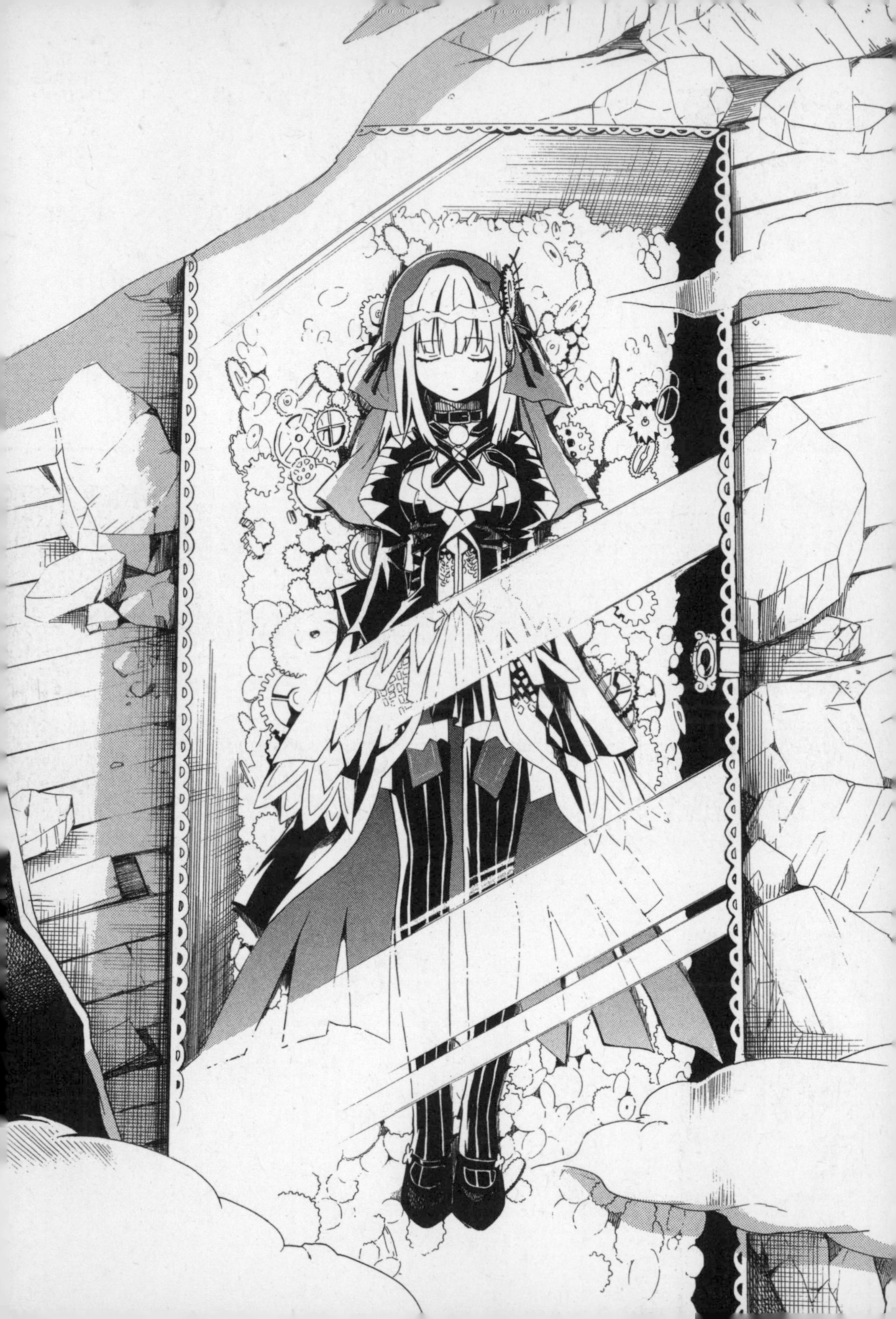

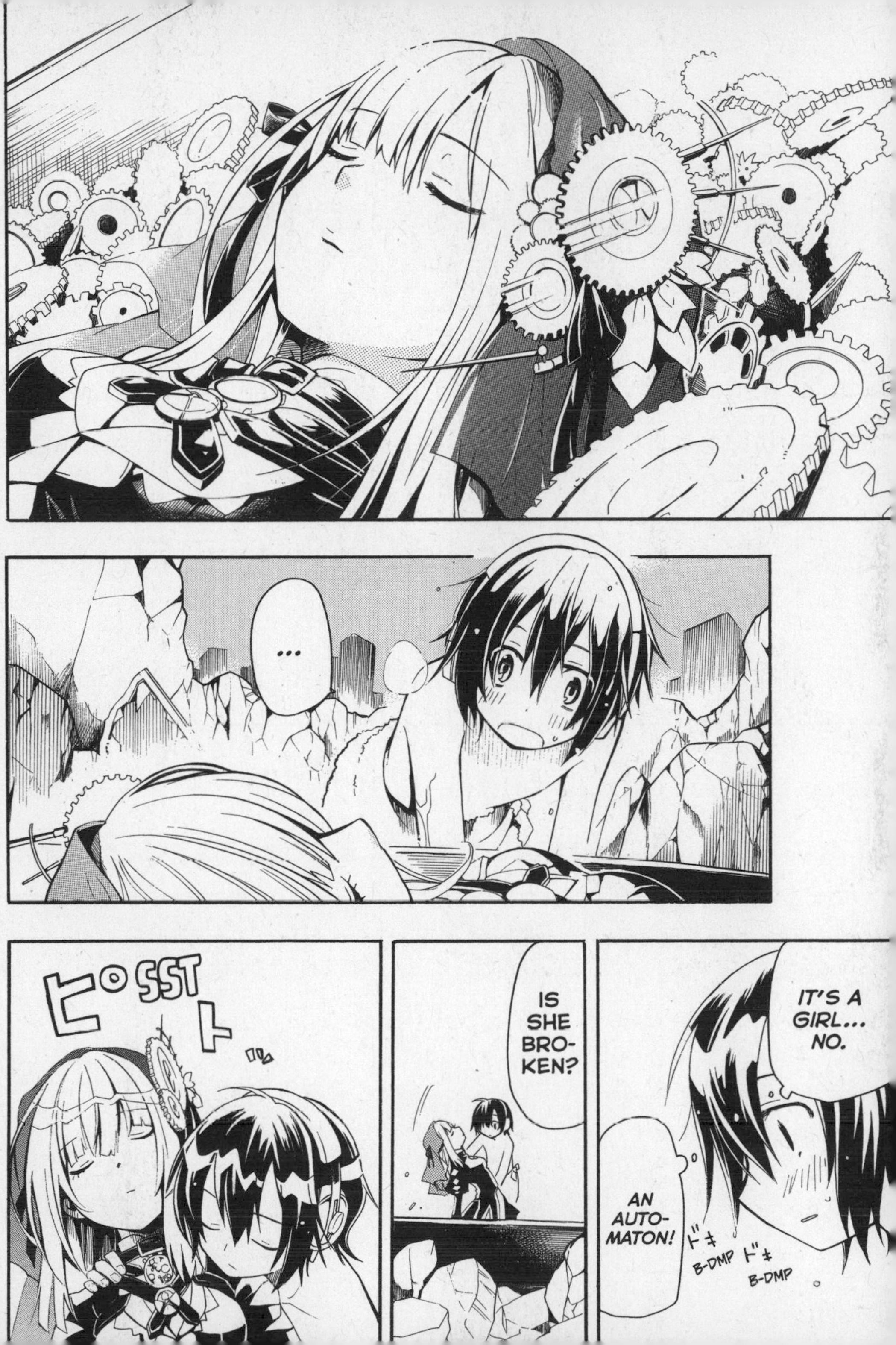
...
IT'S A GIRL... NO.
AN AUTO-MATON!
ドキ B-DMP ドキ B-DMP
IS SHE BRO-KEN?
ピSST ト

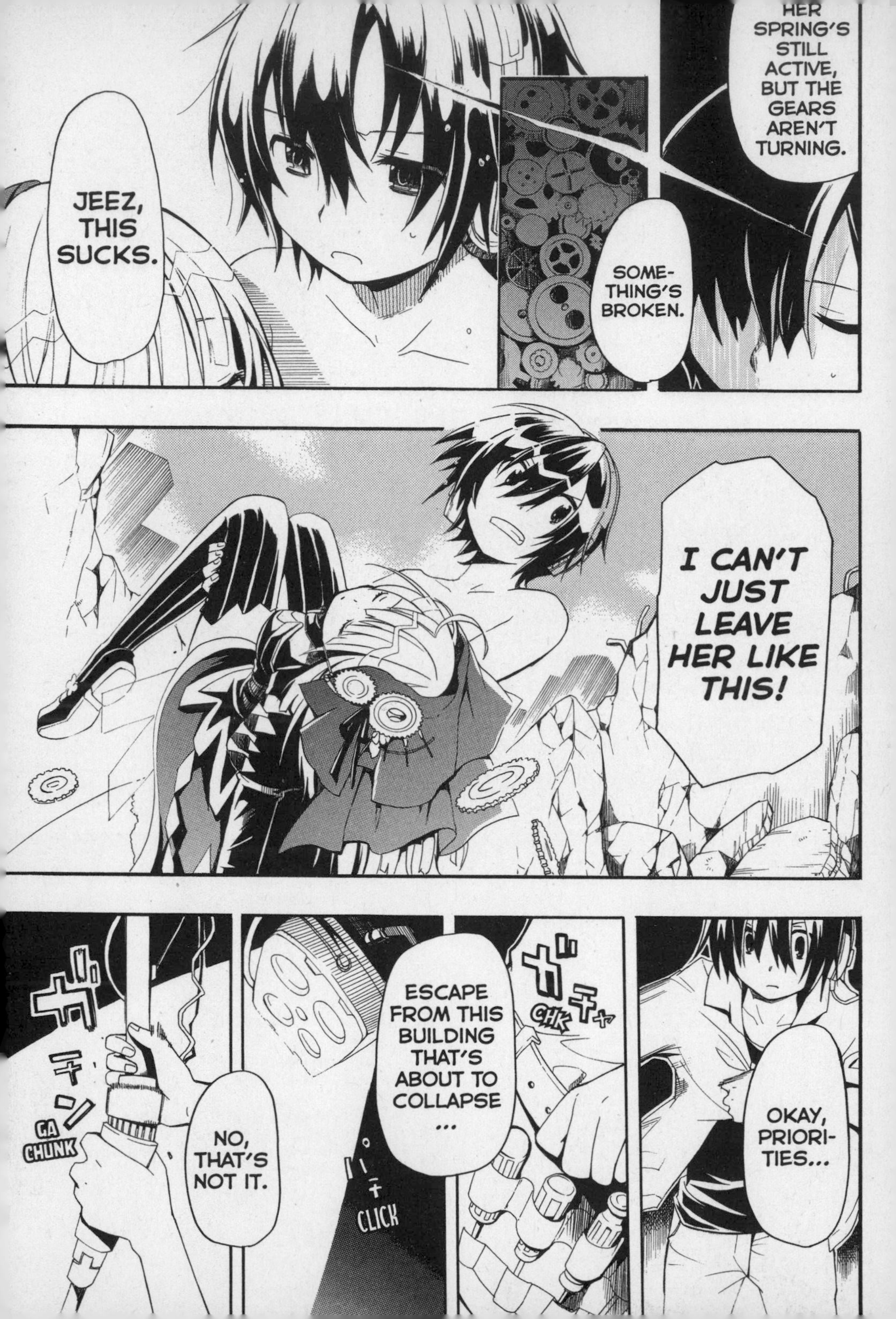
HER SPRING'S STILL ACTIVE, BUT THE GEARS AREN'T TURNING.
SOME-THING'S BROKEN.
JEEZ, THIS SUCKS.
I CAN'T JUST LEAVE HER LIKE THIS!
OKAY, PRIORI-TIES...
CHK
ESCAPE FROM THIS BUILDING THAT'S ABOUT TO COLLAPSE...
CLICK
NO, THAT'S NOT IT.
GA CHUNK

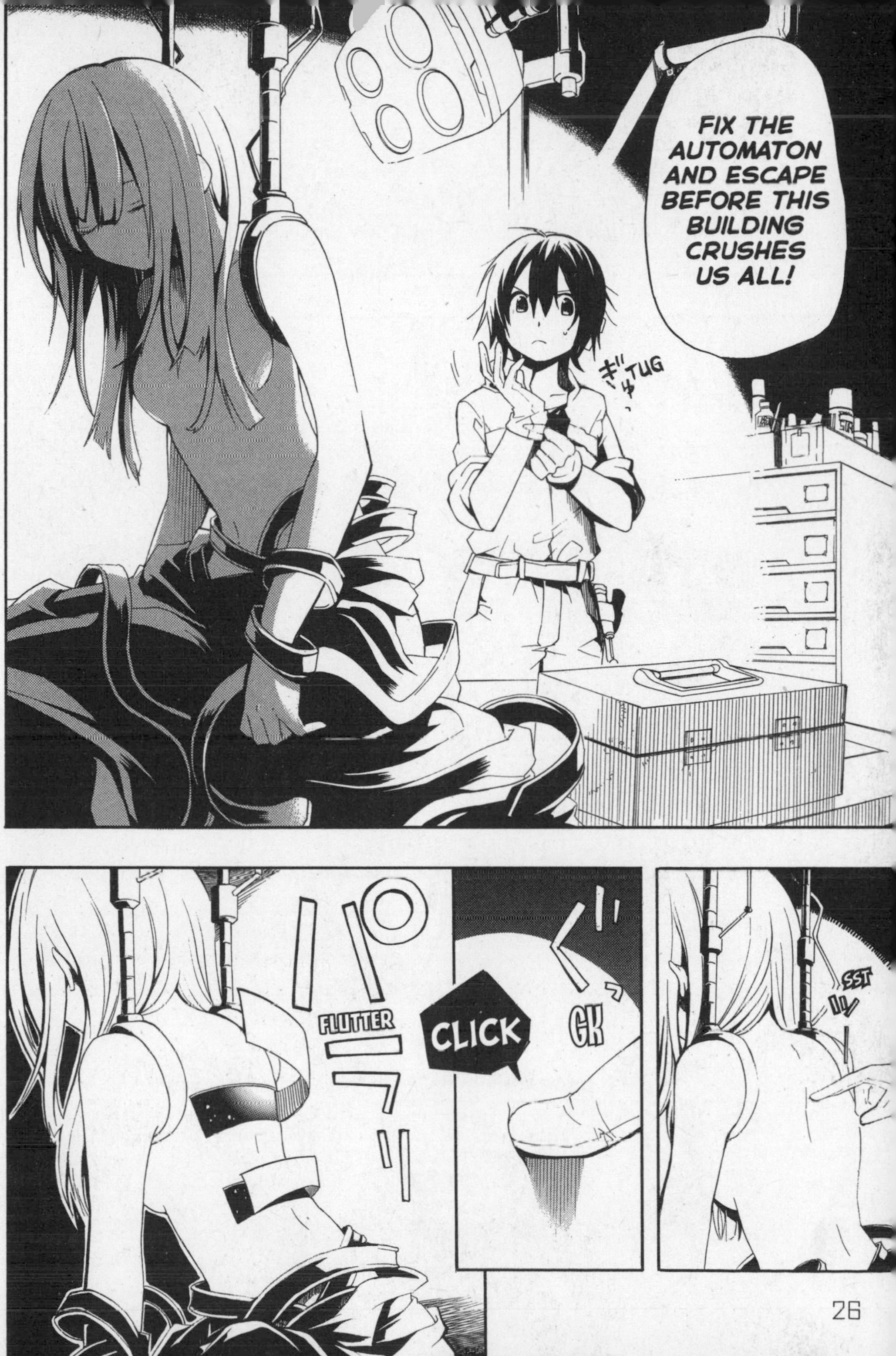
FIX THE AUTOMATON AND ESCAPE BEFORE THIS BUILDING CRUSHES US ALL!
TUG
SST
GK
CLICK
FLUTTER

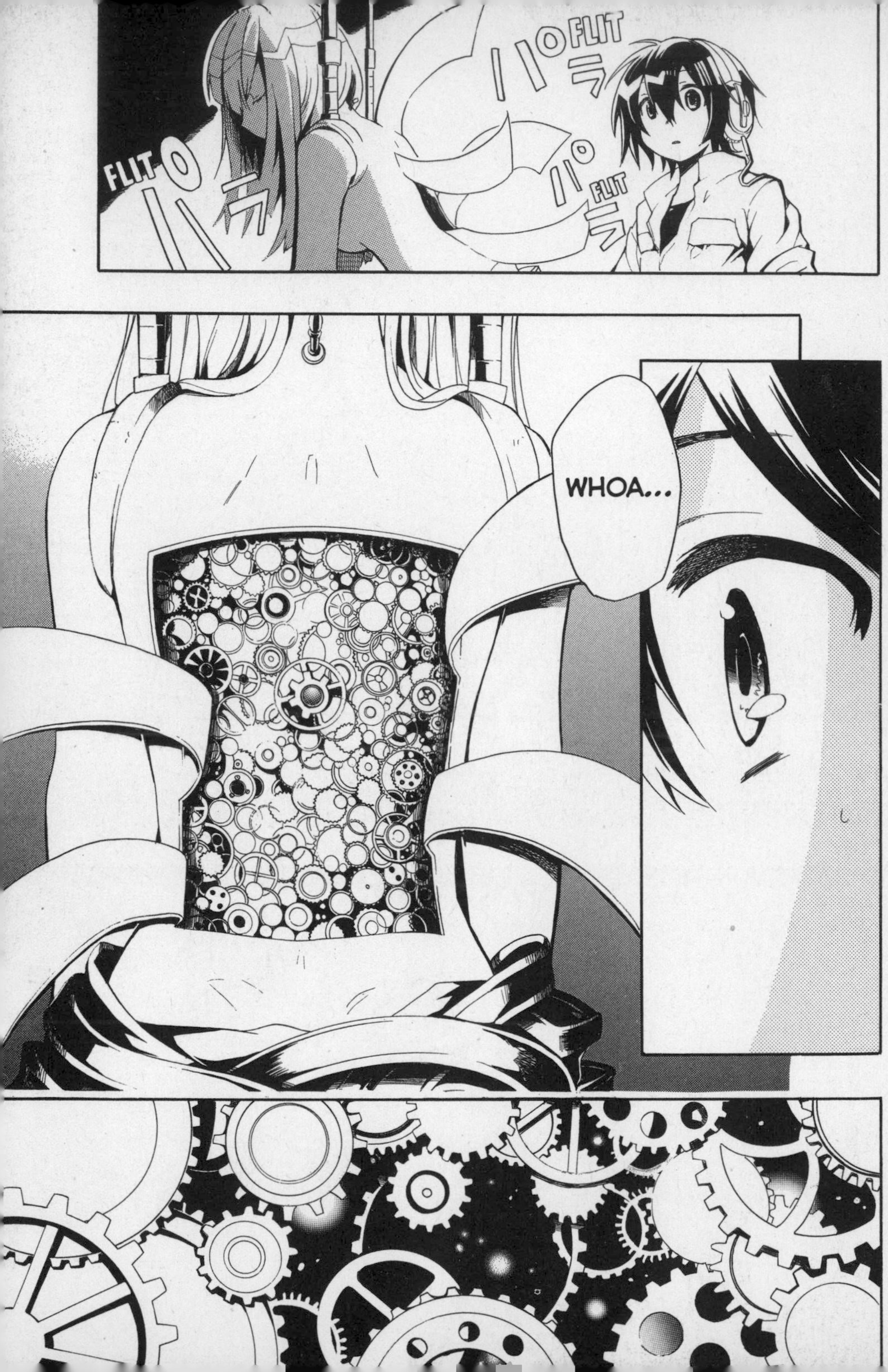
パラ
FLIT
パラ
FLIT
パラ
FLIT
WHOA...

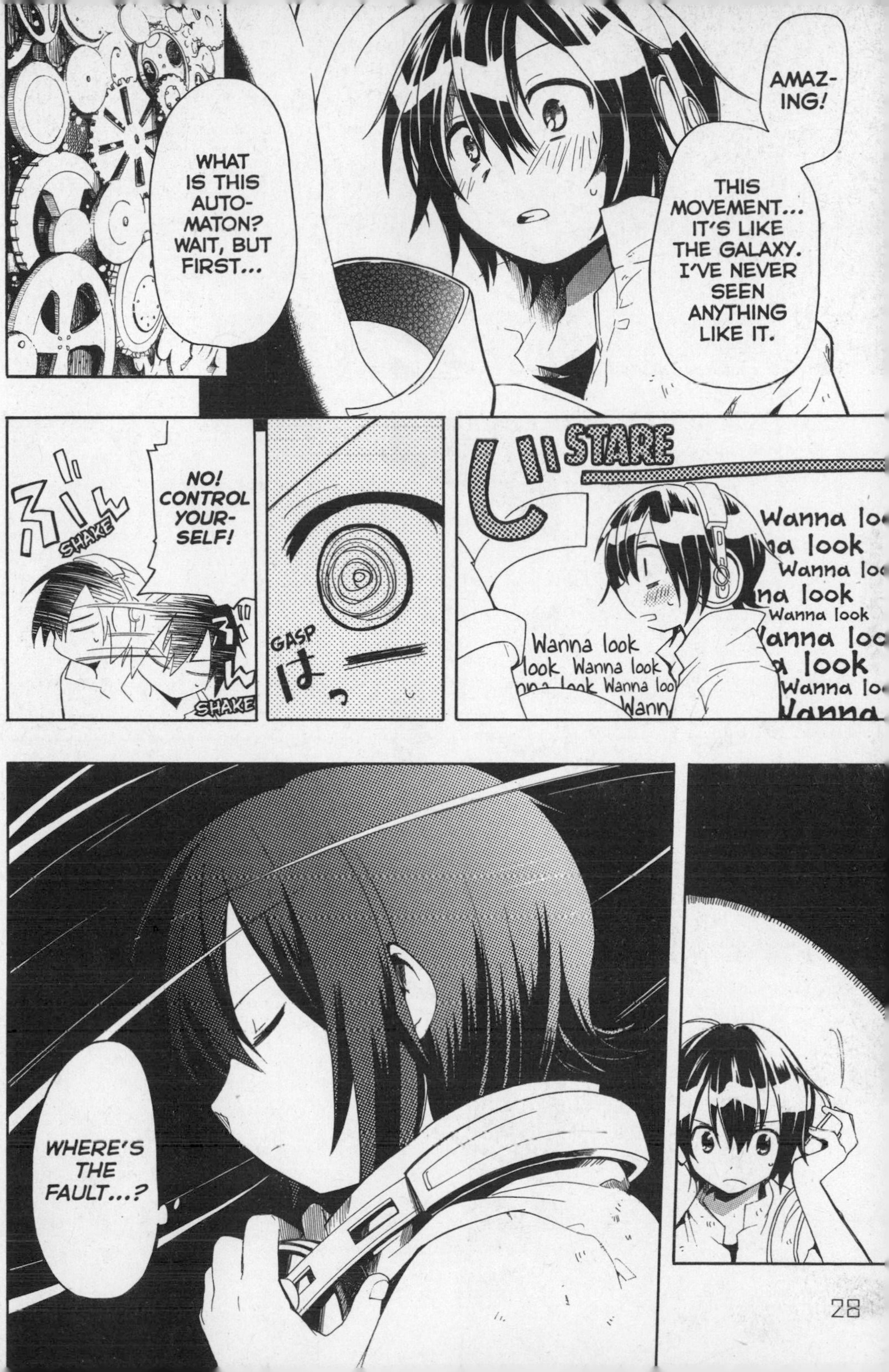
AMAZ-
ING!
THIS MOVEMENT... IT'S LIKE THE GALAXY. I'VE NEVER SEEN ANYTHING LIKE IT.
WHAT IS THIS AUTO-MATON? WAIT, BUT FIRST...
じー STARE
Wanna look Wanna look Wanna look Wanna look Wanna look
Wanna look Wanna look Wanna look
GASP はっ
NO! CONTROL YOUR-SELF!
ぶるん SHAKE
ぶるん SHAKE
WHERE'S THE FAULT...?

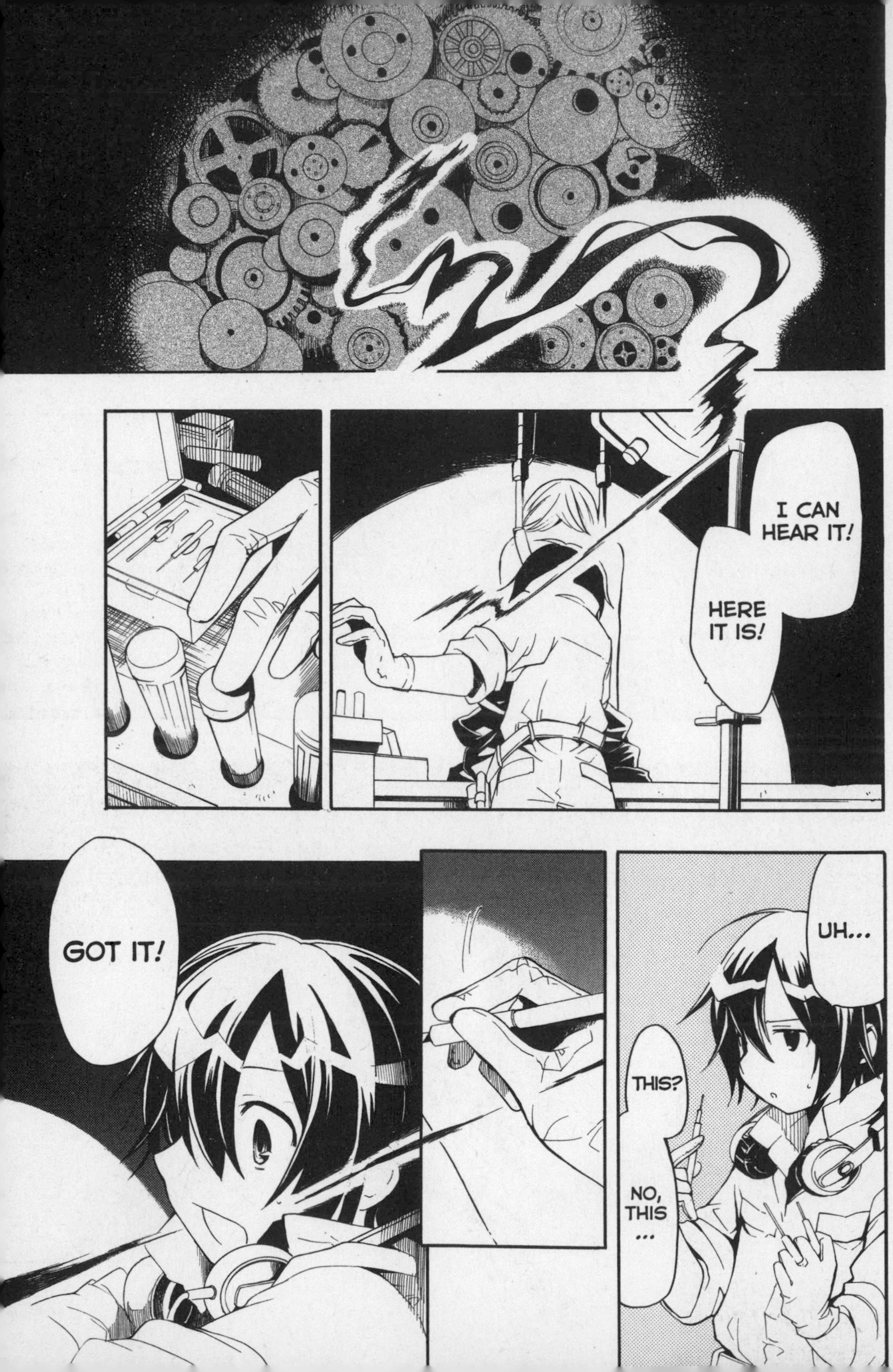
I CAN HEAR IT!
HERE IT IS!
UH...
THIS?
NO, THIS ...
GOT IT!

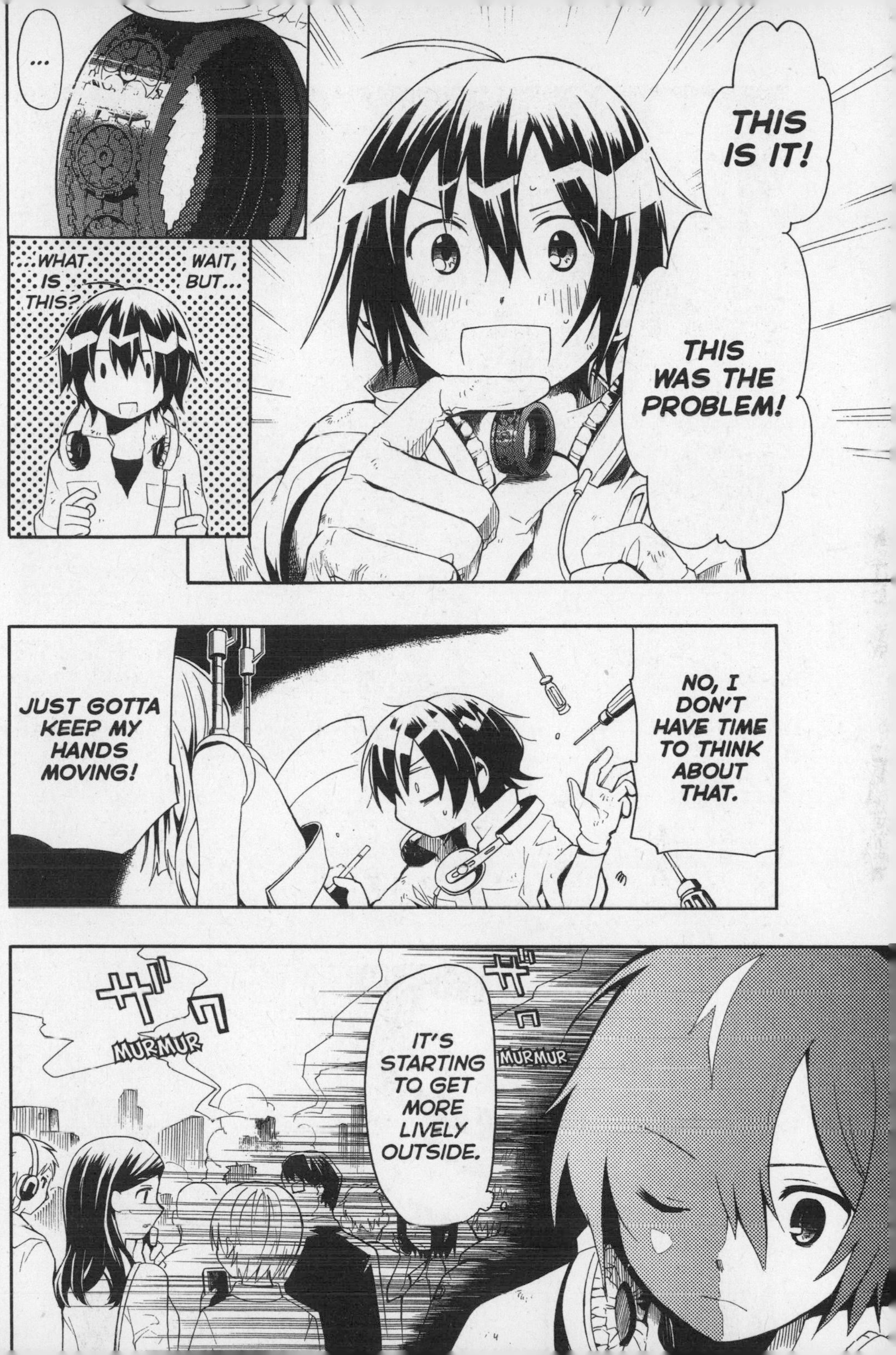
THIS IS IT!
THIS WAS THE PROBLEM!
...
WAIT, BUT...
...WHAT IS THIS?
NO, I DON'T HAVE TIME TO THINK ABOUT THAT.
JUST GOTTA KEEP MY HANDS MOVING!
MURMUR
IT'S STARTING TO GET MORE LIVELY OUTSIDE.
MURMUR

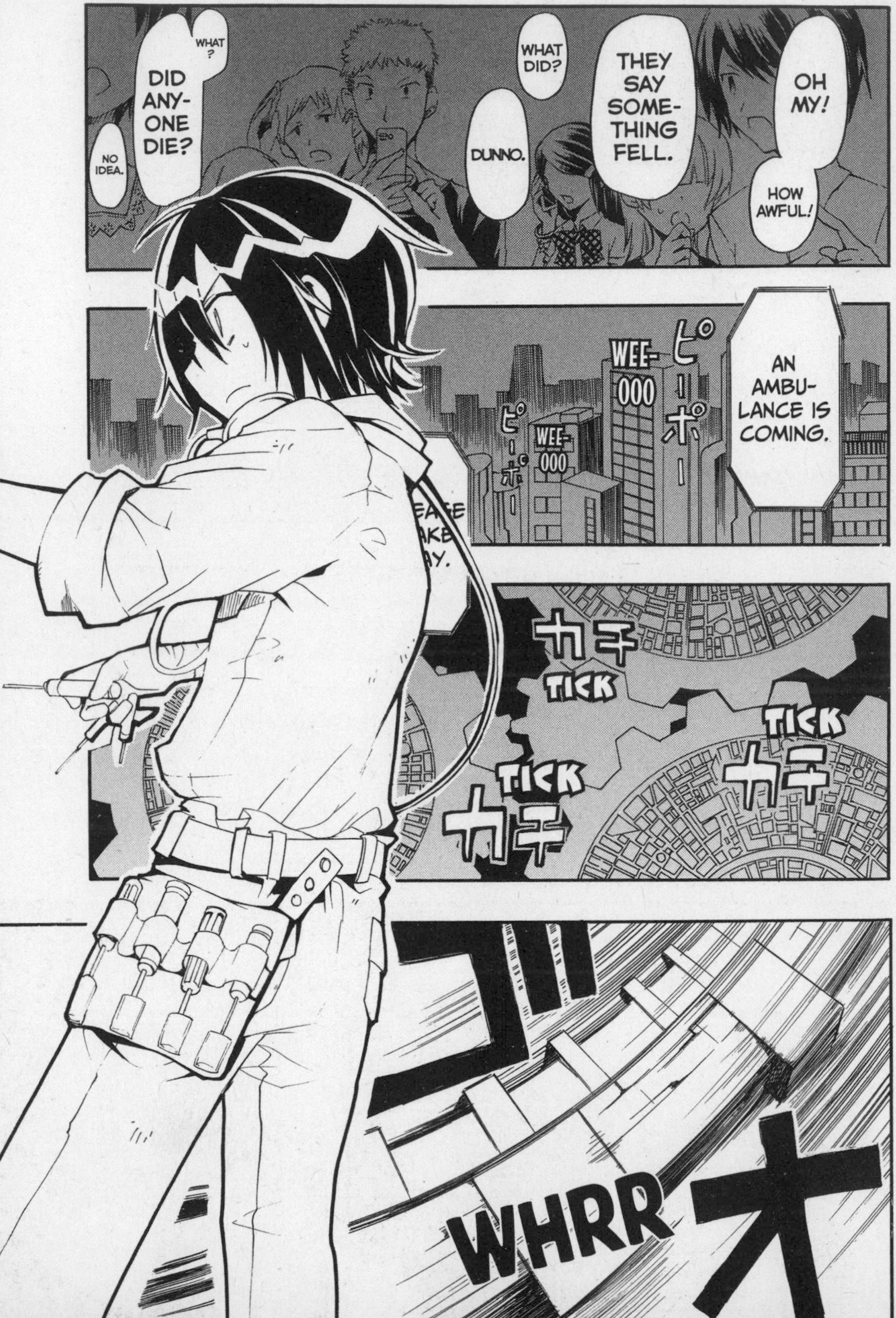
OH MY!
HOW AWFUL!
THEY SAY SOME-THING FELL.
WHAT DID?
DUNNO.
DID ANY-ONE DIE?
WHAT?
NO IDEA.
AN AMBU-LANCE IS COMING.
ピーポー
WEE-OOO
ピーポー
WEE-OOO
カチ
TICK
TICK
カチ
TICK
カチ
WHRR

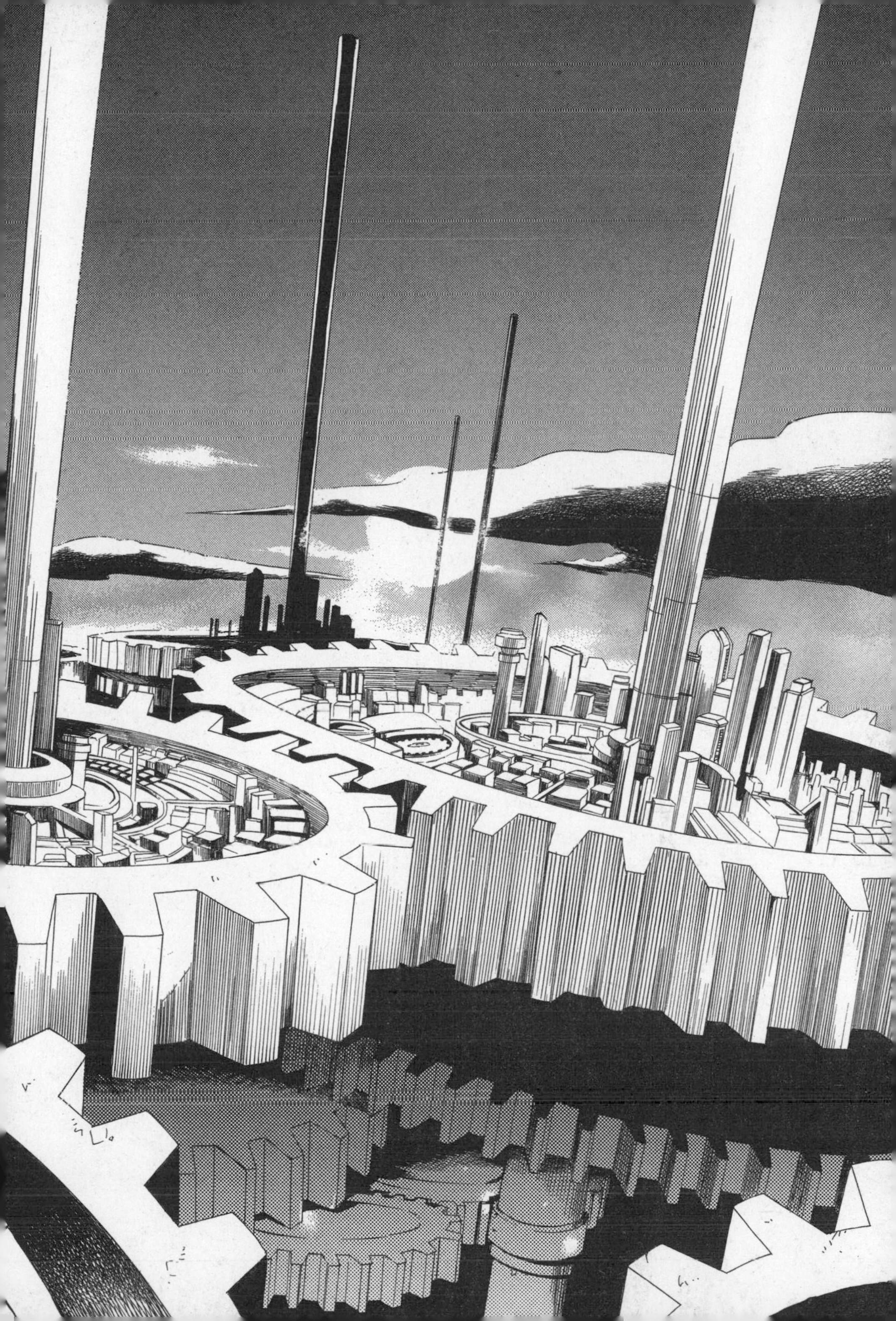

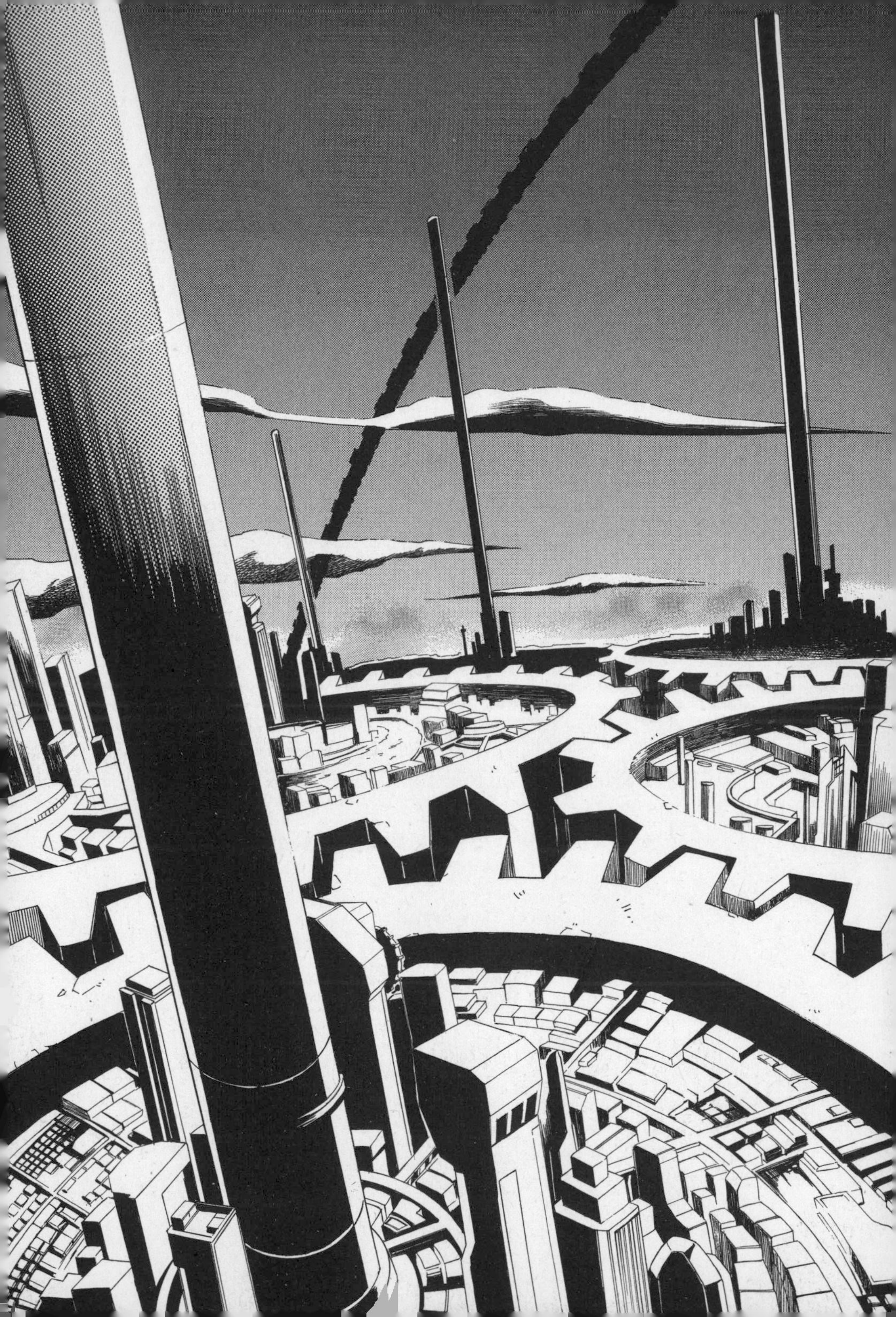

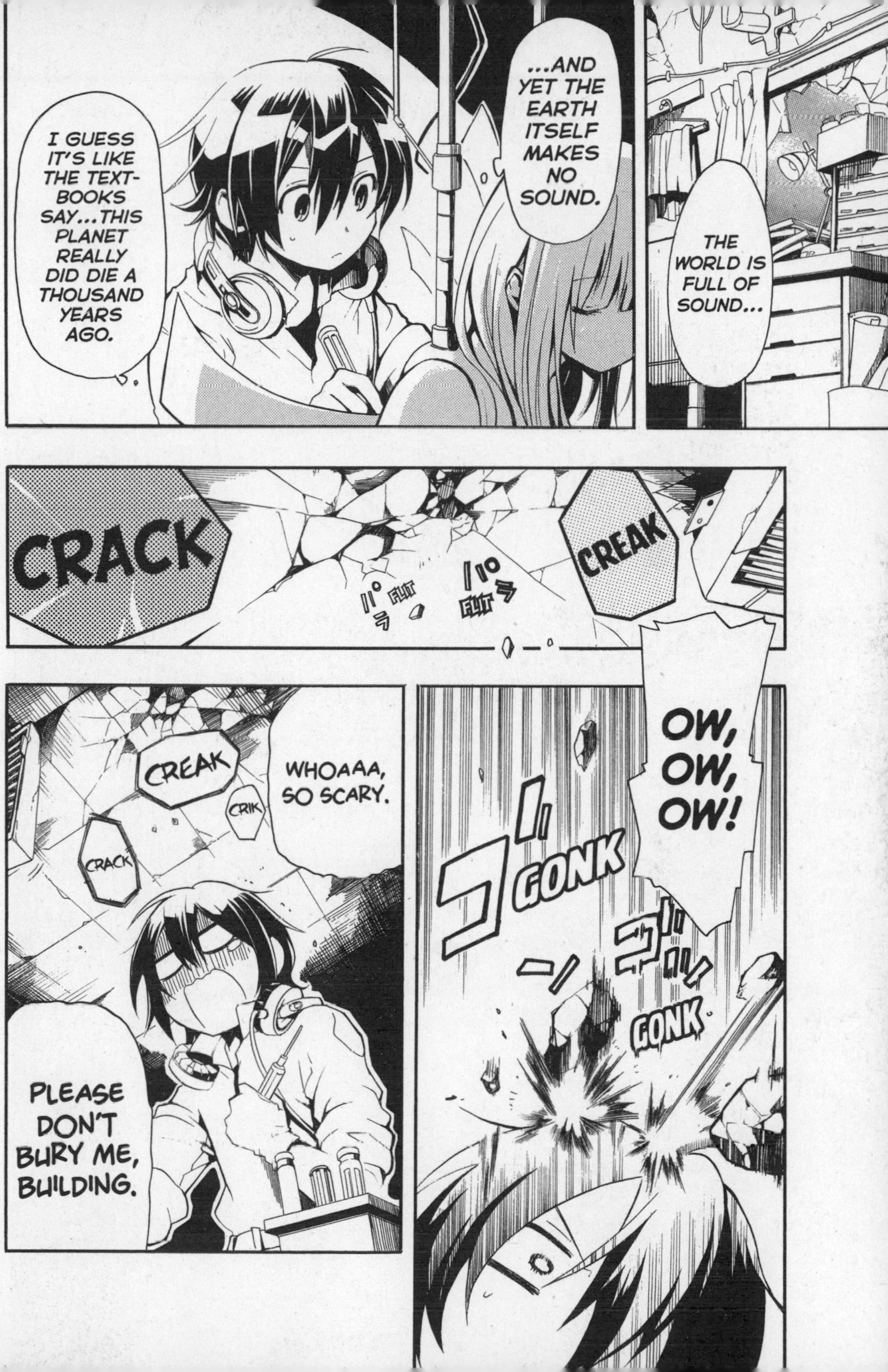
THE WORLD IS FULL OF SOUND...
...AND YET THE EARTH ITSELF MAKES NO SOUND.
I GUESS IT'S LIKE THE TEXT-BOOKS SAY...THIS PLANET REALLY DID DIE A THOUSAND YEARS AGO.
CREAK
パラ FLIT
パラ FLIT
CRACK
OW, OW, OW!
GONK
GONK
WHOAAA, SO SCARY.
CREAK
CRIK
CRACK
PLEASE DON'T BURY ME, BUILDING.

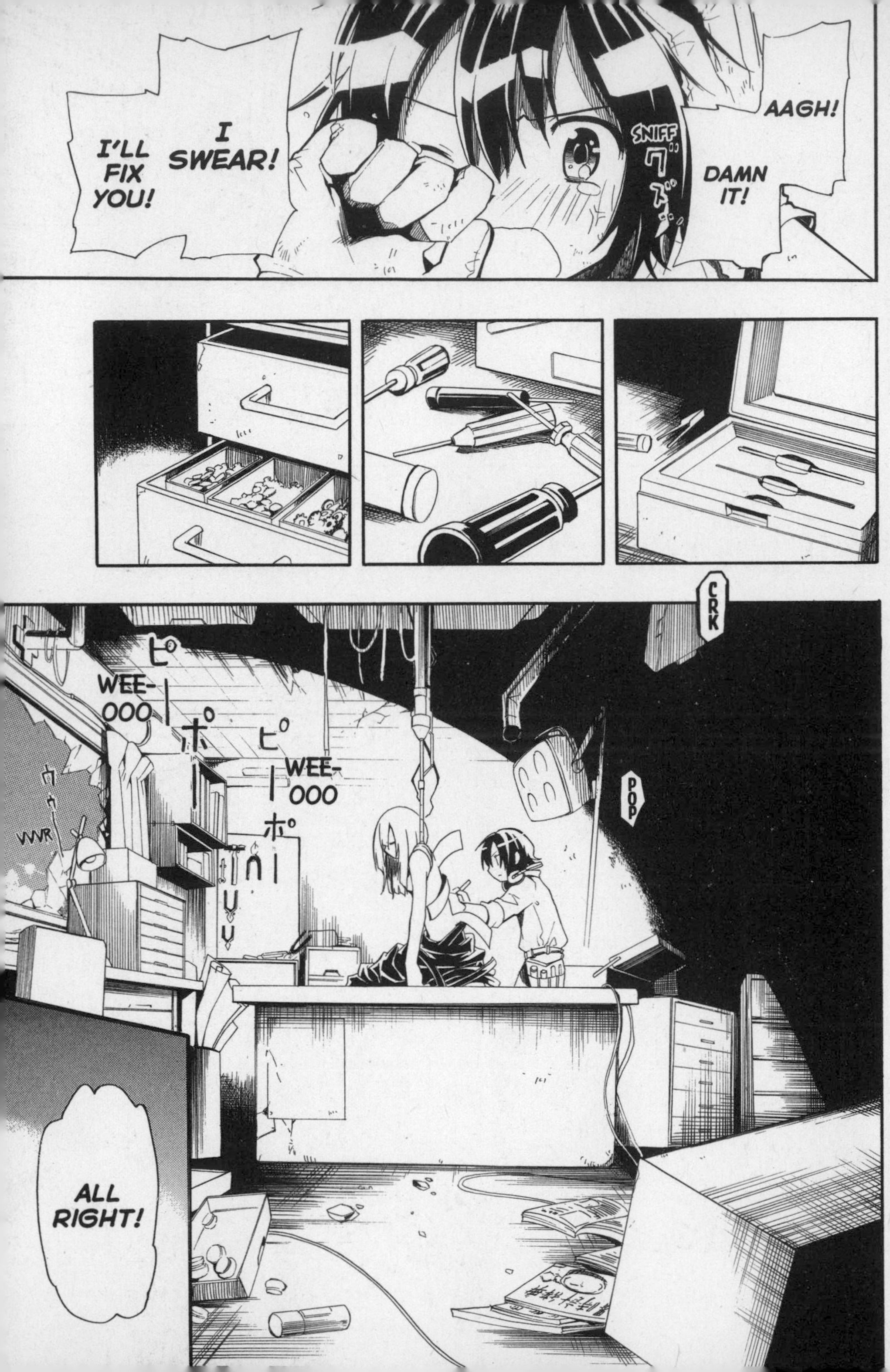
AAGH!
DAMN IT!
SNIFF
I SWEAR!
I'LL FIX YOU!
CRK
POP
ピーポー
WEE-OOO
ピーポー
WEE-OOO
VVVR
ALL RIGHT!

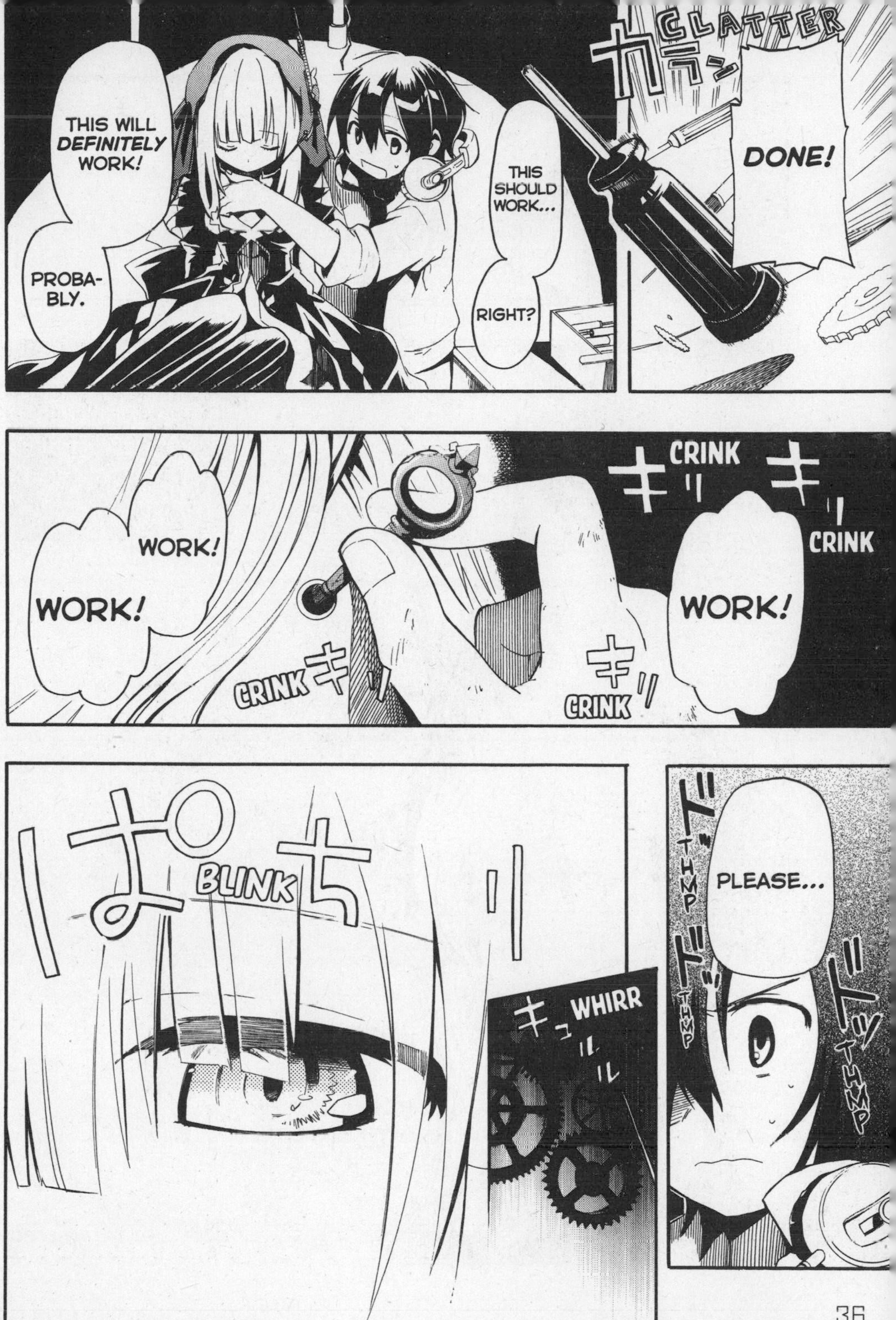
CLATTER
DONE!
THIS SHOULD WORK...
RIGHT?
THIS WILL DEFINITELY WORK!
PROBABLY.
CRINK
CRINK
WORK!
CRINK
WORK!
WORK!
CRINK
THUMP
THUMP
THUMP
PLEASE...
BLINK
WHIRR

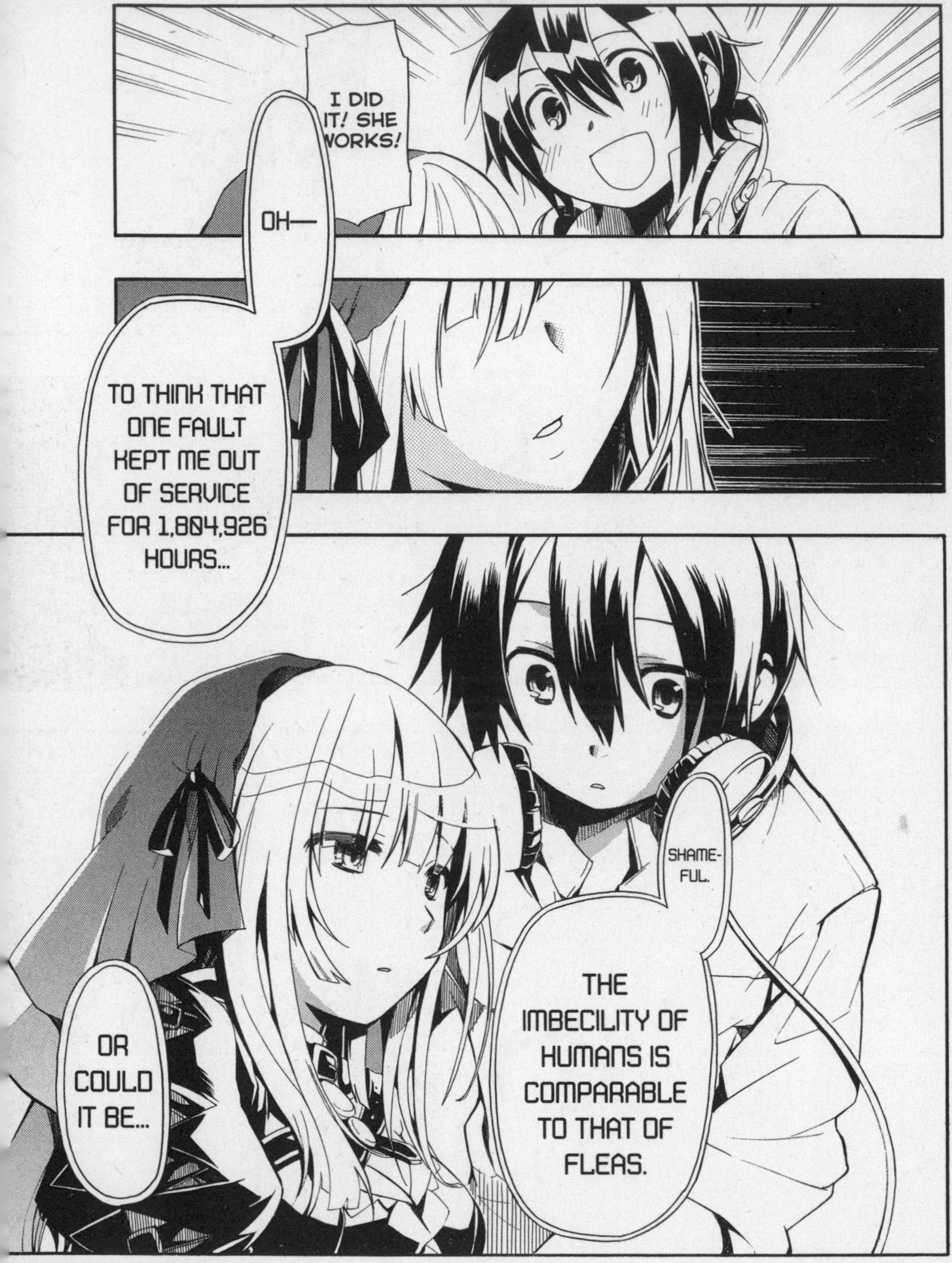
I DID IT! SHE WORKS!
OH—
TO THINK THAT ONE FAULT KEPT ME OUT OF SERVICE FOR 1,804,926 HOURS...
SHAME-FUL.
THE IMBECILITY OF HUMANS IS COMPARABLE TO THAT OF FLEAS.
OR COULD IT BE...

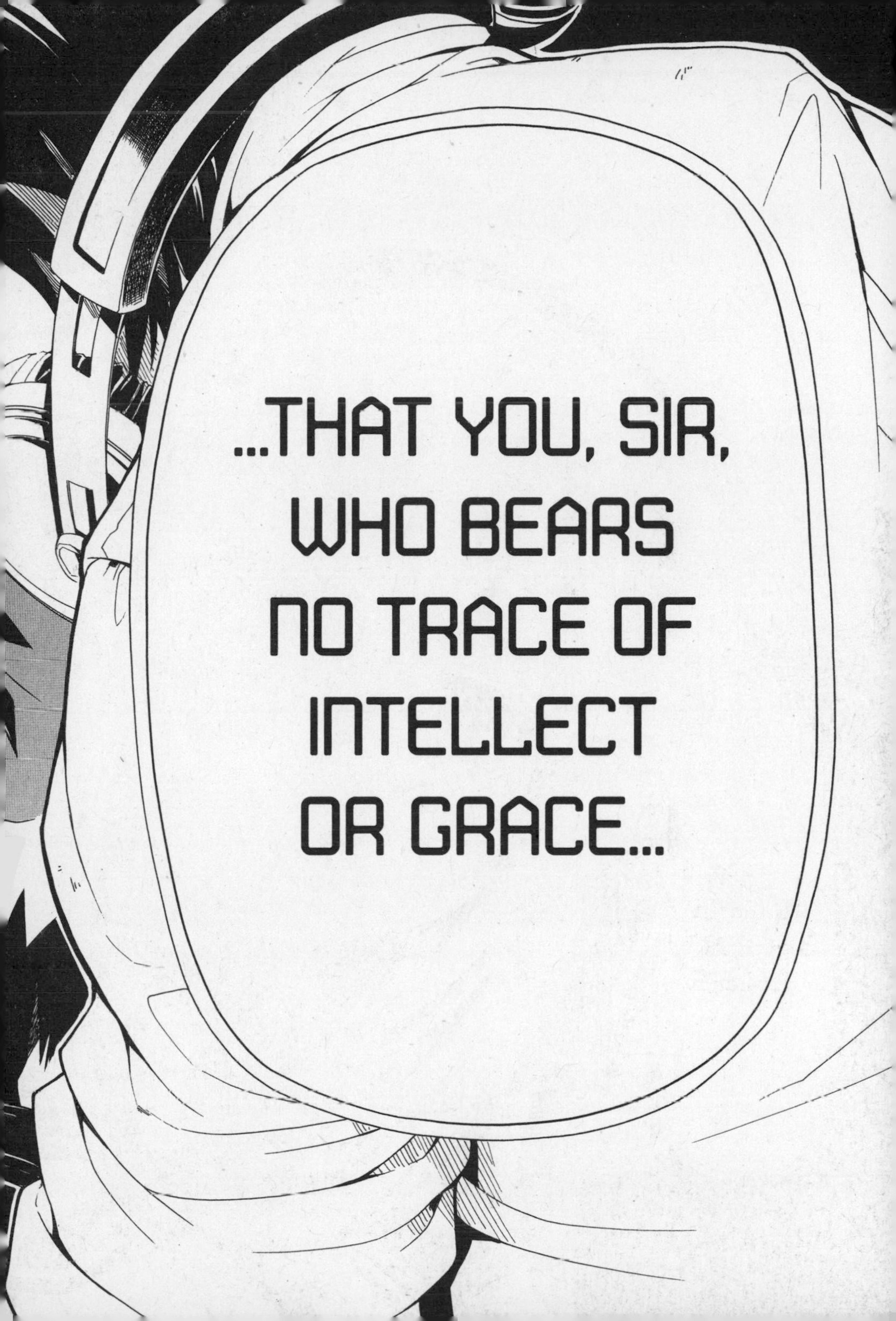
...THAT YOU, SIR, WHO BEARS NO TRACE OF INTELLECT OR GRACE...

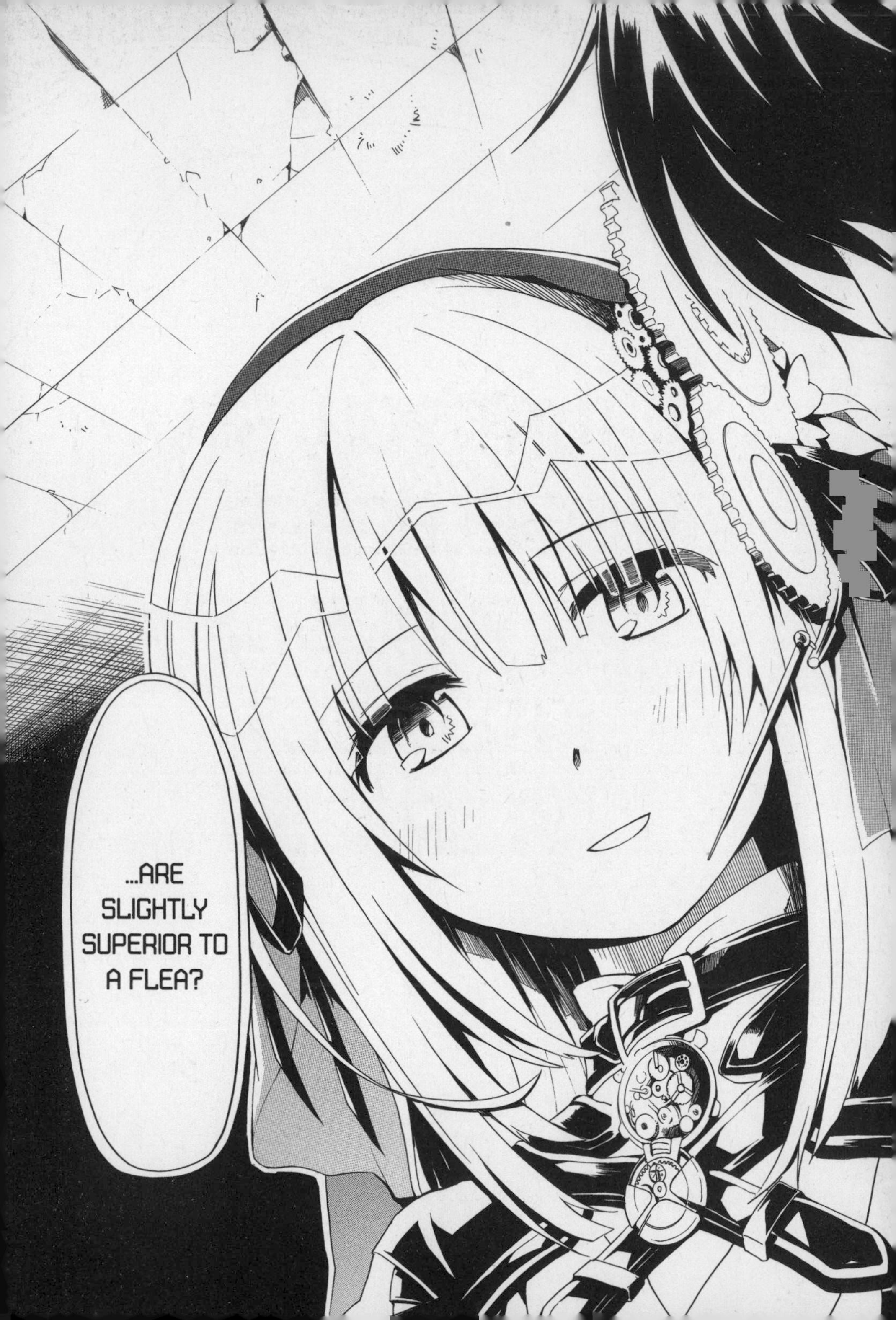
...ARE SLIGHTLY SUPERIOR TO A FLEA?

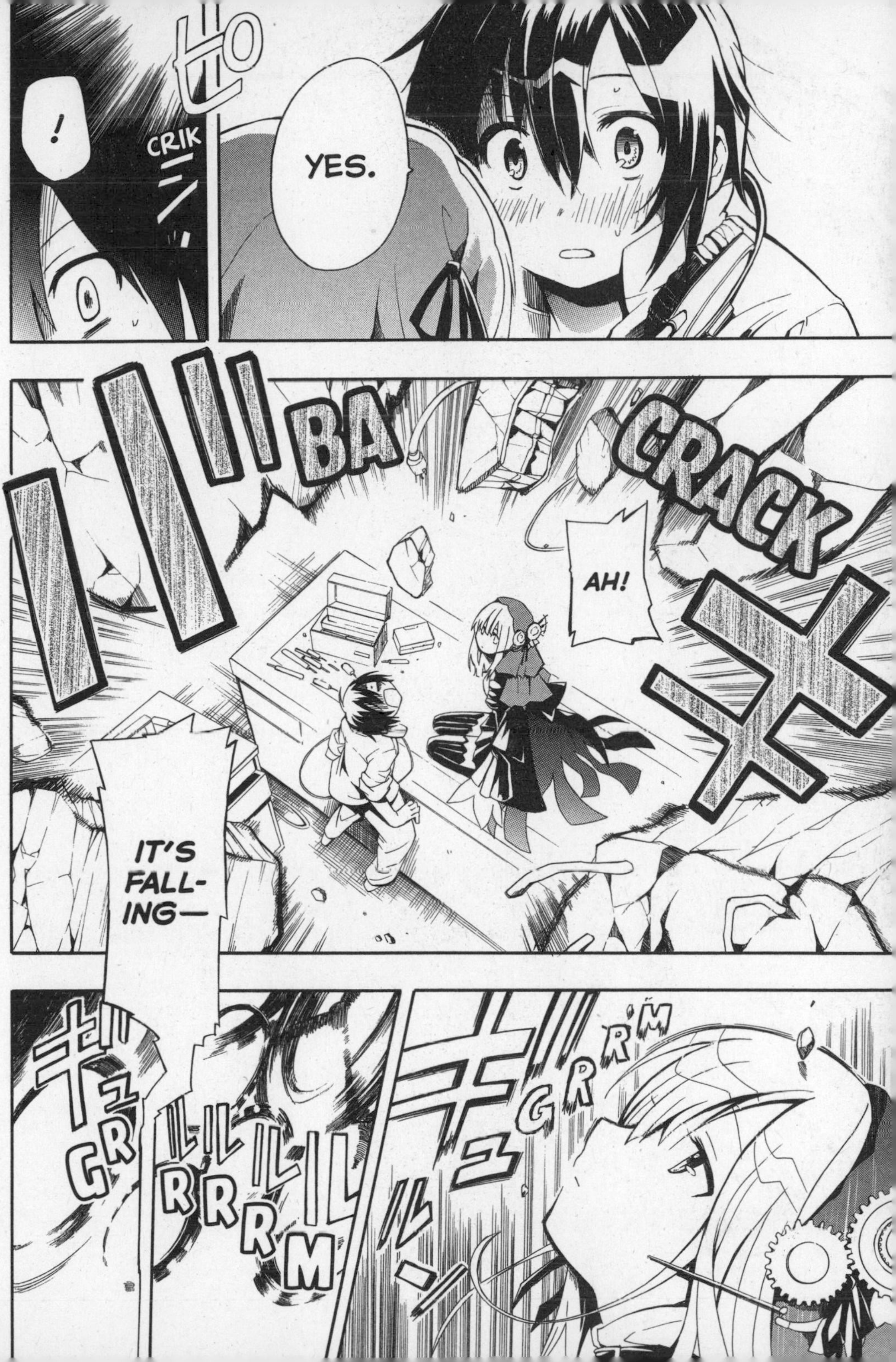
YES.
!
CRIK
BA
CRACK
AH!
IT'S FALLING—
GRRM
GRRRRM

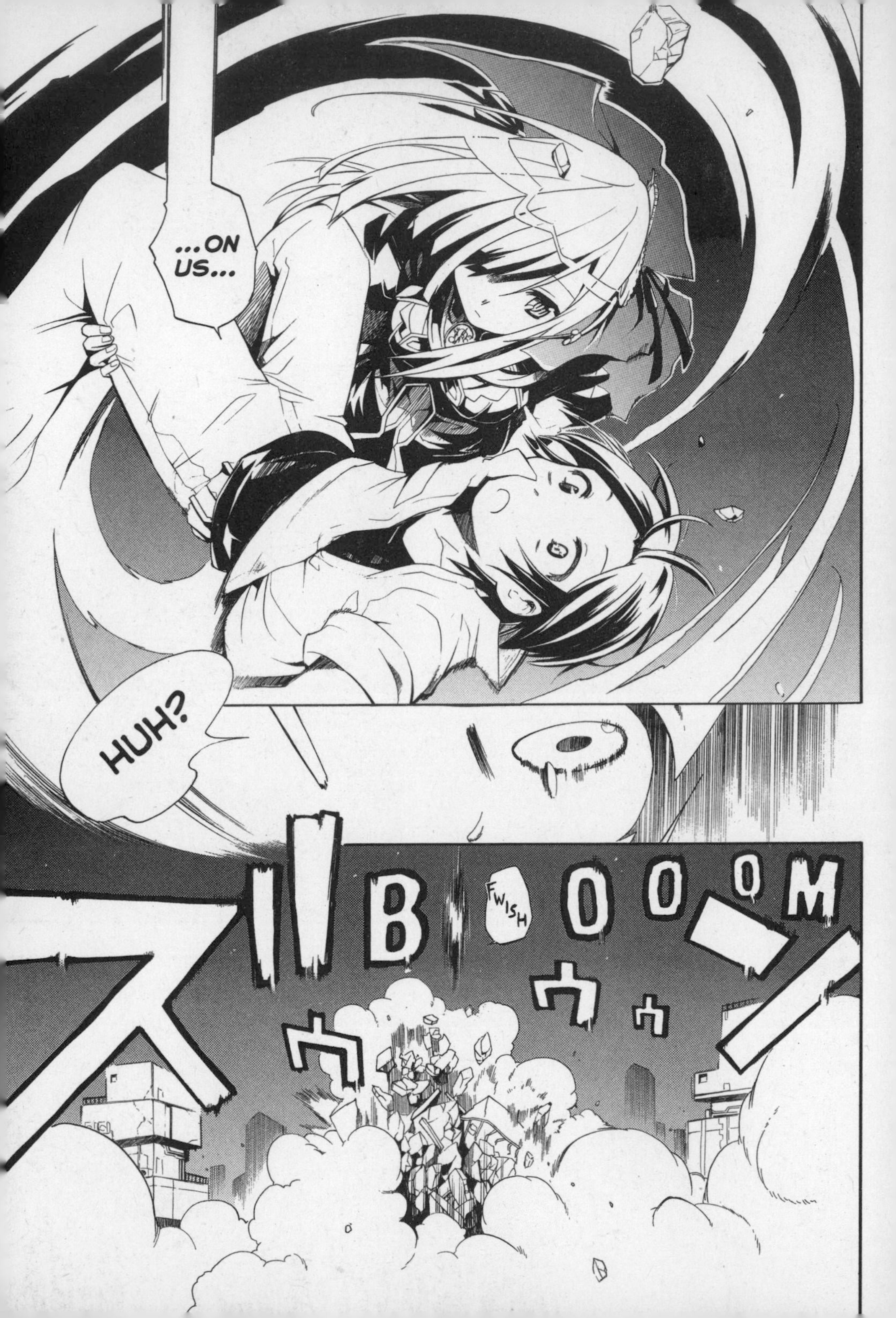
...ON US...
HUH?
BOOOM
FWISH

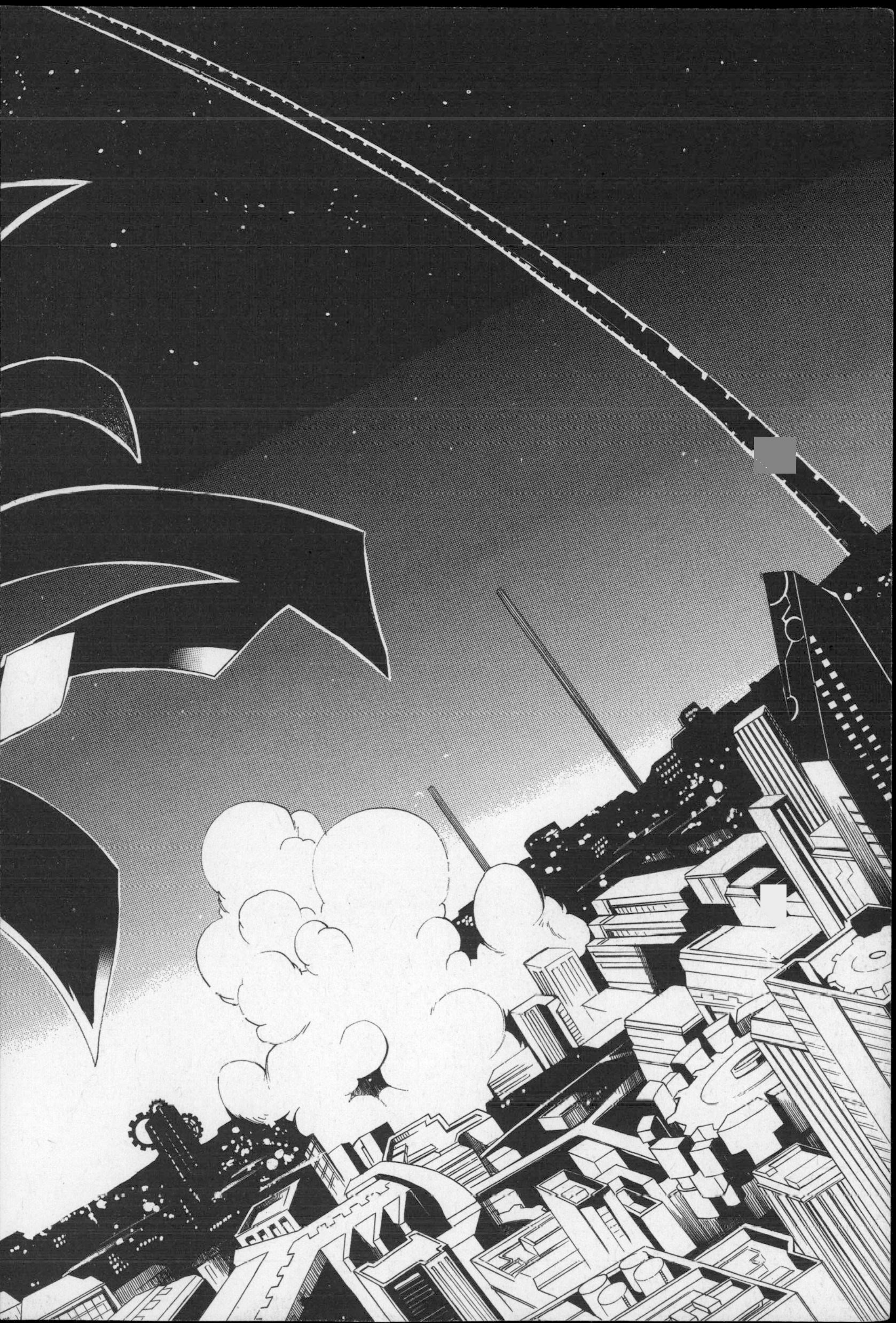

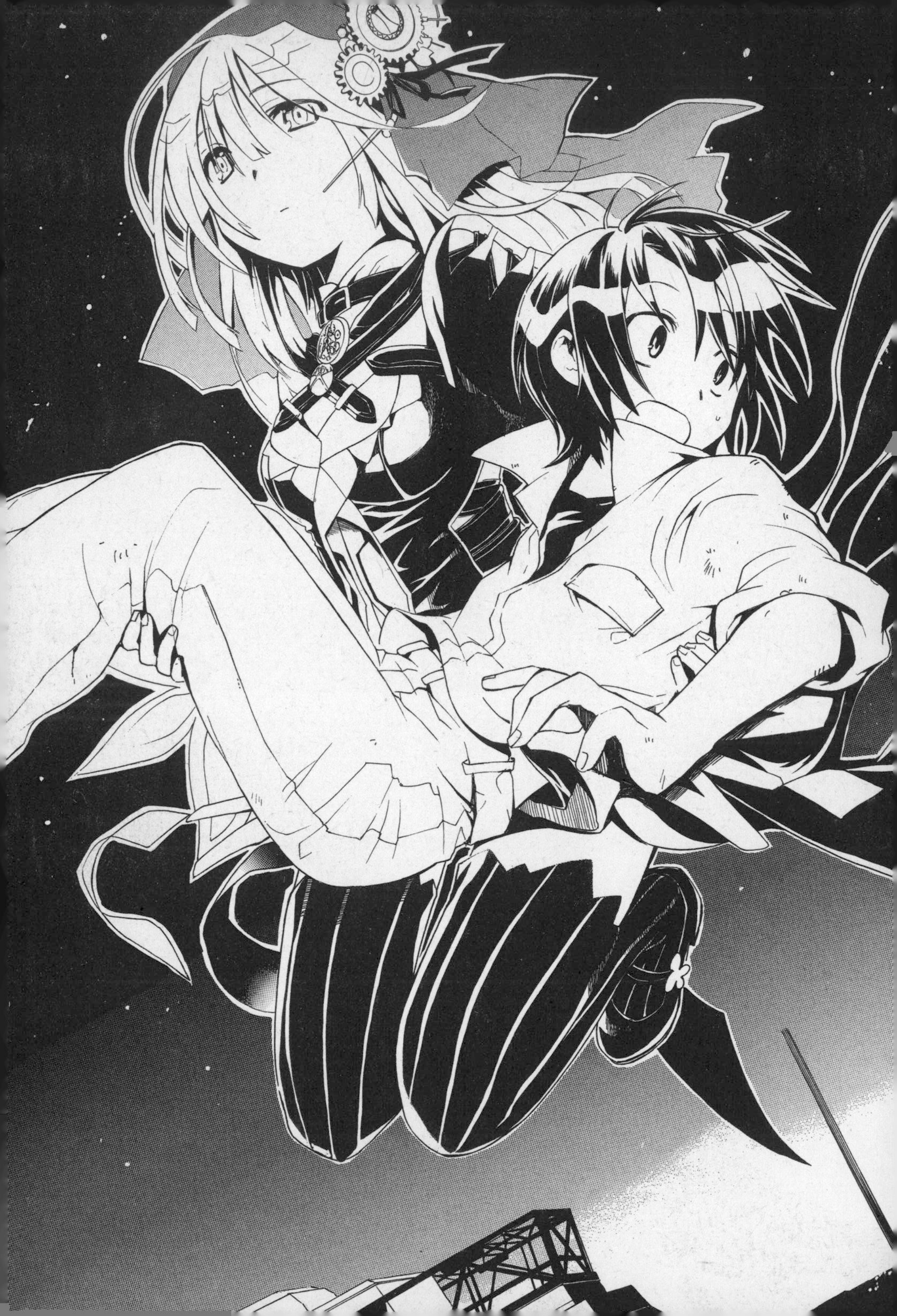

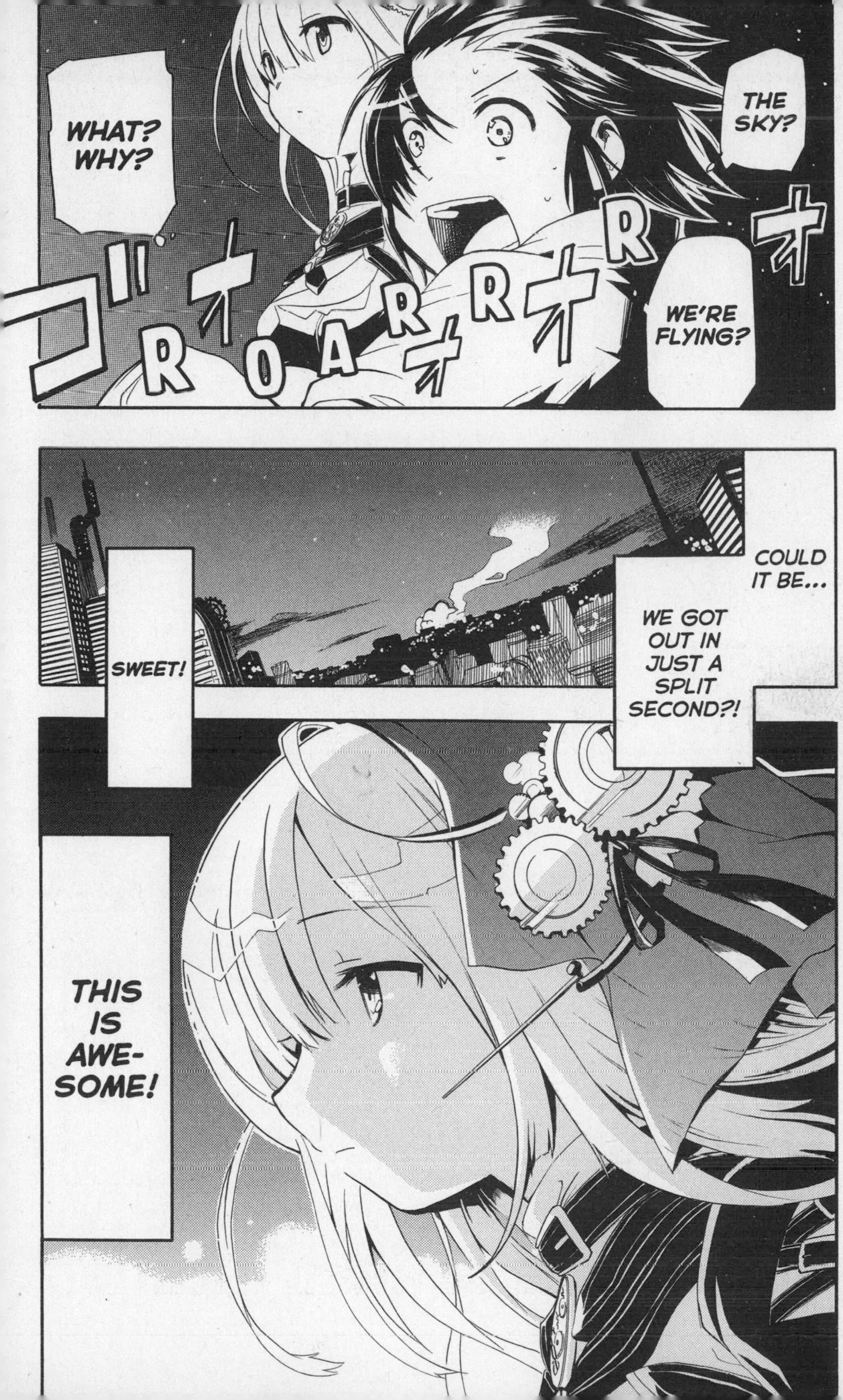
THE SKY?
WHAT? WHY?
ゴオオオオ
ROARRR
WE'RE FLYING?
COULD IT BE...
WE GOT OUT IN JUST A SPLIT SECOND?!
SWEET!
THIS IS AWE-SOME!

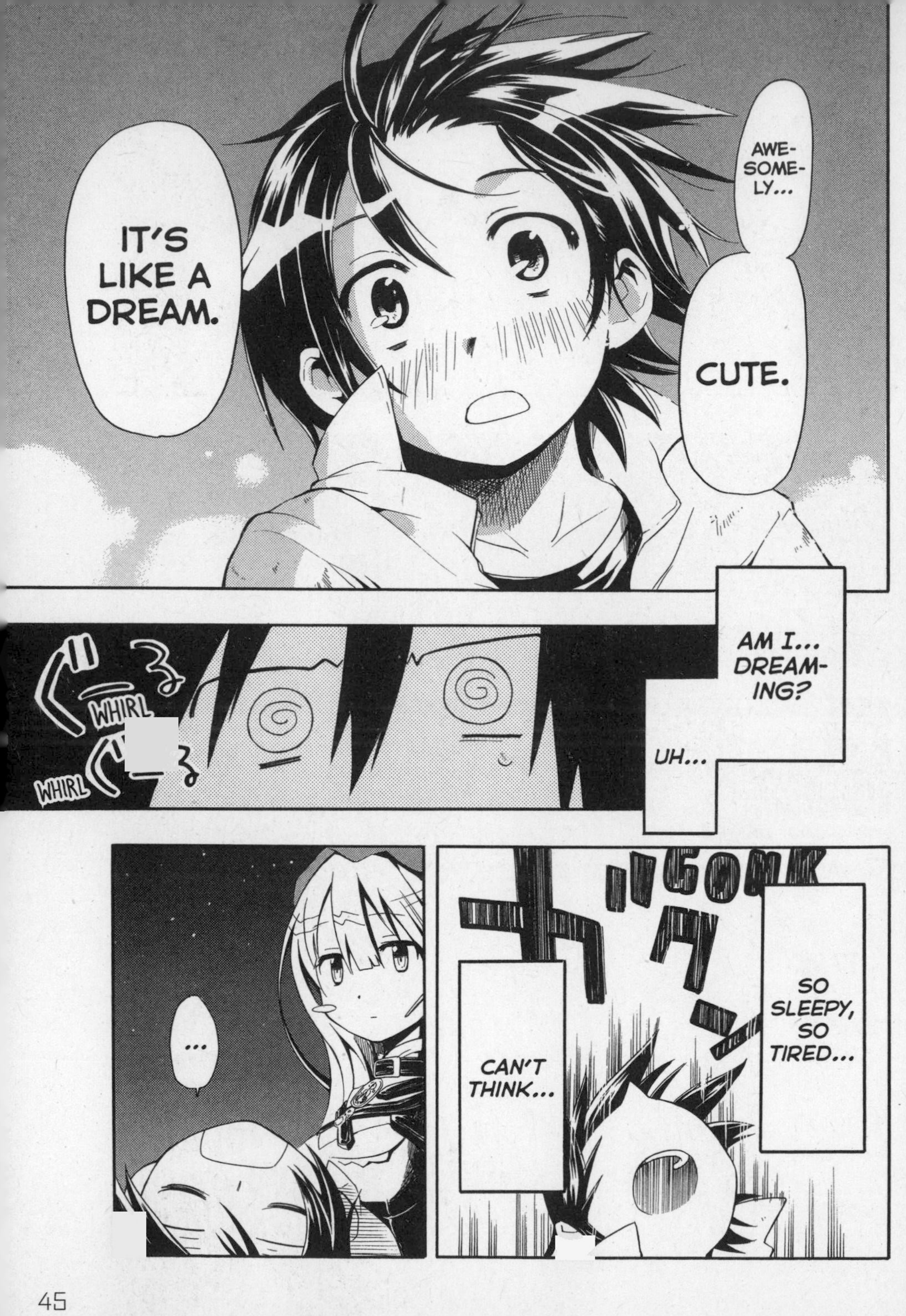
AWE-SOME-LY...
CUTE.
IT'S LIKE A DREAM.
AM I... DREAM-ING?
UH...
WHIRL
WHIRL
GONK
SO SLEEPY, SO TIRED...
CAN'T THINK...
...

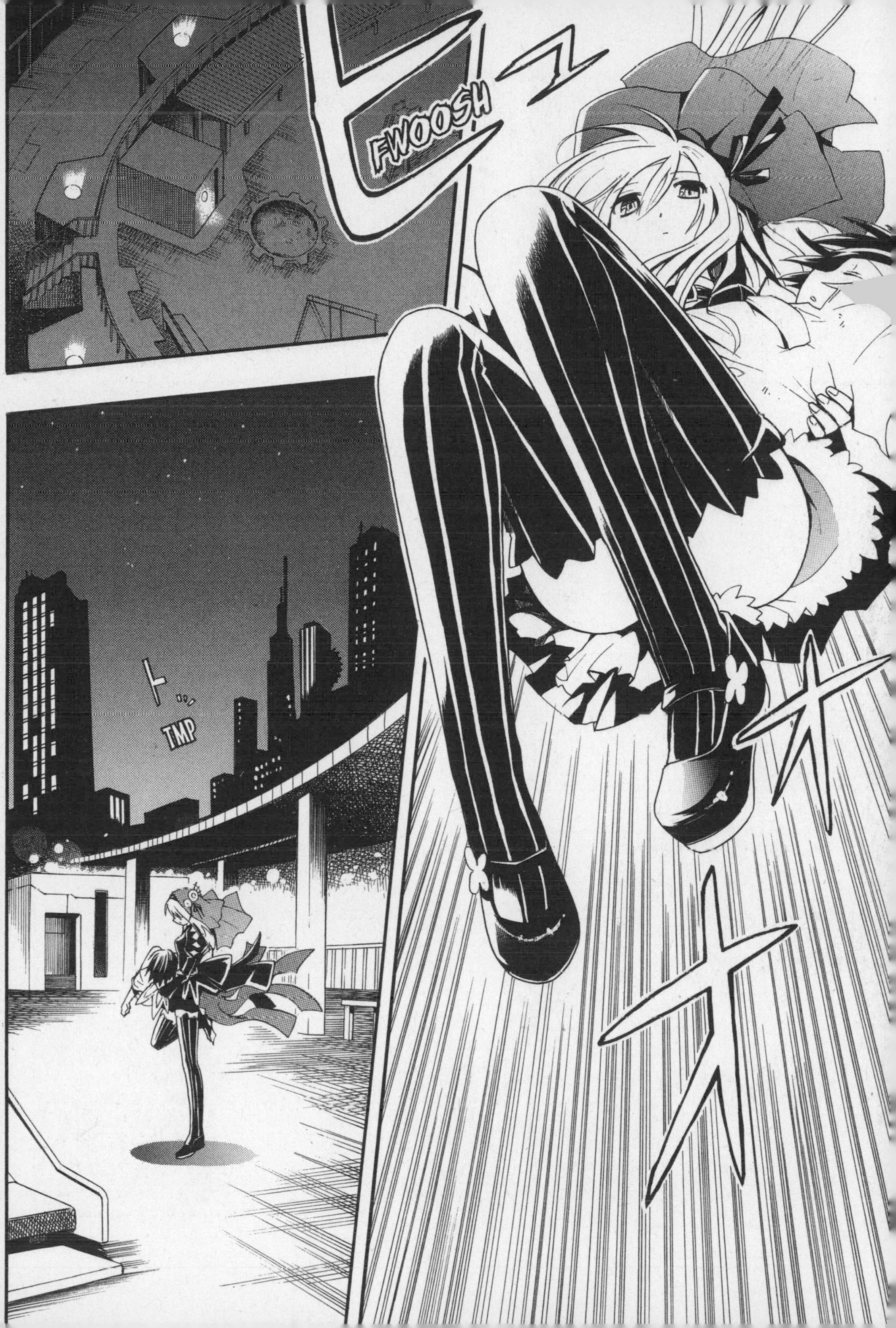
FWOOSH
TMP

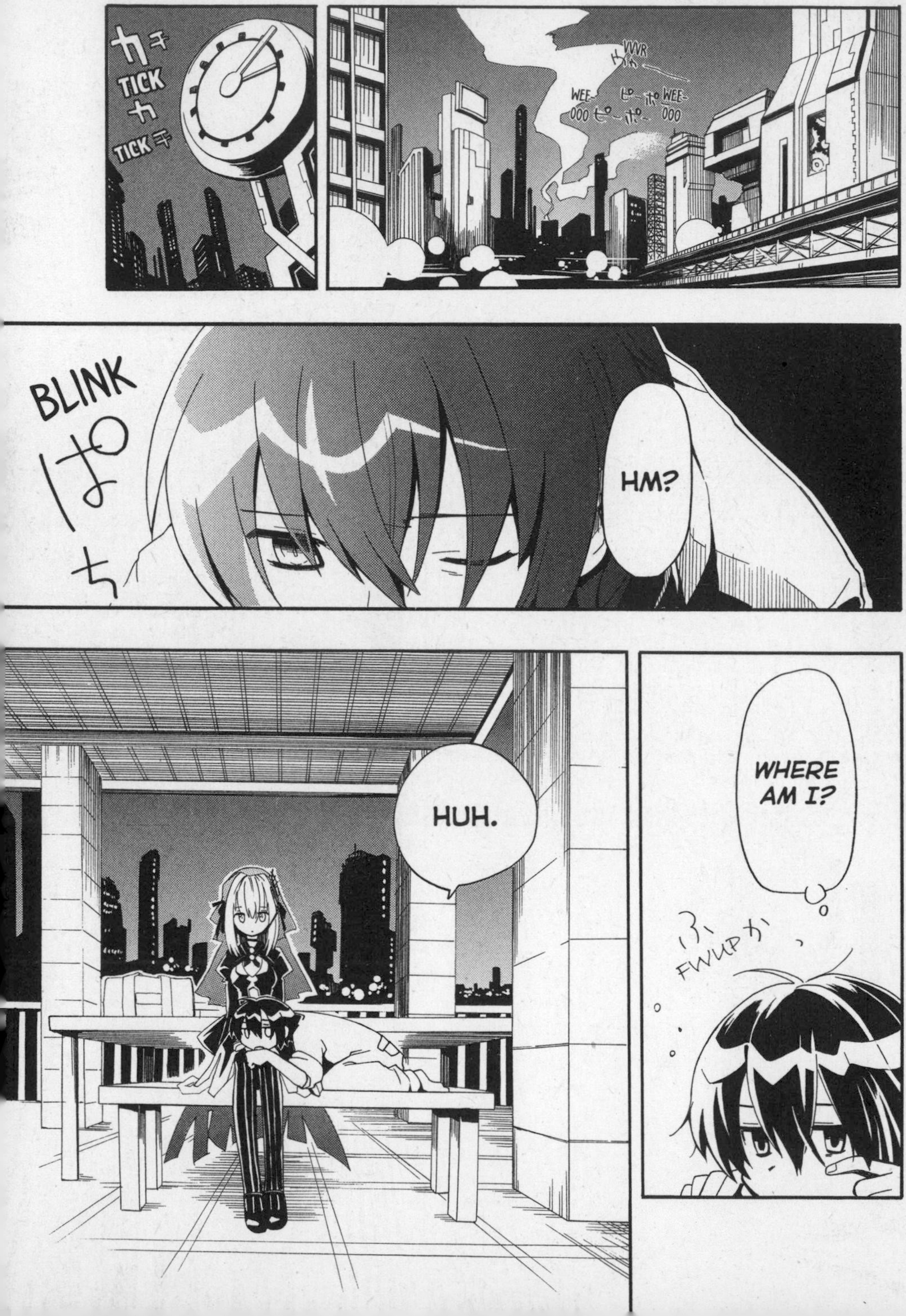
VVVR
WEE-OOO
WEE-OOO
カチ TICK
カチ TICK
BLINK
ぱち
HM?
WHERE AM I?
ふ FWUP
HUH.

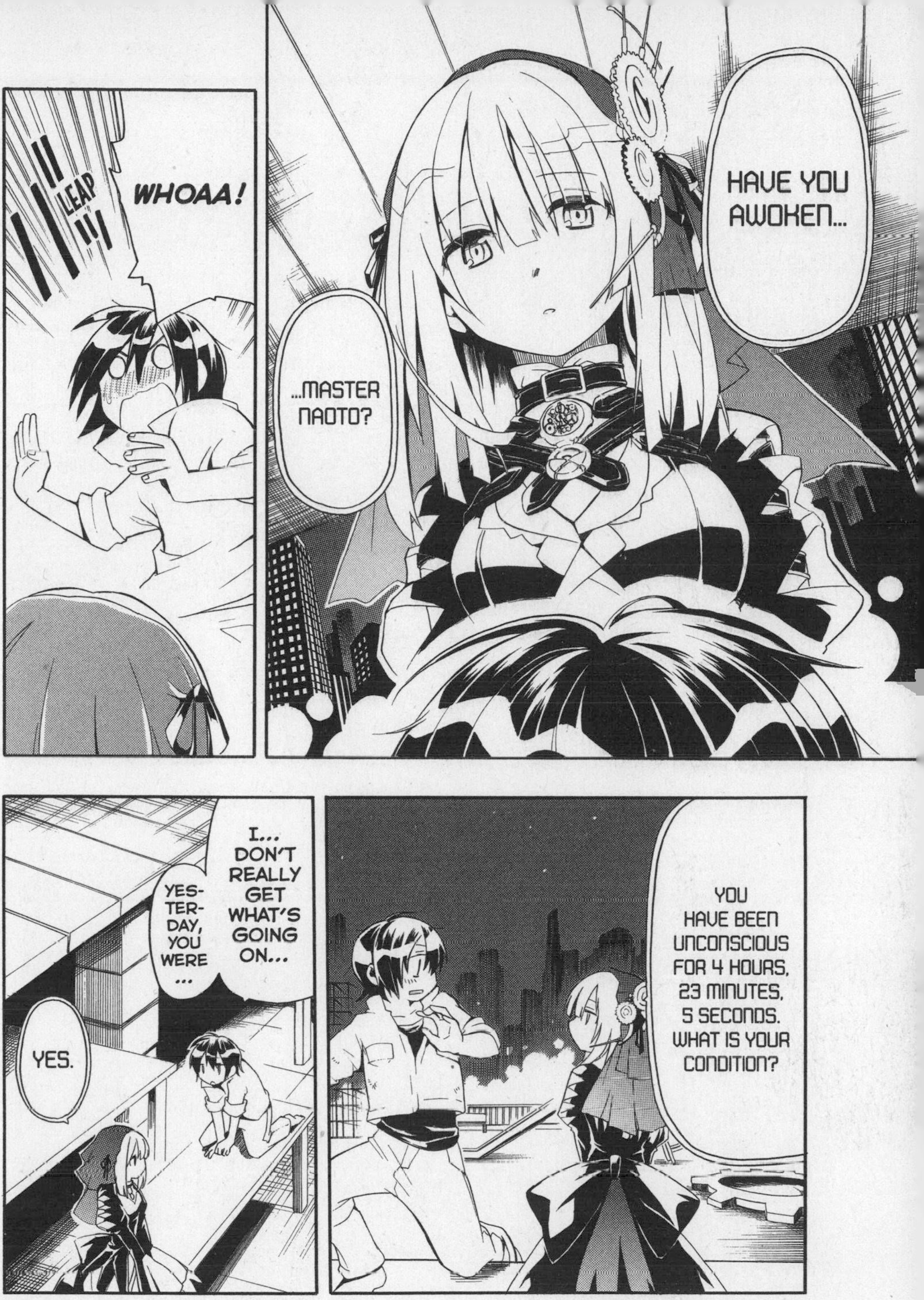
HAVE YOU AWOKEN...
...MASTER NAOTO?
WHOAA!
LEAP
YOU HAVE BEEN UNCONSCIOUS FOR 4 HOURS, 23 MINUTES, 5 SECONDS. WHAT IS YOUR CONDITION?
I... DON'T REALLY GET WHAT'S GOING ON...
YES-TER-DAY, YOU WERE ...
YES.

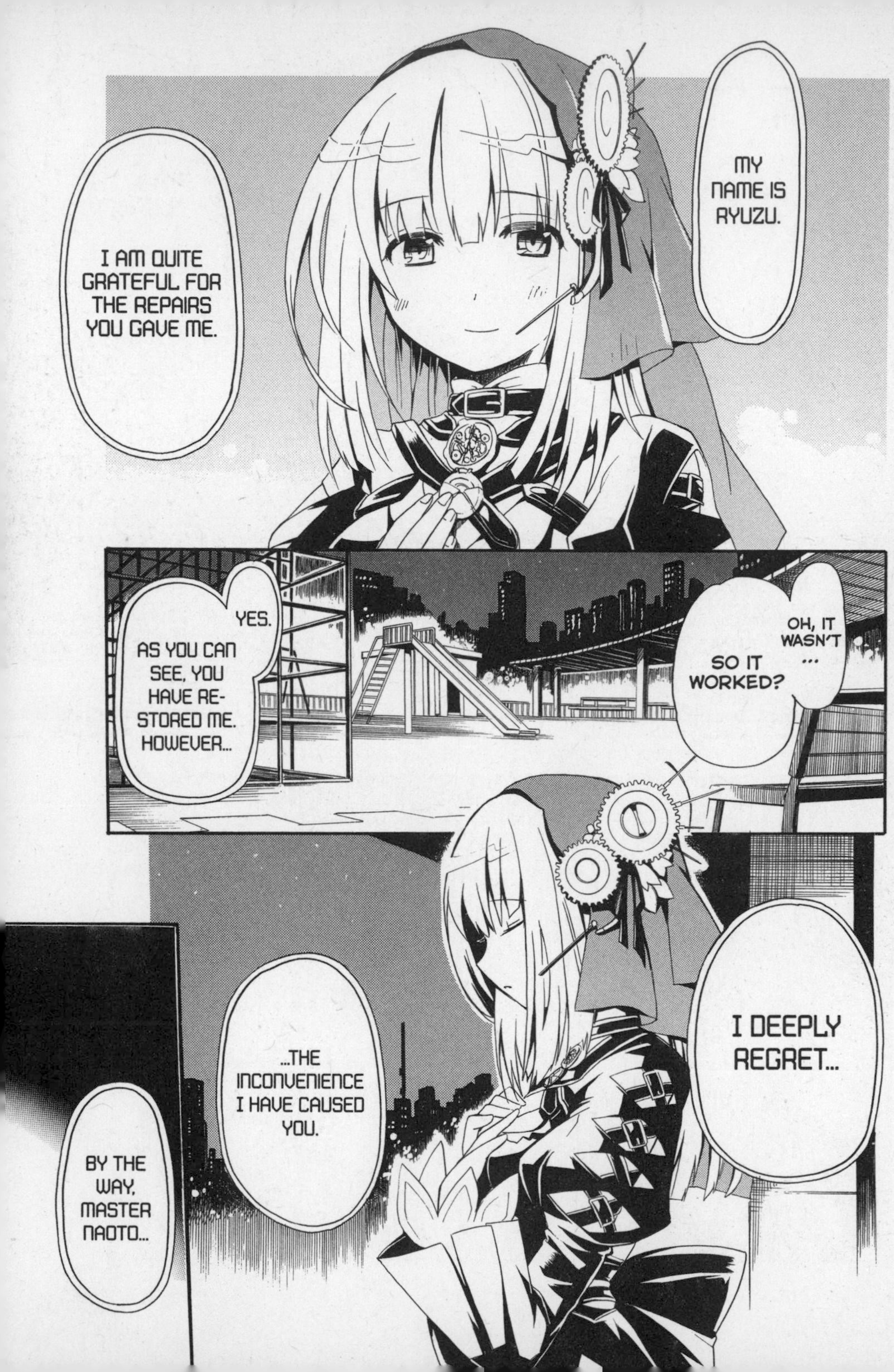
MY NAME IS RYUZU.
I AM QUITE GRATEFUL FOR THE REPAIRS YOU GAVE ME.
OH, IT WASN'T ...
SO IT WORKED?
YES. AS YOU CAN SEE, YOU HAVE RE-STORED ME. HOWEVER...
I DEEPLY REGRET...
...THE INCONVENIENCE I HAVE CAUSED YOU.
BY THE WAY, MASTER NAOTO...

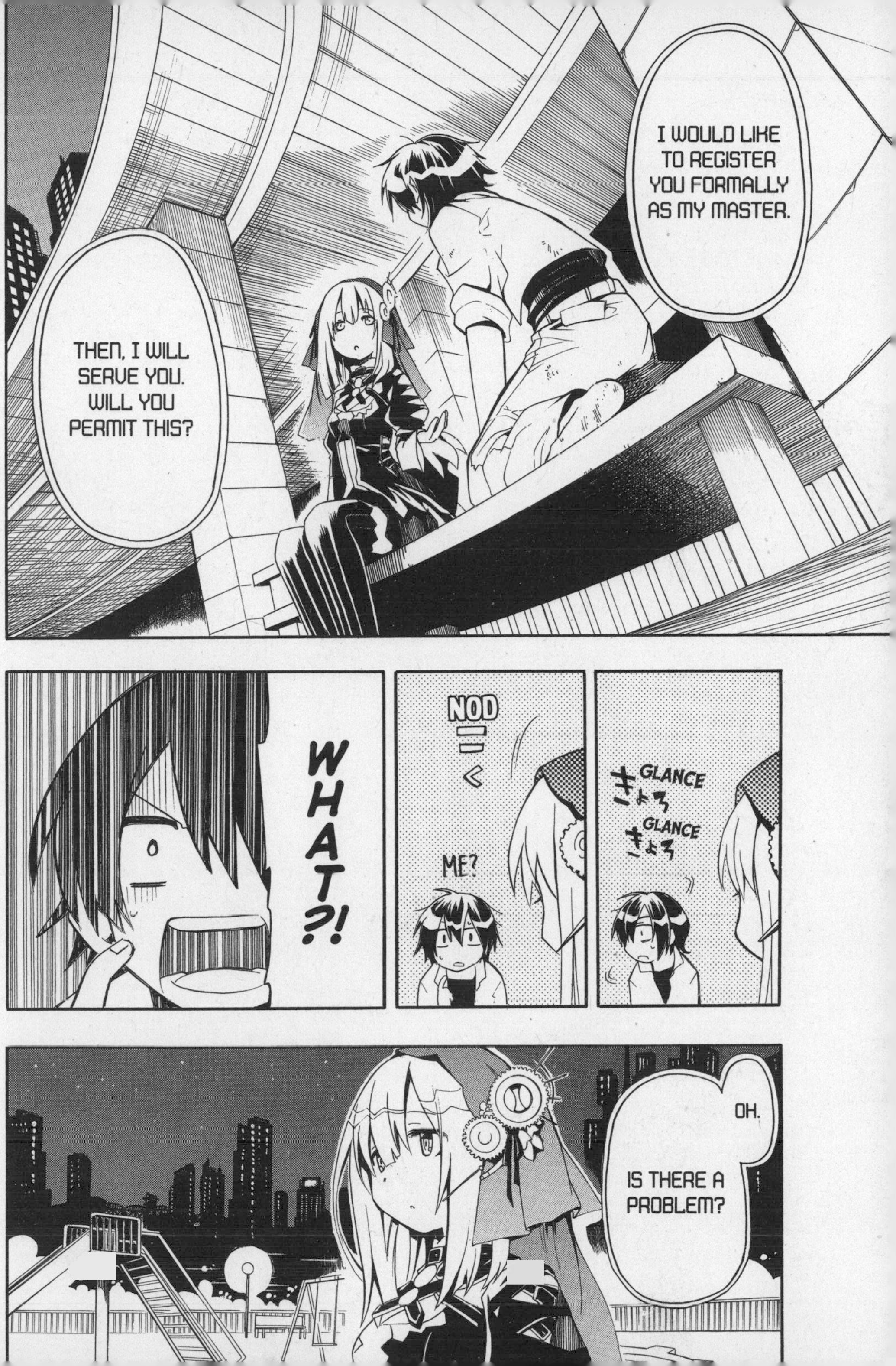
I WOULD LIKE TO REGISTER YOU FORMALLY AS MY MASTER.
THEN, I WILL SERVE YOU. WILL YOU PERMIT THIS?
GLANCE きょろ
GLANCE きょろ
NOD
ME?
WHAT?!
OH.
IS THERE A PROBLEM?

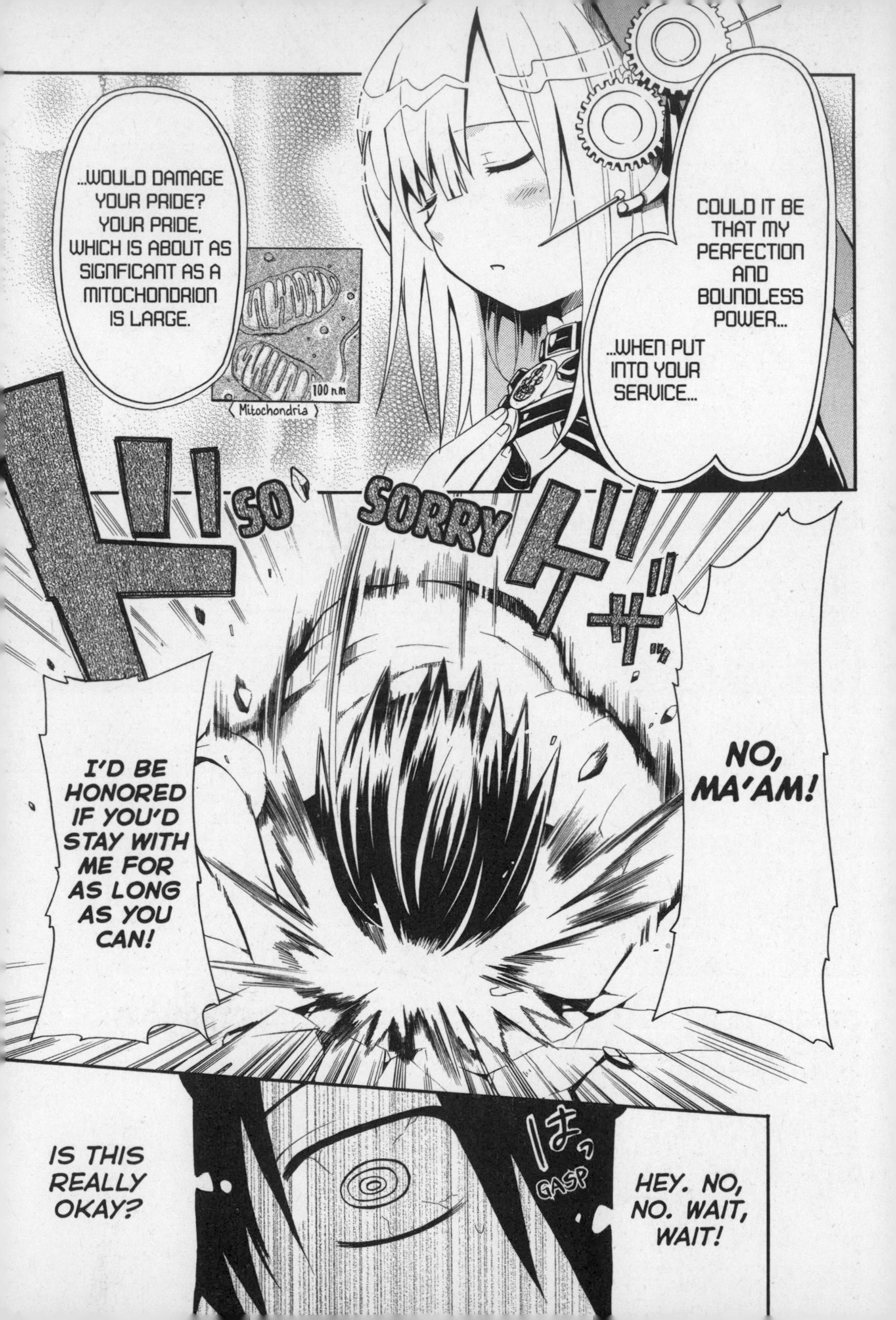
COULD IT BE THAT MY PERFECTION AND BOUNDLESS POWER...
...WHEN PUT INTO YOUR SERVICE...
...WOULD DAMAGE YOUR PRIDE? YOUR PRIDE, WHICH IS ABOUT AS SIGNFICANT AS A MITOCHONDRION IS LARGE.
100 nm
Mitochondria
SO SORRY
NO, MA'AM!
I'D BE HONORED IF YOU'D STAY WITH ME FOR AS LONG AS YOU CAN!
HEY. NO, NO. WAIT, WAIT!
はっ
GASP
IS THIS REALLY OKAY?

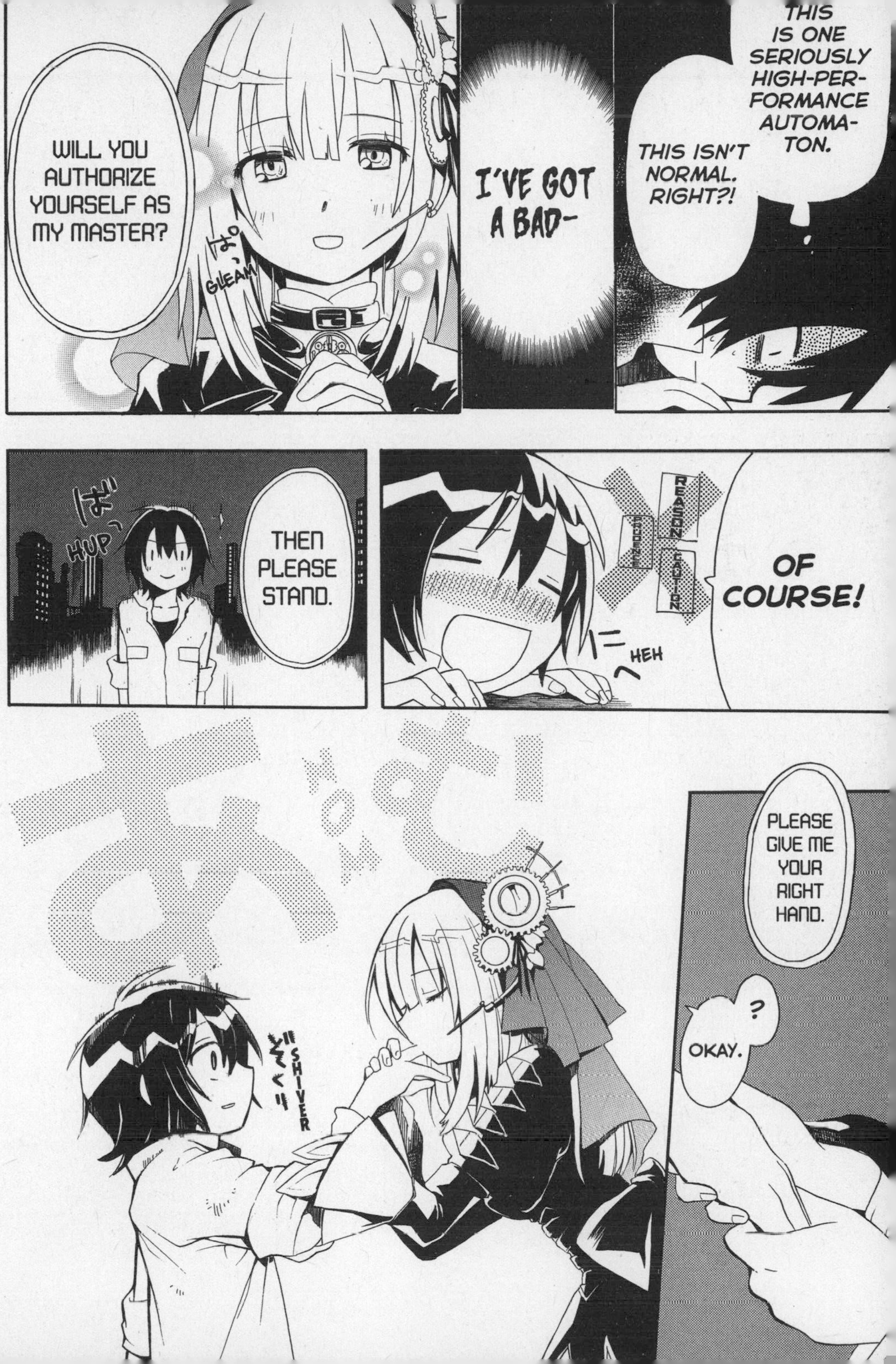
THIS IS ONE SERIOUSLY HIGH-PERFORMANCE AUTOMATON.
THIS ISN'T NORMAL. RIGHT?!
I'VE GOT A BAD-
WILL YOU AUTHORIZE YOURSELF AS MY MASTER?
ぱ、
GLEAM
OF COURSE!
REASON
CAUTION
PRUDENCE
へ
HEH
THEN PLEASE STAND.
ば、
HUP
PLEASE GIVE ME YOUR RIGHT HAND.
?
OKAY.
SHIVER

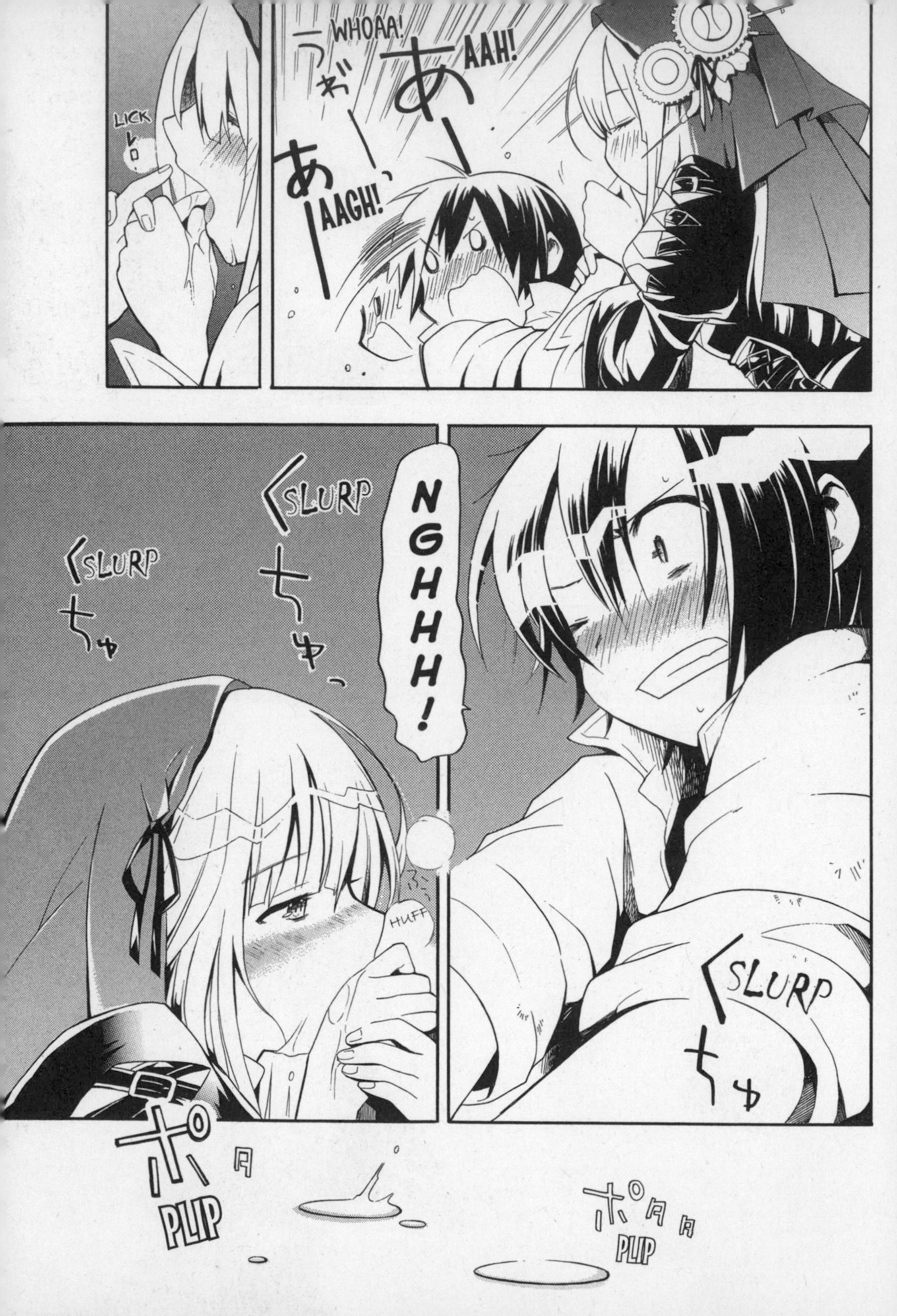
WHOAA!
AAH!
AAGH!
LICK
NGHHHH!
SLURP
SLURP
SLURP
HUFF
PLIP
PLIP

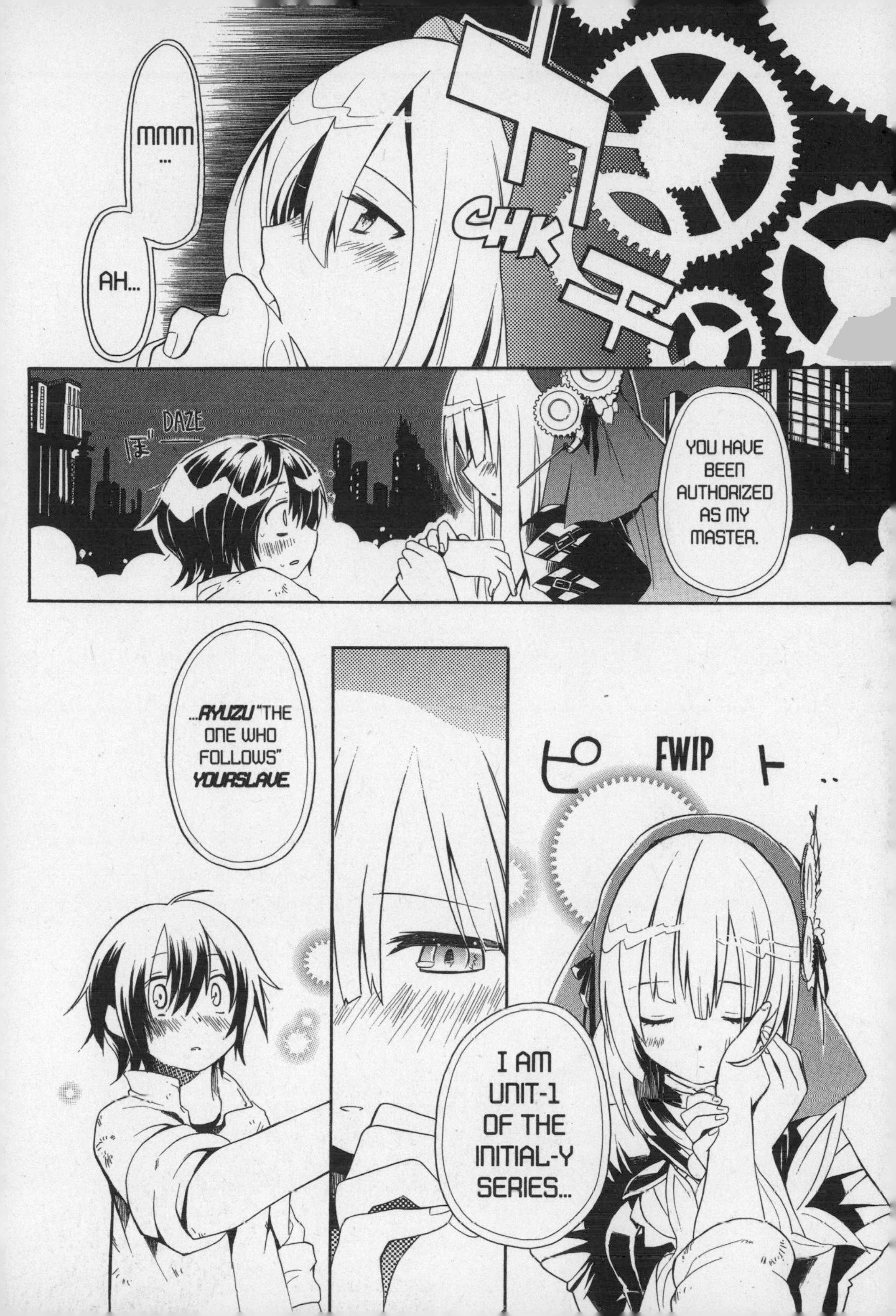

CHK
mmm...
AH...
YOU HAVE BEEN AUTHORIZED AS MY MASTER.
DAZE
FWIP
I AM UNIT-1 OF THE INITIAL-Y SERIES...
...RYUZU "THE ONE WHO FOLLOWS" YOURSLAVE.

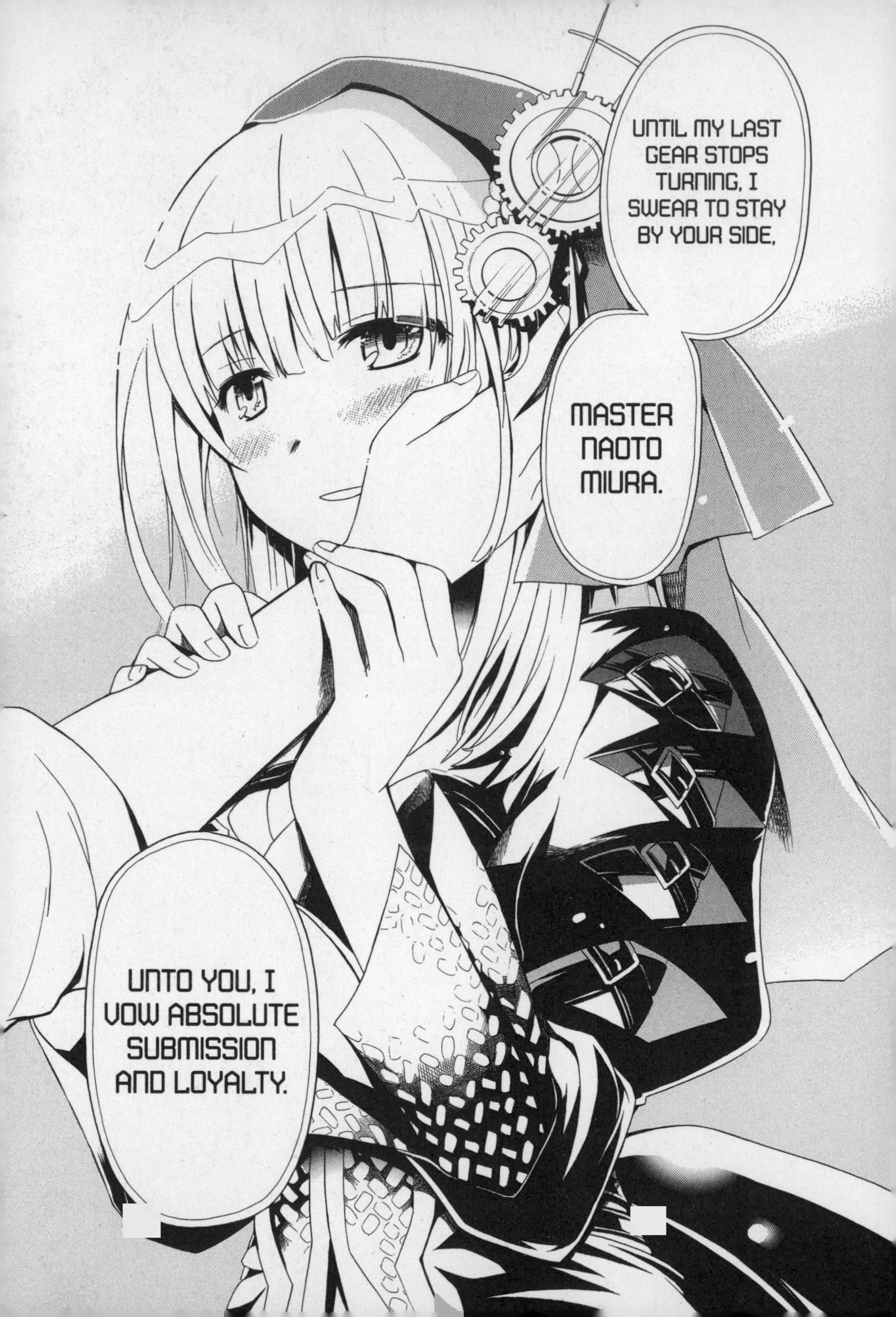
UNTIL MY LAST GEAR STOPS TURNING, I SWEAR TO STAY BY YOUR SIDE,
MASTER NAOTO MIURA.
UNTO YOU, I VOW ABSOLUTE SUBMISSION AND LOYALTY.

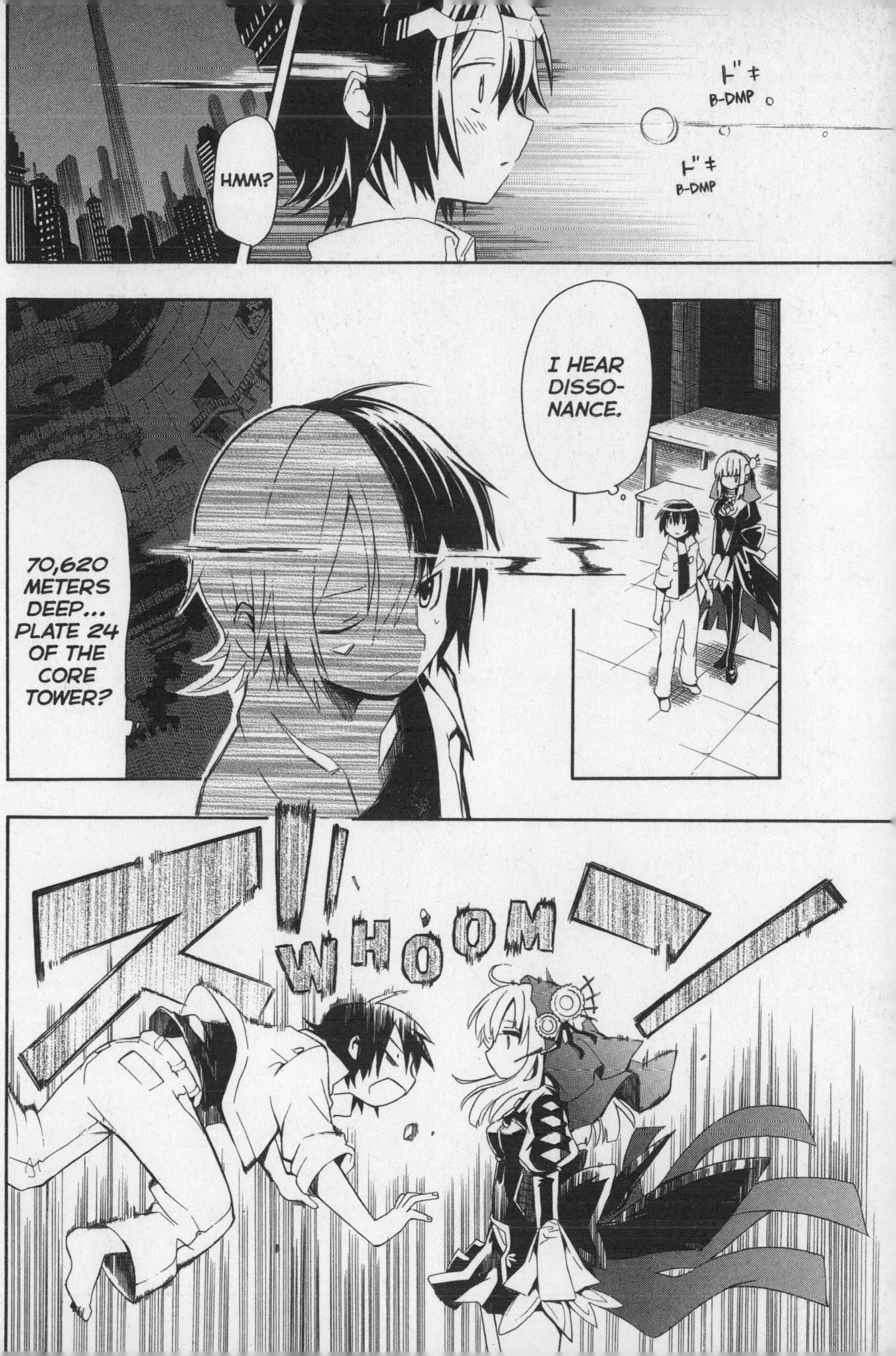
ドキ
B-DMP
ドキ
B-DMP
HMM?
I HEAR DISSO-NANCE.
70,620 METERS DEEP... PLATE 24 OF THE CORE TOWER?
WHOOM

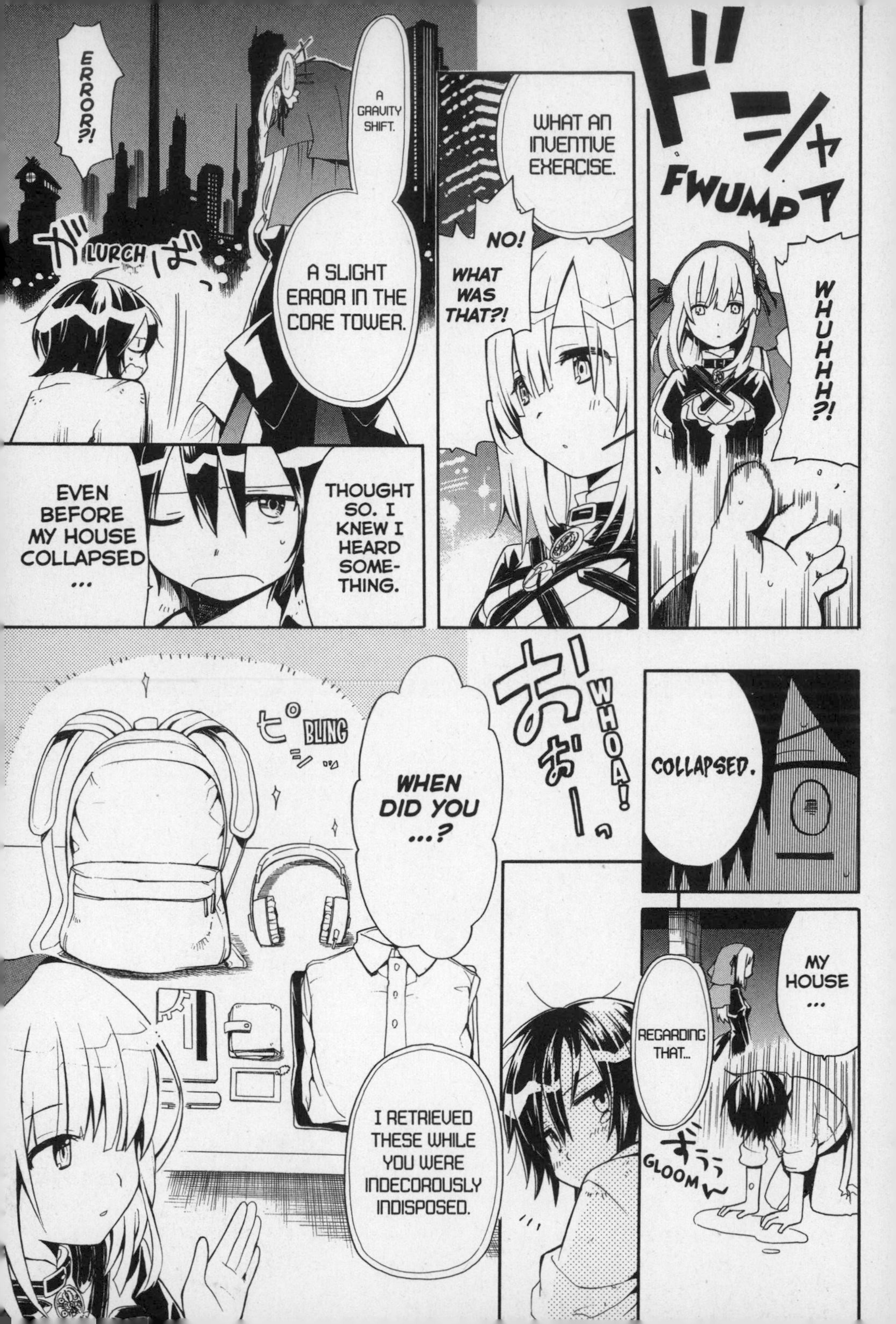
ドシャア
FWUMP
WHUHHHH?!
WHAT AN INVENTIVE EXERCISE.
NO! WHAT WAS THAT?!
A GRAVITY SHIFT.
A SLIGHT ERROR IN THE CORE TOWER.
ERROR?!
LURCH
THOUGHT SO. I KNEW I HEARD SOME-THING.
EVEN BEFORE MY HOUSE COLLAPSED ...
COLLAPSED.
MY HOUSE ...
REGARDING THAT...
GLOOM
おぉー
WHOA!
WHEN DID YOU ...?
BLING
I RETRIEVED THESE WHILE YOU WERE INDECOROUSLY INDISPOSED.

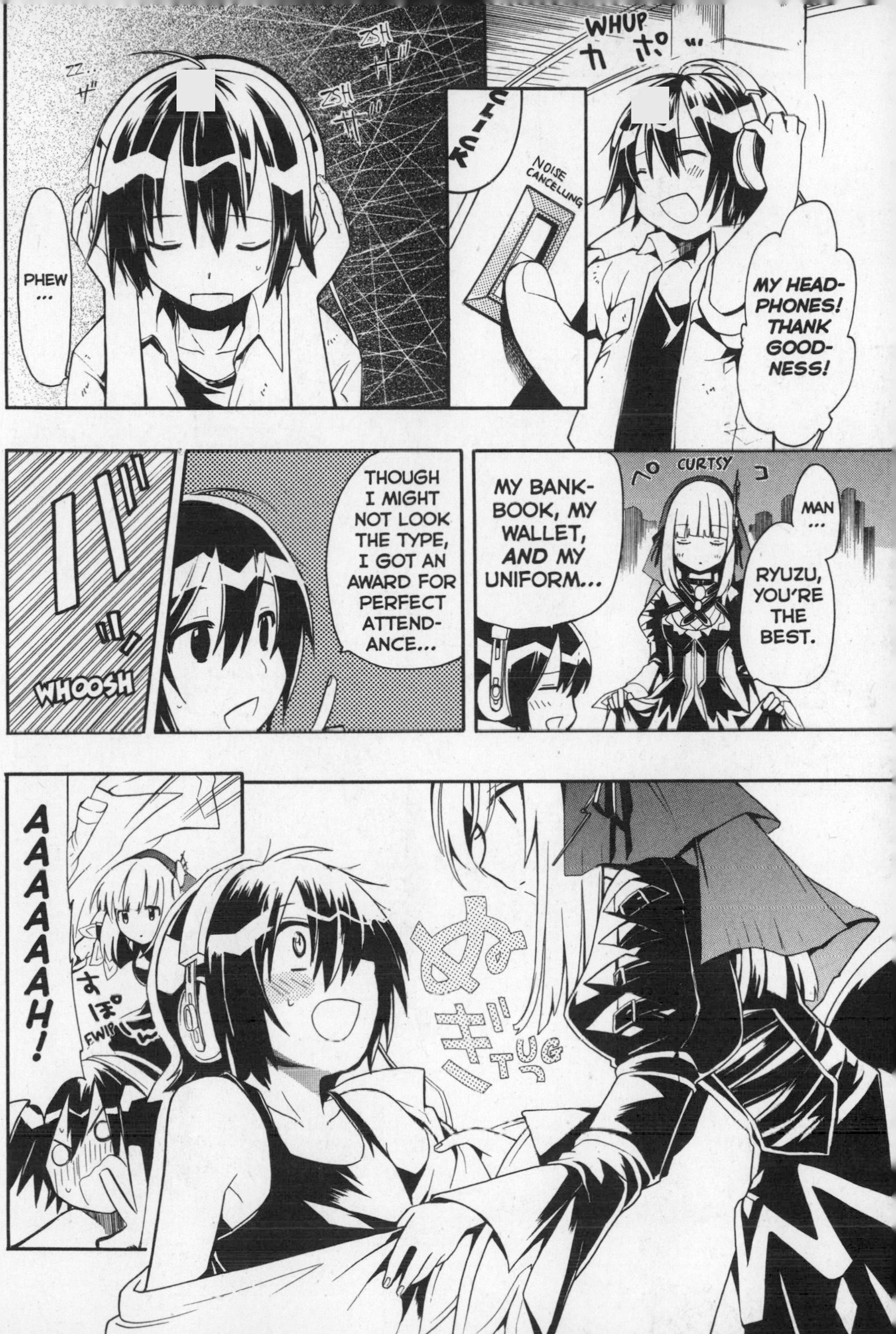
WHUP
カポ
MY HEAD-PHONES! THANK GOOD-NESS!
CLICK
NOISE CANCELLING
ZZ... ザ
ZSH ザ
ZSH ザ
PHEW...
CURTSY
ペコ
MAN...
RYUZU, YOU'RE THE BEST.
MY BANK-BOOK, MY WALLET, AND MY UNIFORM...
THOUGH I MIGHT NOT LOOK THE TYPE, I GOT AN AWARD FOR PERFECT ATTEND-ANCE...
WHOOSH
めぎっ
TUG
すぽ
FWIP
AAAAAAAH!

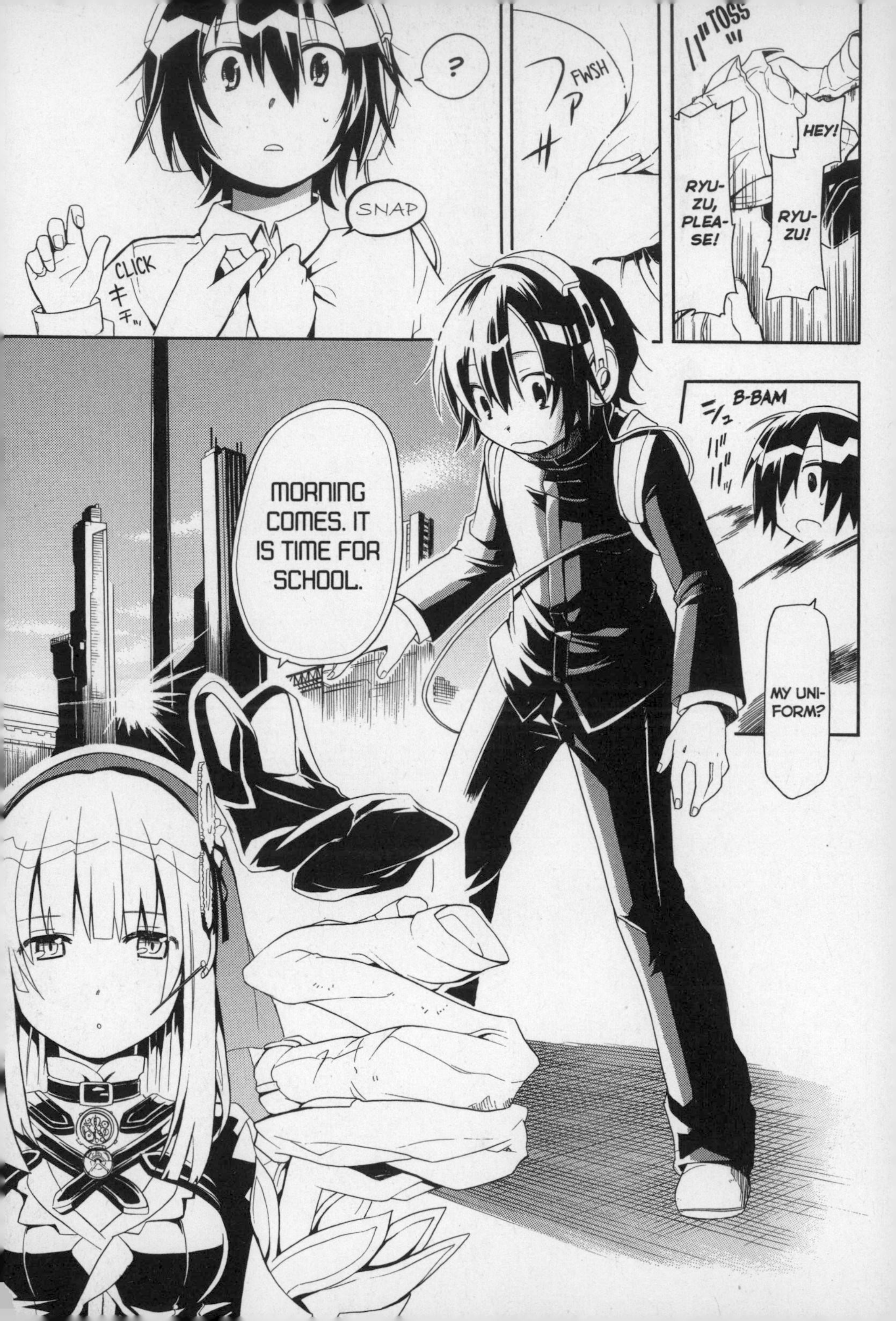
TOSS
HEY!
RYU-ZU!
RYU-ZU, PLEASE!
FWSH
?
SNAP
CLICK
B-BAM
MY UNI-FORM?
MORNING COMES. IT IS TIME FOR SCHOOL.

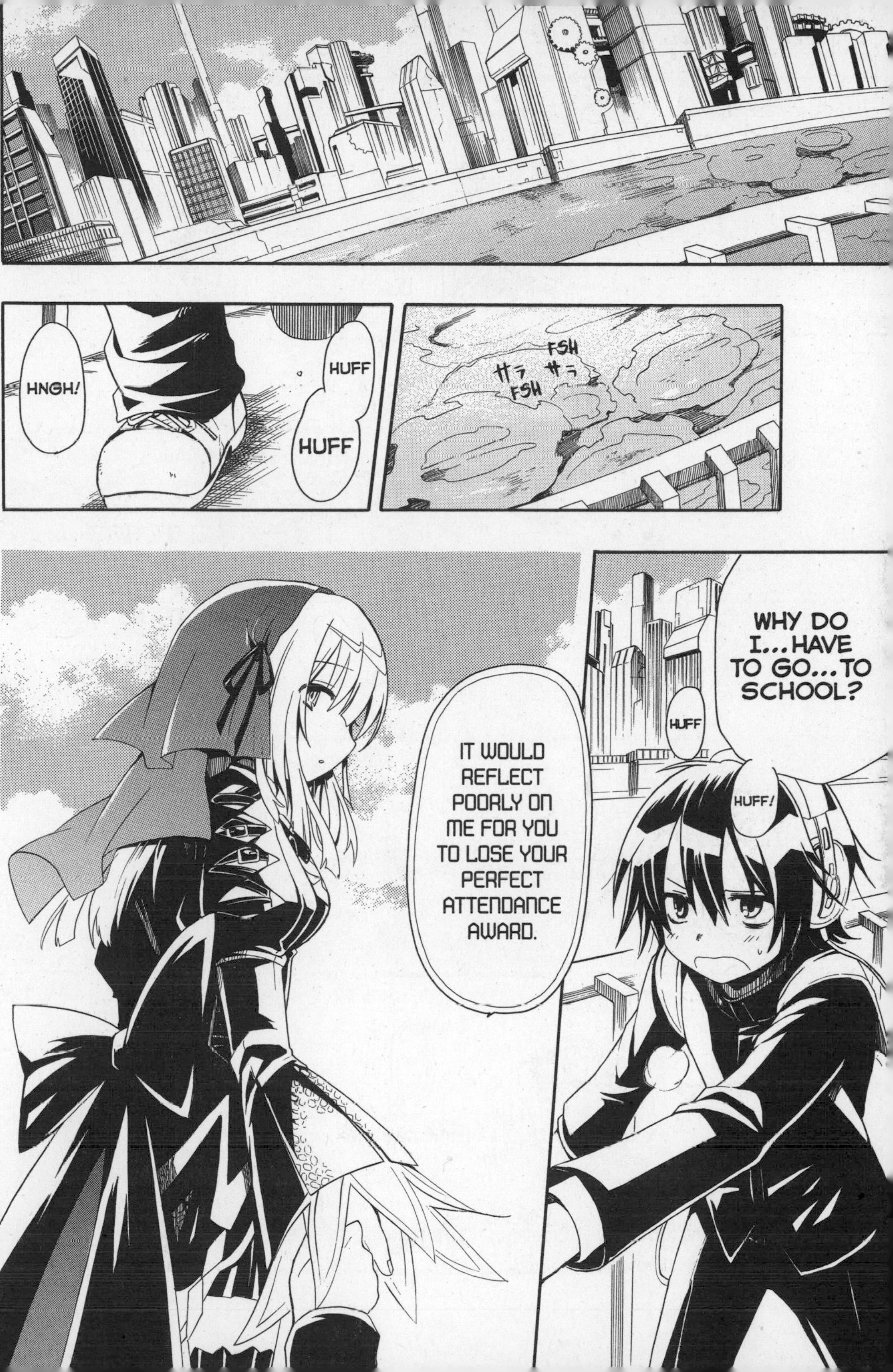
FSH
サラ サラ
FSH
HUFF
HUFF
HNGH!
WHY DO I...HAVE TO GO...TO SCHOOL?
HUFF
HUFF!
IT WOULD REFLECT POORLY ON ME FOR YOU TO LOSE YOUR PERFECT ATTENDANCE AWARD.

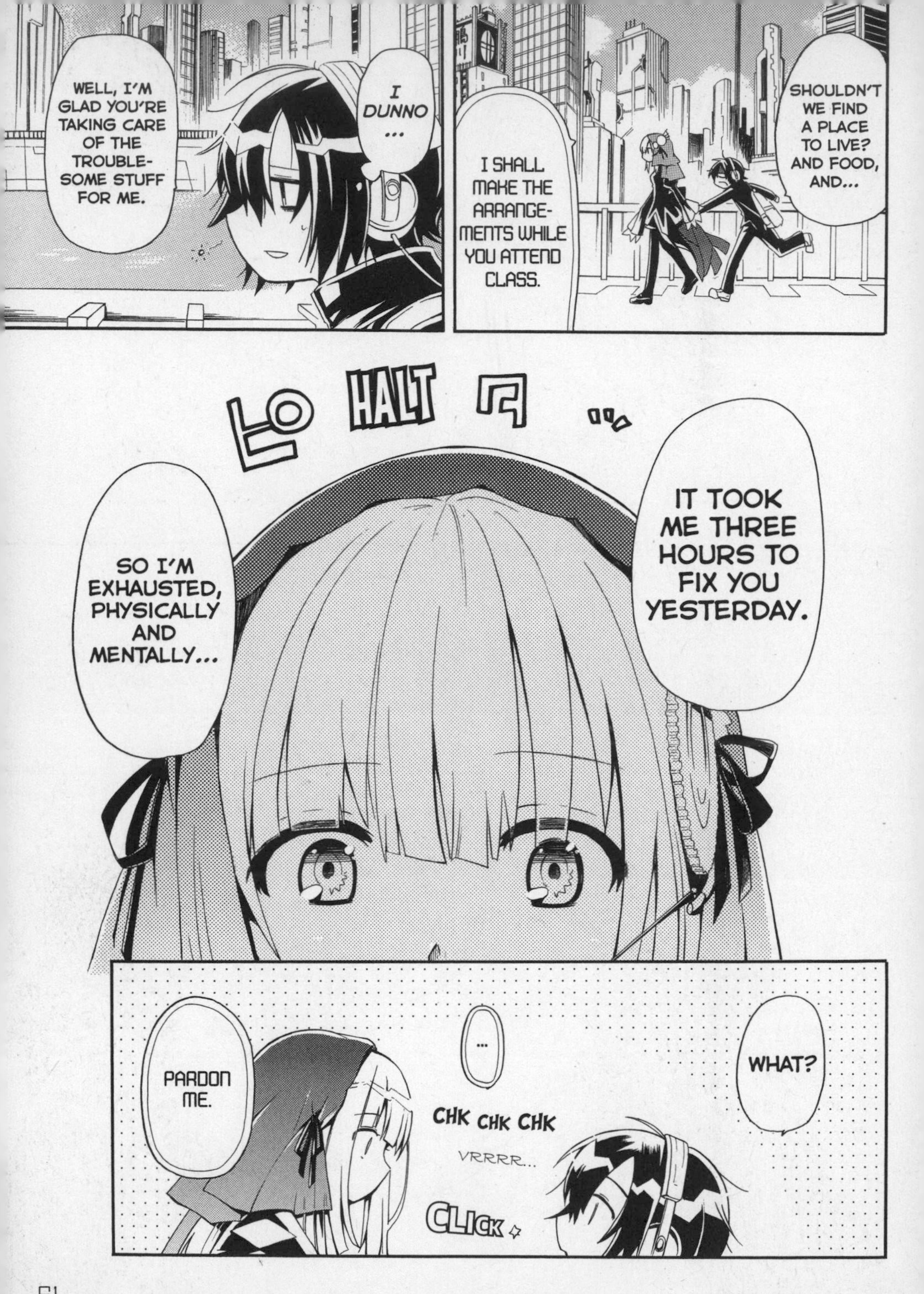
SHOULDN'T WE FIND A PLACE TO LIVE? AND FOOD, AND...
I SHALL MAKE THE ARRANGE-MENTS WHILE YOU ATTEND CLASS.
I DUNNO...
WELL, I'M GLAD YOU'RE TAKING CARE OF THE TROUBLE-SOME STUFF FOR ME.
HALT
IT TOOK ME THREE HOURS TO FIX YOU YESTERDAY.
SO I'M EXHAUSTED, PHYSICALLY AND MENTALLY...
WHAT?
...
CHK CHK CHK
VRRRR...
CLICK
PARDON ME.

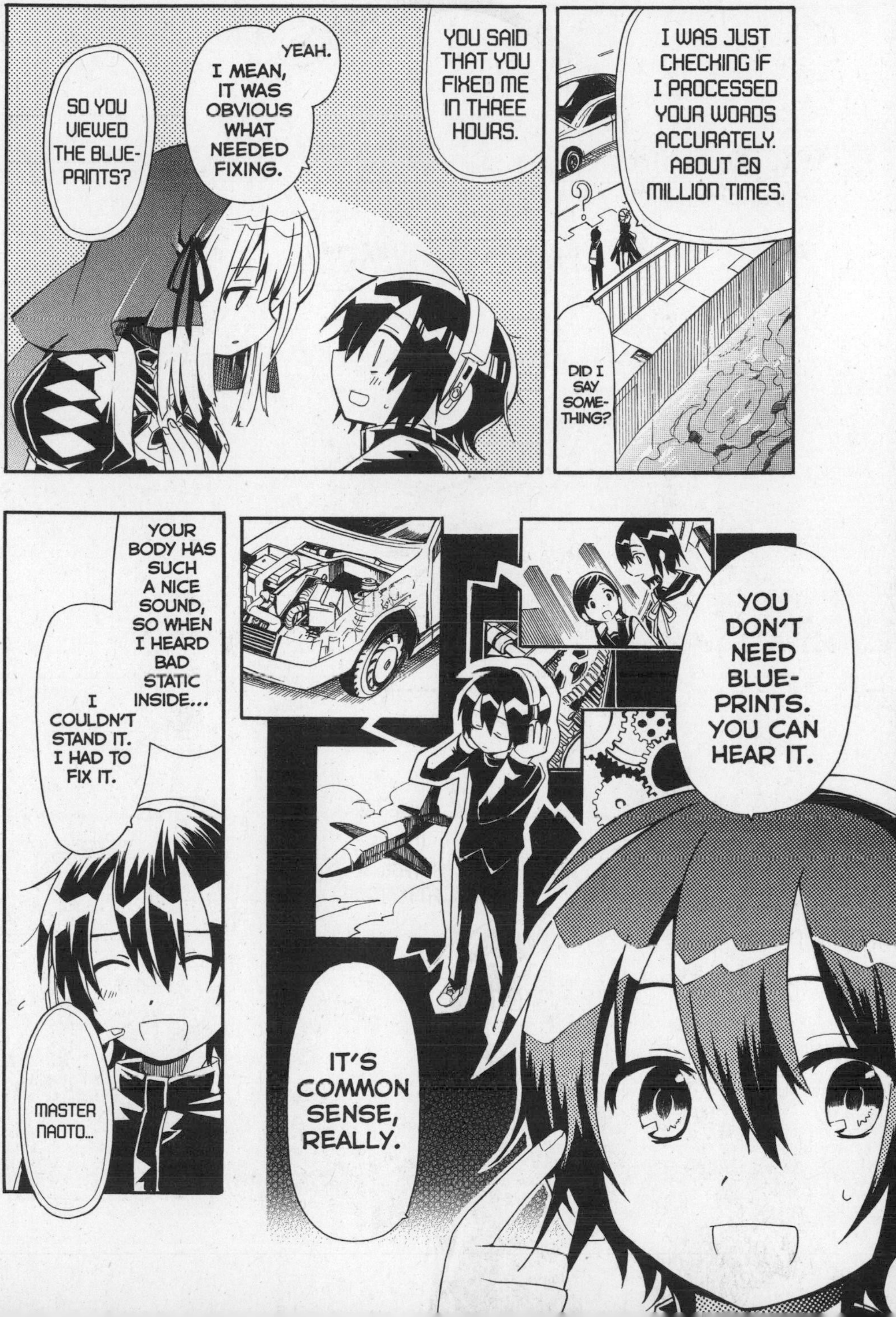
I WAS JUST CHECKING IF I PROCESSED YOUR WORDS ACCURATELY. ABOUT 20 MILLION TIMES.
DID I SAY SOME-THING?
YOU SAID THAT YOU FIXED ME IN THREE HOURS.
YEAH. I MEAN, IT WAS OBVIOUS WHAT NEEDED FIXING.
SO YOU VIEWED THE BLUE-PRINTS?
YOU DON'T NEED BLUE-PRINTS. YOU CAN HEAR IT.
IT'S COMMON SENSE, REALLY.
YOUR BODY HAS SUCH A NICE SOUND, SO WHEN I HEARD BAD STATIC INSIDE...
I COULDN'T STAND IT. I HAD TO FIX IT.
MASTER NAOTO...

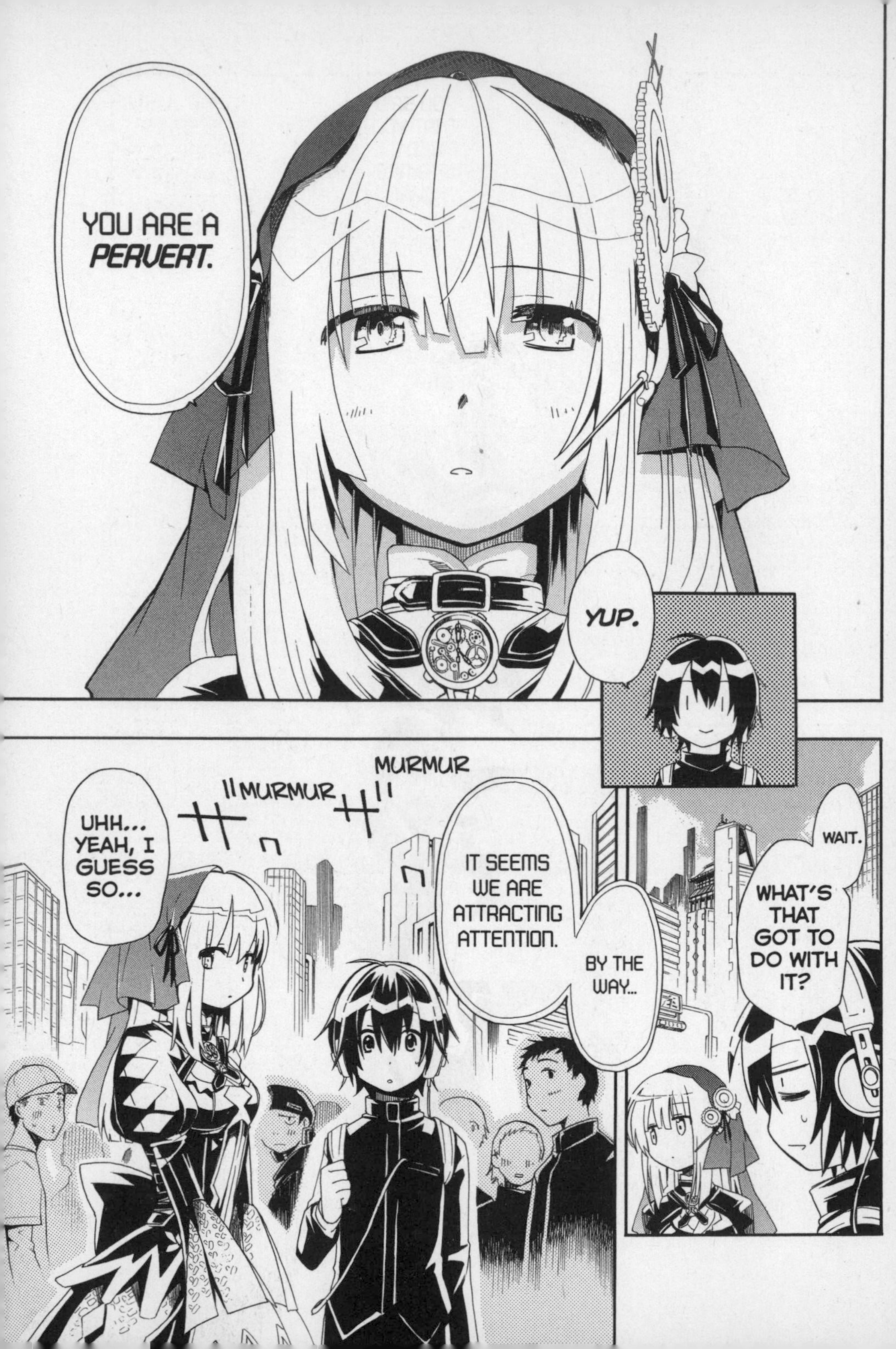
YOU ARE A *PERVERT.*
YUP.
WAIT.
WHAT'S THAT GOT TO DO WITH IT?
MURMUR
MURMUR
IT SEEMS WE ARE ATTRACTING ATTENTION.
BY THE WAY...
UHH... YEAH, I GUESS SO...

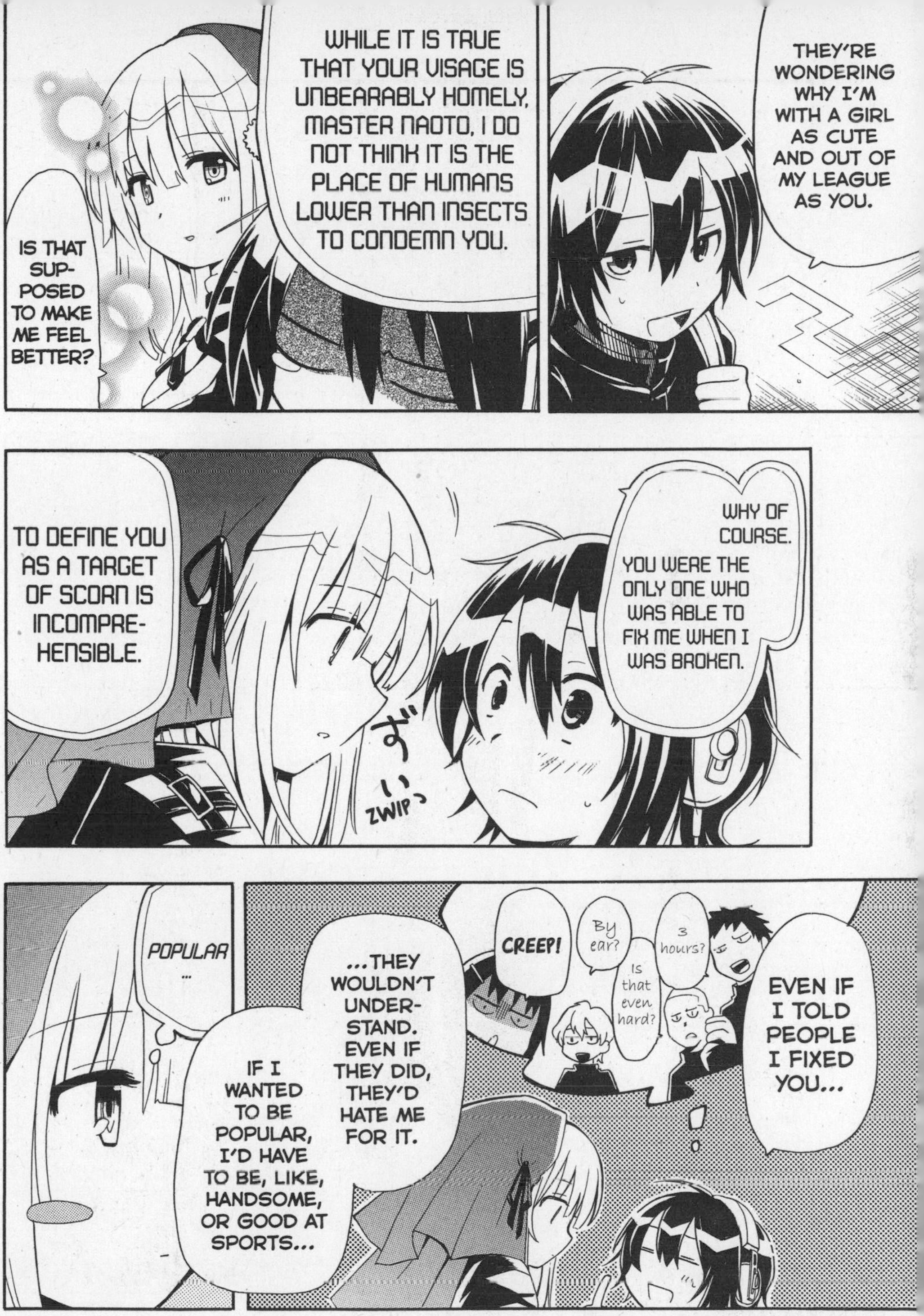
THEY'RE WONDERING WHY I'M WITH A GIRL AS CUTE AND OUT OF MY LEAGUE AS YOU.
WHILE IT IS TRUE THAT YOUR VISAGE IS UNBEARABLY HOMELY, MASTER NAOTO, I DO NOT THINK IT IS THE PLACE OF HUMANS LOWER THAN INSECTS TO CONDEMN YOU.
IS THAT SUP-POSED TO MAKE ME FEEL BETTER?
WHY OF COURSE. YOU WERE THE ONLY ONE WHO WAS ABLE TO FIX ME WHEN I WAS BROKEN.
TO DEFINE YOU AS A TARGET OF SCORN IS INCOMPRE-HENSIBLE.
ずい
ZWIP
EVEN IF I TOLD PEOPLE I FIXED YOU...
3 hours?
Is that even hard?
By ear?
CREEP!
...THEY WOULDN'T UNDER-STAND. EVEN IF THEY DID, THEY'D HATE ME FOR IT.
IF I WANTED TO BE POPULAR, I'D HAVE TO BE, LIKE, HANDSOME, OR GOOD AT SPORTS...
POPULAR ...

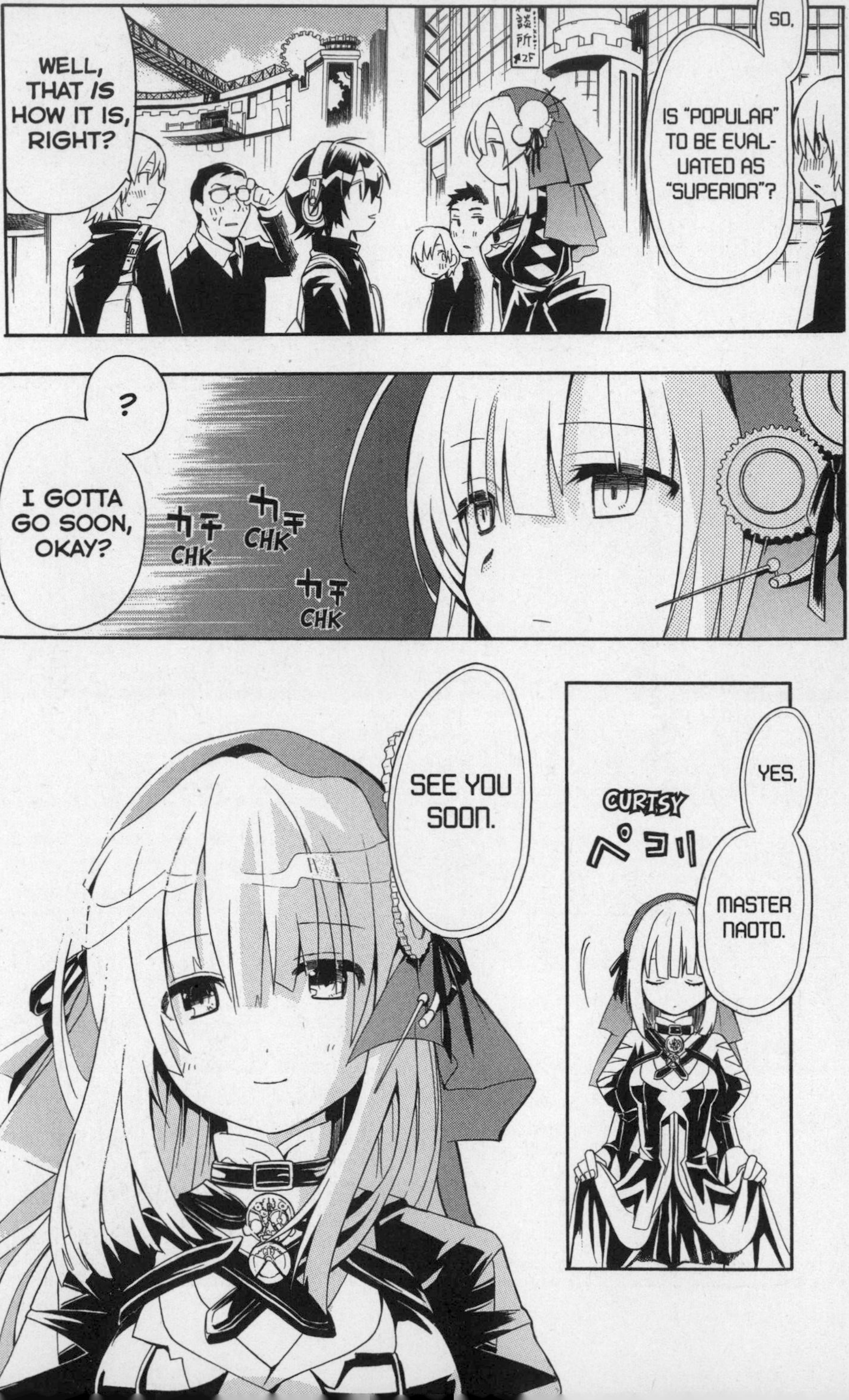
SO,
IS "POPULAR" TO BE EVAL-UATED AS "SUPERIOR"?
WELL, THAT IS HOW IT IS, RIGHT?
?
カチ CHK
カチ CHK
カチ CHK
I GOTTA GO SOON, OKAY?
YES,
MASTER NAOTO.
ペコリ CURTSY
SEE YOU SOON.

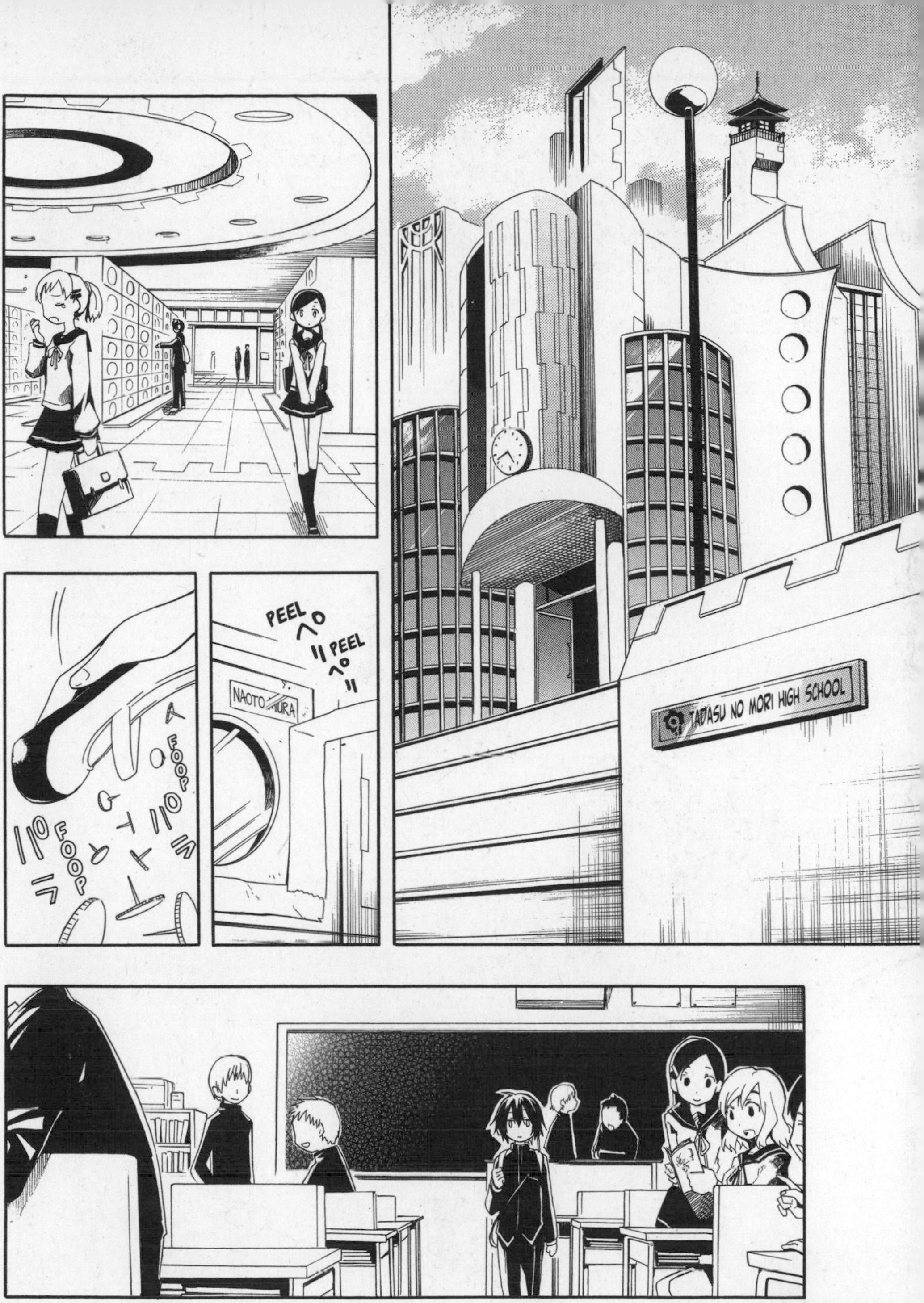
TADASU NO MORI HIGH SCHOOL
PEEL
PEEL
NAOTO MIURA
FOOP
FOOP

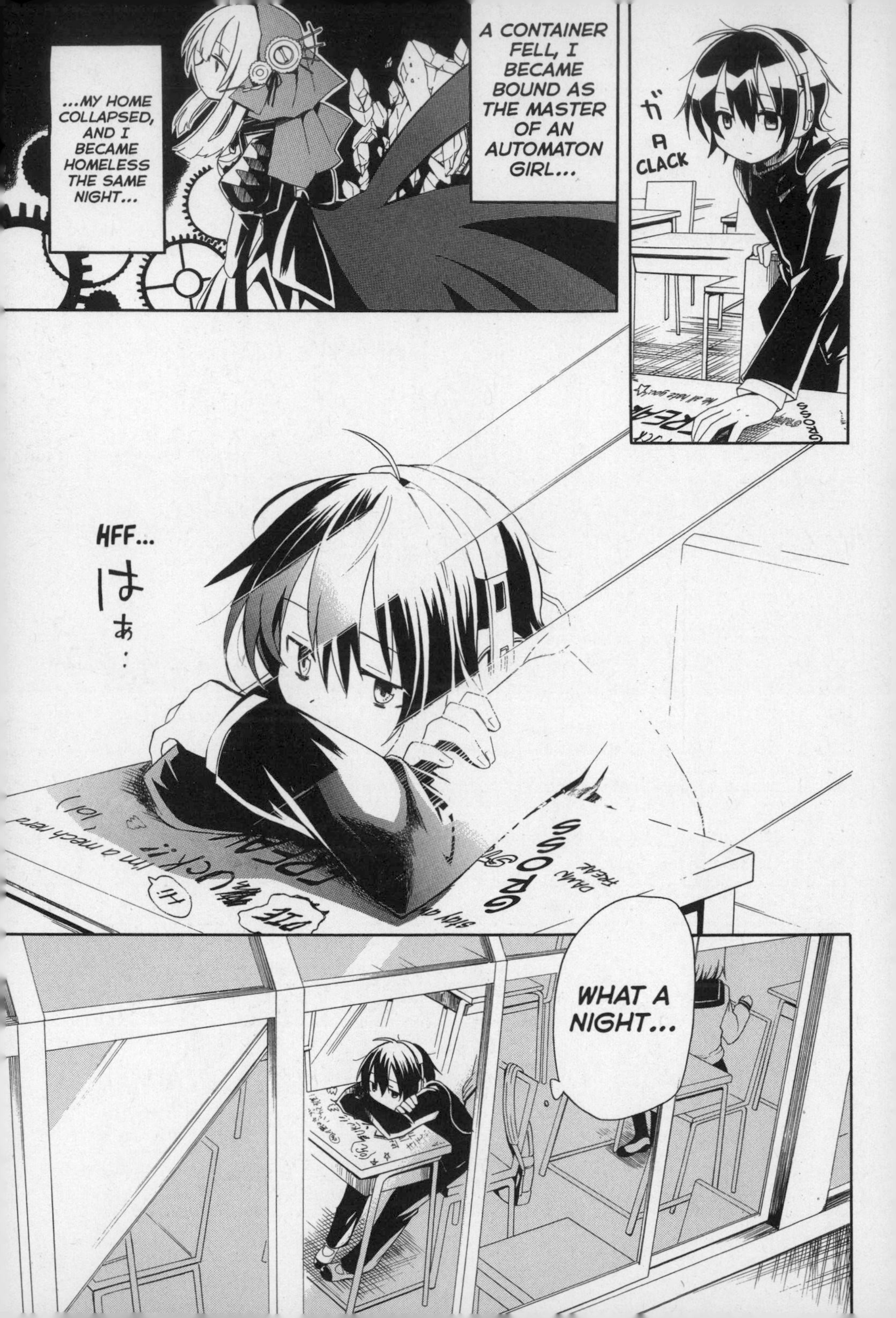
ガ
A CLACK
A CONTAINER FELL, I BECAME BOUND AS THE MASTER OF AN AUTOMATON GIRL...
...MY HOME COLLAPSED, AND I BECAME HOMELESS THE SAME NIGHT...
HFF...
はぁ：
WHAT A NIGHT...

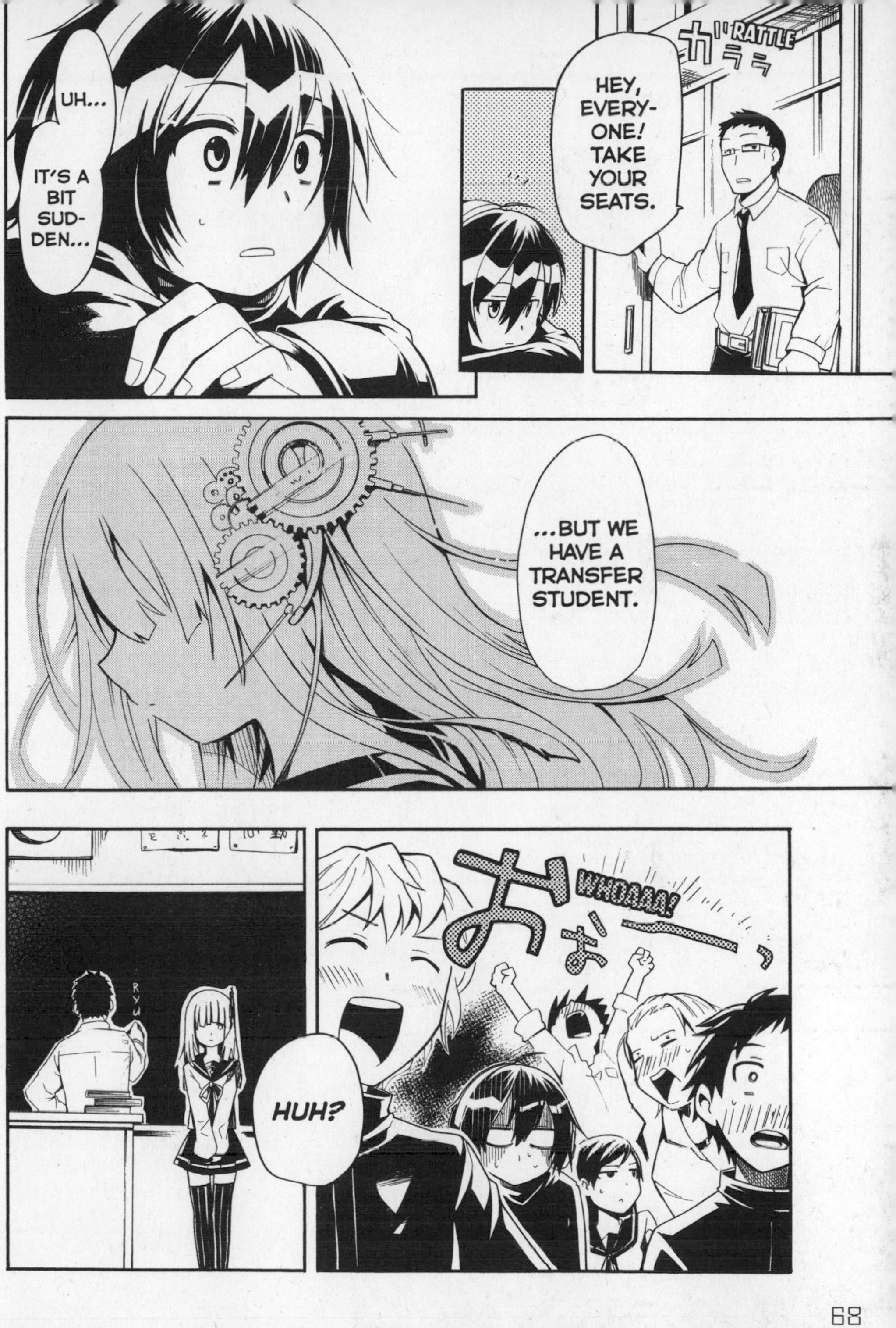
RATTLE
HEY, EVERYONE! TAKE YOUR SEATS.
UH...
IT'S A BIT SUDDEN...
...BUT WE HAVE A TRANSFER STUDENT.
WHOAAA!
HUH?

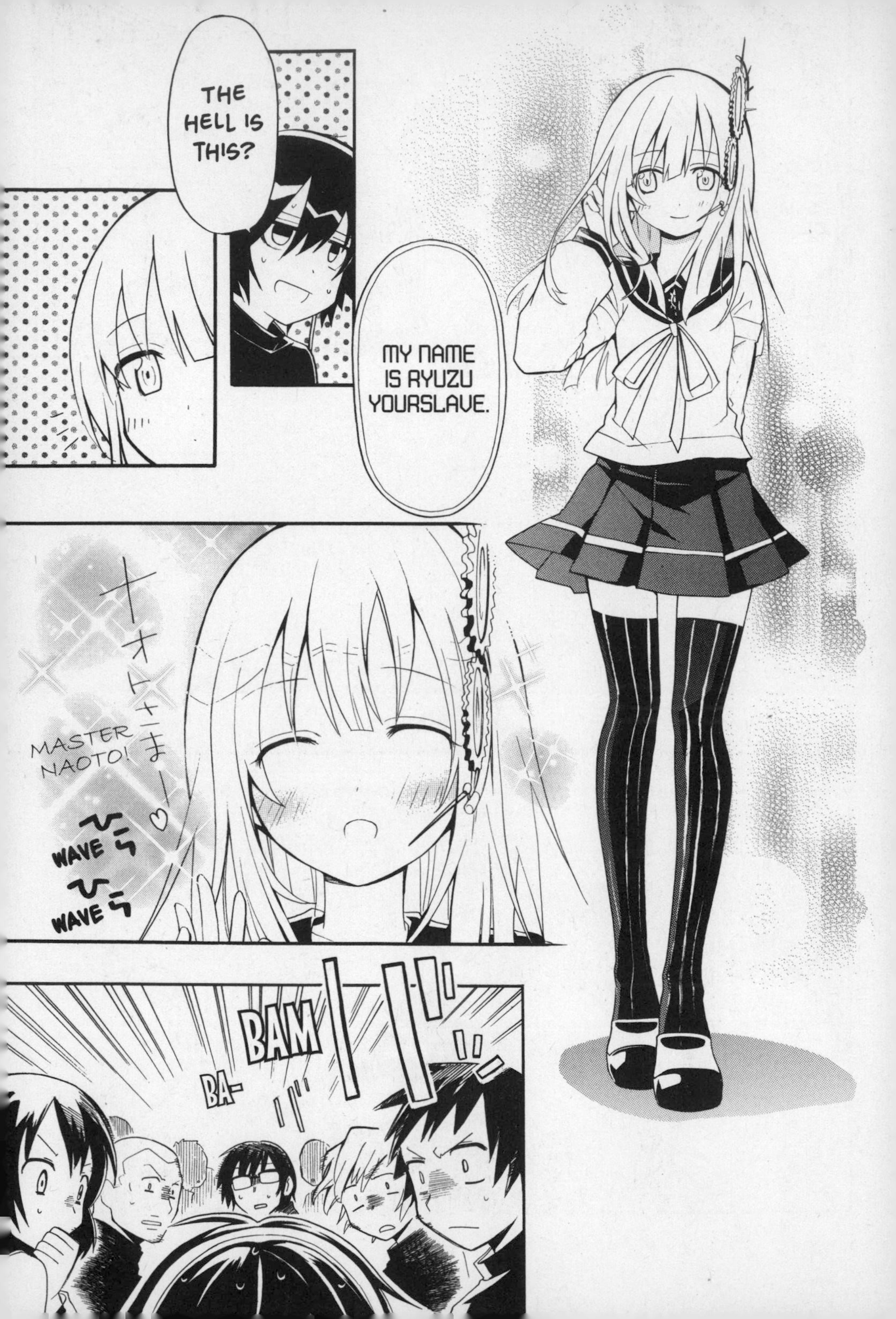
MY NAME IS RYUZU YOURSLAVE.
THE HELL IS THIS?
MASTER NAOTO!
WAVE
WAVE
BAM
BA-

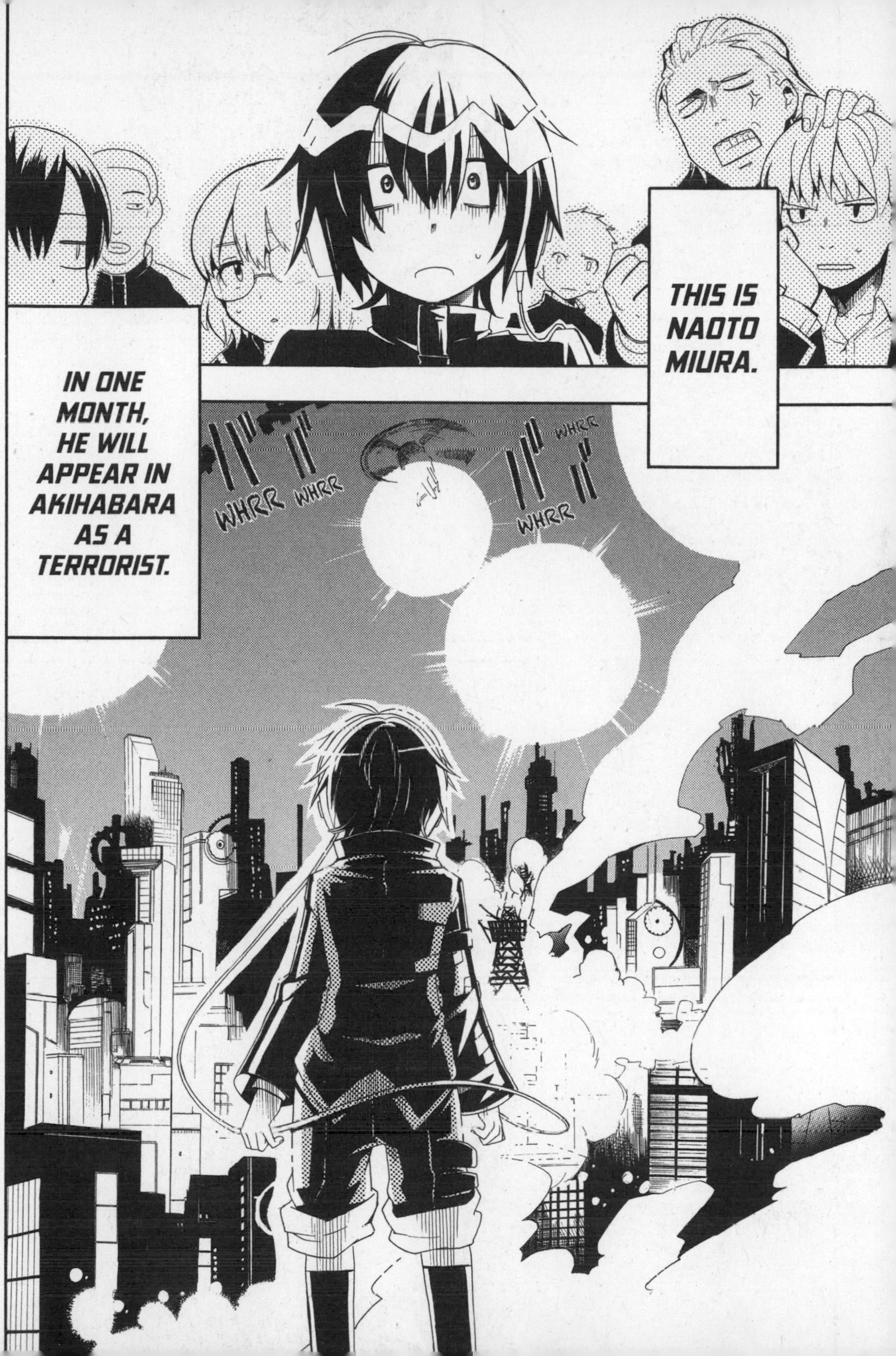
THIS IS NAOTO MIURA.
IN ONE MONTH, HE WILL APPEAR IN AKIHABARA AS A TERRORIST.
WHRR
WHRR
WHRR WHRR

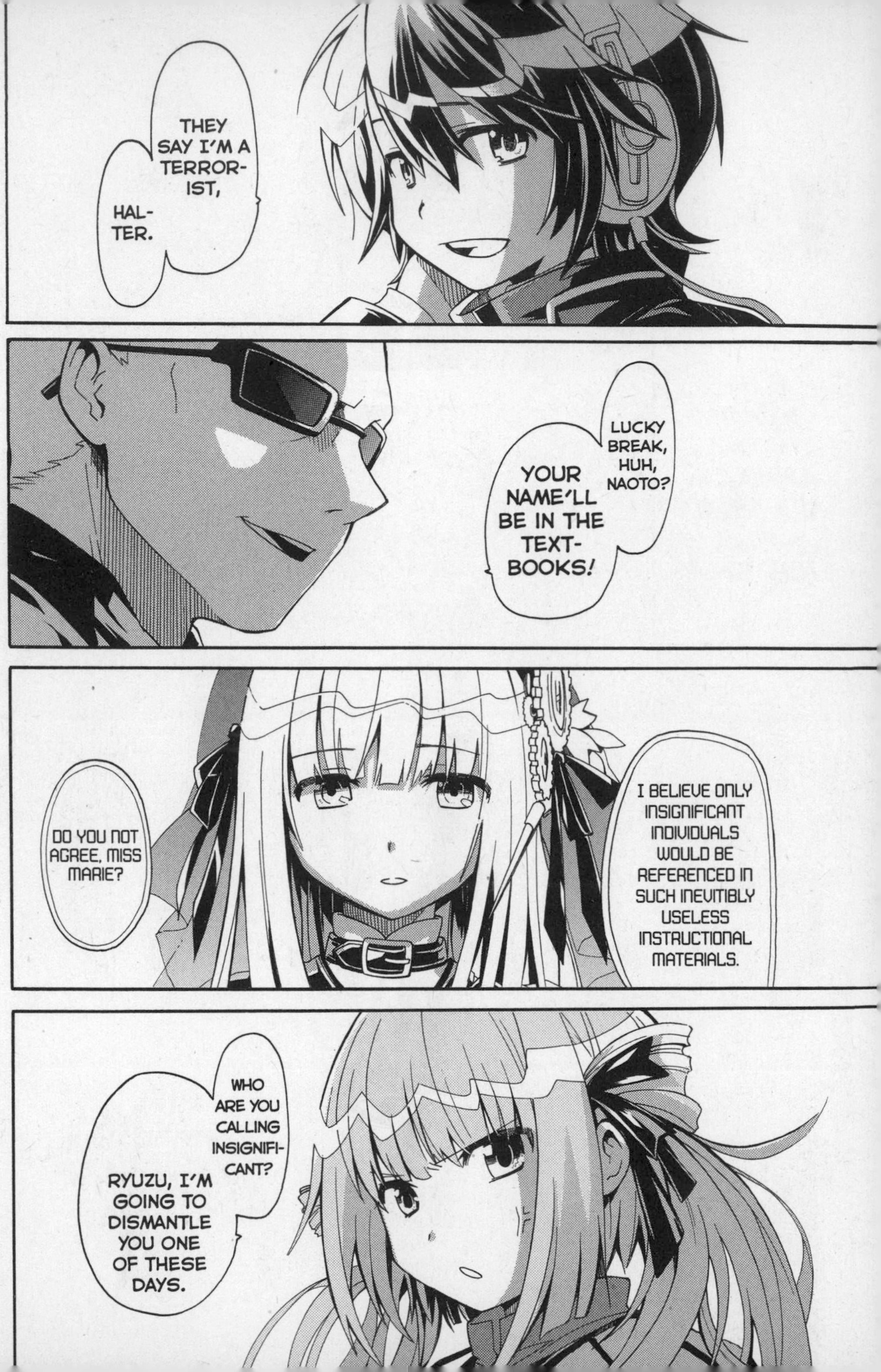
THEY SAY I'M A TERRORIST, HALTER.
LUCKY BREAK, HUH, NAOTO?
YOUR NAME'LL BE IN THE TEXTBOOKS!
I BELIEVE ONLY INSIGNIFICANT INDIVIDUALS WOULD BE REFERENCED IN SUCH INEVITIBLY USELESS INSTRUCTIONAL MATERIALS.
DO YOU NOT AGREE, MISS MARIE?
WHO ARE YOU CALLING INSIGNIFICANT?
RYUZU, I'M GOING TO DISMANTLE YOU ONE OF THESE DAYS.

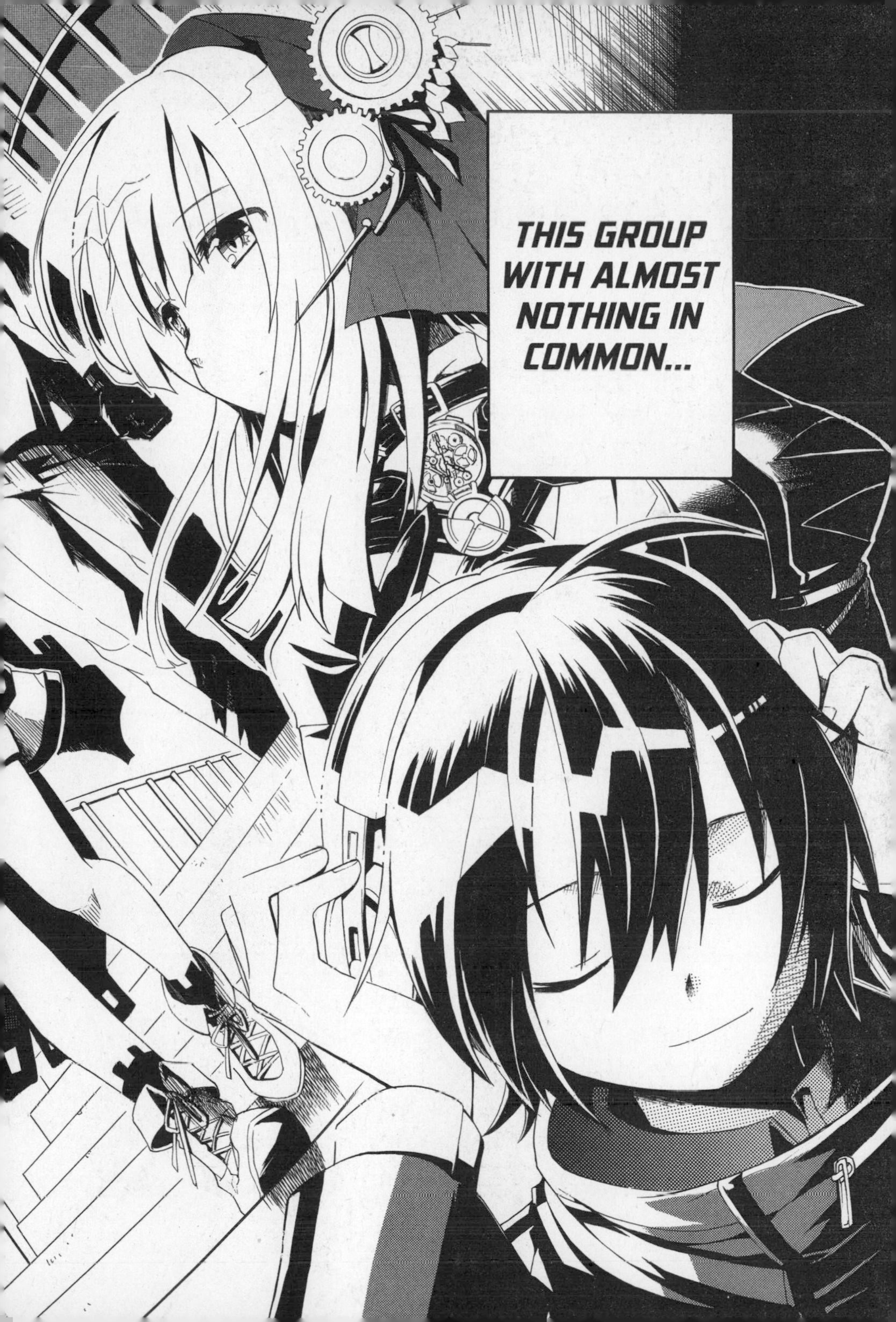
THIS GROUP WITH ALMOST NOTHING IN COMMON...

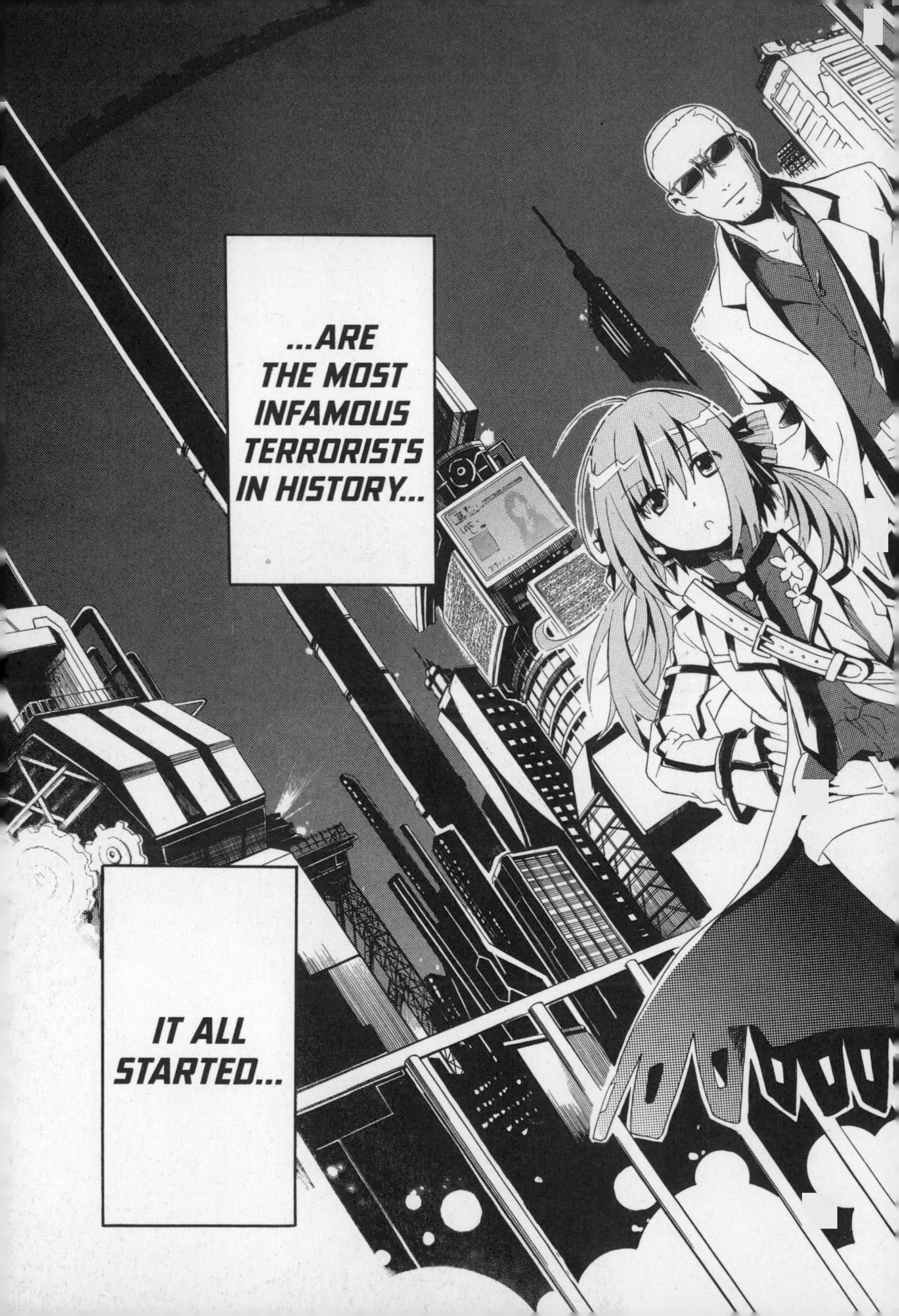
...ARE THE MOST INFAMOUS TERRORISTS IN HISTORY...
IT ALL STARTED...

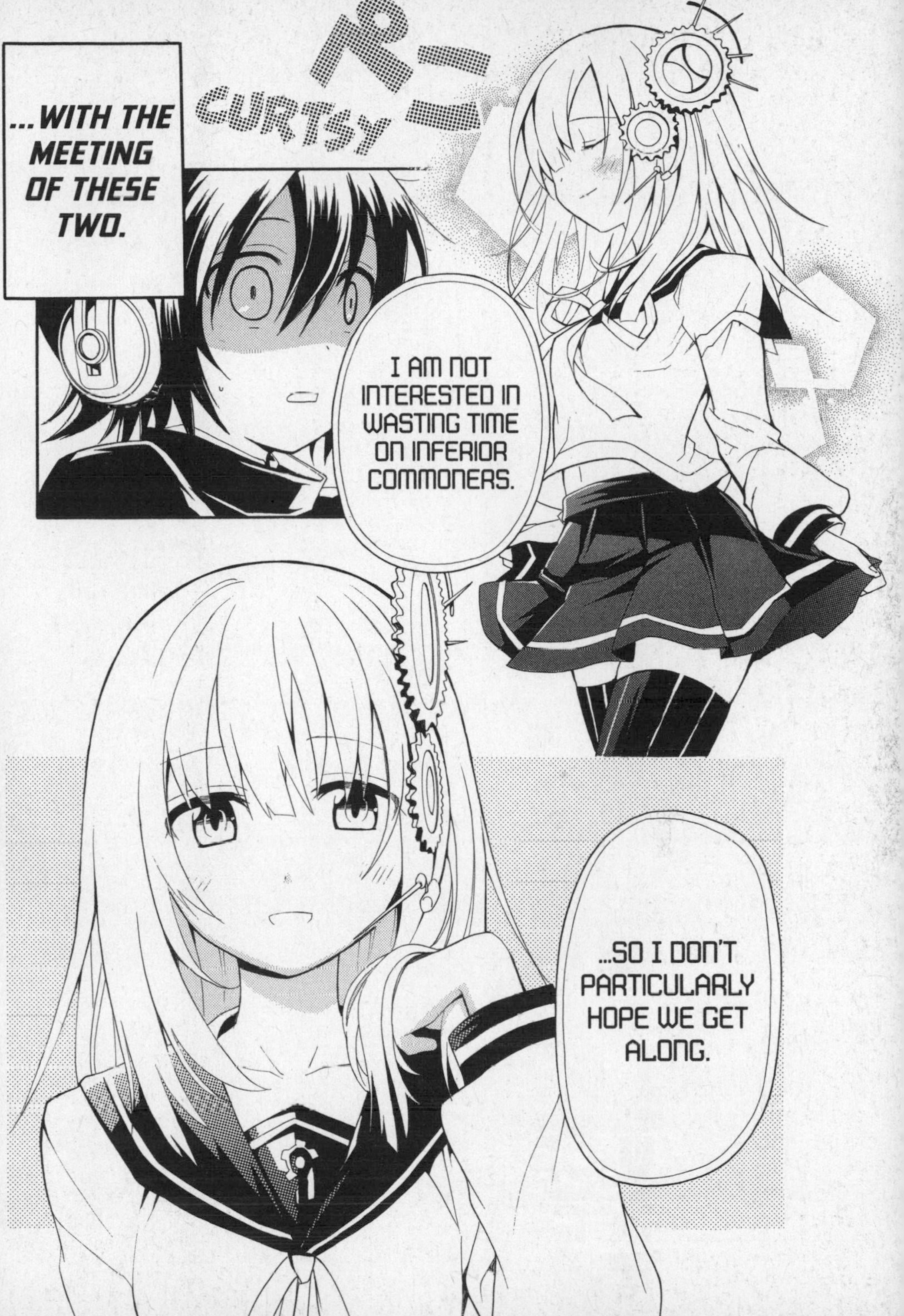
CURTSY
...WITH THE MEETING OF THESE TWO.
I AM NOT INTERESTED IN WASTING TIME ON INFERIOR COMMONERS.
...SO I DON'T PARTICULARLY HOPE WE GET ALONG.

Clockwork Planet

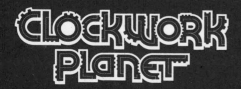

CLOCKWORK PLANET

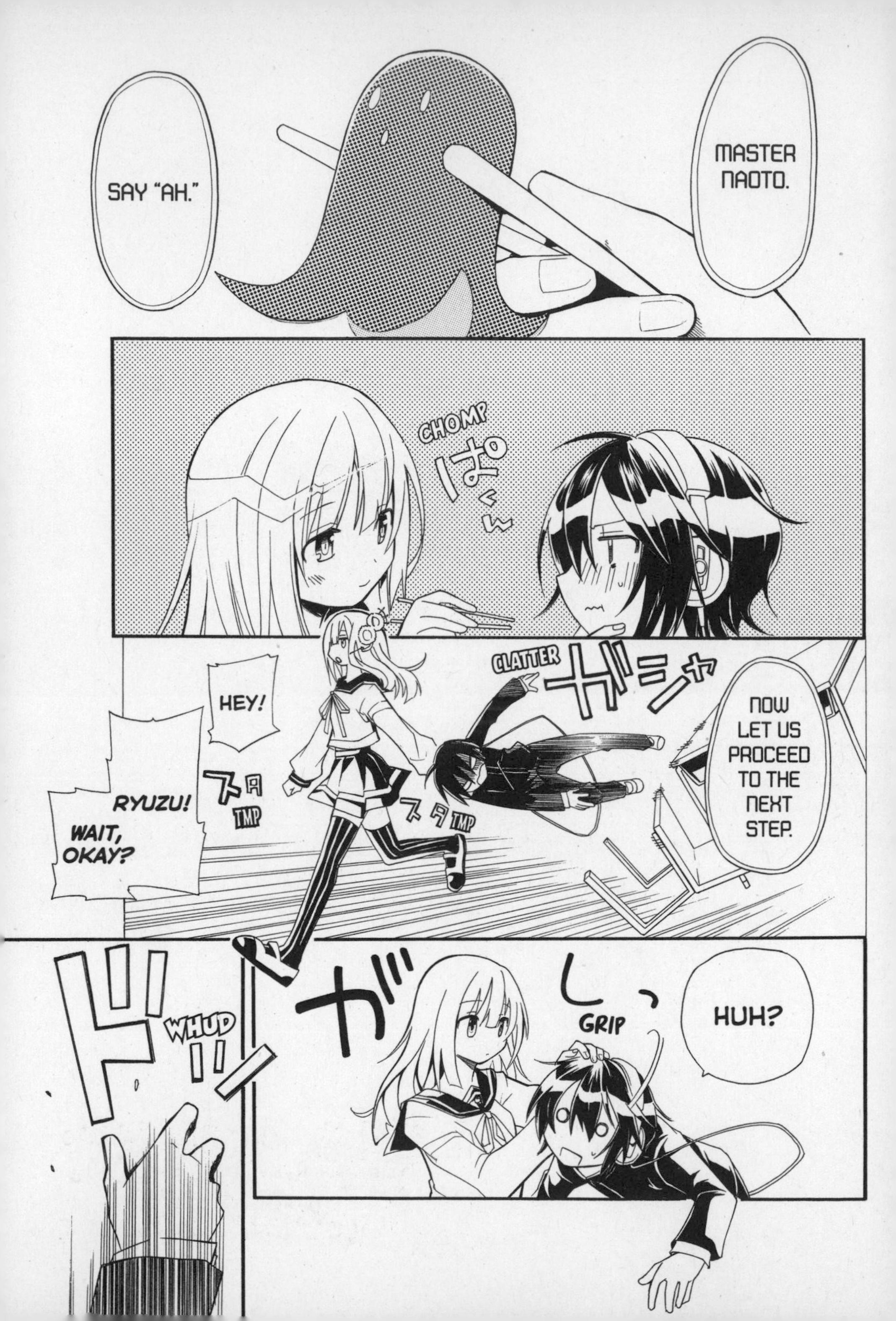
MASTER NAOTO.
SAY "AH."
CHOMP
ぱくん
CLATTER
ガシャ
NOW LET US PROCEED TO THE NEXT STEP.
HEY!
スタ
TMP
スタ
TMP
RYUZU! WAIT, OKAY?
HUH?
GRIP
がしっ
WHUD
ドッ

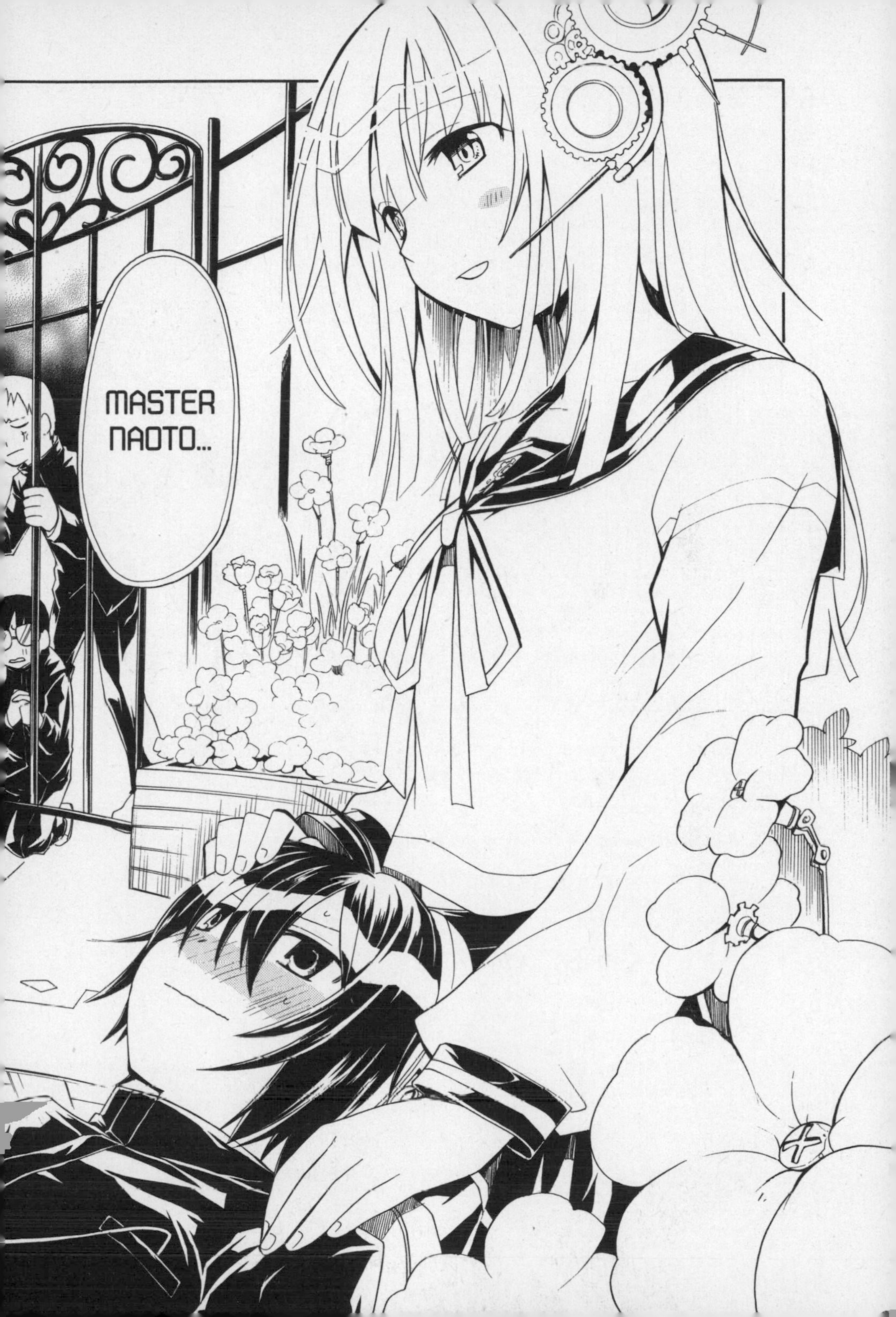
MASTER NAOTO...

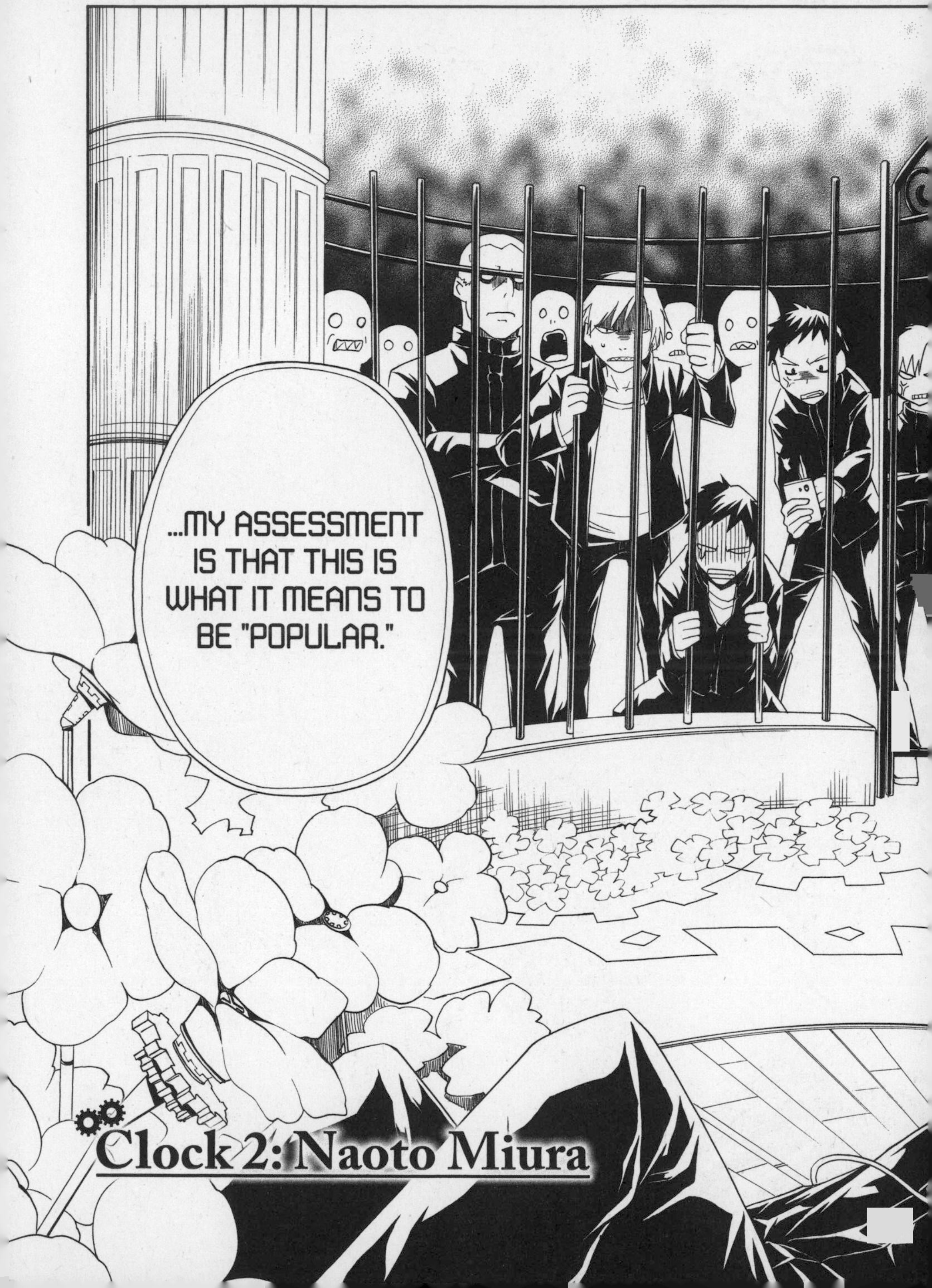
...MY ASSESSMENT IS THAT THIS IS WHAT IT MEANS TO BE "POPULAR."

Clock 2: Naoto Miura

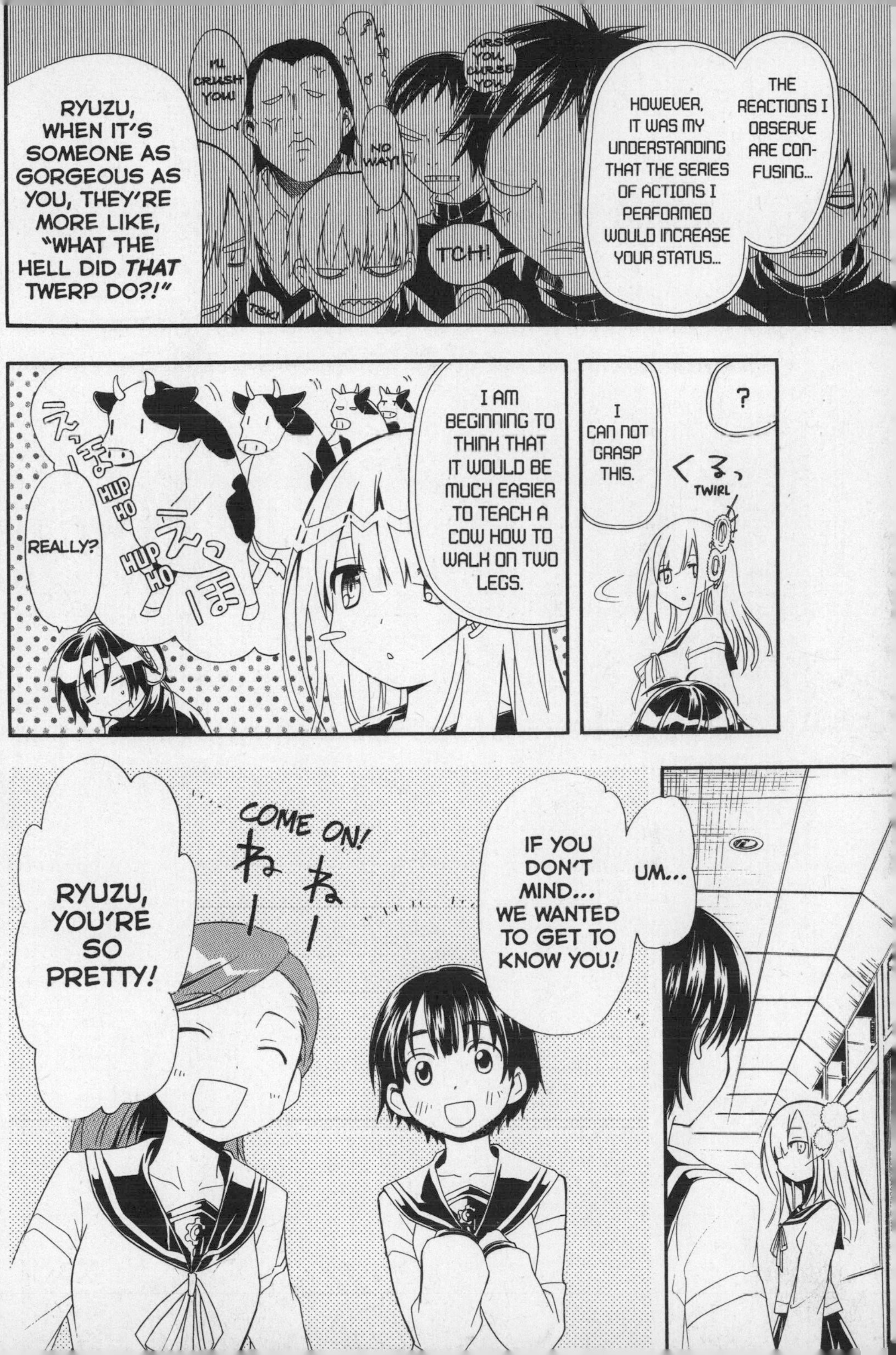
THE REACTIONS I OBSERVE ARE CON-FUSING...
HOWEVER, IT WAS MY UNDERSTANDING THAT THE SERIES OF ACTIONS I PERFORMED WOULD INCREASE YOUR STATUS...
CURSE YOU, CURSE YOU
TCH!
NO WAY!
I'LL CRUSH YOU!
RYUZU, WHEN IT'S SOMEONE AS GORGEOUS AS YOU, THEY'RE MORE LIKE, "WHAT THE HELL DID *THAT* TWERP DO?!"
TSK!
?
くるっ
TWIRL
I CAN NOT GRASP THIS.
I AM BEGINNING TO THINK THAT IT WOULD BE MUCH EASIER TO TEACH A COW HOW TO WALK ON TWO LEGS.
えっほ
HUP HO
えっほ
HUP HO
REALLY?
UM...
IF YOU DON'T MIND... WE WANTED TO GET TO KNOW YOU!
ねー ねー
COME ON!
RYUZU, YOU'RE SO PRETTY!

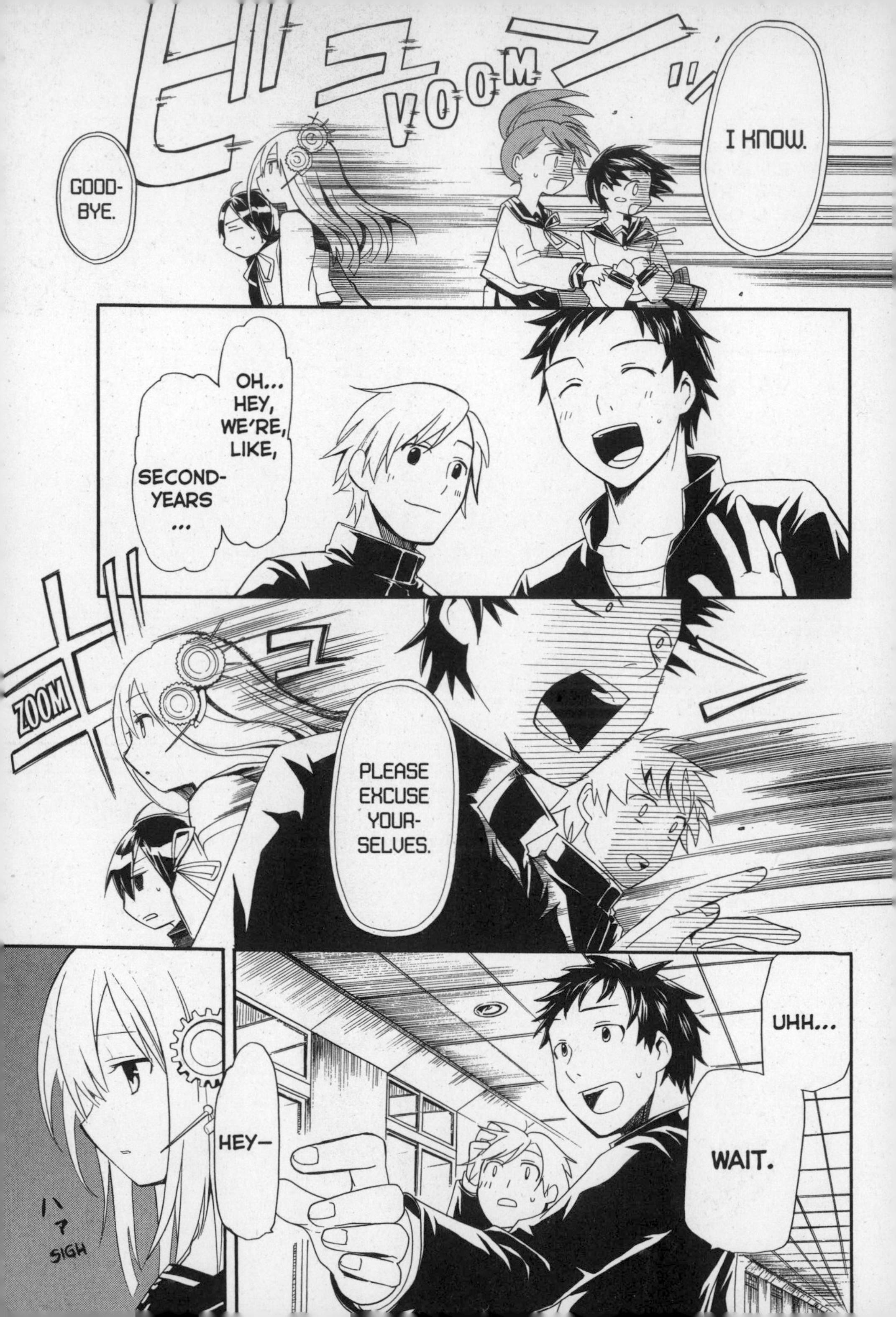
I KNOW.
VOOM
GOOD-BYE.
OH... HEY, WE'RE, LIKE, SECOND-YEARS...
PLEASE EXCUSE YOUR-SELVES.
ZOOM
UHH...
WAIT.
HEY—
SIGH

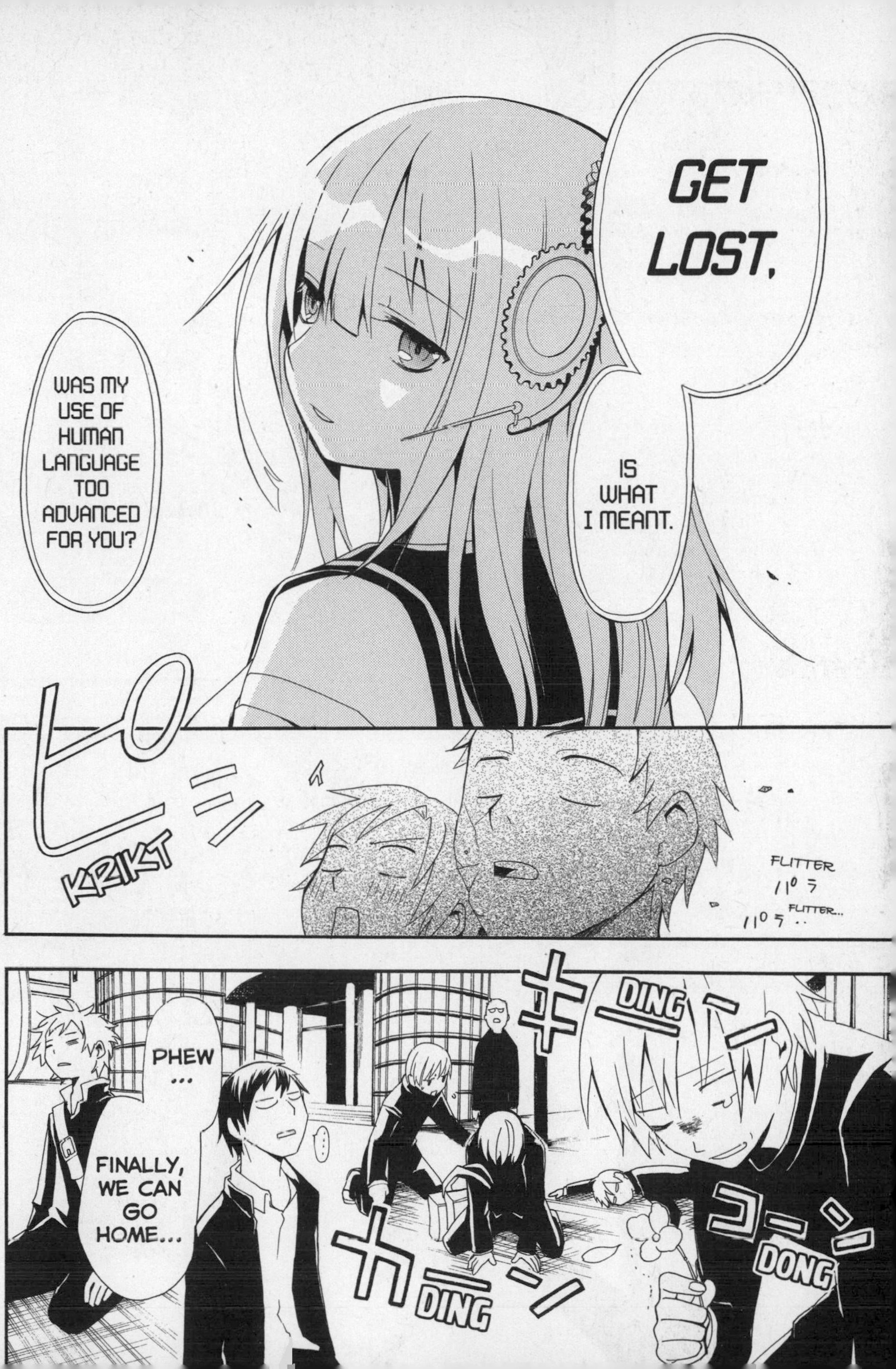
GET LOST,
IS WHAT I MEANT.
WAS MY USE OF HUMAN LANGUAGE TOO ADVANCED FOR YOU?
FLITTER
パラ
FLITTER...
パラ..
KRIKT
DING
DONG
PHEW...
FINALLY, WE CAN GO HOME...
DING

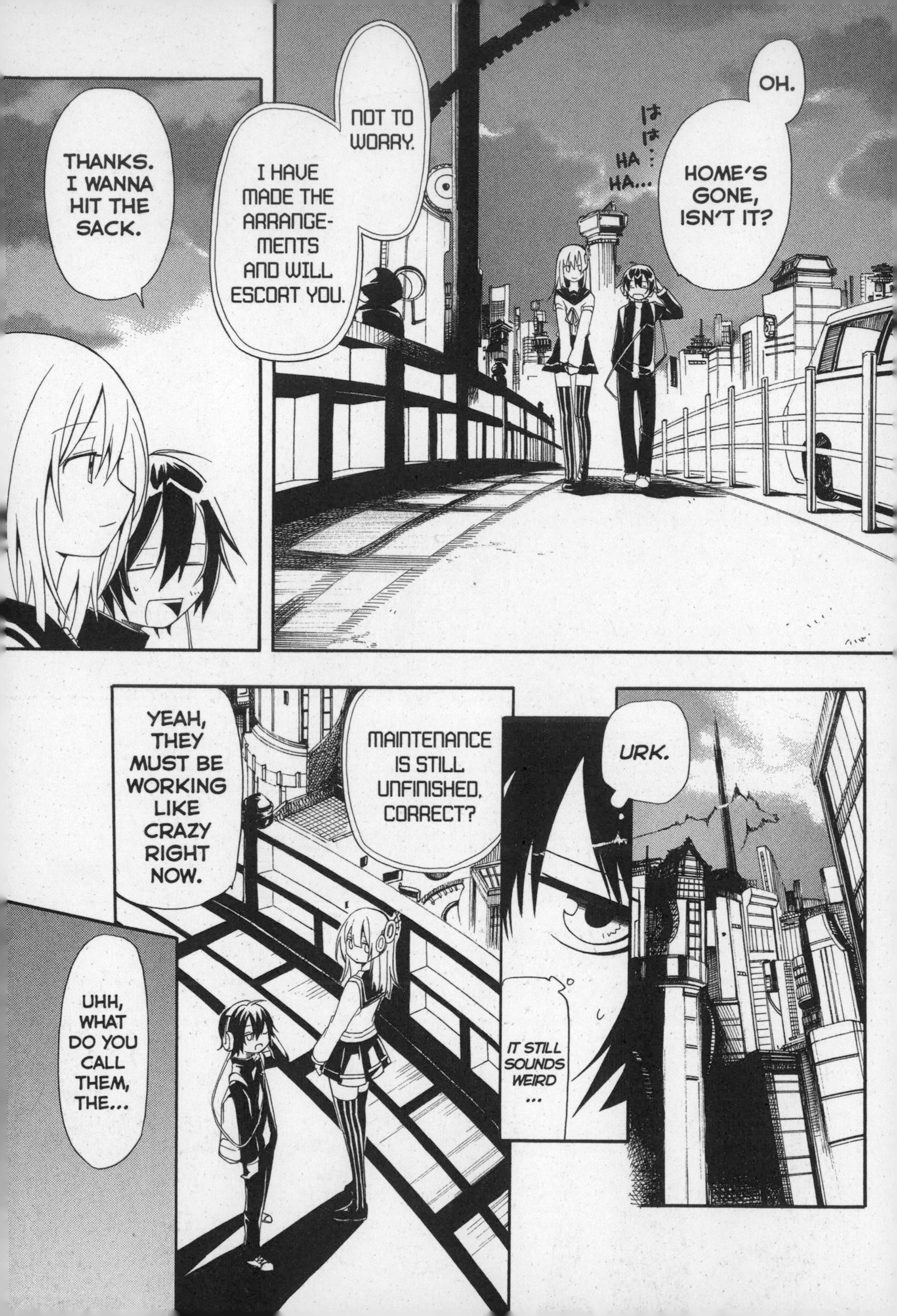
OH.
はは
HA HA...
HOME'S GONE, ISN'T IT?
NOT TO WORRY.
I HAVE MADE THE ARRANGE-MENTS AND WILL ESCORT YOU.
THANKS. I WANNA HIT THE SACK.
URK.
IT STILL SOUNDS WEIRD...
MAINTENANCE IS STILL UNFINISHED, CORRECT?
YEAH, THEY MUST BE WORKING LIKE CRAZY RIGHT NOW.
UHH, WHAT DO YOU CALL THEM, THE...

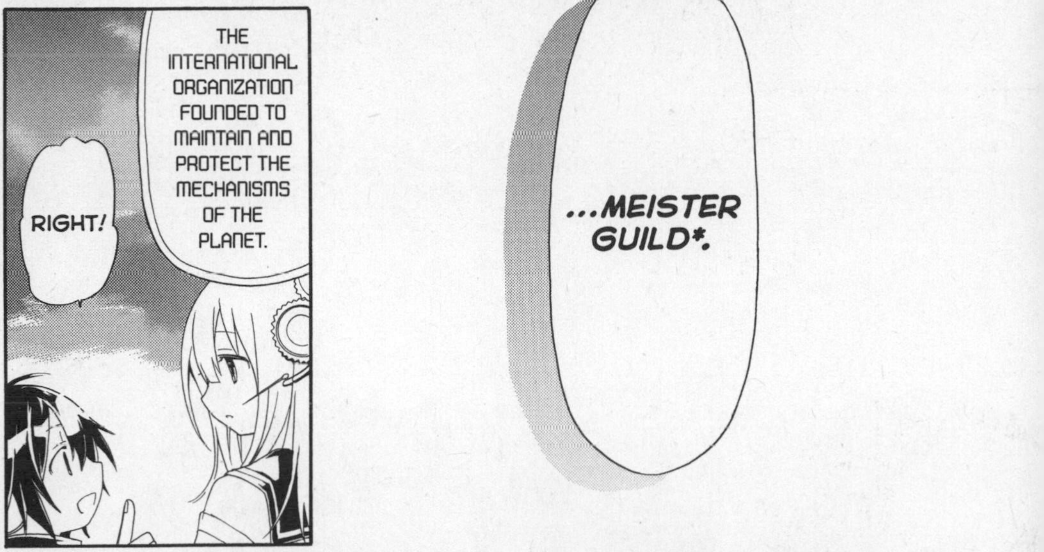
...MEISTER GUILD*.
THE INTERNATIONAL ORGANIZATION FOUNDED TO MAINTAIN AND PROTECT THE MECHANISMS OF THE PLANET.
RIGHT!

*Engineers Without Borders.

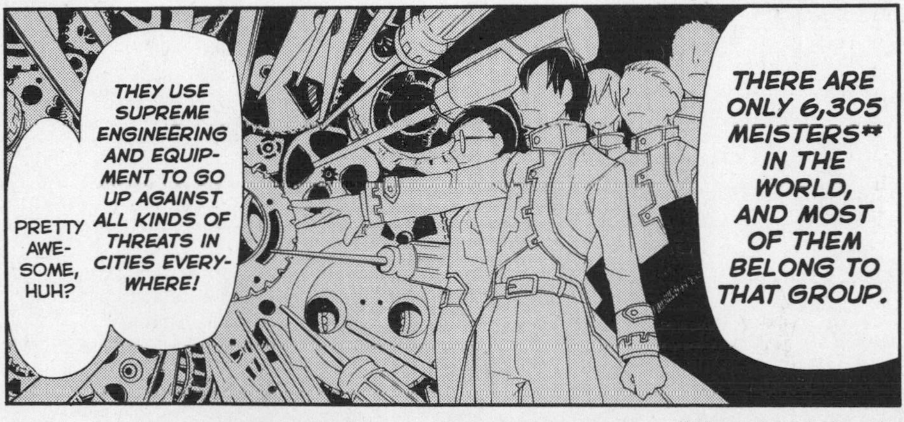
THERE ARE ONLY 6,305 MEISTERS** IN THE WORLD, AND MOST OF THEM BELONG TO THAT GROUP.
THEY USE SUPREME ENGINEERING AND EQUIPMENT TO GO UP AGAINST ALL KINDS OF THREATS IN CITIES EVERYWHERE!
PRETTY AWESOME, HUH?

**First-class clocksmiths.

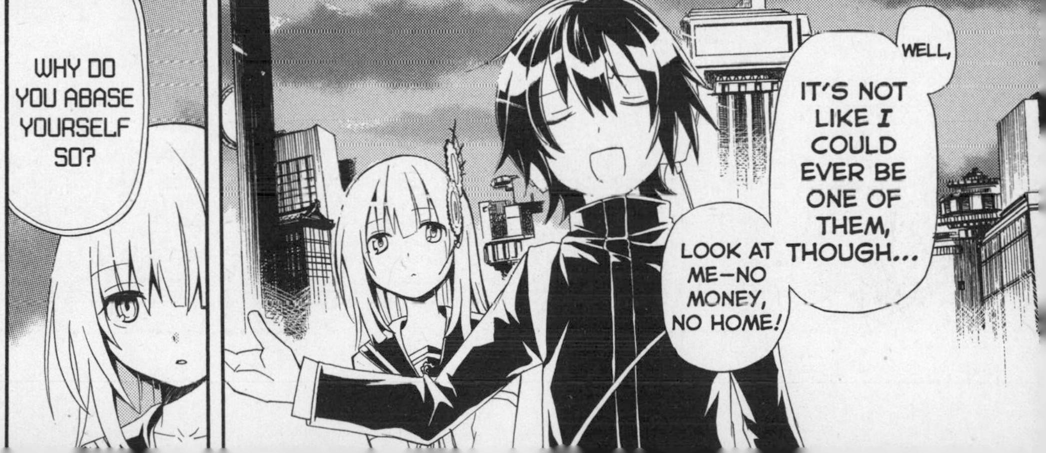
WELL,
IT'S NOT LIKE I COULD EVER BE ONE OF THEM, THOUGH...
LOOK AT ME—NO MONEY, NO HOME!
WHY DO YOU ABASE YOURSELF SO?

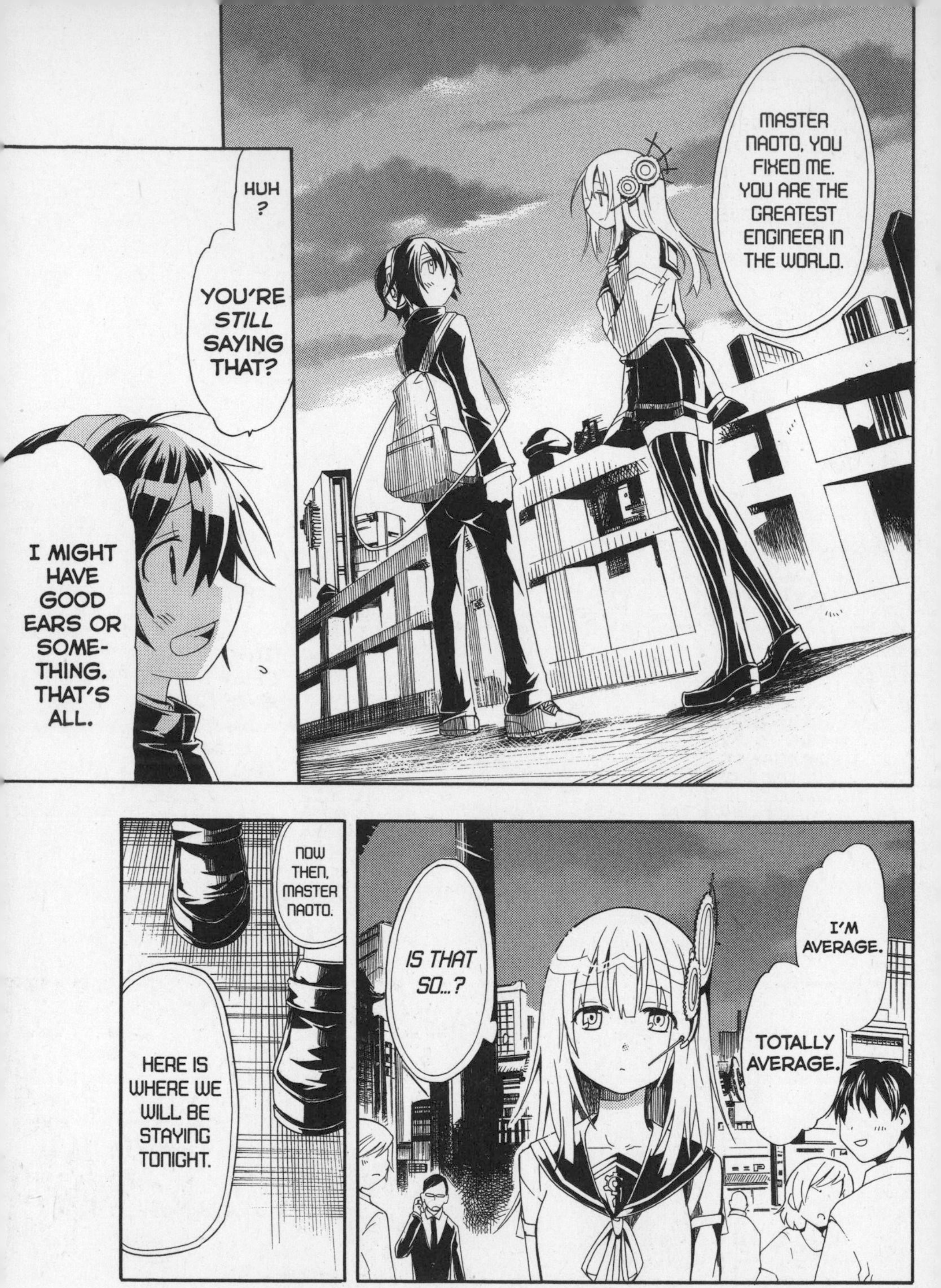
MASTER NAOTO, YOU FIXED ME. YOU ARE THE GREATEST ENGINEER IN THE WORLD.
HUH?
YOU'RE *STILL* SAYING THAT?
I MIGHT HAVE GOOD EARS OR SOME-THING. THAT'S ALL.
I'M AVERAGE.
TOTALLY AVERAGE.
IS THAT SO...?
NOW THEN, MASTER NAOTO.
HERE IS WHERE WE WILL BE STAYING TONIGHT.

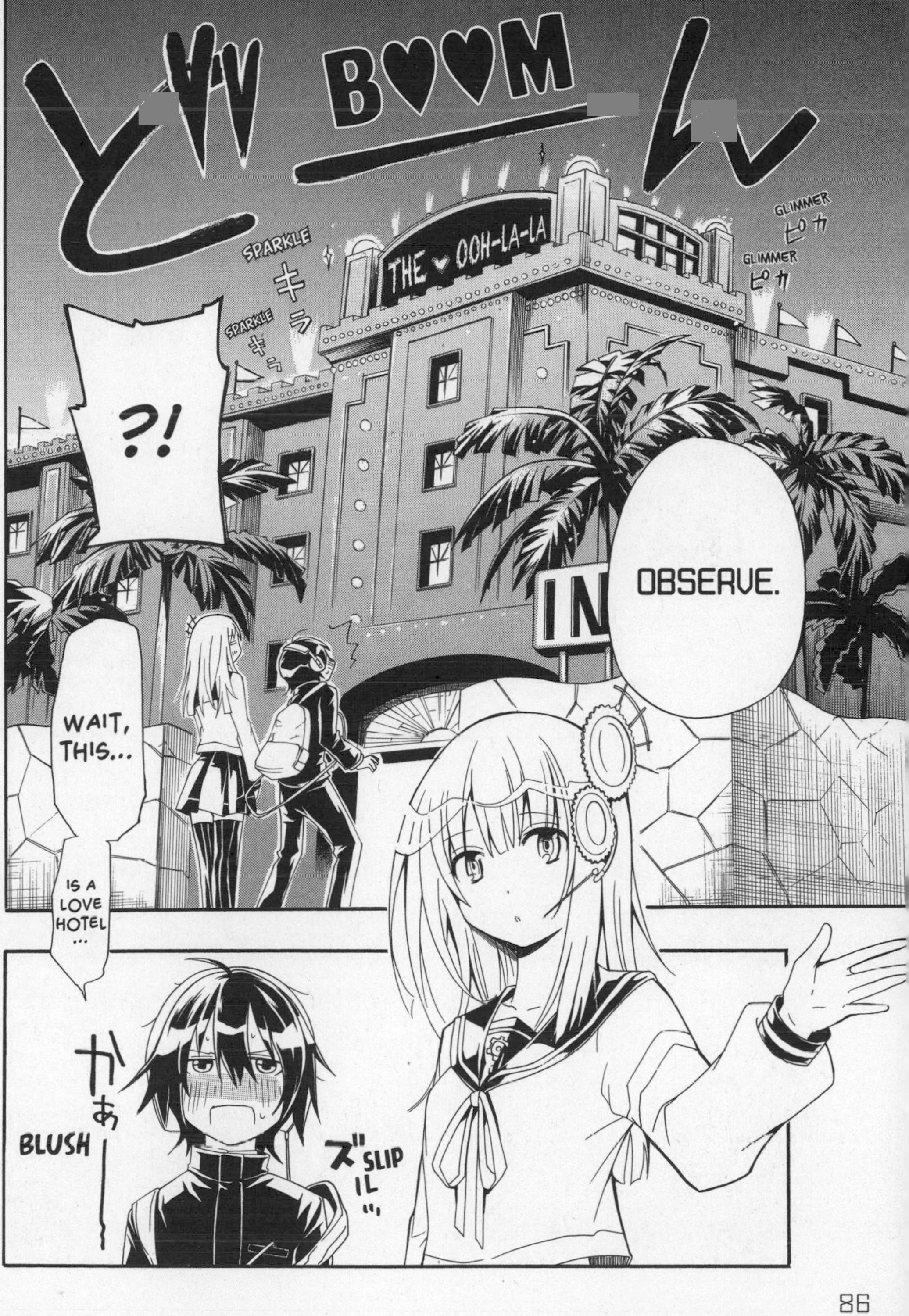

BOOM
GLIMMER ピカ
GLIMMER ピカ
THE ♥ OOH-LA-LA
SPARKLE キラ
SPARKLE キラ
?!
IN
OBSERVE.
WAIT, THIS...
IS A LOVE HOTEL ...
SLIP ズル
BLUSH かぁ

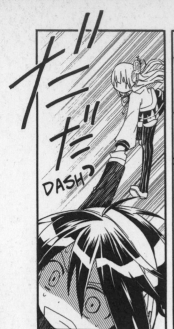

YES.
1. THE OOH-LA-LA
2. BUSINESS KYOTO
3. ORIENTAL HOTEL K
COMFORT
AMENITIES
PRICE
I HAVE DETERMINED THAT THIS LOVE HOTEL, THE OOH-LA-LA, IS CURRENTLY THE MOST INEXPENSIVE AND COMFORTABLE IN GRID—
DASH?
IF ANYONE SEES ME LEAVING FROM HERE, I'LL GET EXPELLED!
BUT THE AMENITIES ARE ALSO SUPERIOR...
NO WAY!
LOOK!
WE CAN STAY AT A MANGA CAFÉ!
NOW HIRING!
AND IT'LL BE CHEAP WITH THE NIGHT PACKAGE...
PACKAGE
300YEN
HUH?
RYUZU?

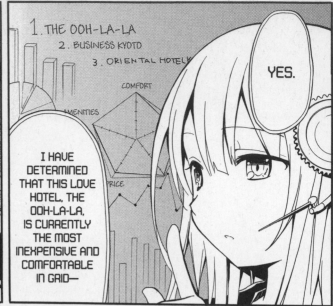

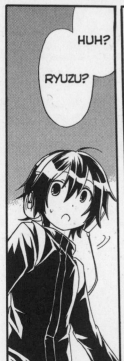

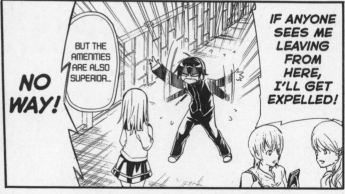

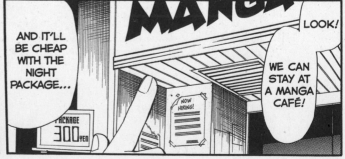

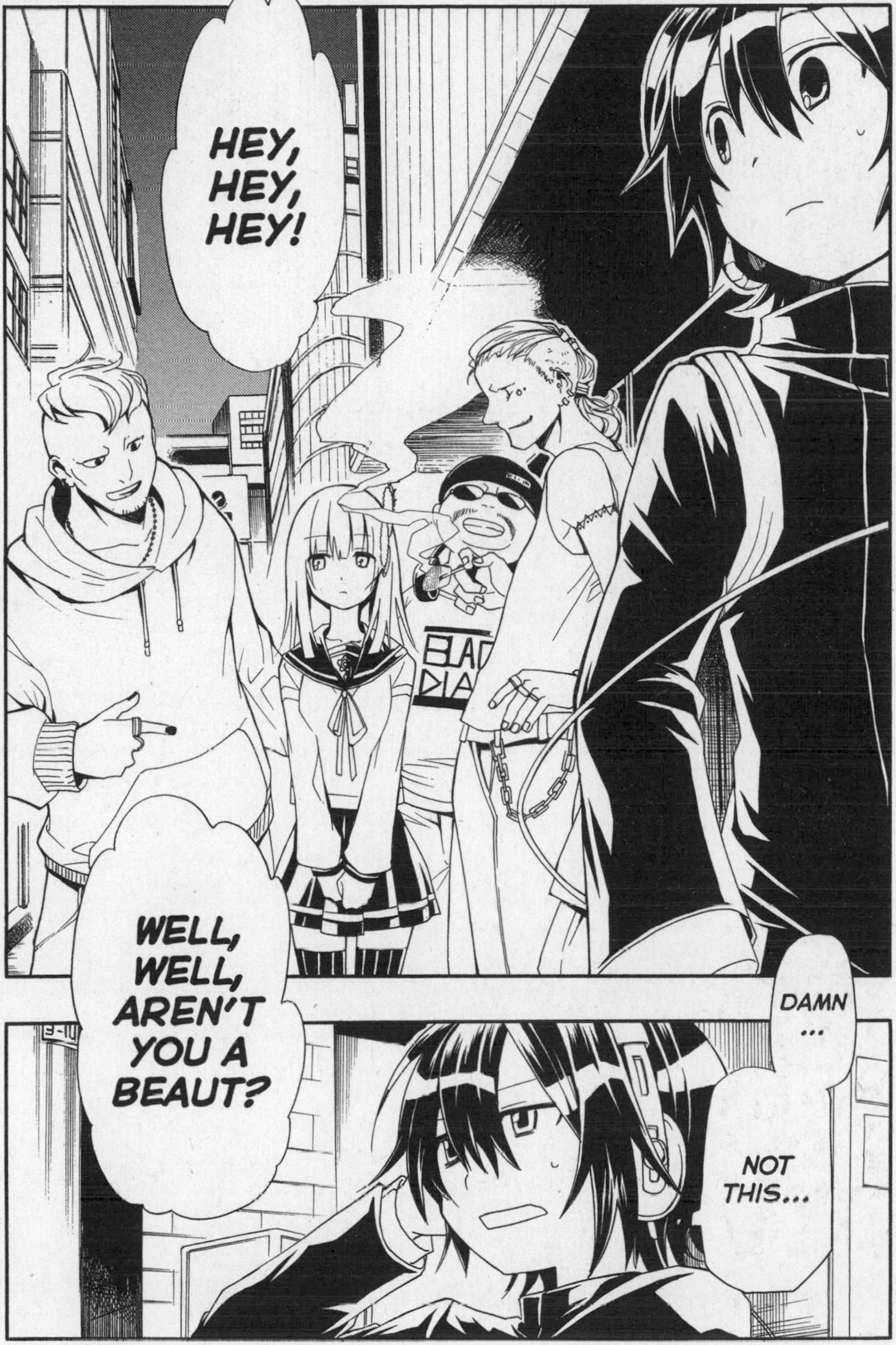
HEY, HEY, HEY!
WELL, WELL, AREN'T YOU A BEAUT?
DAMN...
NOT THIS...

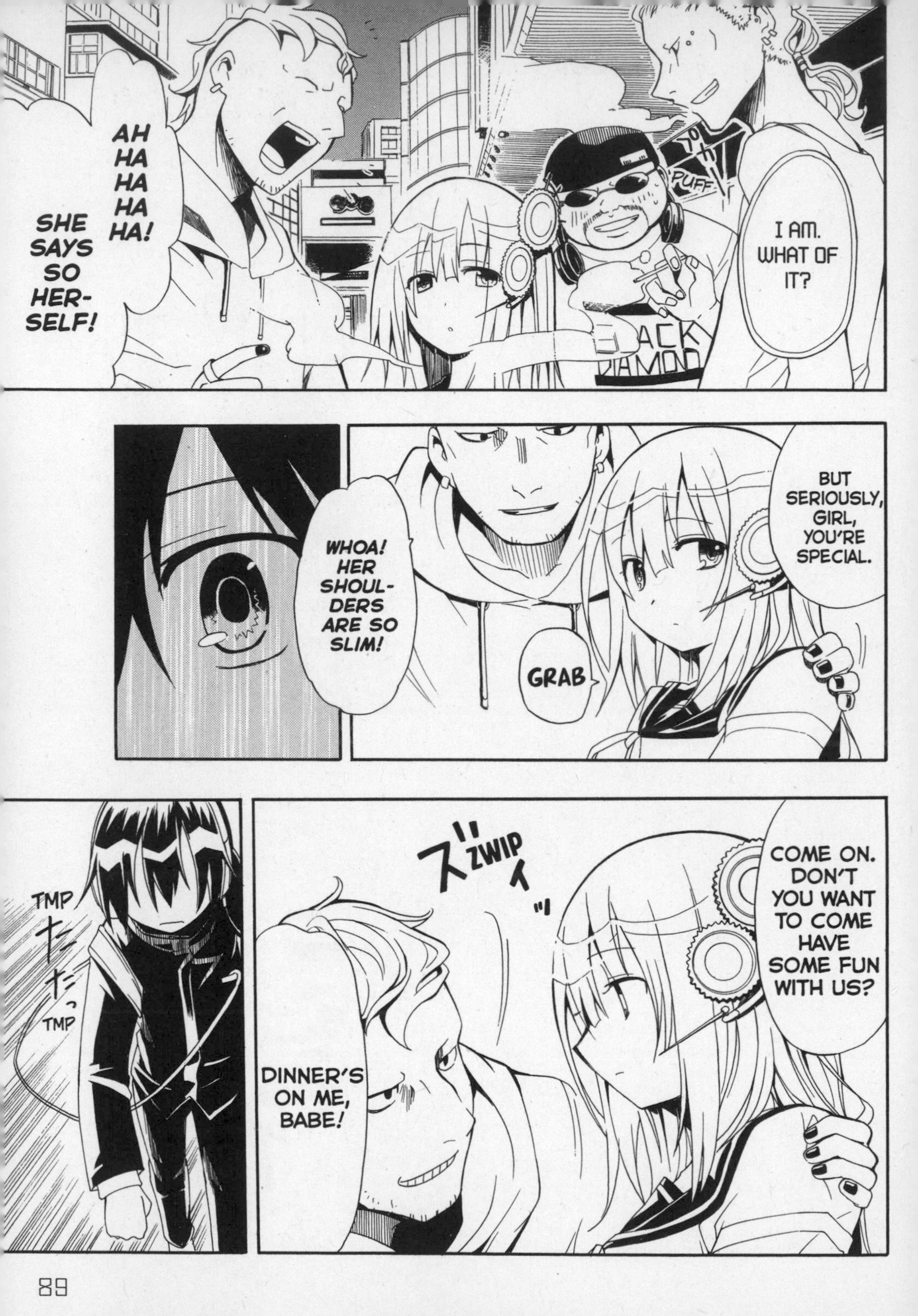
I AM. WHAT OF IT?
PUFF
AH HA HA HA HA!
SHE SAYS SO HER-SELF!
BUT SERIOUSLY, GIRL, YOU'RE SPECIAL.
GRAB
WHOA! HER SHOUL-DERS ARE SO SLIM!
COME ON. DON'T YOU WANT TO COME HAVE SOME FUN WITH US?
ZWIP
DINNER'S ON ME, BABE!
TMP
TMP

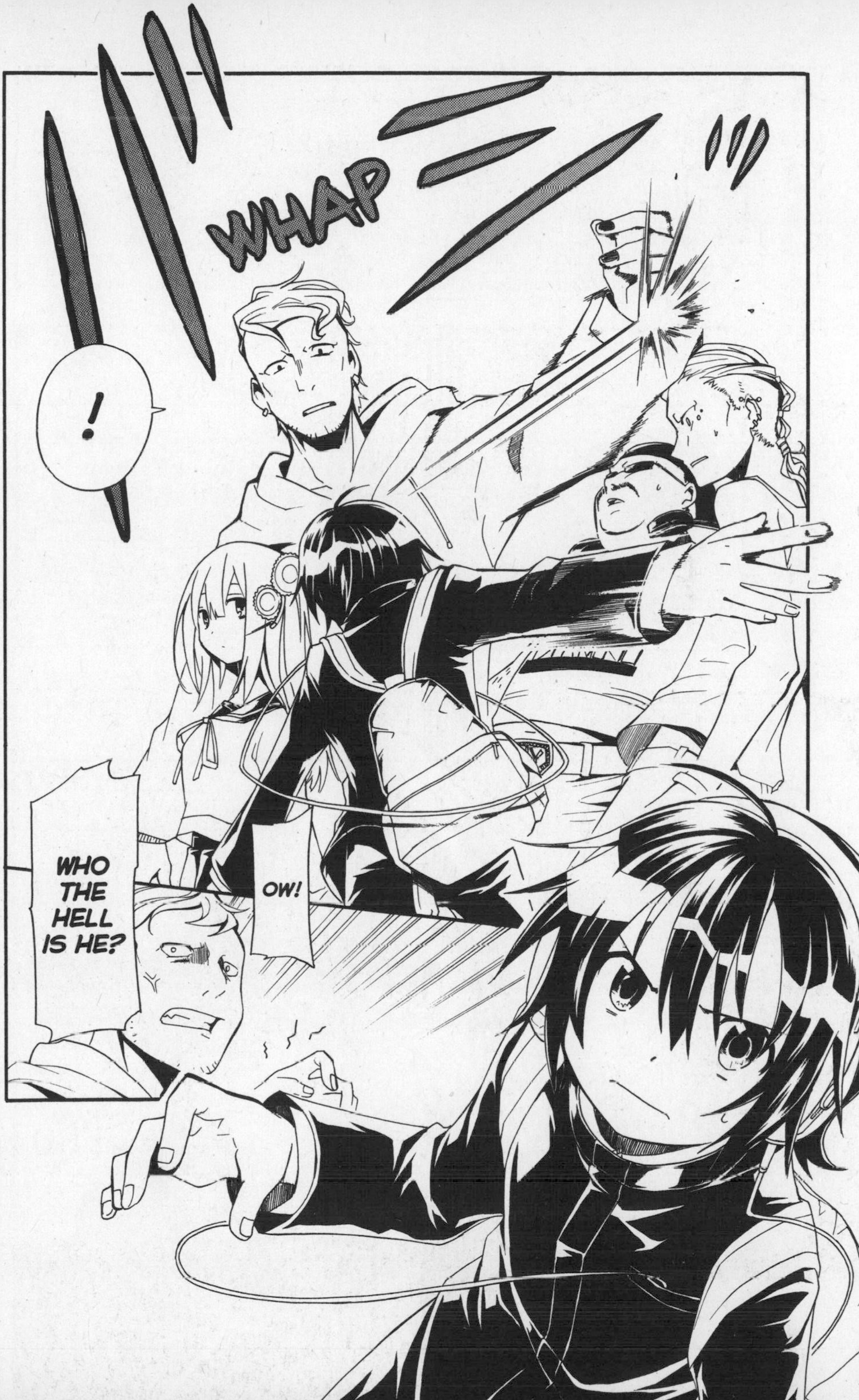
WHAP
!
OW!
WHO THE HELL IS HE?

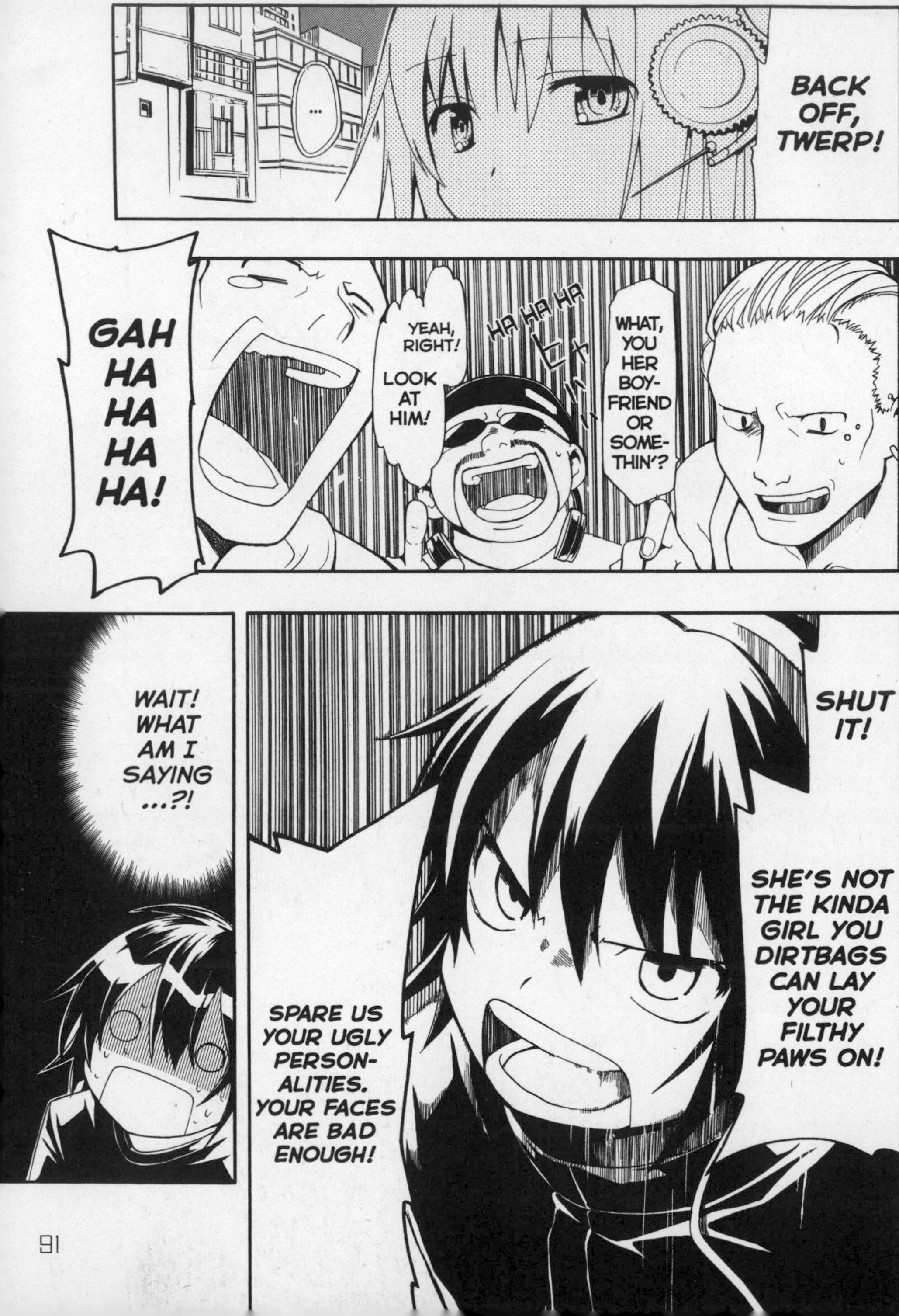
BACK OFF, TWERP!
...
WHAT, YOU HER BOY-FRIEND OR SOME-THIN'?
HA HA HA
YEAH, RIGHT!
LOOK AT HIM!
GAH HA HA HA HA!
SHUT IT!
SHE'S NOT THE KINDA GIRL YOU DIRTBAGS CAN LAY YOUR FILTHY PAWS ON!
SPARE US YOUR UGLY PERSON-ALITIES. YOUR FACES ARE BAD ENOUGH!
WAIT! WHAT AM I SAYING ...?!

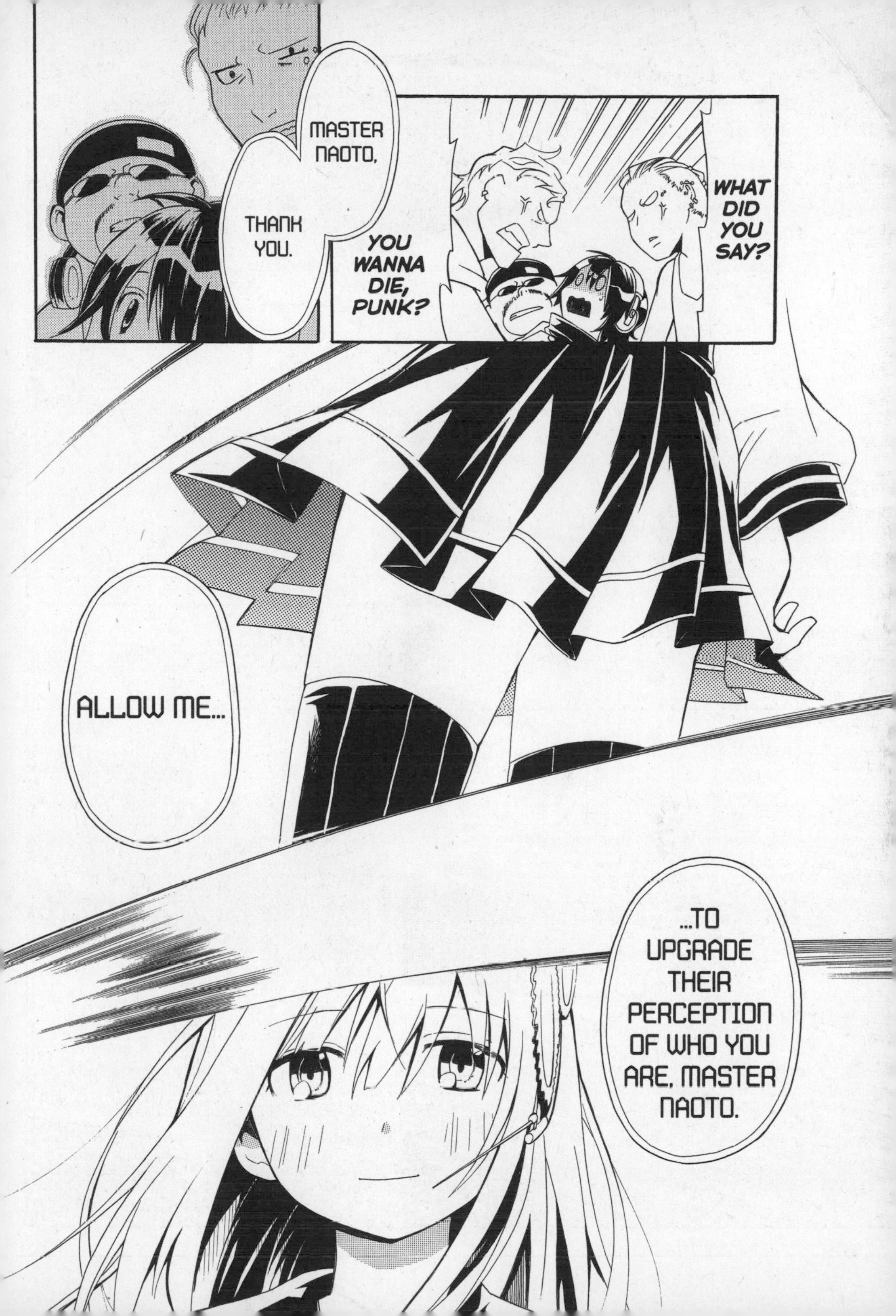
WHAT DID YOU SAY?
YOU WANNA DIE, PUNK?
MASTER NAOTO,
THANK YOU.
ALLOW ME...
...TO UPGRADE THEIR PERCEPTION OF WHO YOU ARE, MASTER NAOTO.

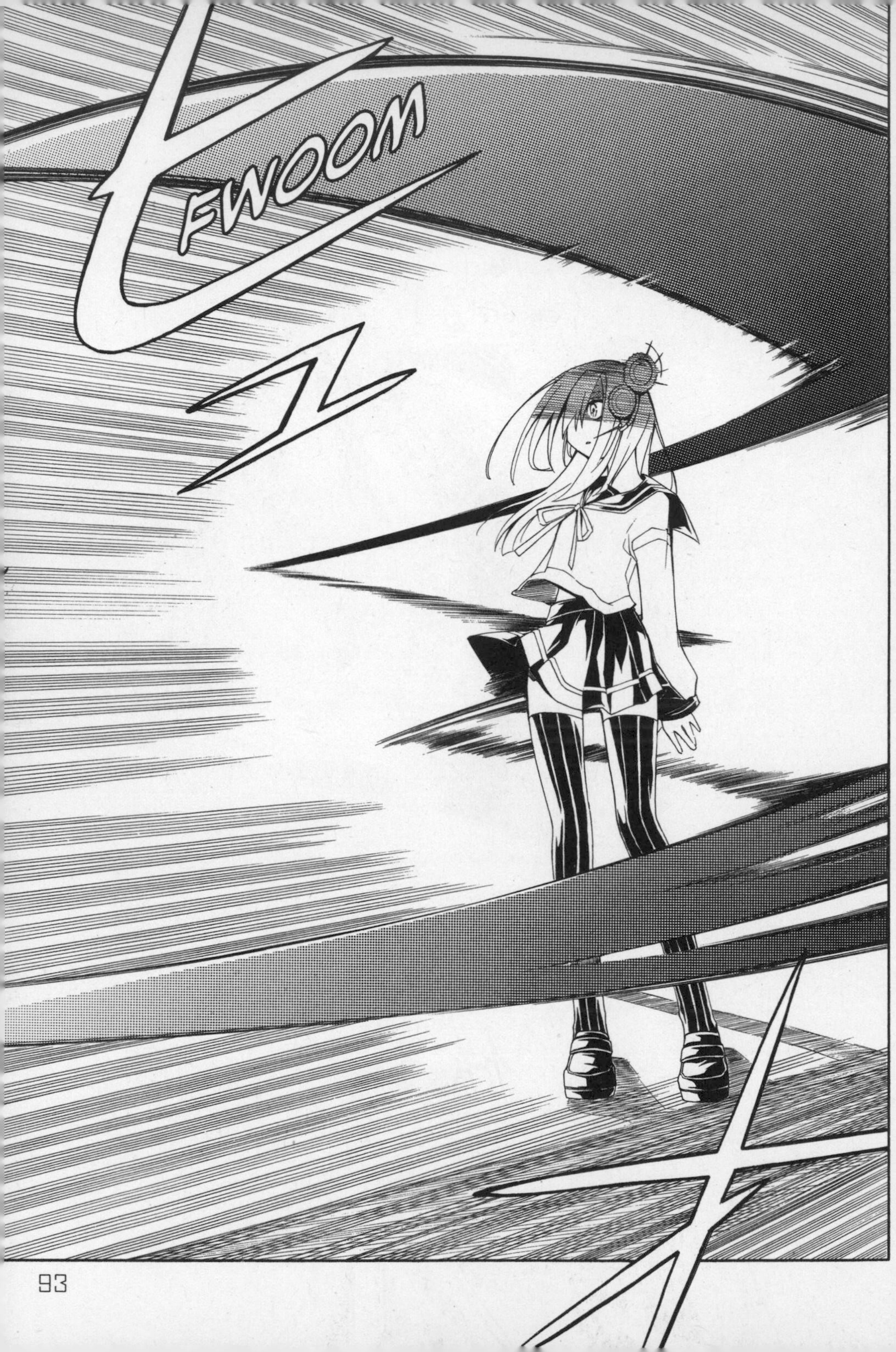
FWOOM

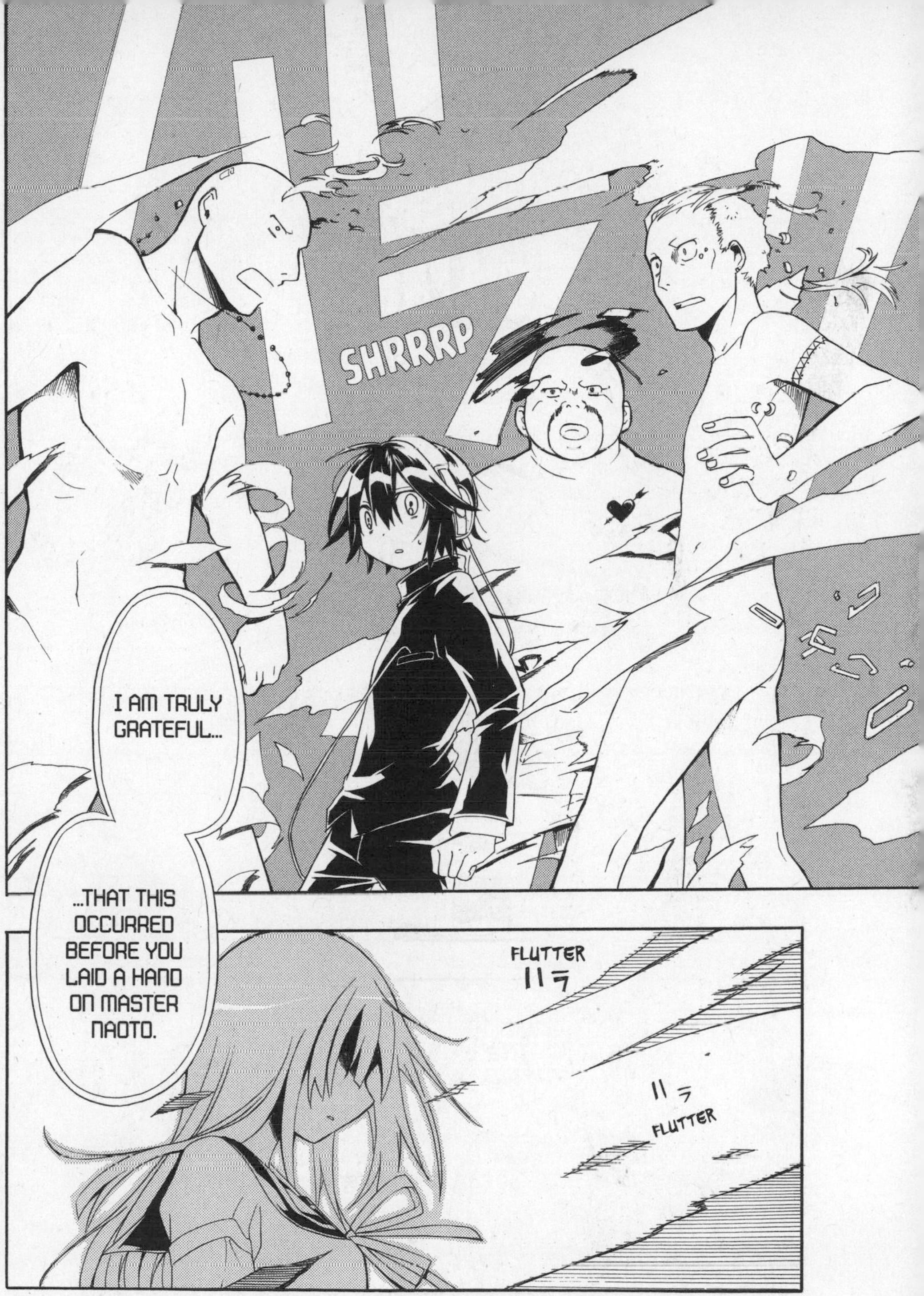
SHRRRP
I AM TRULY GRATEFUL...
...THAT THIS OCCURRED BEFORE YOU LAID A HAND ON MASTER NAOTO.
FLUTTER
FLUTTER

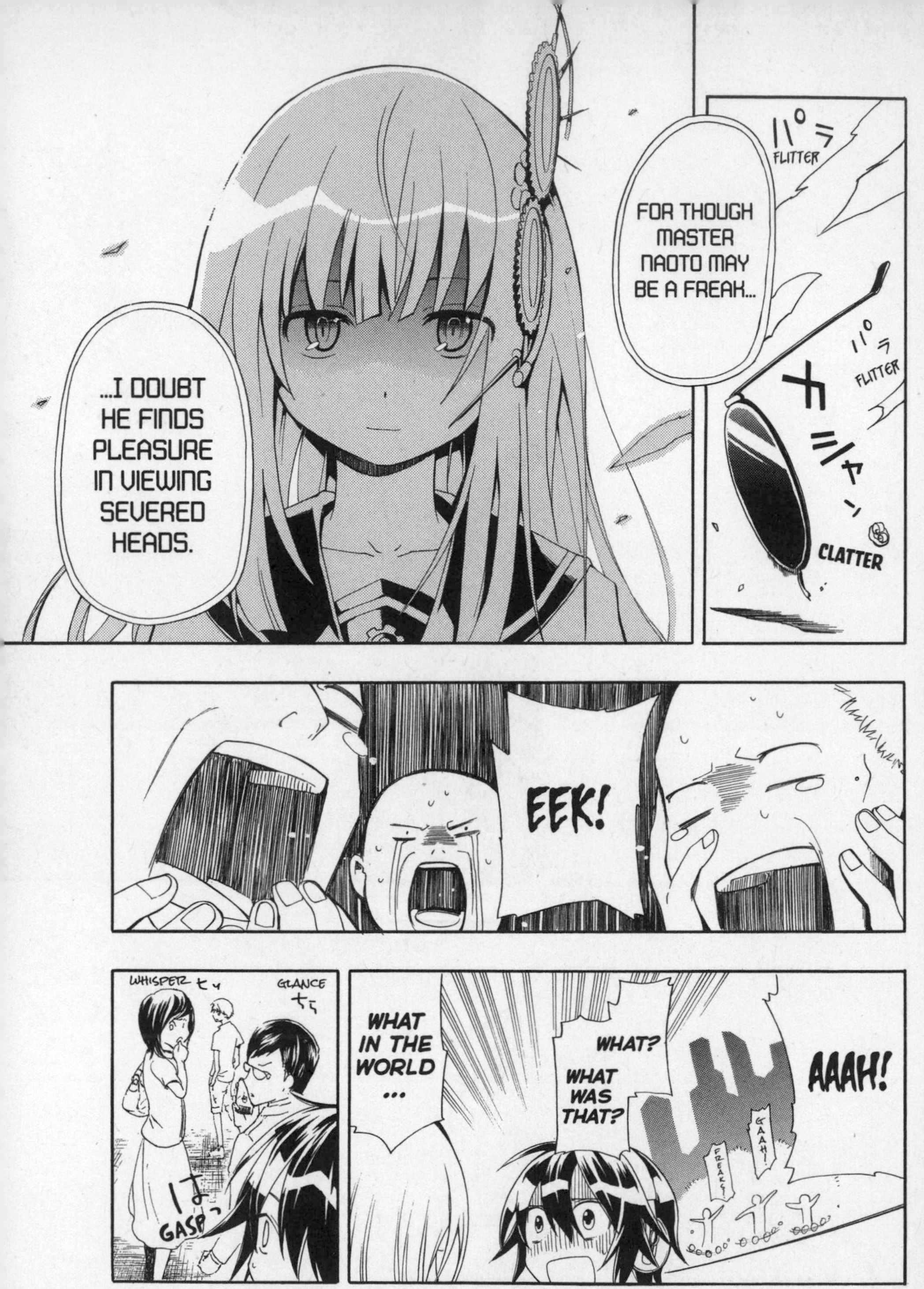
FOR THOUGH MASTER NAOTO MAY BE A FREAK...
パラ
FLITTER
パラ
FLITTER
カシャン
CLATTER
...I DOUBT HE FINDS PLEASURE IN VIEWING SEVERED HEADS.
EEK!
AAAH!
WHAT?
WHAT WAS THAT?
WHAT IN THE WORLD ...
GAAAH!
FREAKS!
GLANCE
チラ
WHISPER
ヒソ
はっ
GASP

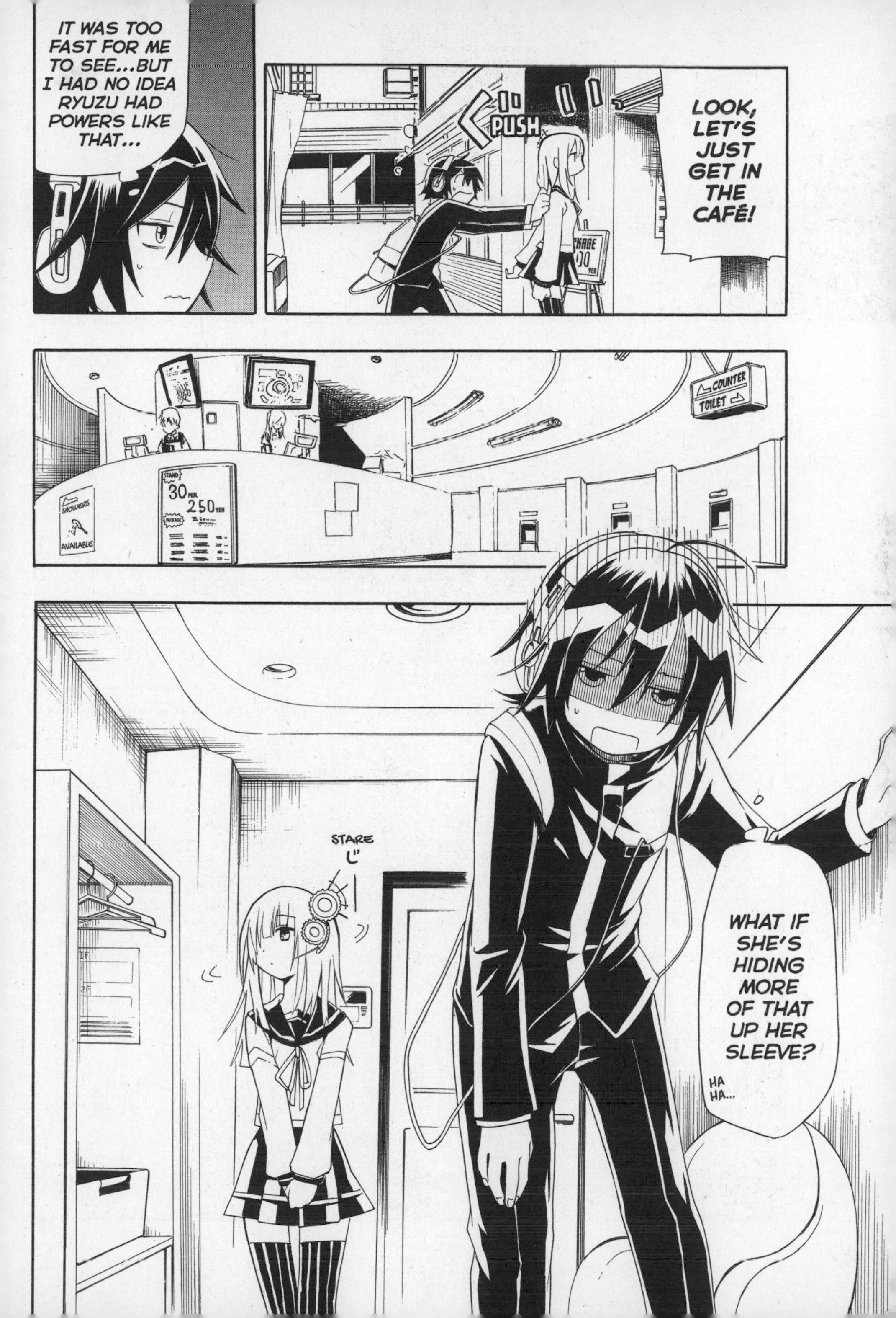
LOOK, LET'S JUST GET IN THE CAFÉ!
PUSH
IT WAS TOO FAST FOR ME TO SEE...BUT I HAD NO IDEA RYUZU HAD POWERS LIKE THAT...
COUNTER
TOILET
STAND
30 MIN.
250 YEN
PACKAGE
SHOWERS
AVAILABLE
WHAT IF SHE'S HIDING MORE OF THAT UP HER SLEEVE?
HA HA...
STARE
じ

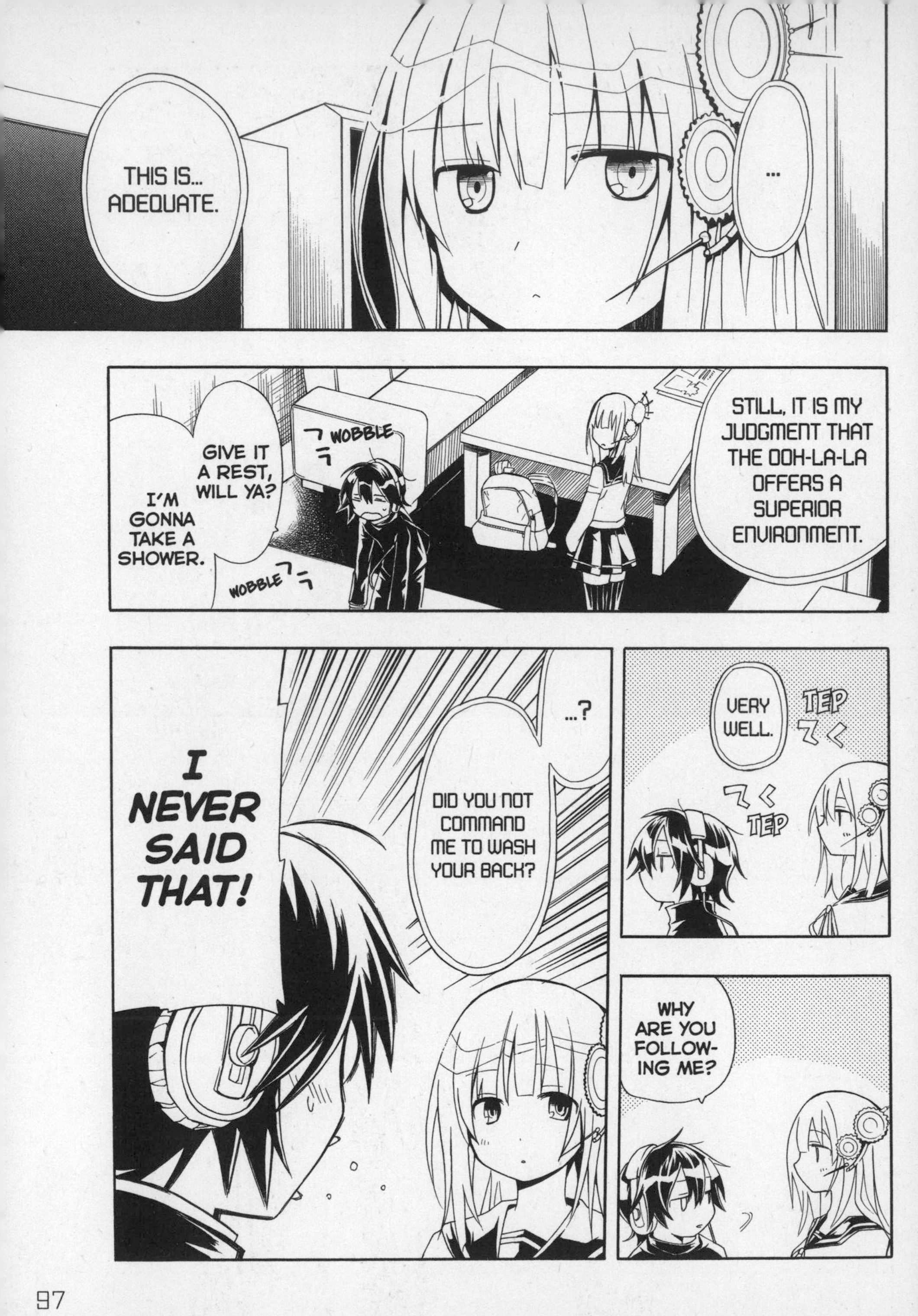
...
THIS IS... ADEQUATE.
STILL, IT IS MY JUDGMENT THAT THE OOH-LA-LA OFFERS A SUPERIOR ENVIRONMENT.
WOBBLE
GIVE IT A REST, WILL YA? I'M GONNA TAKE A SHOWER.
WOBBLE
VERY WELL.
TEP
TEP
WHY ARE YOU FOLLOW-ING ME?
...?
DID YOU NOT COMMAND ME TO WASH YOUR BACK?
I NEVER SAID THAT!

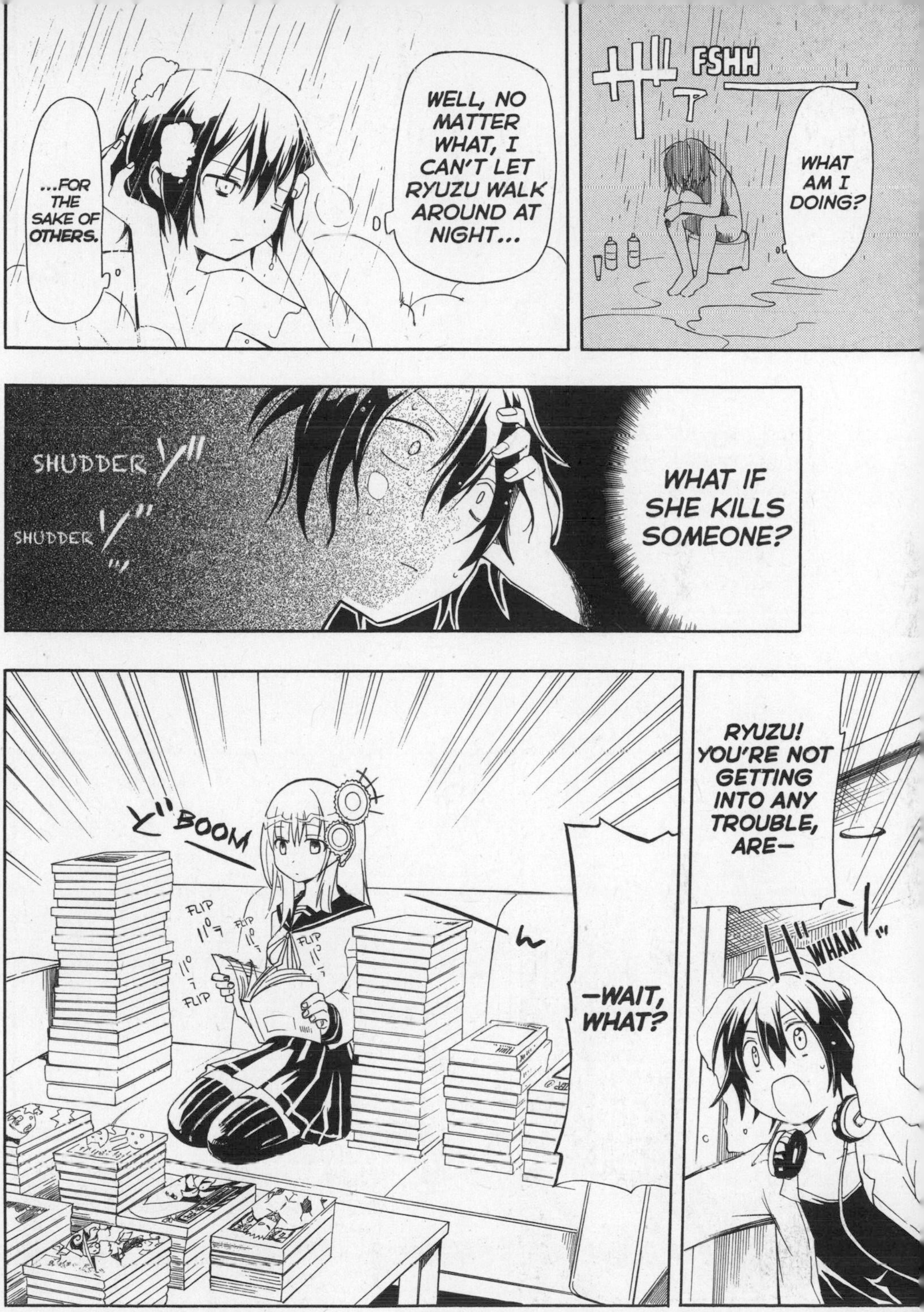
FSHH
WHAT AM I DOING?
WELL, NO MATTER WHAT, I CAN'T LET RYUZU WALK AROUND AT NIGHT...
...FOR THE SAKE OF OTHERS.
WHAT IF SHE KILLS SOMEONE?
SHUDDER
SHUDDER
RYUZU! YOU'RE NOT GETTING INTO ANY TROUBLE, ARE—
WHAM
—WAIT, WHAT?
BOOM
FLIP
FLIP
FLIP
FLIP

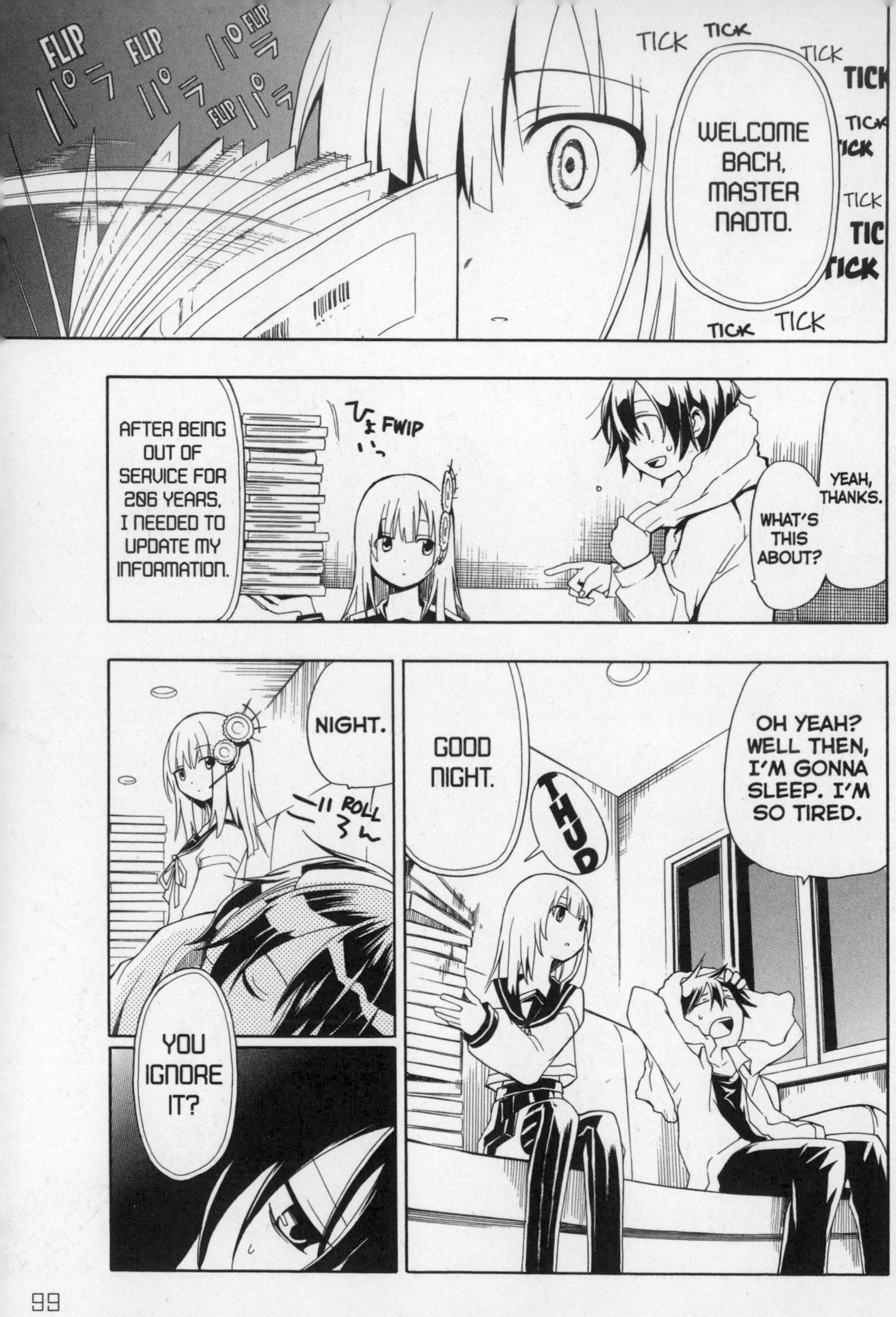
TICK TICK TICK TICK TICK TICK TICK TICK TIC TICK TICK TICK
WELCOME BACK, MASTER NAOTO.
FLIP FLIP FLIP FLIP
YEAH, THANKS.
WHAT'S THIS ABOUT?
FWIP
AFTER BEING OUT OF SERVICE FOR 206 YEARS, I NEEDED TO UPDATE MY INFORMATION.
OH YEAH? WELL THEN, I'M GONNA SLEEP. I'M SO TIRED.
GOOD NIGHT.
THUD
NIGHT.
ROLL
YOU IGNORE IT?

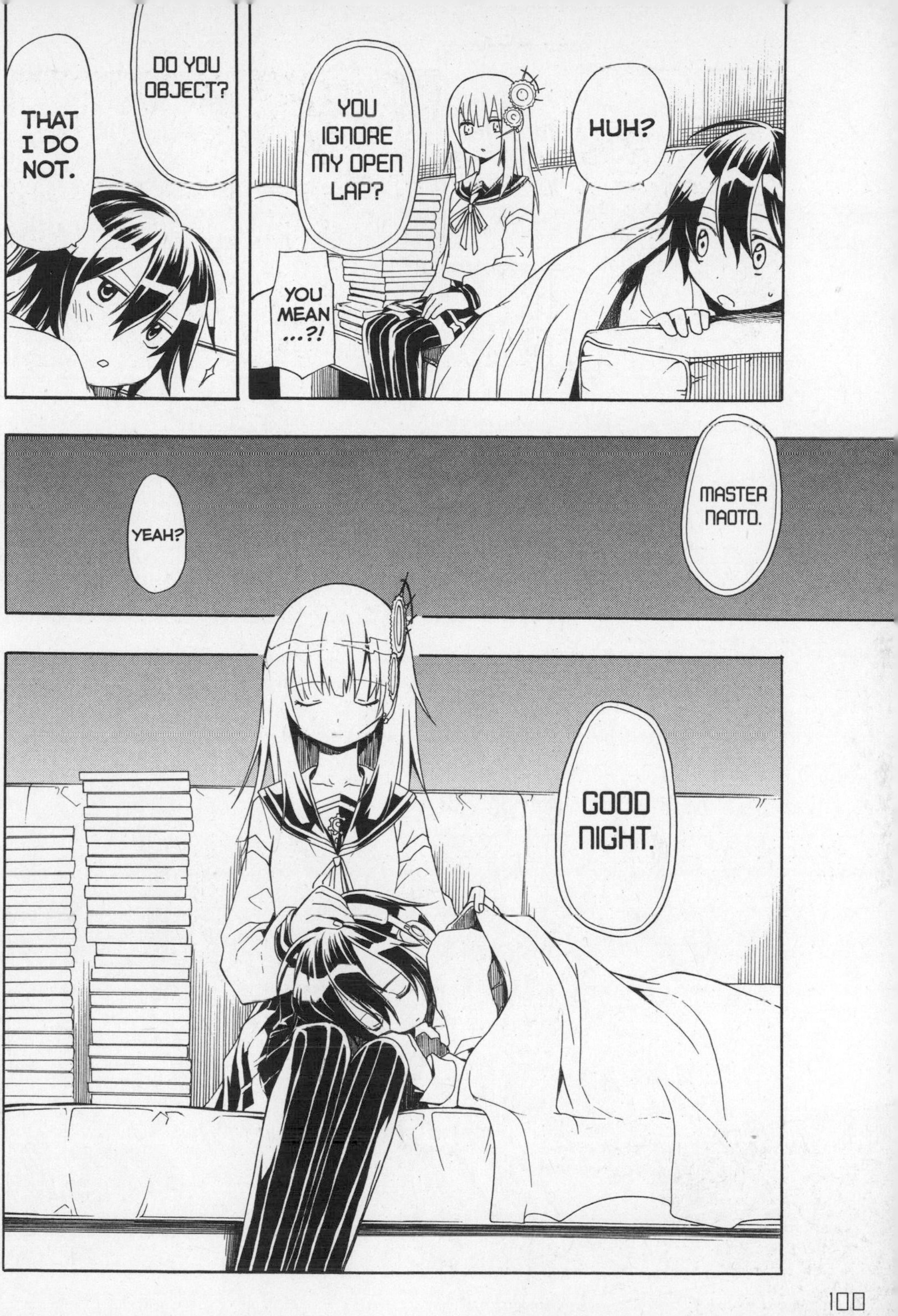
HUH?
YOU IGNORE MY OPEN LAP?
YOU MEAN ...?!
DO YOU OBJECT?
THAT I DO NOT.
MASTER NAOTO.
YEAH?
GOOD NIGHT.

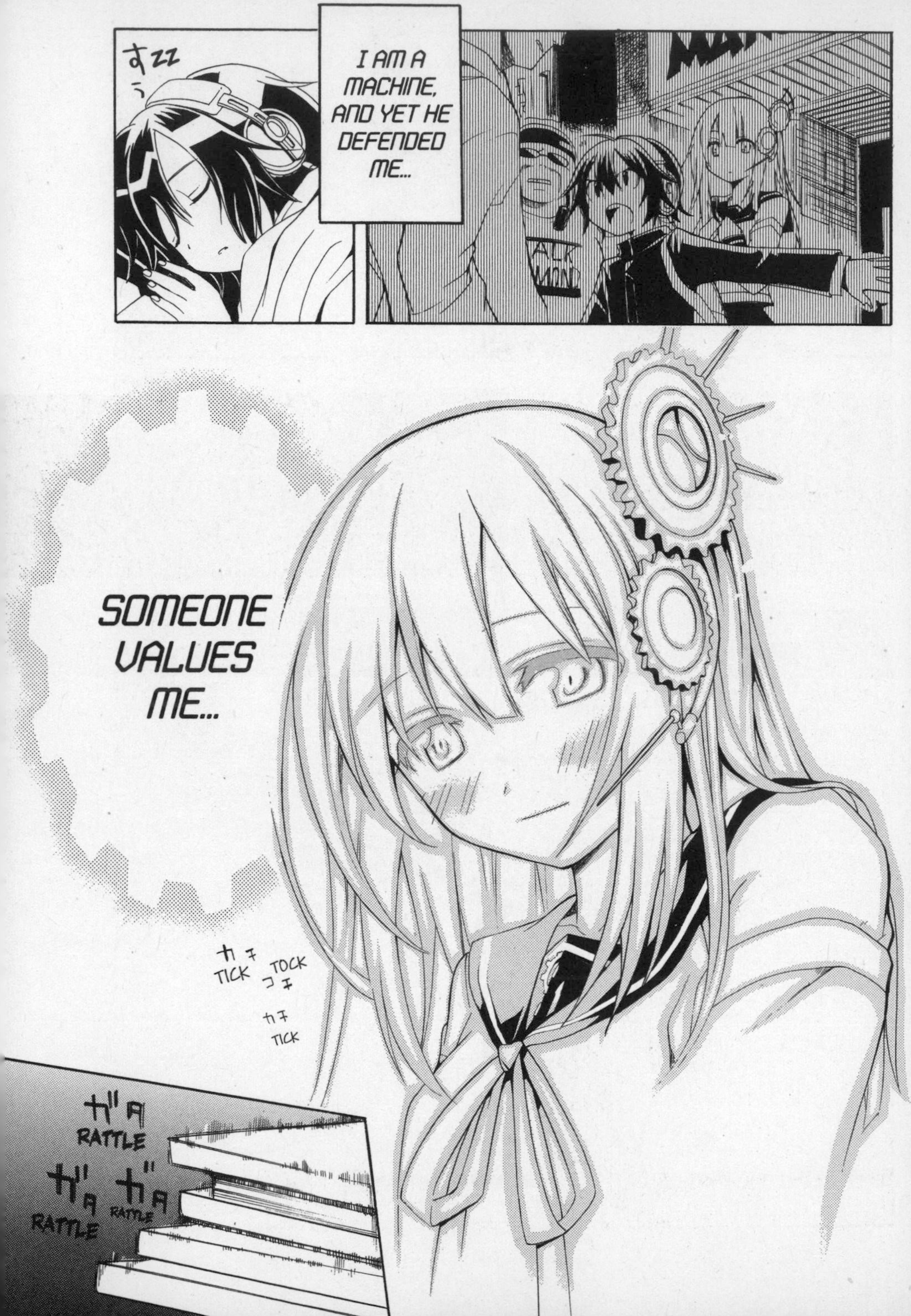
I AM A MACHINE, AND YET HE DEFENDED ME...
すzz
SOMEONE VALUES ME...
カチ TICK
TOCK コチ
カチ TICK
ガタ RATTLE
ガタ RATTLE
ガタ RATTLE

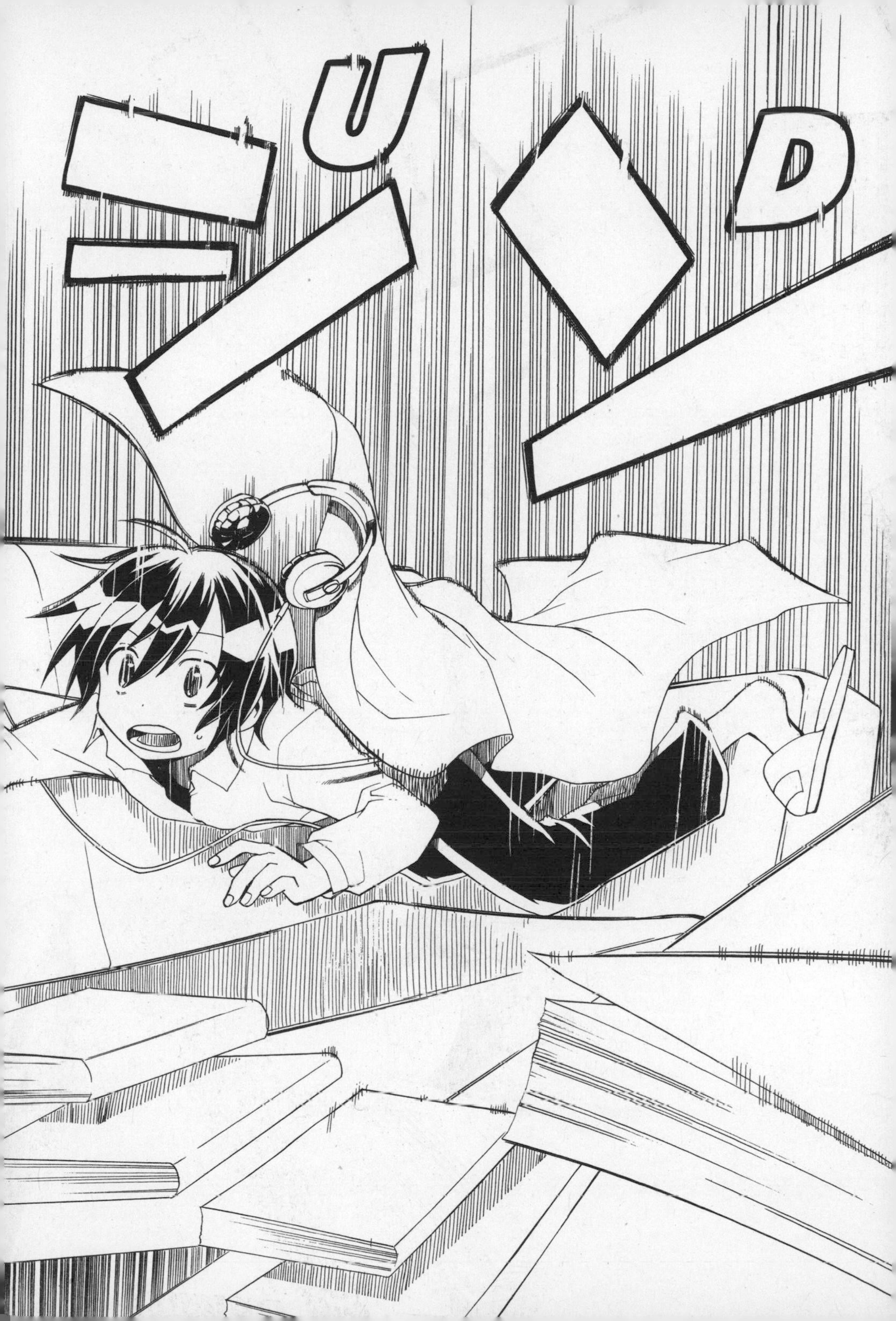
THUD

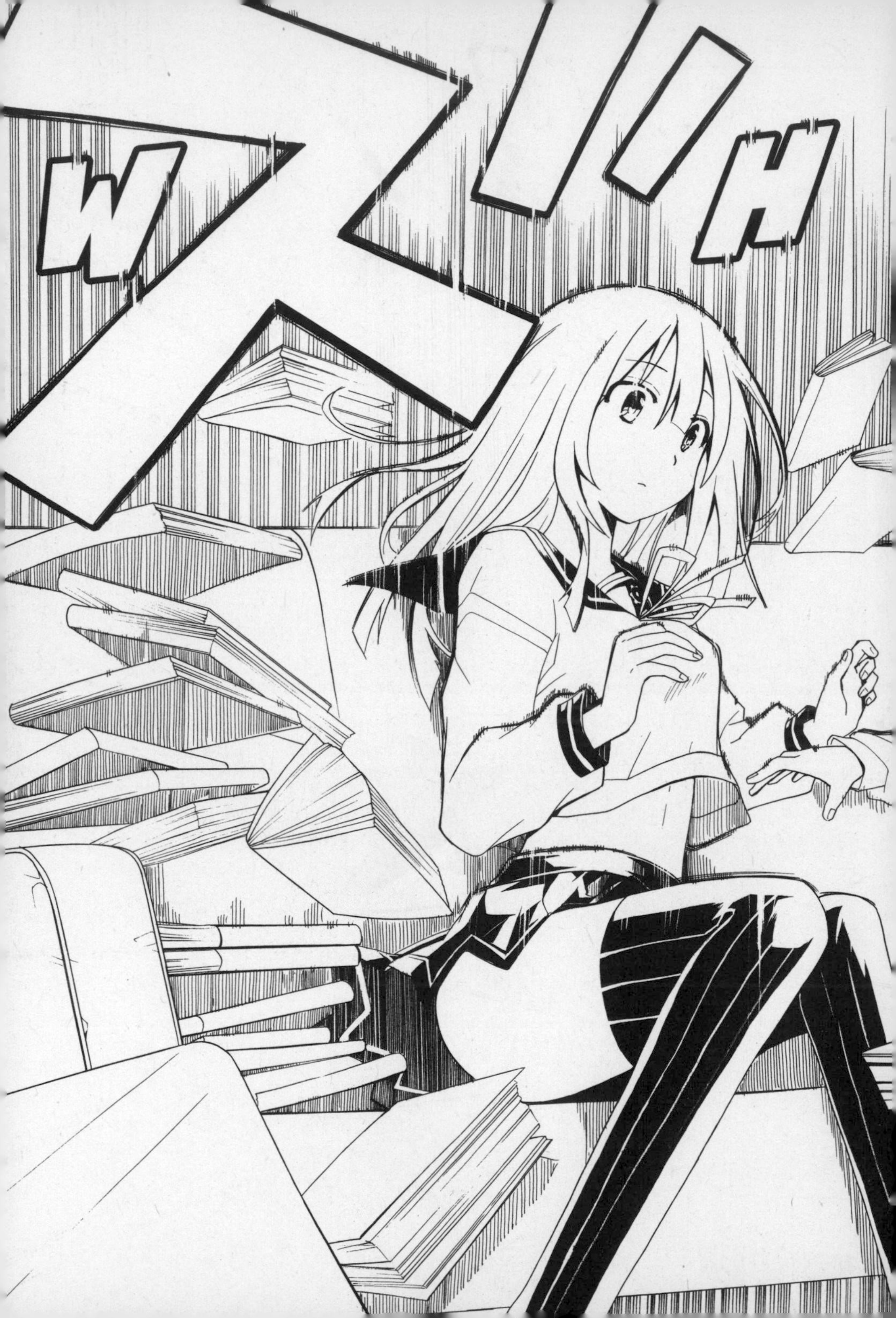
WHH

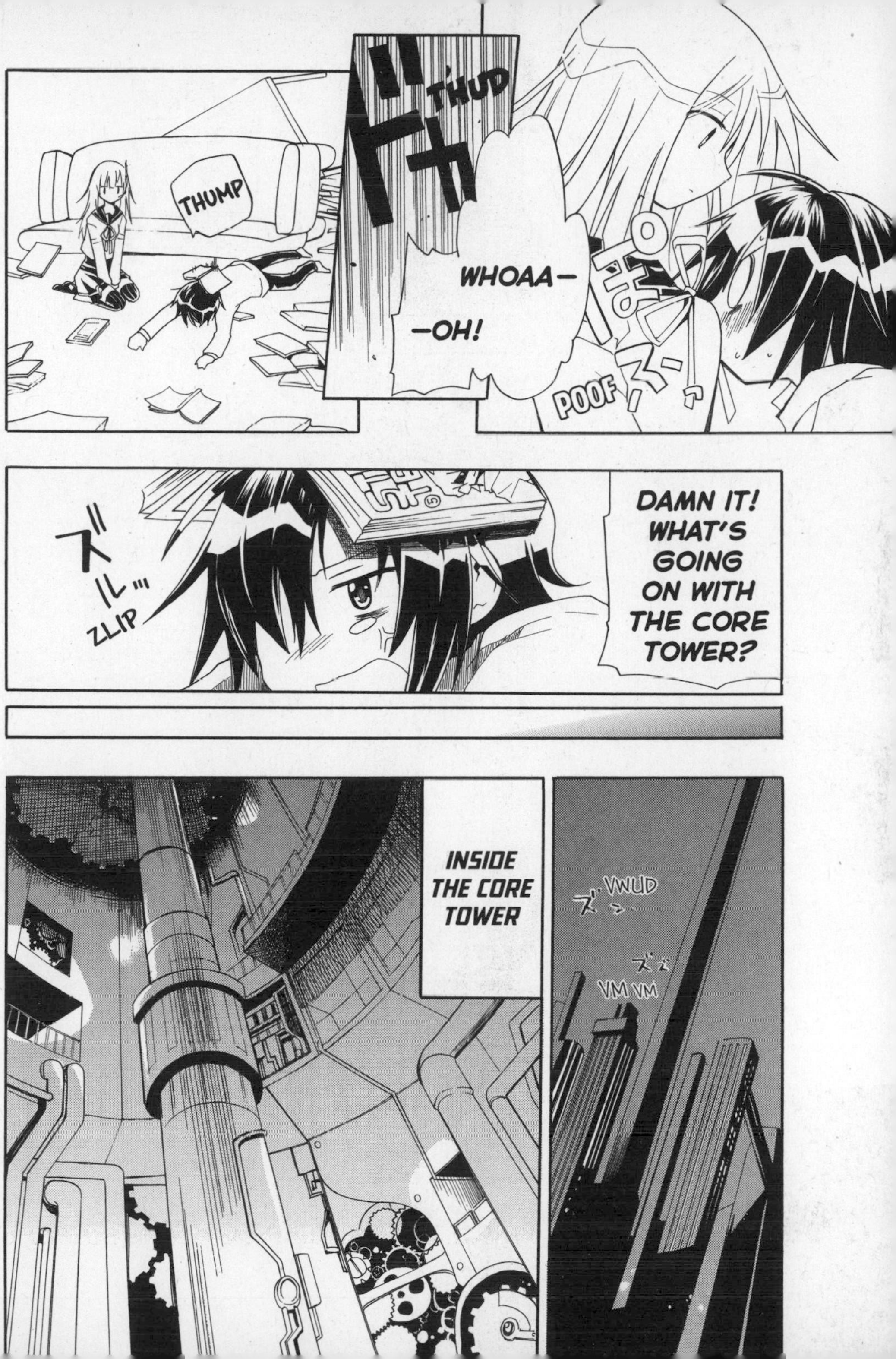
THUD
WHOAA—
—OH!
POOF
THUMP
DAMN IT! WHAT'S GOING ON WITH THE CORE TOWER?
ZLIP
VWUD
VM VM
INSIDE THE CORE TOWER

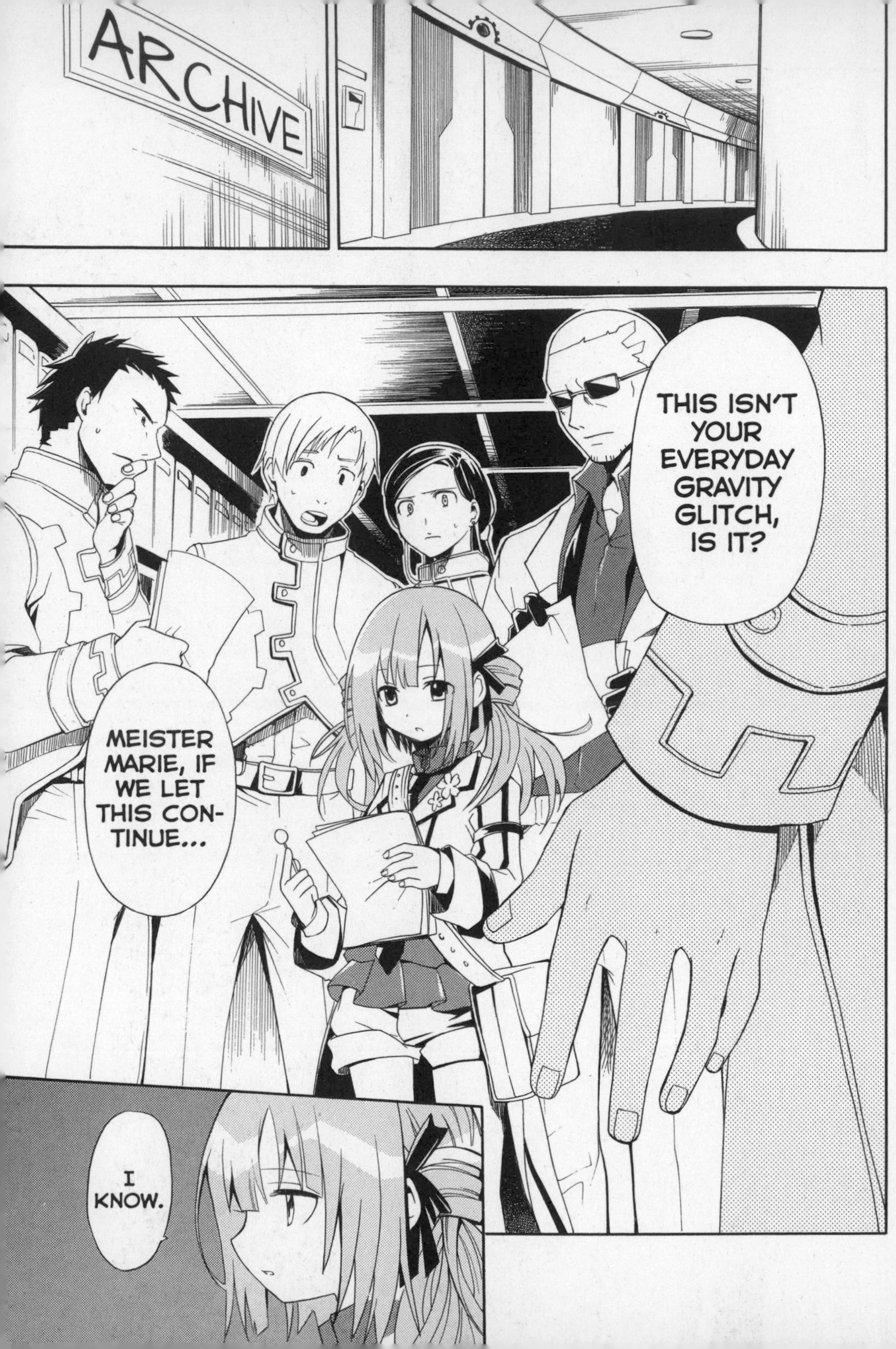
ARCHIVE
THIS ISN'T YOUR EVERYDAY GRAVITY GLITCH, IS IT?
MEISTER MARIE, IF WE LET THIS CON-TINUE...
I KNOW.

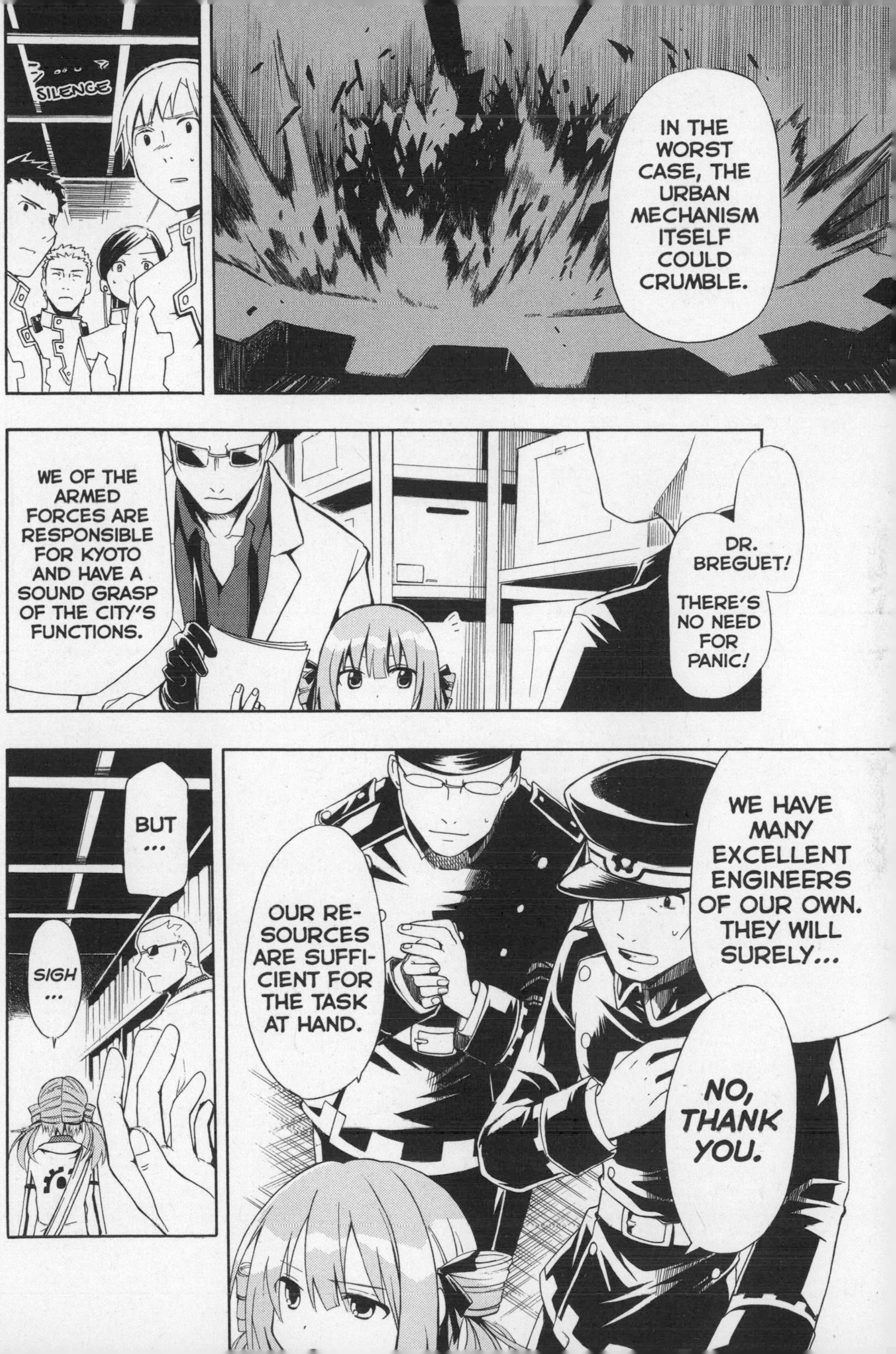
IN THE WORST CASE, THE URBAN MECHANISM ITSELF COULD CRUMBLE.
SILENCE
DR. BREGUET!
THERE'S NO NEED FOR PANIC!
WE OF THE ARMED FORCES ARE RESPONSIBLE FOR KYOTO AND HAVE A SOUND GRASP OF THE CITY'S FUNCTIONS.
WE HAVE MANY EXCELLENT ENGINEERS OF OUR OWN. THEY WILL SURELY...
OUR RE-SOURCES ARE SUFFI-CIENT FOR THE TASK AT HAND.
NO, THANK YOU.
BUT...
SIGH...

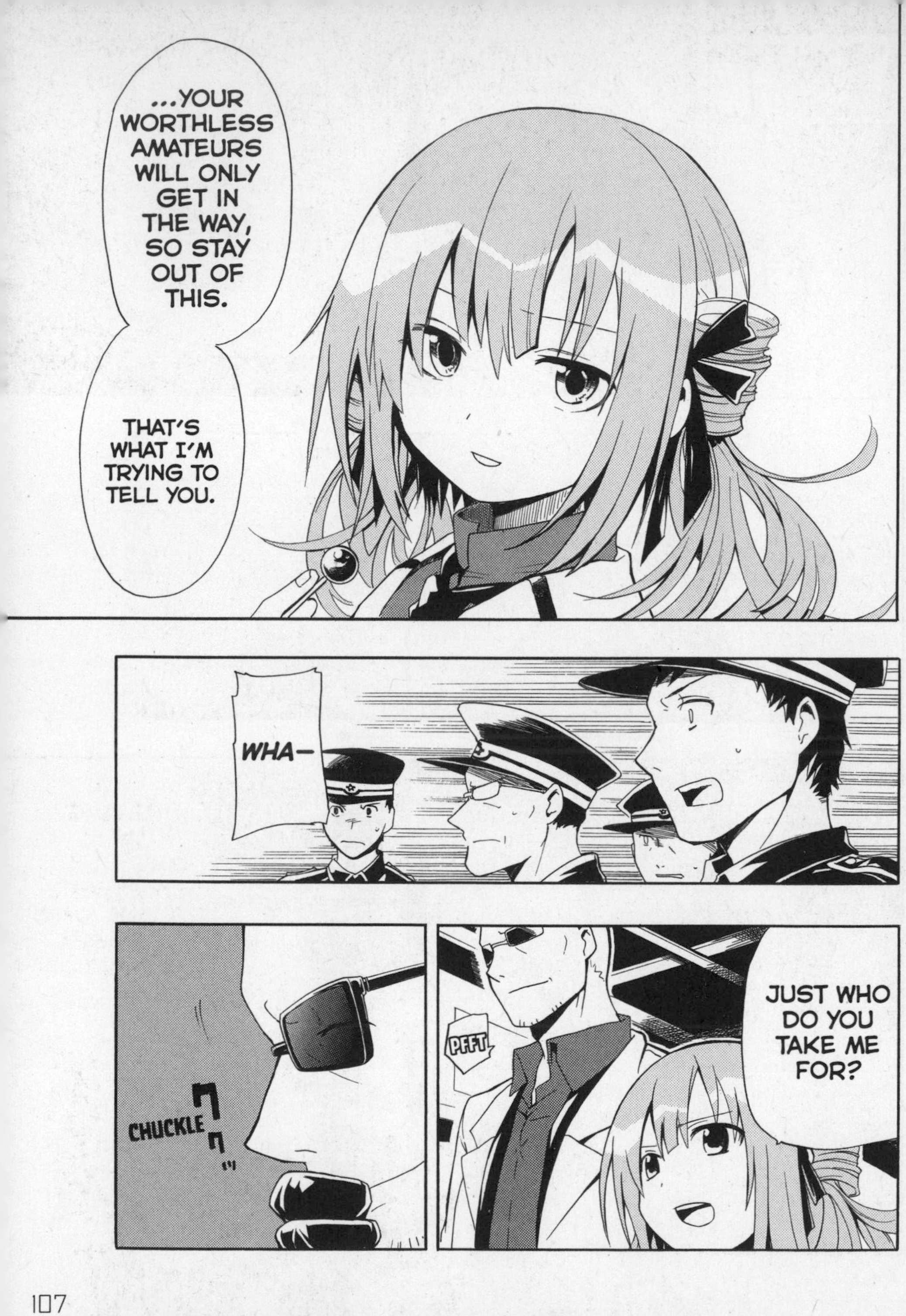
...YOUR WORTHLESS AMATEURS WILL ONLY GET IN THE WAY, SO STAY OUT OF THIS.
THAT'S WHAT I'M TRYING TO TELL YOU.
WHA-
JUST WHO DO YOU TAKE ME FOR?
PFFT
CHUCKLE

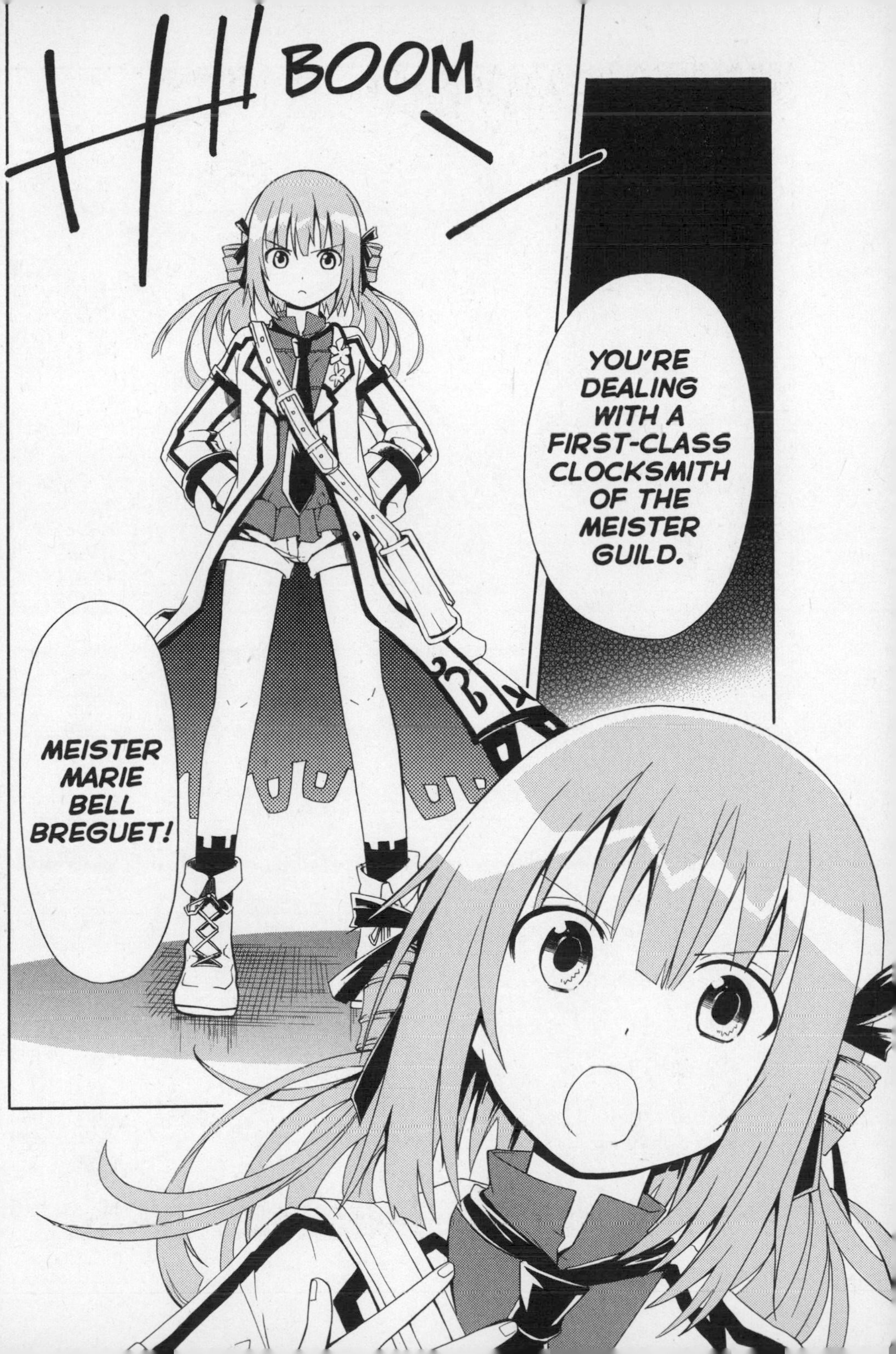
BOOM
YOU'RE DEALING WITH A FIRST-CLASS CLOCKSMITH OF THE MEISTER GUILD.
MEISTER MARIE BELL BREGUET!

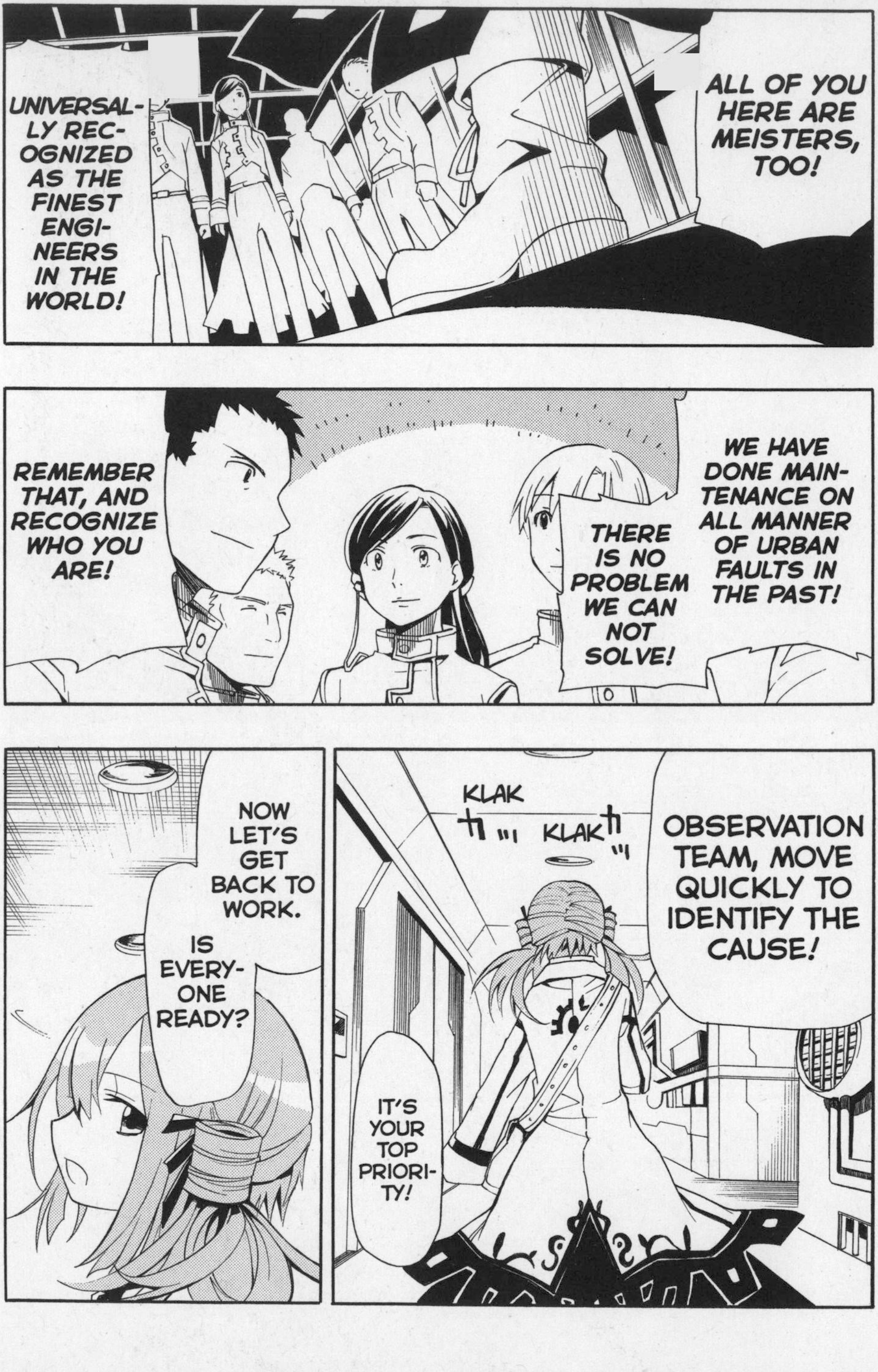
ALL OF YOU HERE ARE MEISTERS, TOO!
UNIVERSALLY RECOGNIZED AS THE FINEST ENGINEERS IN THE WORLD!
WE HAVE DONE MAINTENANCE ON ALL MANNER OF URBAN FAULTS IN THE PAST!
THERE IS NO PROBLEM WE CAN NOT SOLVE!
REMEMBER THAT, AND RECOGNIZE WHO YOU ARE!
KLAK
KLAK
OBSERVATION TEAM, MOVE QUICKLY TO IDENTIFY THE CAUSE!
IT'S YOUR TOP PRIORITY!
NOW LET'S GET BACK TO WORK.
IS EVERYONE READY?

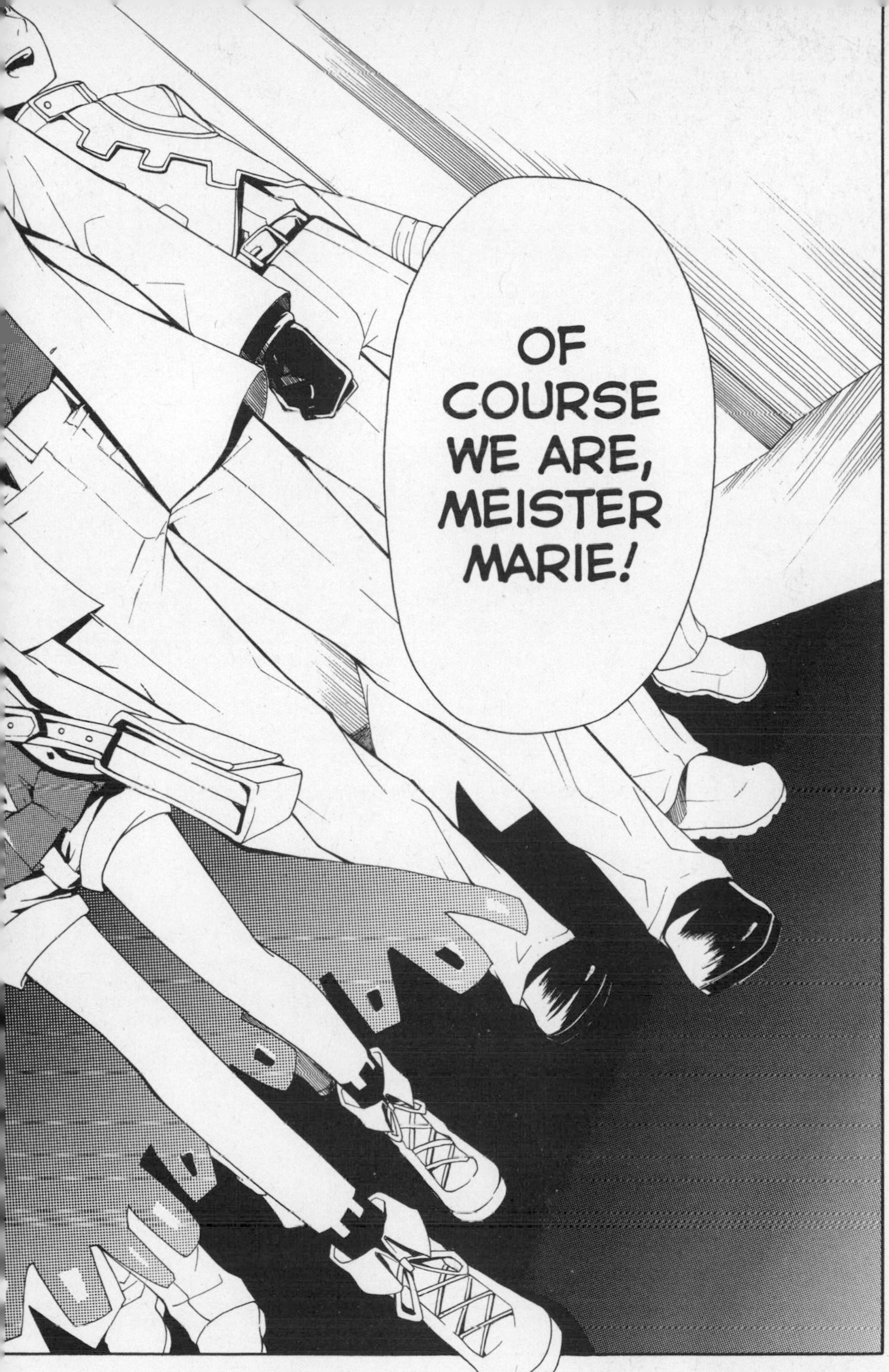
OF COURSE WE ARE, MEISTER MARIE!

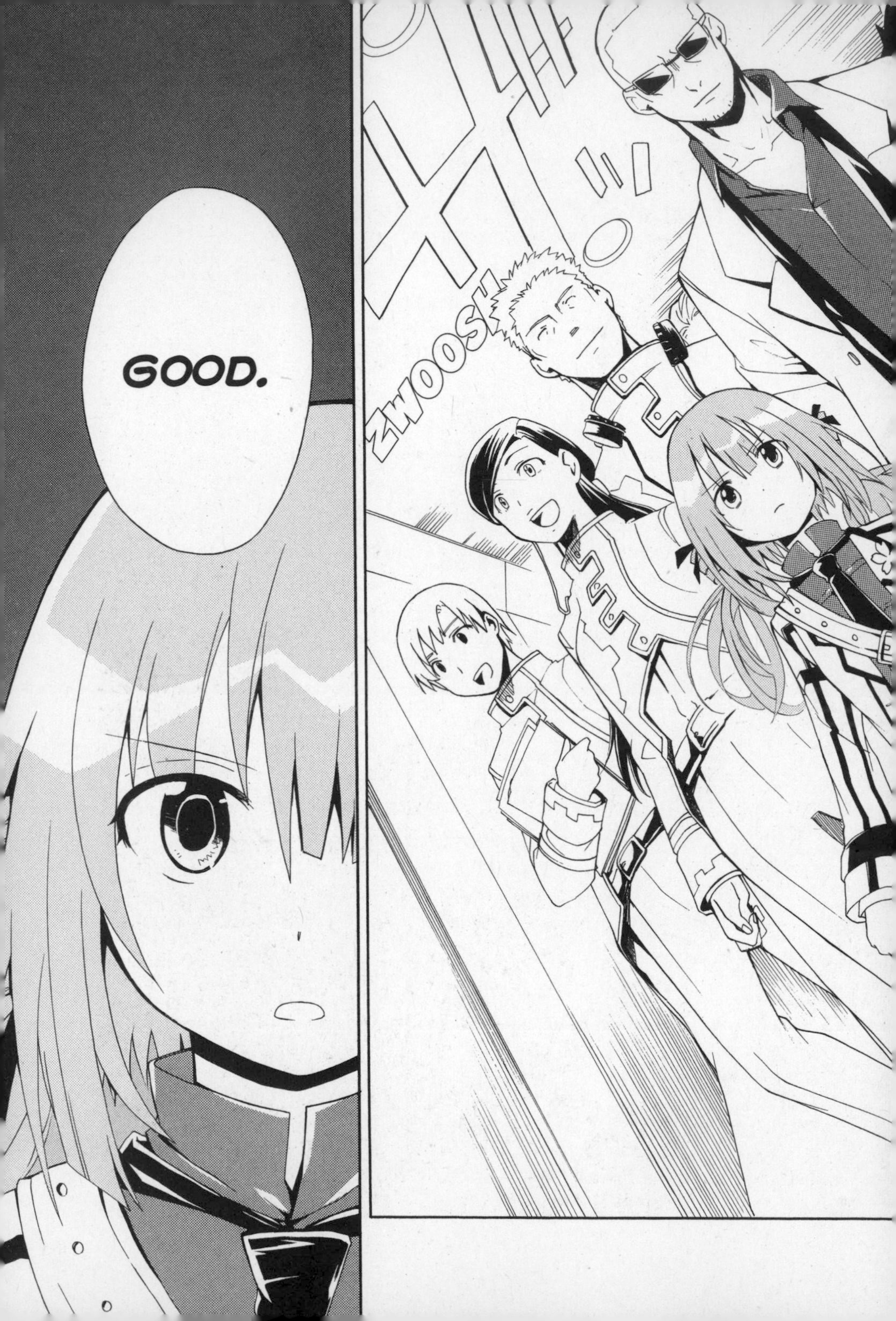
ZWOOSH
GOOD.

Clockwork Planet

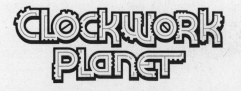

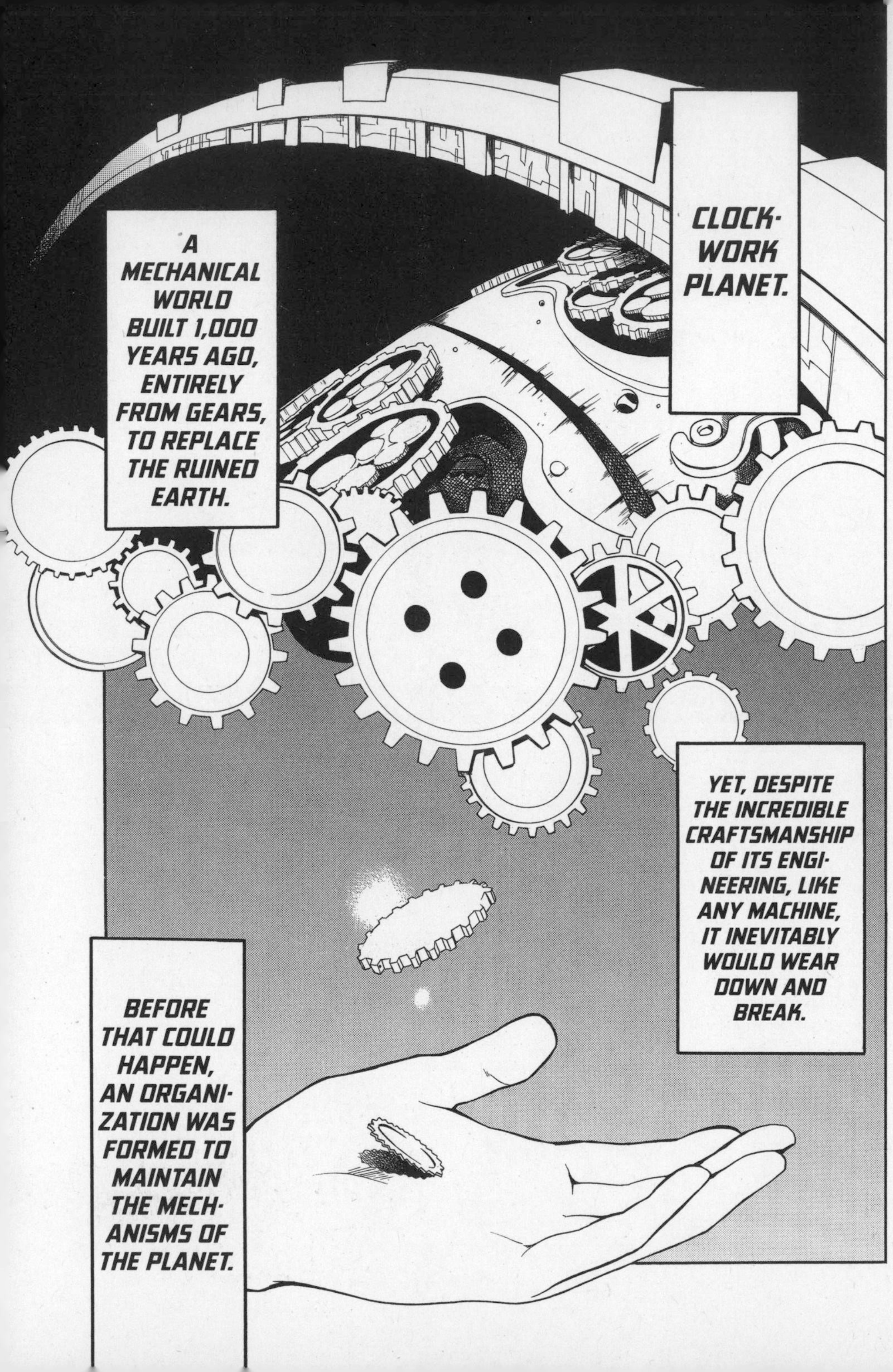
CLOCK-WORK PLANET.
A MECHANICAL WORLD BUILT 1,000 YEARS AGO, ENTIRELY FROM GEARS, TO REPLACE THE RUINED EARTH.
YET, DESPITE THE INCREDIBLE CRAFTSMANSHIP OF ITS ENGI-NEERING, LIKE ANY MACHINE, IT INEVITABLY WOULD WEAR DOWN AND BREAK.
BEFORE THAT COULD HAPPEN, AN ORGANI-ZATION WAS FORMED TO MAINTAIN THE MECH-ANISMS OF THE PLANET.

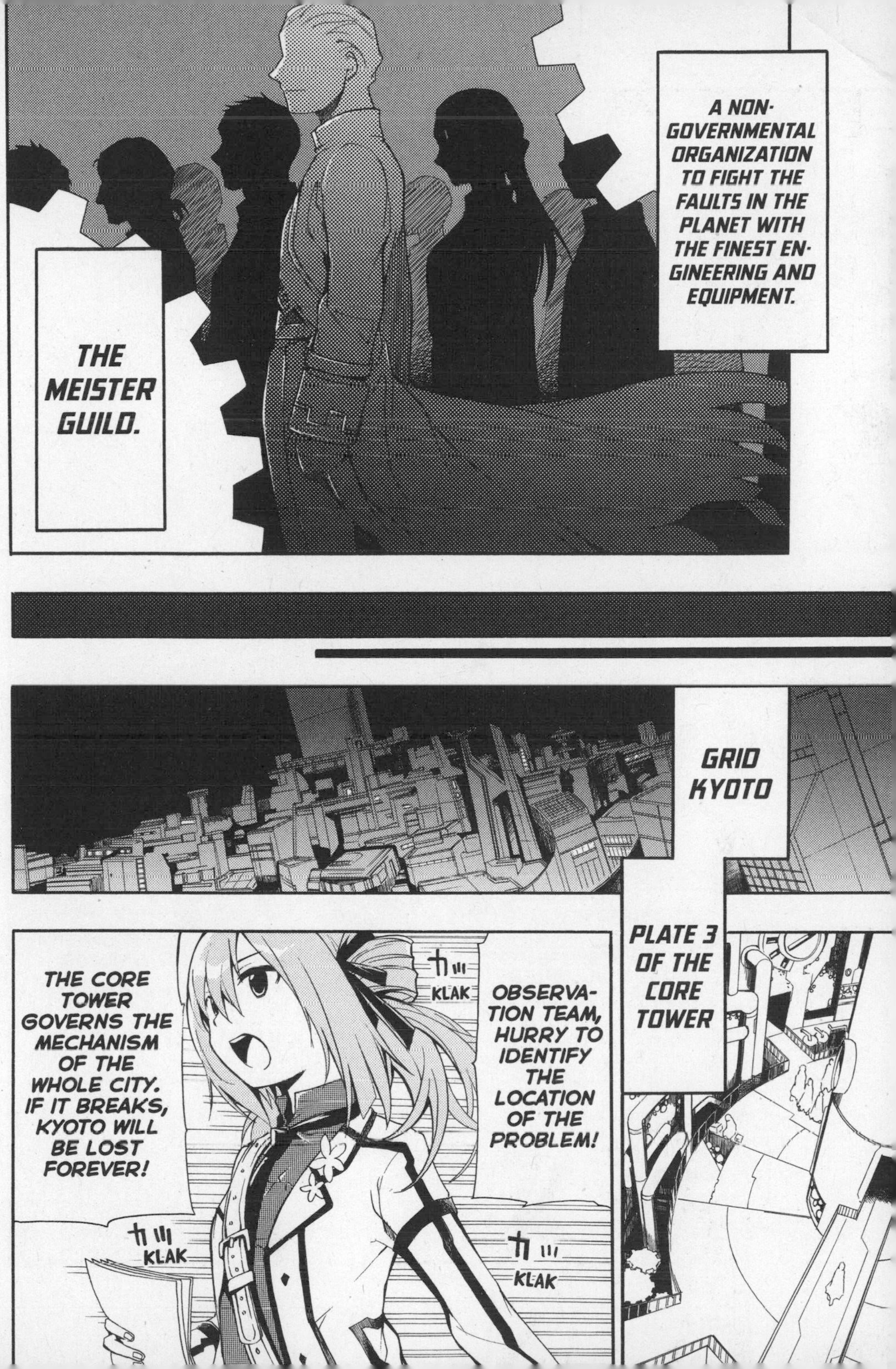
A NON-GOVERNMENTAL ORGANIZATION TO FIGHT THE FAULTS IN THE PLANET WITH THE FINEST ENGINEERING AND EQUIPMENT.
THE MEISTER GUILD.
GRID KYOTO
PLATE 3 OF THE CORE TOWER
OBSERVATION TEAM, HURRY TO IDENTIFY THE LOCATION OF THE PROBLEM!
KLAK
THE CORE TOWER GOVERNS THE MECHANISM OF THE WHOLE CITY. IF IT BREAKS, KYOTO WILL BE LOST FOREVER!
KLAK
KLAK

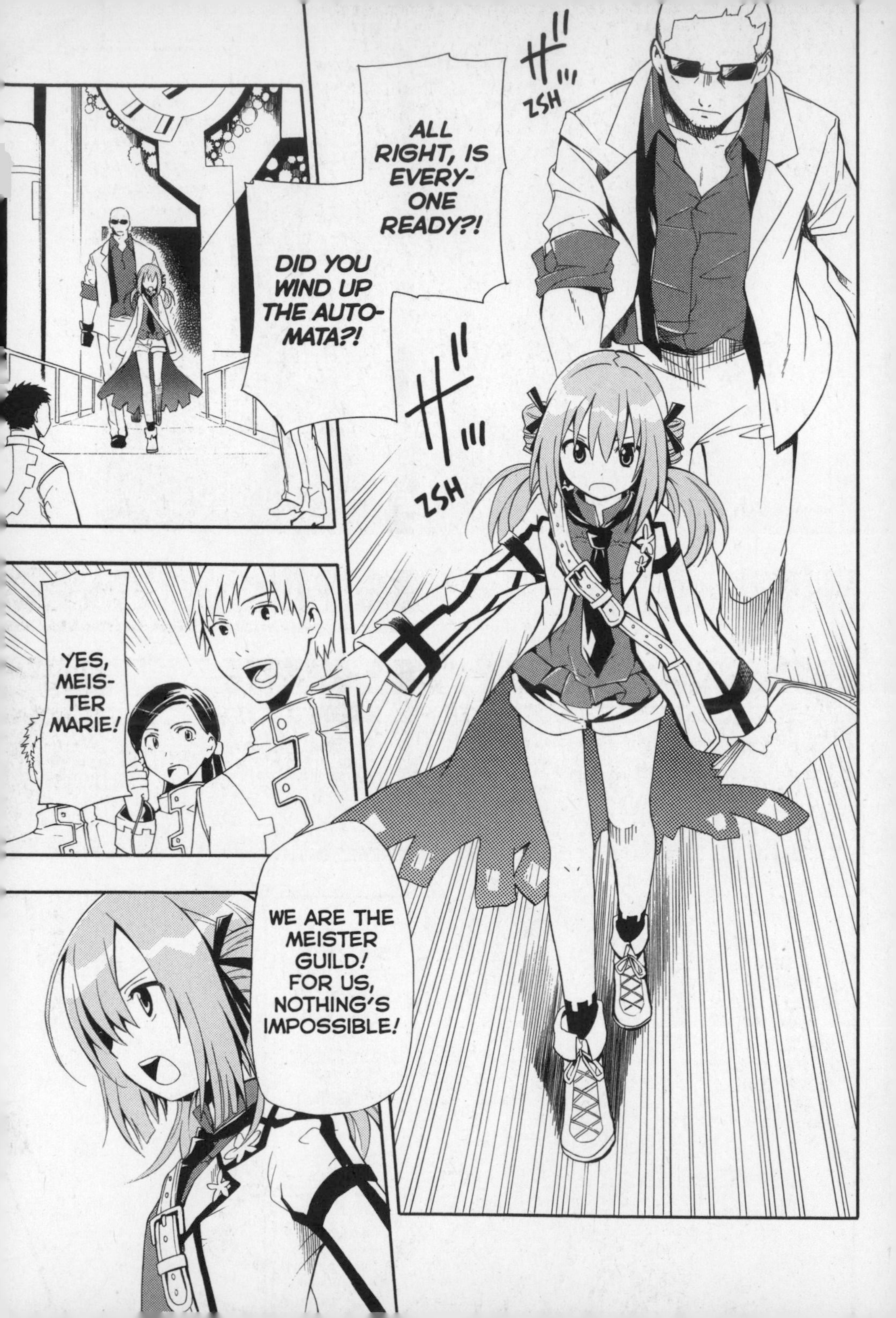
ZSH
ALL RIGHT, IS EVERY-ONE READY?!
DID YOU WIND UP THE AUTO-MATA?!
ZSH
YES, MEIS-TER MARIE!
WE ARE THE MEISTER GUILD! FOR US, NOTHING'S IMPOSSIBLE!

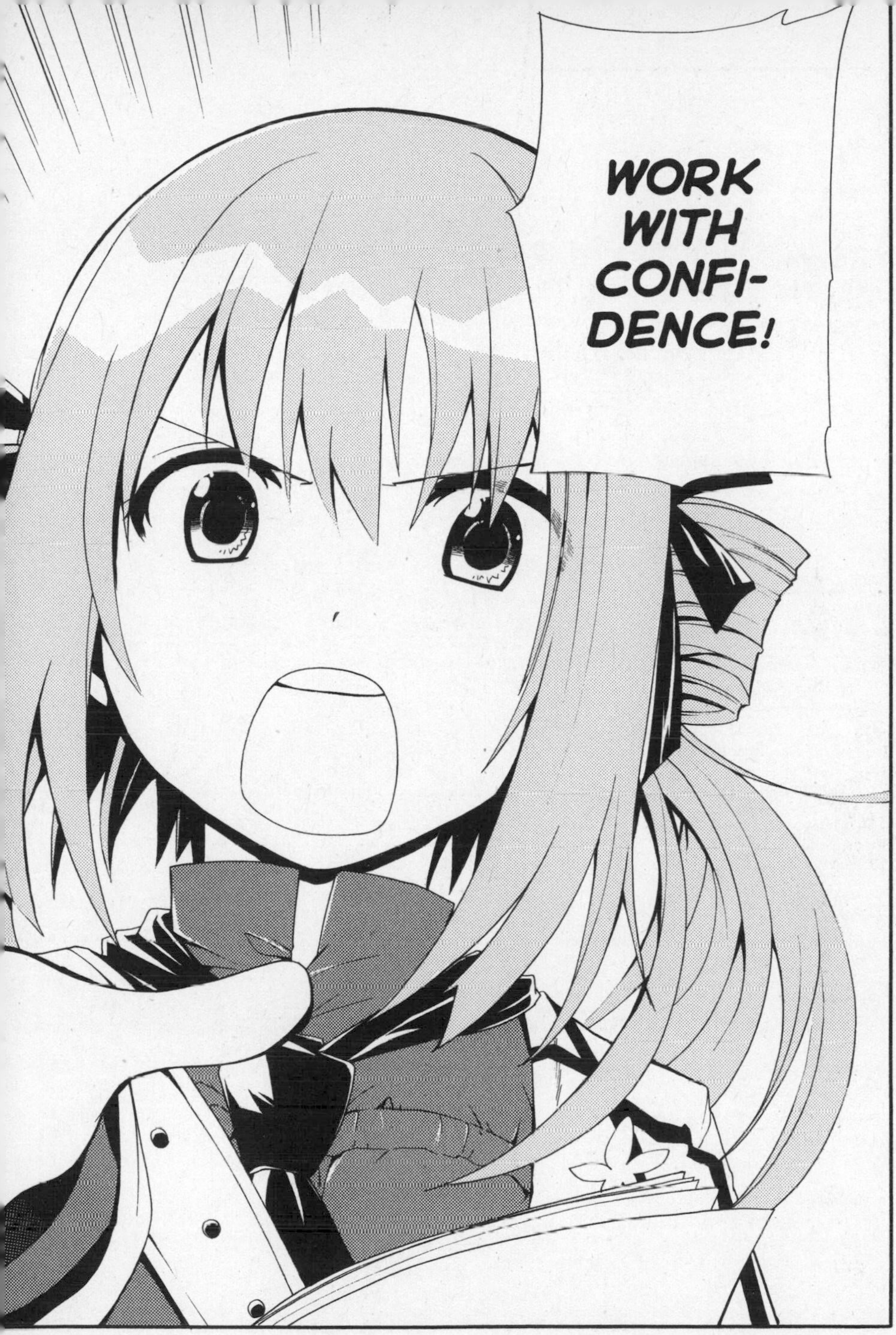
WORK WITH CONFI- DENCE!

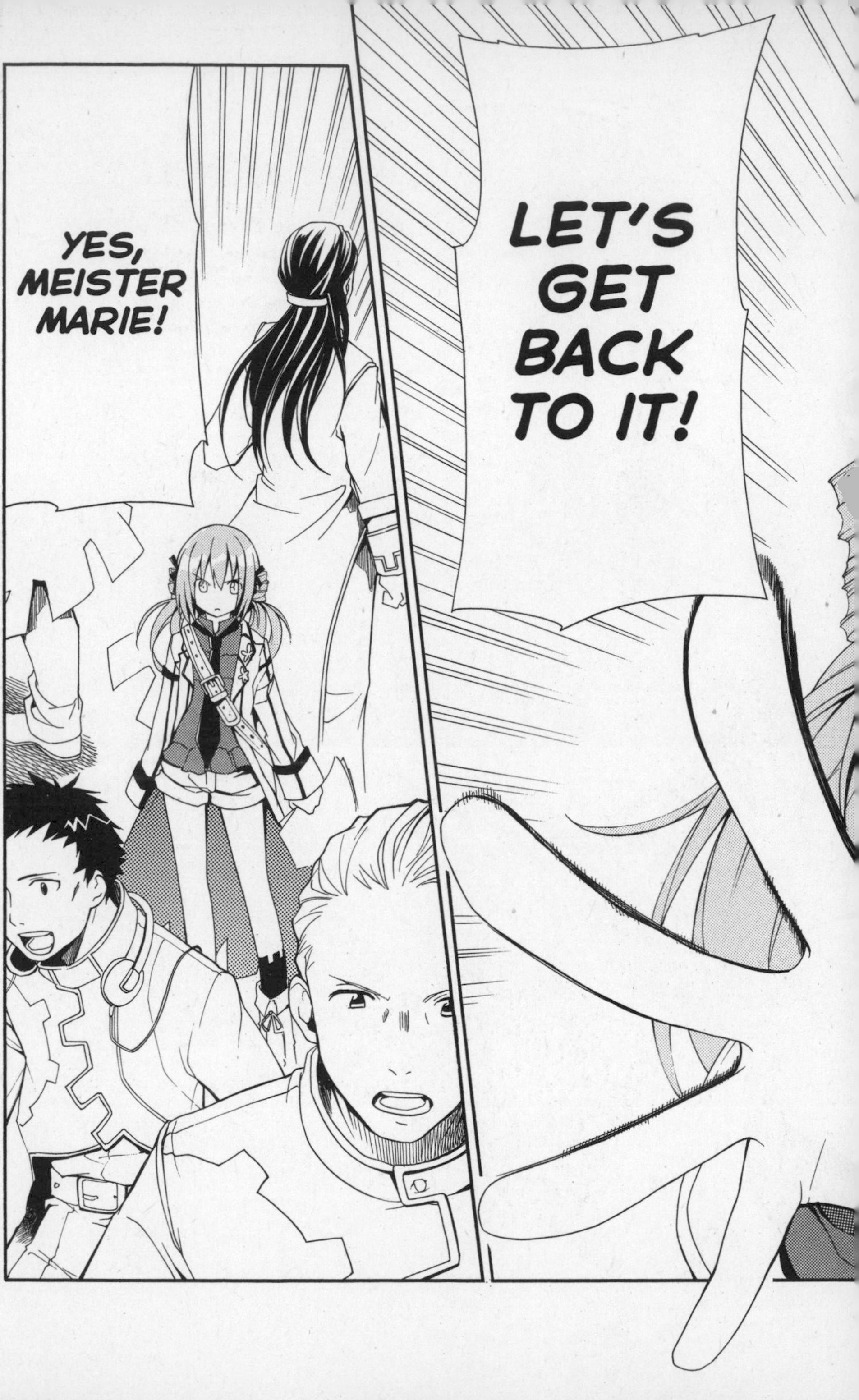
LET'S GET BACK TO IT!
YES, MEISTER MARIE!

Clock 3: Marie Bell Breguet

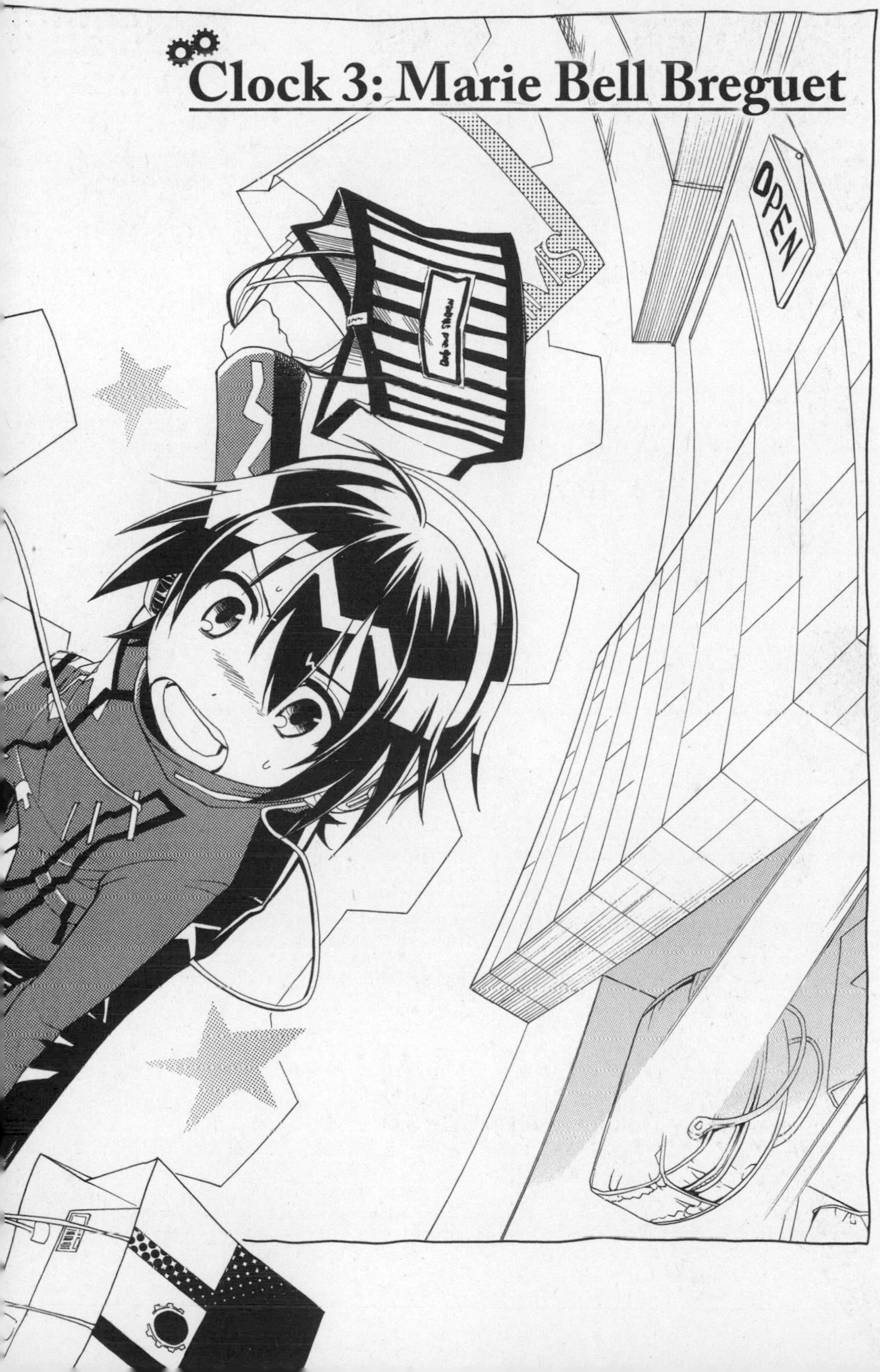
OPEN

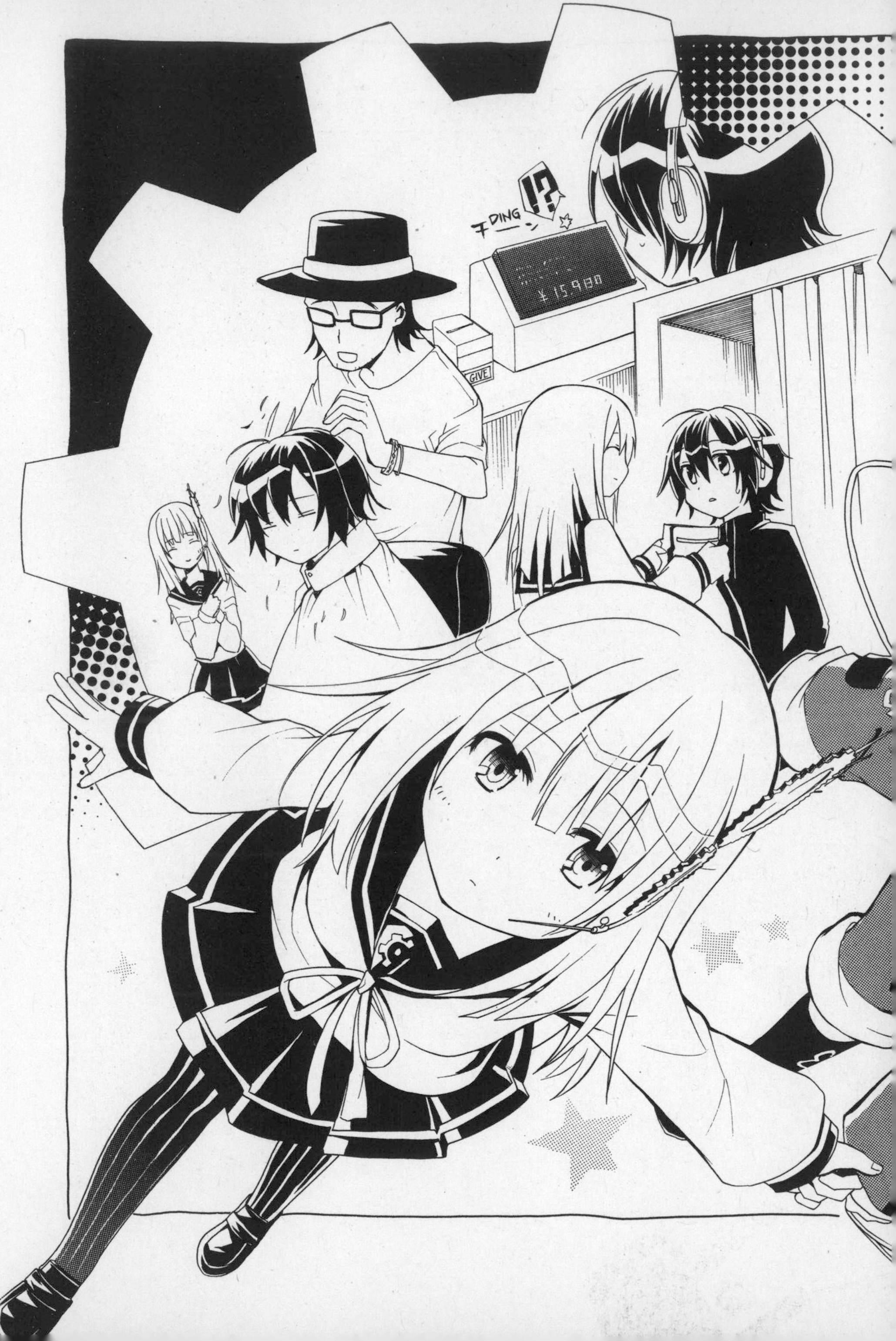

!?
DING
チーン
¥15,980
GIVE

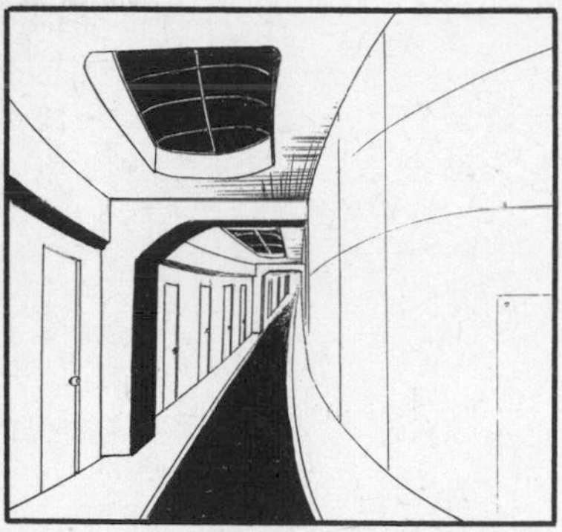

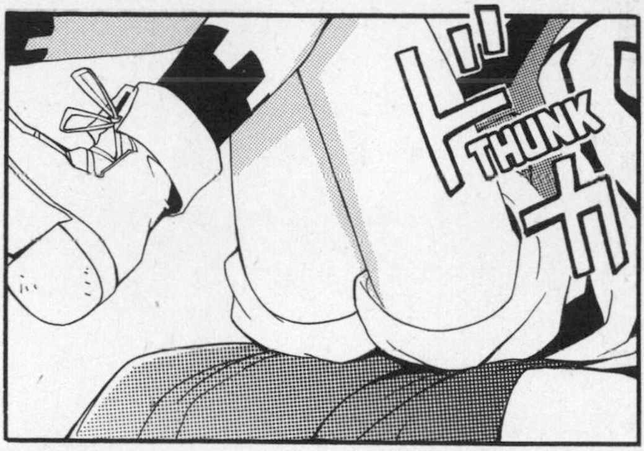
THUNK

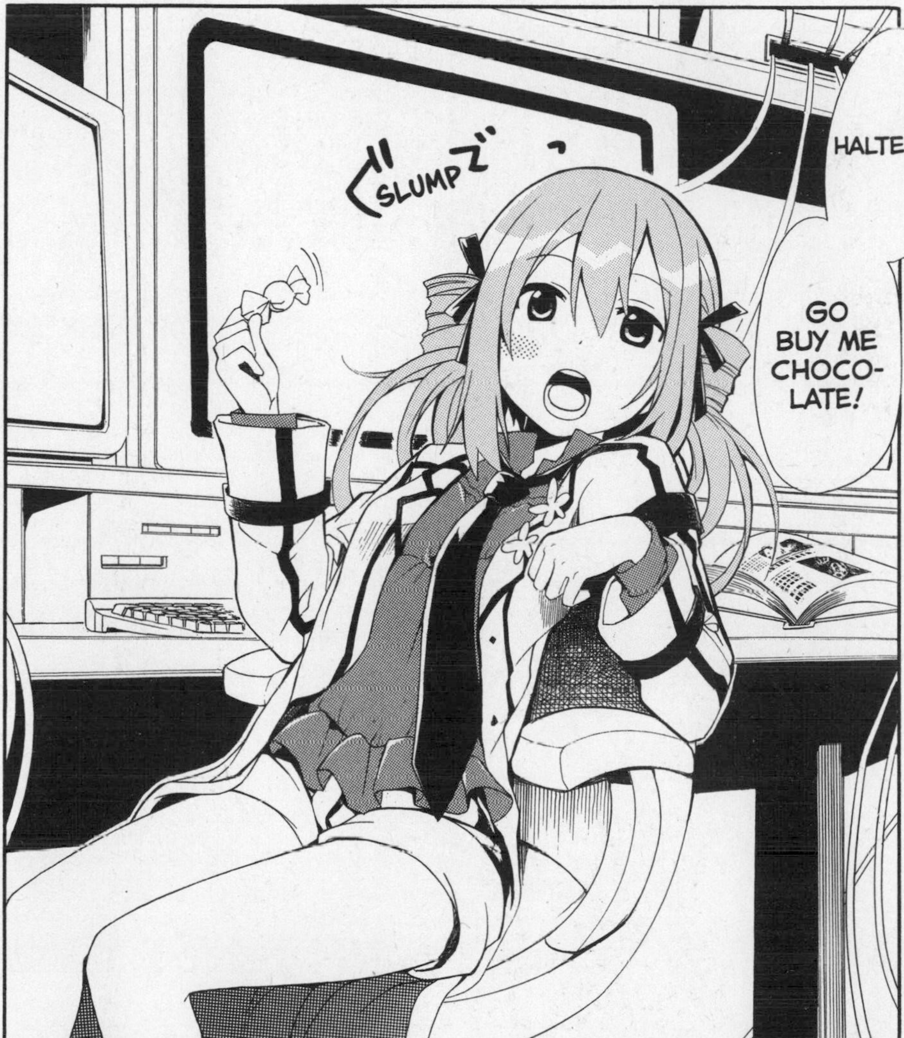
SLUMP
HALTER!
GO BUY ME CHOCOLATE!

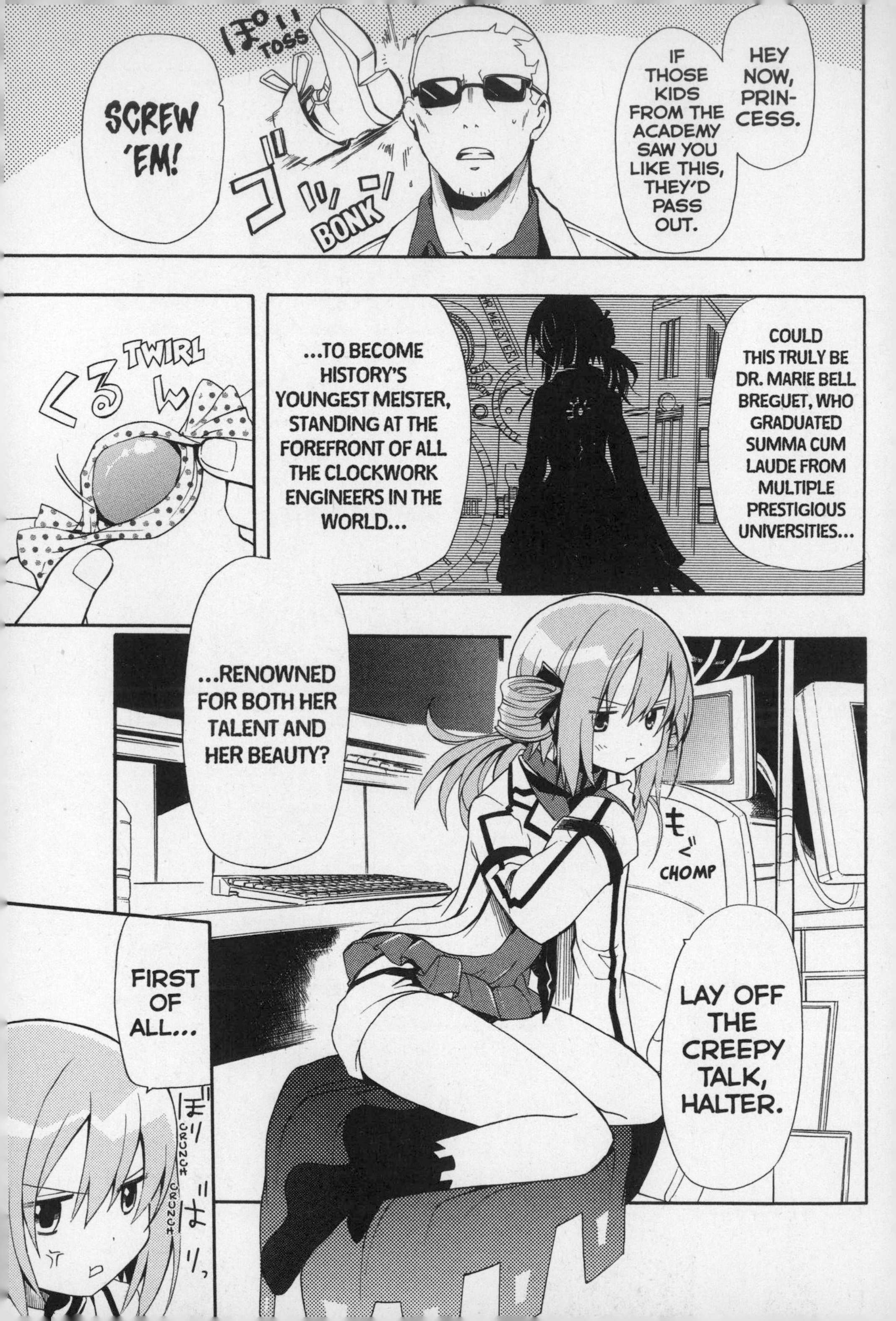
HEY NOW, PRINCESS.
IF THOSE KIDS FROM THE ACADEMY SAW YOU LIKE THIS, THEY'D PASS OUT.
TOSS
SCREW 'EM!
BONK
COULD THIS TRULY BE DR. MARIE BELL BREGUET, WHO GRADUATED SUMMA CUM LAUDE FROM MULTIPLE PRESTIGIOUS UNIVERSITIES...
...TO BECOME HISTORY'S YOUNGEST MEISTER, STANDING AT THE FOREFRONT OF ALL THE CLOCKWORK ENGINEERS IN THE WORLD...
TWIRL
...RENOWNED FOR BOTH HER TALENT AND HER BEAUTY?
CHOMP
LAY OFF THE CREEPY TALK, HALTER.
FIRST OF ALL...
CRUNCH
CRUNCH

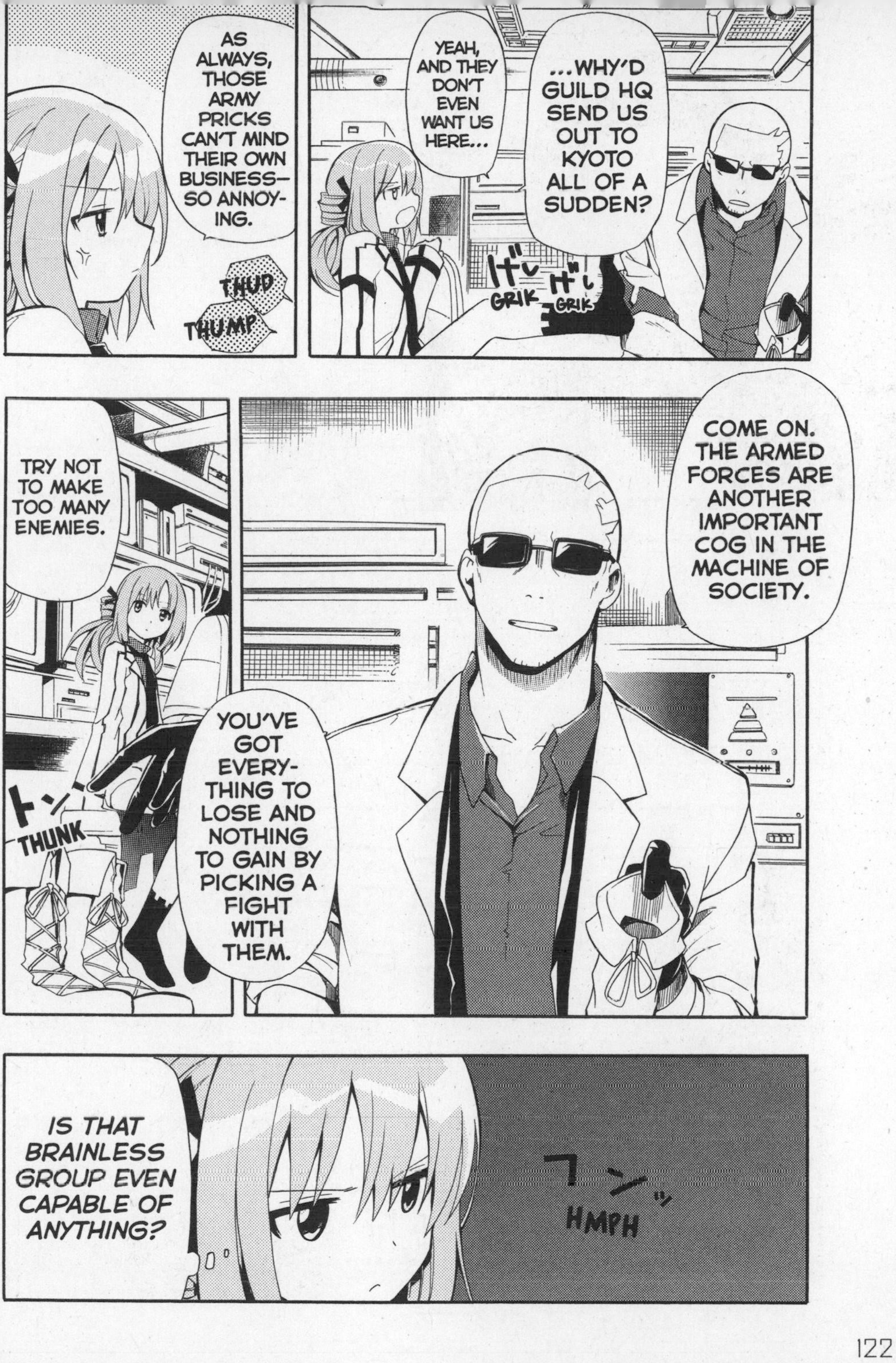
...WHY'D GUILD HQ SEND US OUT TO KYOTO ALL OF A SUDDEN?
YEAH, AND THEY DON'T EVEN WANT US HERE...
げし げし
GRIK GRIK
AS ALWAYS, THOSE ARMY PRICKS CAN'T MIND THEIR OWN BUSINESS—SO ANNOYING.
THUD
THUMP
COME ON. THE ARMED FORCES ARE ANOTHER IMPORTANT COG IN THE MACHINE OF SOCIETY.
YOU'VE GOT EVERYTHING TO LOSE AND NOTHING TO GAIN BY PICKING A FIGHT WITH THEM.
TRY NOT TO MAKE TOO MANY ENEMIES.
トン
THUNK
フンッ
HMPH
IS THAT BRAINLESS GROUP EVEN CAPABLE OF ANYTHING?

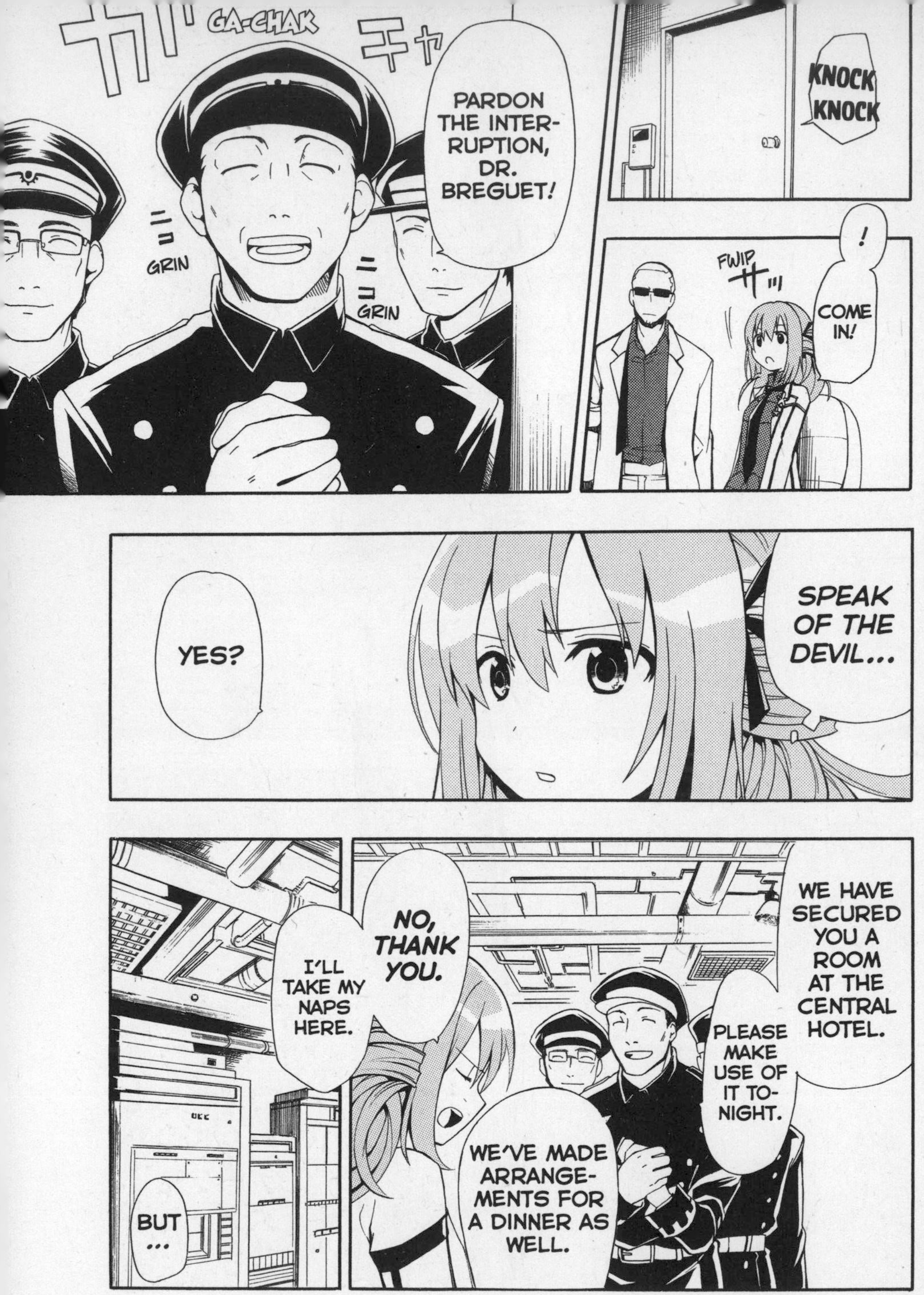
KNOCK KNOCK
FWIP
サッ
!
COME IN!
GA-CHAK
ガチャ
PARDON THE INTERRUPTION, DR. BREGUET!
ニコ
GRIN
ニコ
GRIN
SPEAK OF THE DEVIL...
YES?
WE HAVE SECURED YOU A ROOM AT THE CENTRAL HOTEL.
PLEASE MAKE USE OF IT TONIGHT.
NO, THANK YOU.
I'LL TAKE MY NAPS HERE.
WE'VE MADE ARRANGEMENTS FOR A DINNER AS WELL.
BUT...

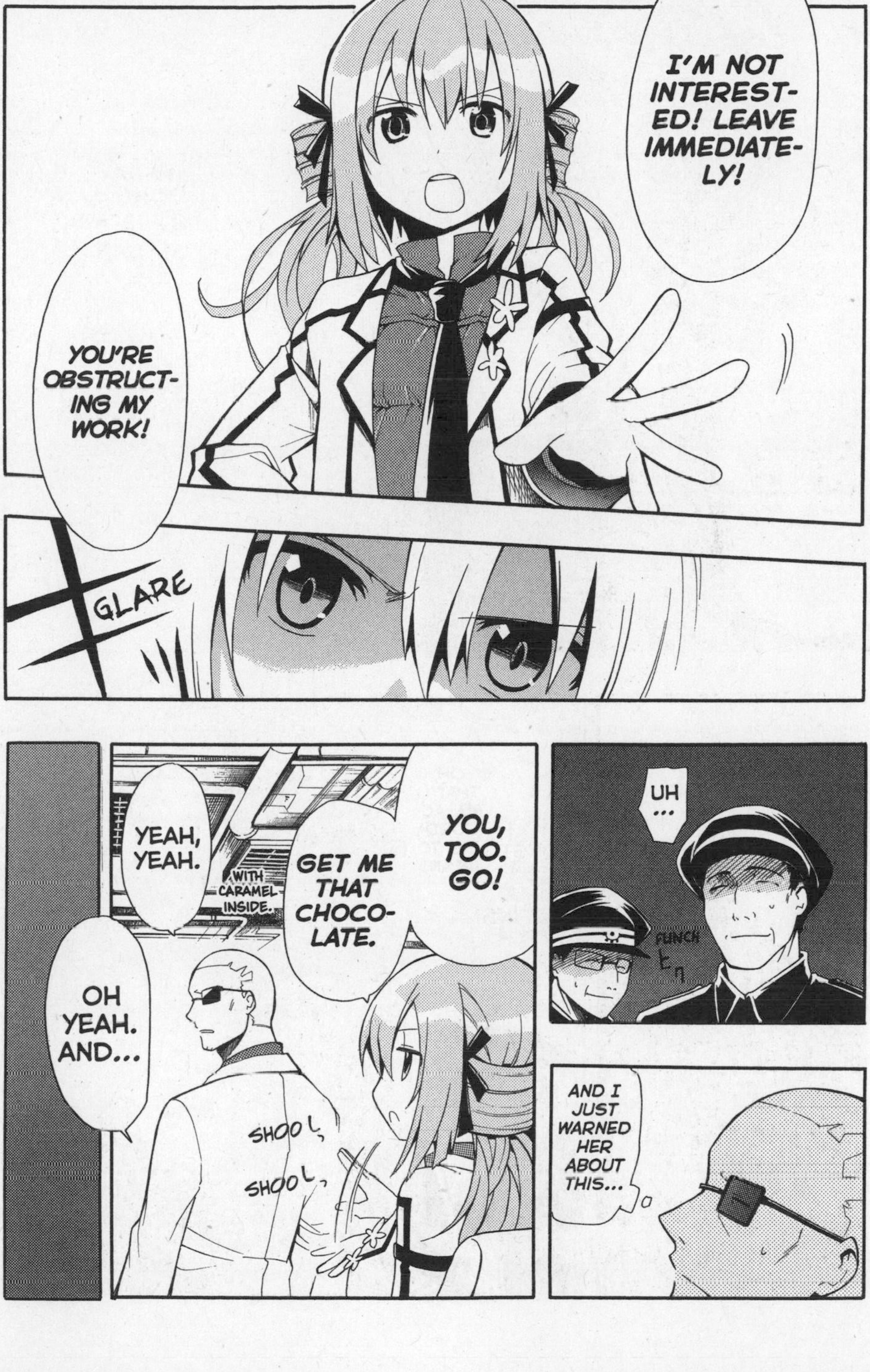
I'M NOT INTEREST-ED! LEAVE IMMEDIATE-LY!
YOU'RE OBSTRUCT-ING MY WORK!
GLARE
UH...
FLINCH
AND I JUST WARNED HER ABOUT THIS...
YOU, TOO. GO!
GET ME THAT CHOCO-LATE.
WITH CARAMEL INSIDE.
YEAH, YEAH.
OH YEAH. AND...
SHOO
SHOO

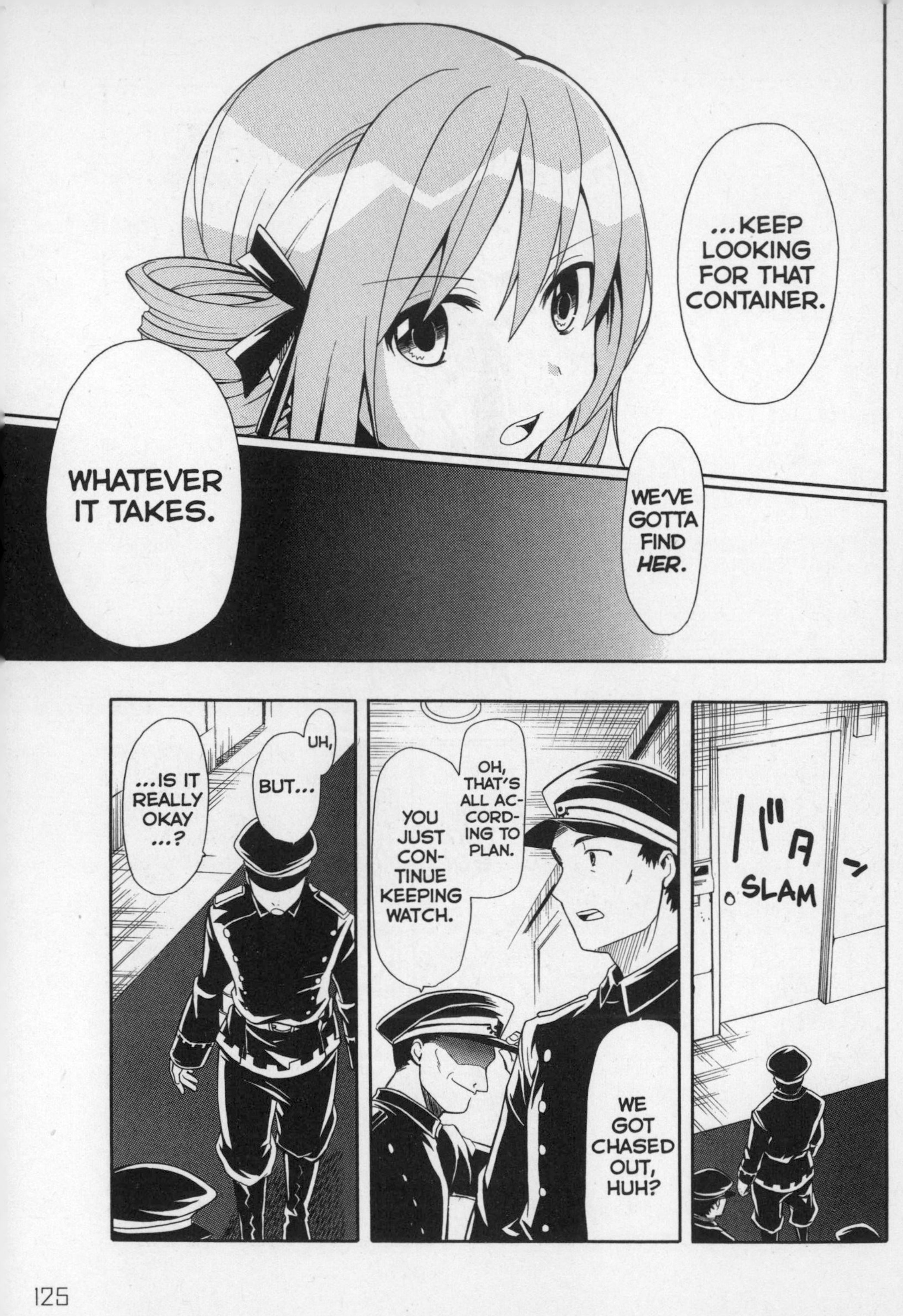
...KEEP LOOKING FOR THAT CONTAINER.
WE'VE GOTTA FIND *HER*.
WHATEVER IT TAKES.
バタン
SLAM
WE GOT CHASED OUT, HUH?
OH, THAT'S ALL AC-CORD-ING TO PLAN.
YOU JUST CON-TINUE KEEPING WATCH.
UH, BUT...
...IS IT REALLY OKAY ...?

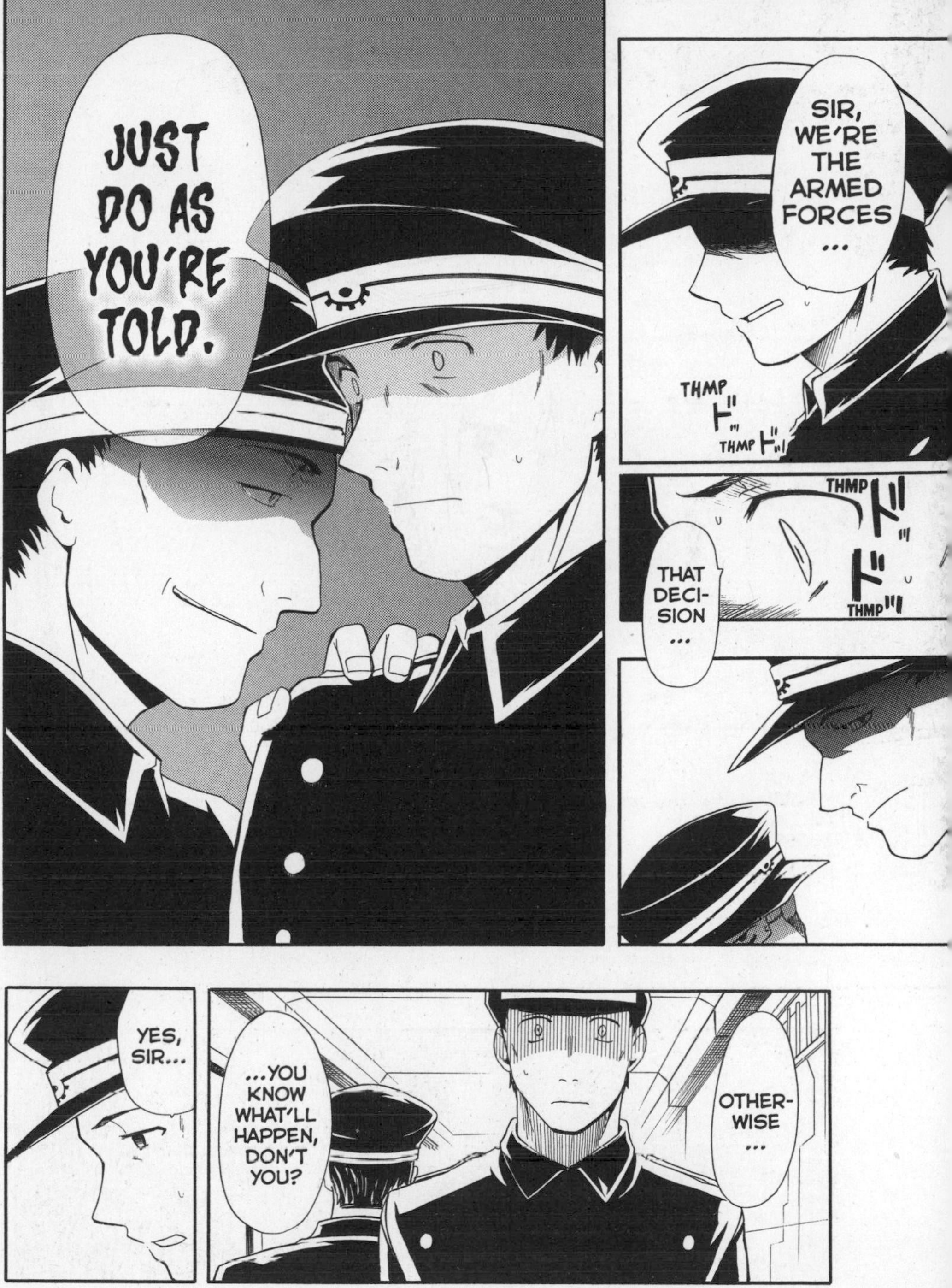
SIR, WE'RE THE ARMED FORCES ...
THMP ドッ
THMP ドッ
THAT DECISION ...
THMP ドッ
THMP ドッ
JUST DO AS YOU'RE TOLD.
OTHER-WISE ...
...YOU KNOW WHAT'LL HAPPEN, DON'T YOU?
YES, SIR...

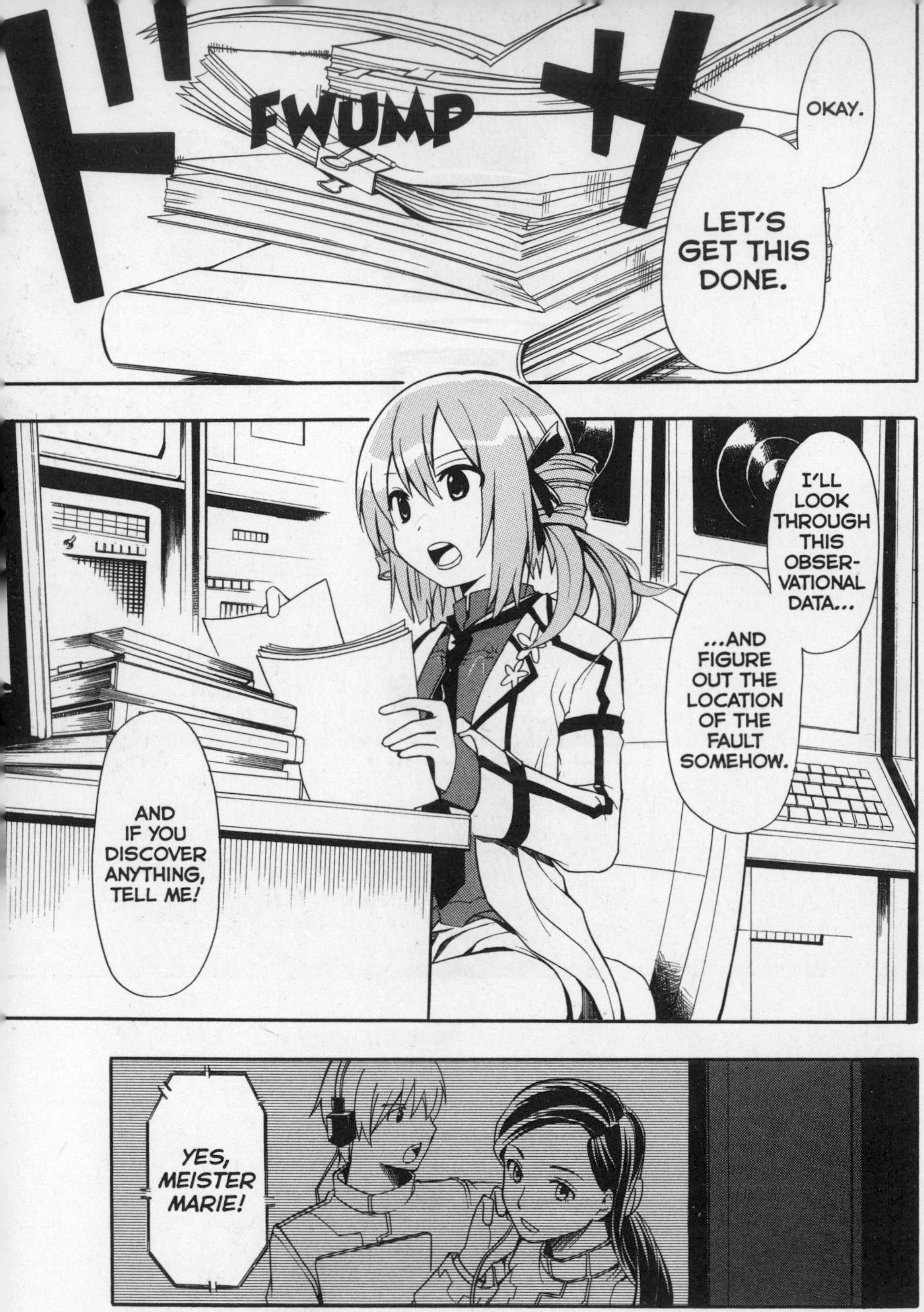
OKAY.
LET'S GET THIS DONE.
FWUMP
I'LL LOOK THROUGH THIS OBSER-VATIONAL DATA...
...AND FIGURE OUT THE LOCATION OF THE FAULT SOMEHOW.
AND IF YOU DISCOVER ANYTHING, TELL ME!
YES, MEISTER MARIE!

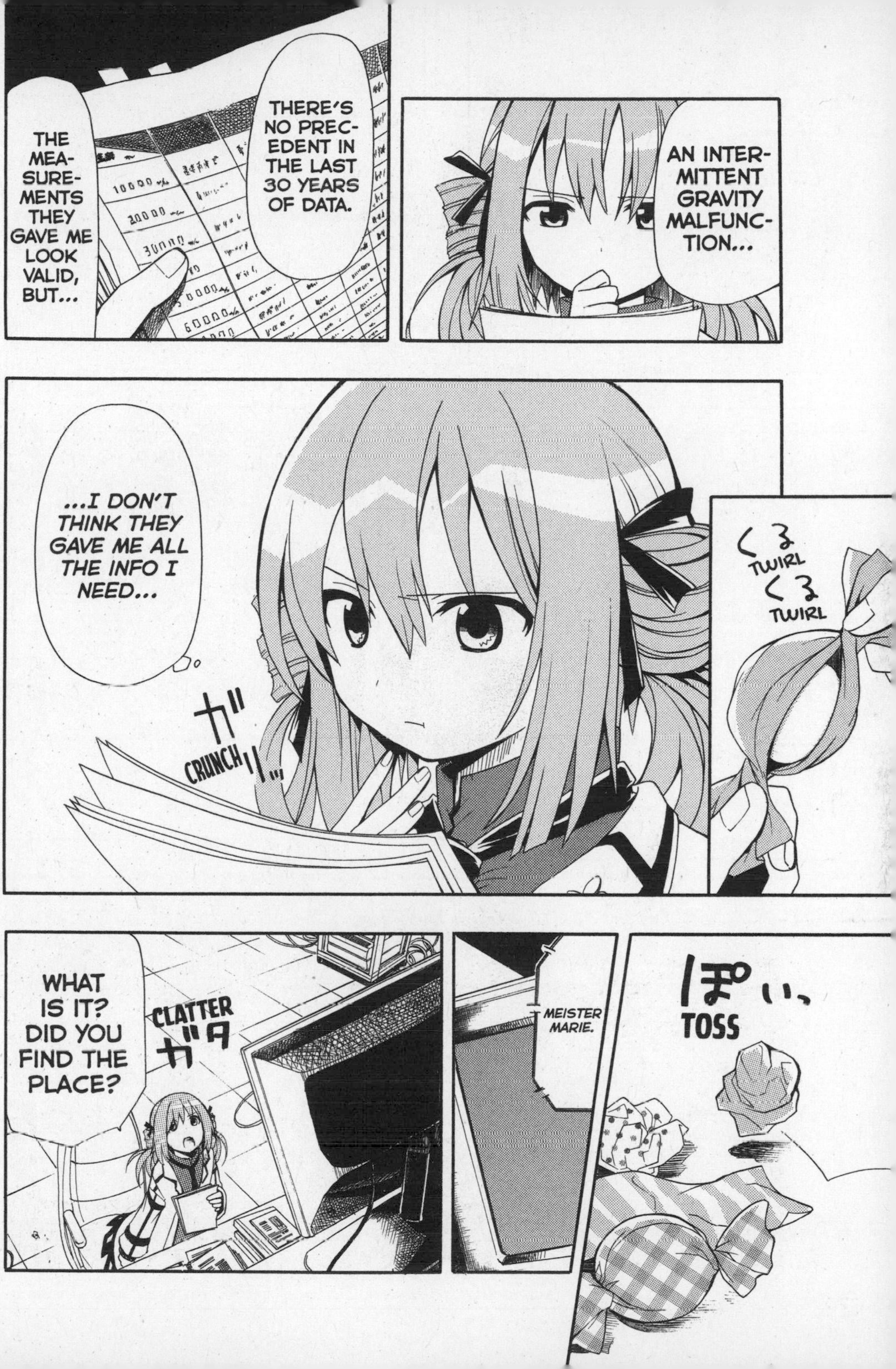
AN INTERMITTENT GRAVITY MALFUNCTION...
THERE'S NO PRECEDENT IN THE LAST 30 YEARS OF DATA.
THE MEASUREMENTS THEY GAVE ME LOOK VALID, BUT...
くる TWIRL くる TWIRL
...I DON'T THINK THEY GAVE ME ALL THE INFO I NEED...
ガ CRUNCH
ぽい TOSS
MEISTER MARIE.
CLATTER ガタ
WHAT IS IT? DID YOU FIND THE PLACE?

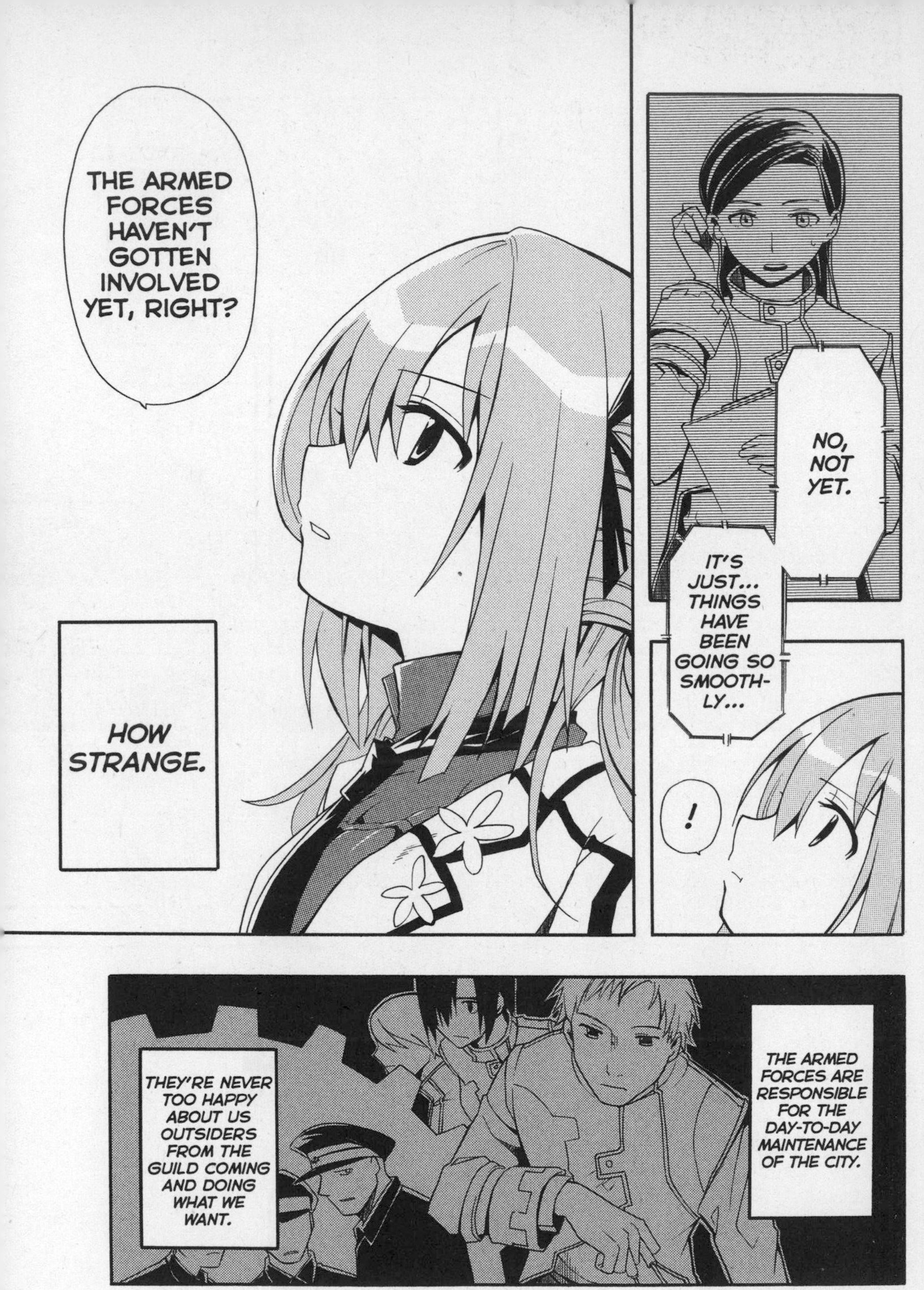
THE ARMED FORCES HAVEN'T GOTTEN INVOLVED YET, RIGHT?
NO, NOT YET.
IT'S JUST... THINGS HAVE BEEN GOING SO SMOOTHLY...
!
HOW STRANGE.
THE ARMED FORCES ARE RESPONSIBLE FOR THE DAY-TO-DAY MAINTENANCE OF THE CITY.
THEY'RE NEVER TOO HAPPY ABOUT US OUTSIDERS FROM THE GUILD COMING AND DOING WHAT WE WANT.

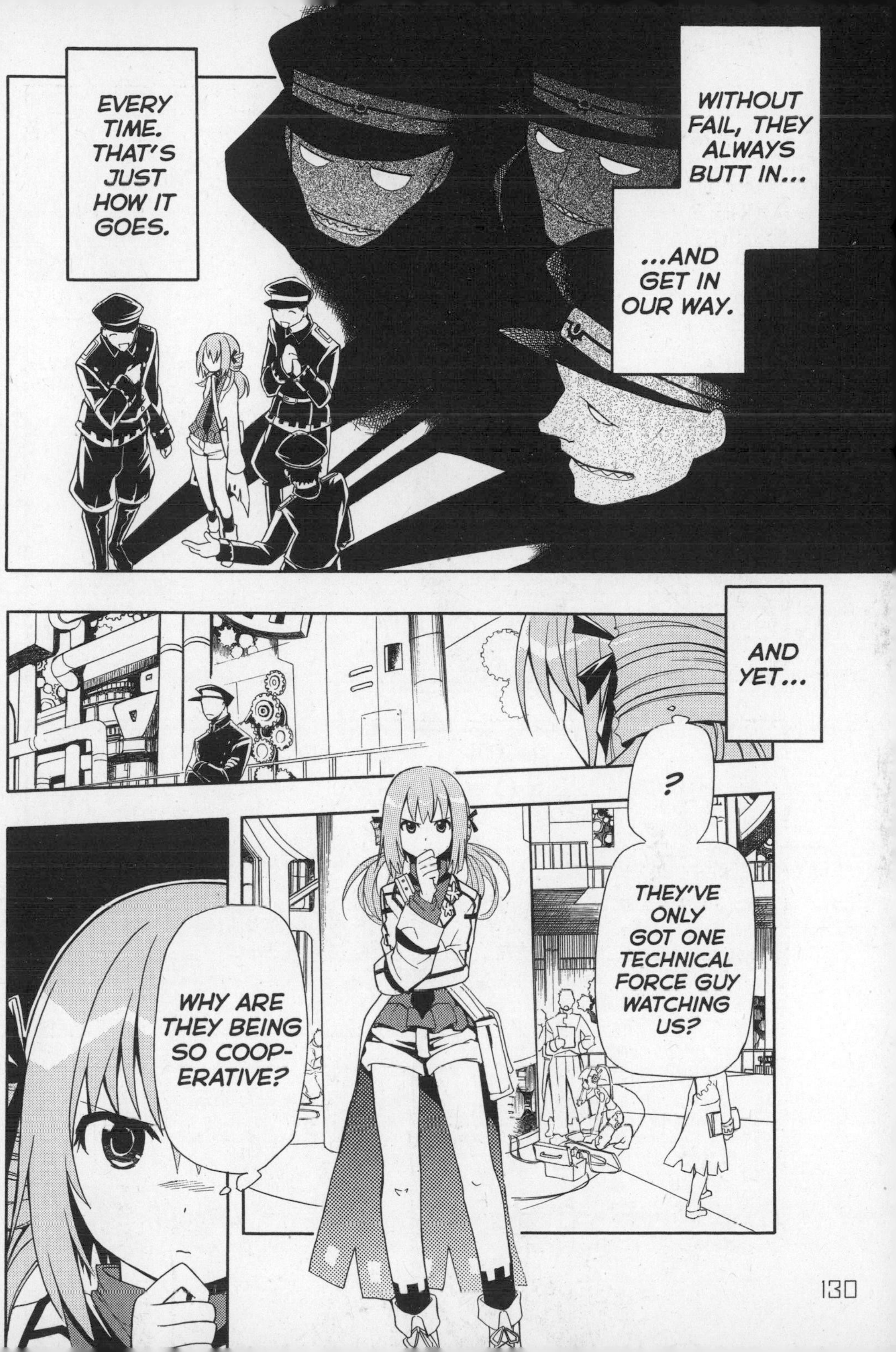
WITHOUT FAIL, THEY ALWAYS BUTT IN...
...AND GET IN OUR WAY.
EVERY TIME. THAT'S JUST HOW IT GOES.
AND YET...
?
THEY'VE ONLY GOT ONE TECHNICAL FORCE GUY WATCHING US?
WHY ARE THEY BEING SO COOP-ERATIVE?

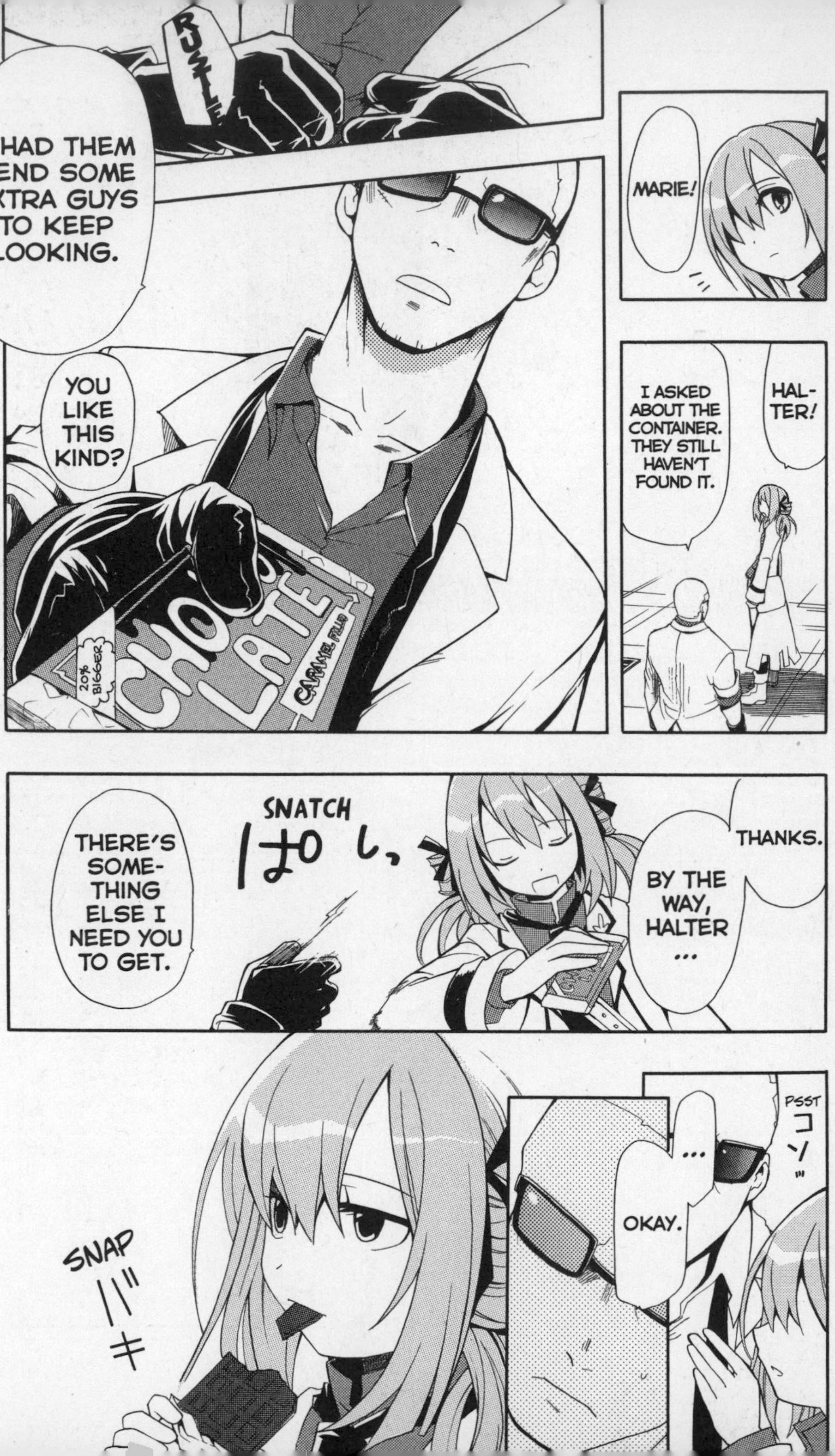
MARIE!
HAL-TER!
I ASKED ABOUT THE CONTAINER. THEY STILL HAVEN'T FOUND IT.
RUSTLE
I HAD THEM SEND SOME EXTRA GUYS TO KEEP LOOKING.
YOU LIKE THIS KIND?
CHOCOLATE
CARAMEL FILLED
20% BIGGER
THANKS.
BY THE WAY, HALTER ...
SNATCH
はしっ
THERE'S SOME-THING ELSE I NEED YOU TO GET.
PSST
コソッ
...
OKAY.
SNAP
バキ

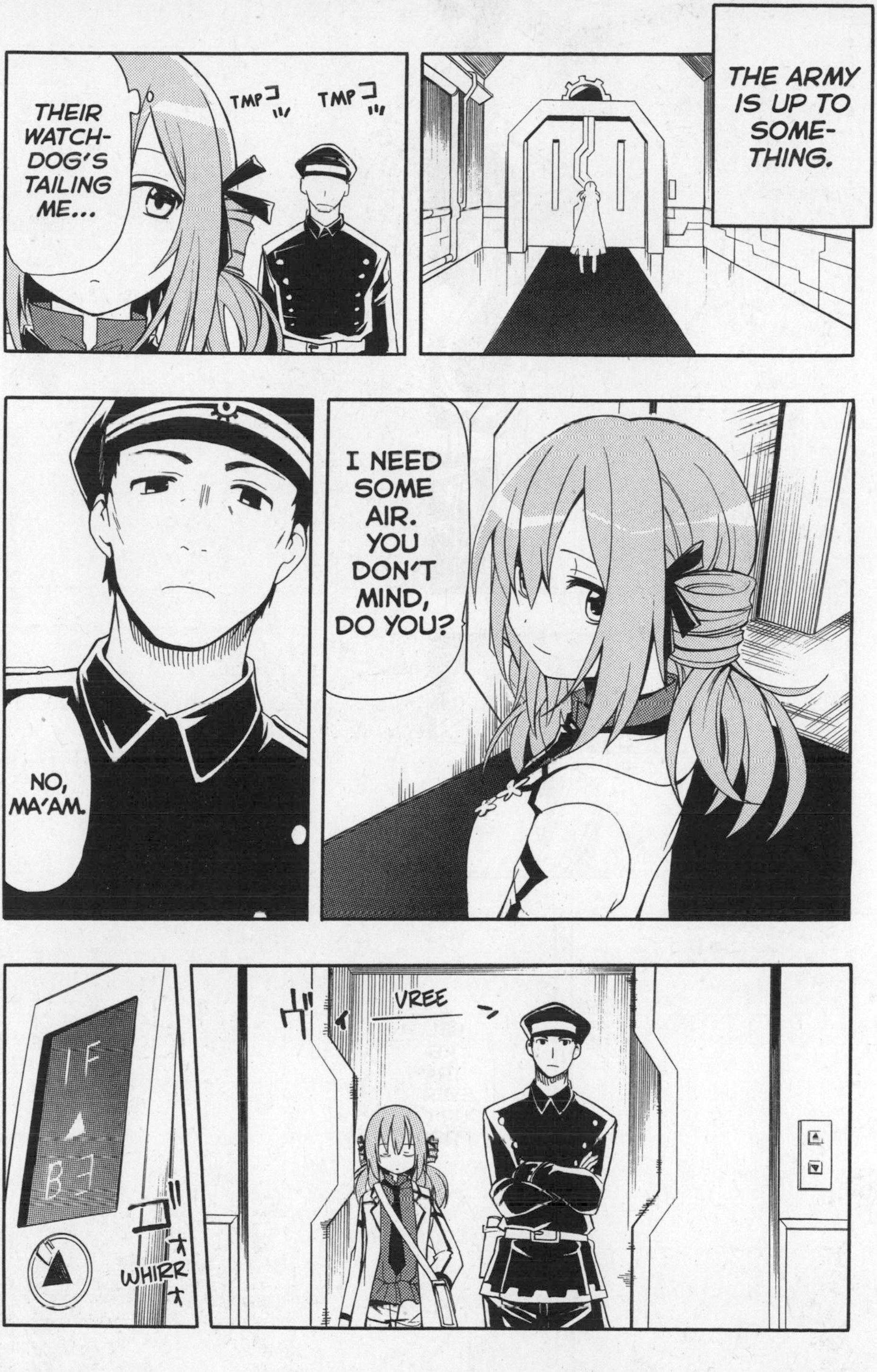
THE ARMY IS UP TO SOME-THING.
TMP
TMP
THEIR WATCH-DOG'S TAILING ME...
I NEED SOME AIR. YOU DON'T MIND, DO YOU?
NO, MA'AM.
ヴィ
VREE
ゴォ
WHIRR

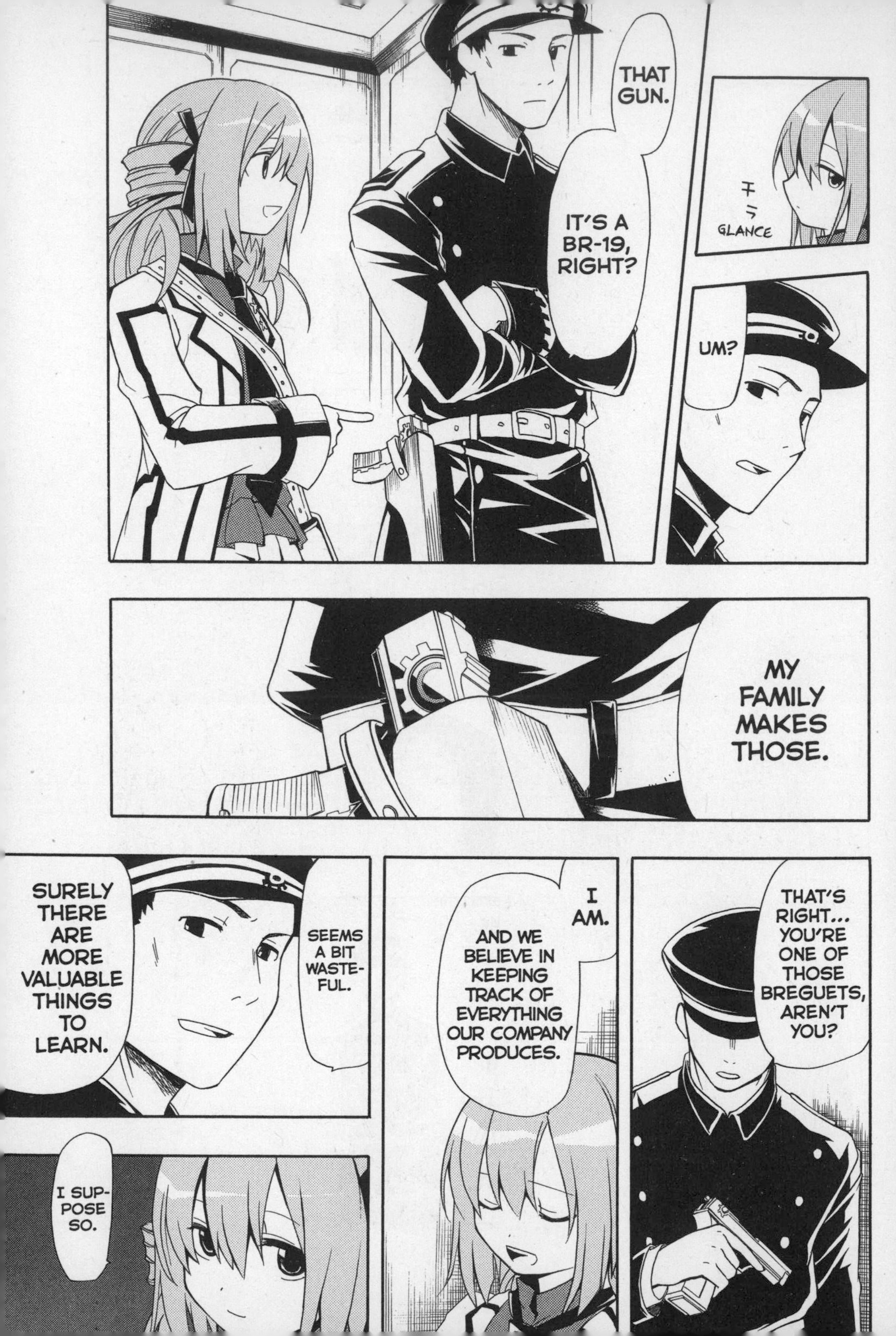
チラ
GLANCE
UM?
THAT GUN.
IT'S A BR-19, RIGHT?
MY FAMILY MAKES THOSE.
THAT'S RIGHT... YOU'RE ONE OF THOSE BREGUETS, AREN'T YOU?
I AM.
AND WE BELIEVE IN KEEPING TRACK OF EVERYTHING OUR COMPANY PRODUCES.
SEEMS A BIT WASTE-FUL.
SURELY THERE ARE MORE VALUABLE THINGS TO LEARN.
I SUP-POSE SO.

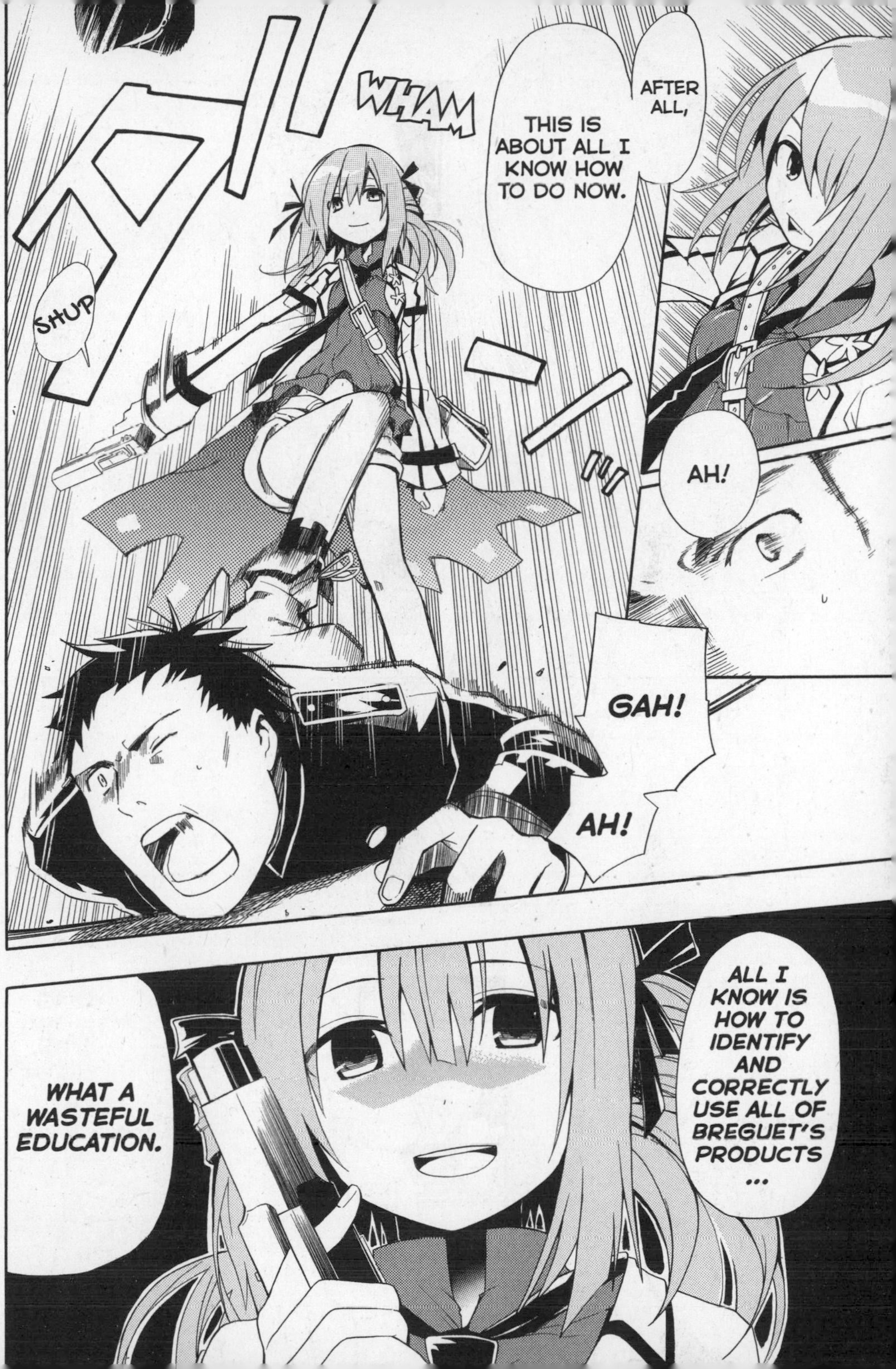
AFTER ALL, THIS IS ABOUT ALL I KNOW HOW TO DO NOW.
AH!
WHAM
SHUP
GAH!
AH!
ALL I KNOW IS HOW TO IDENTIFY AND CORRECTLY USE ALL OF BREGUET'S PRODUCTS ...
WHAT A WASTEFUL EDUCATION.

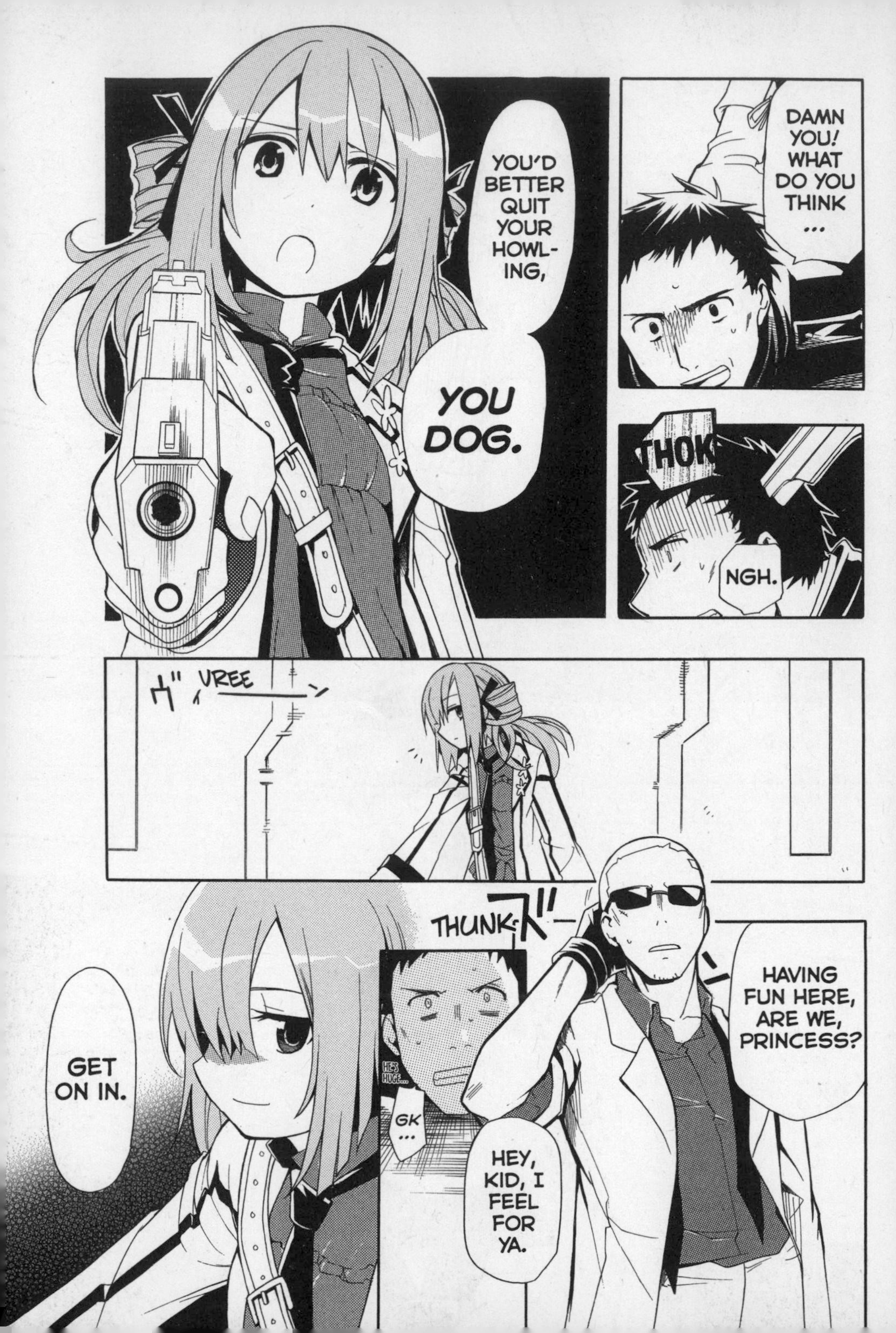

DAMN YOU! WHAT DO YOU THINK ...
THOK
NGH.
YOU'D BETTER QUIT YOUR HOWL-ING,
YOU DOG.
VREE
THUNK
HAVING FUN HERE, ARE WE, PRINCESS?
HE'S HUGE...
GK ...
HEY, KID, I FEEL FOR YA.
GET ON IN.

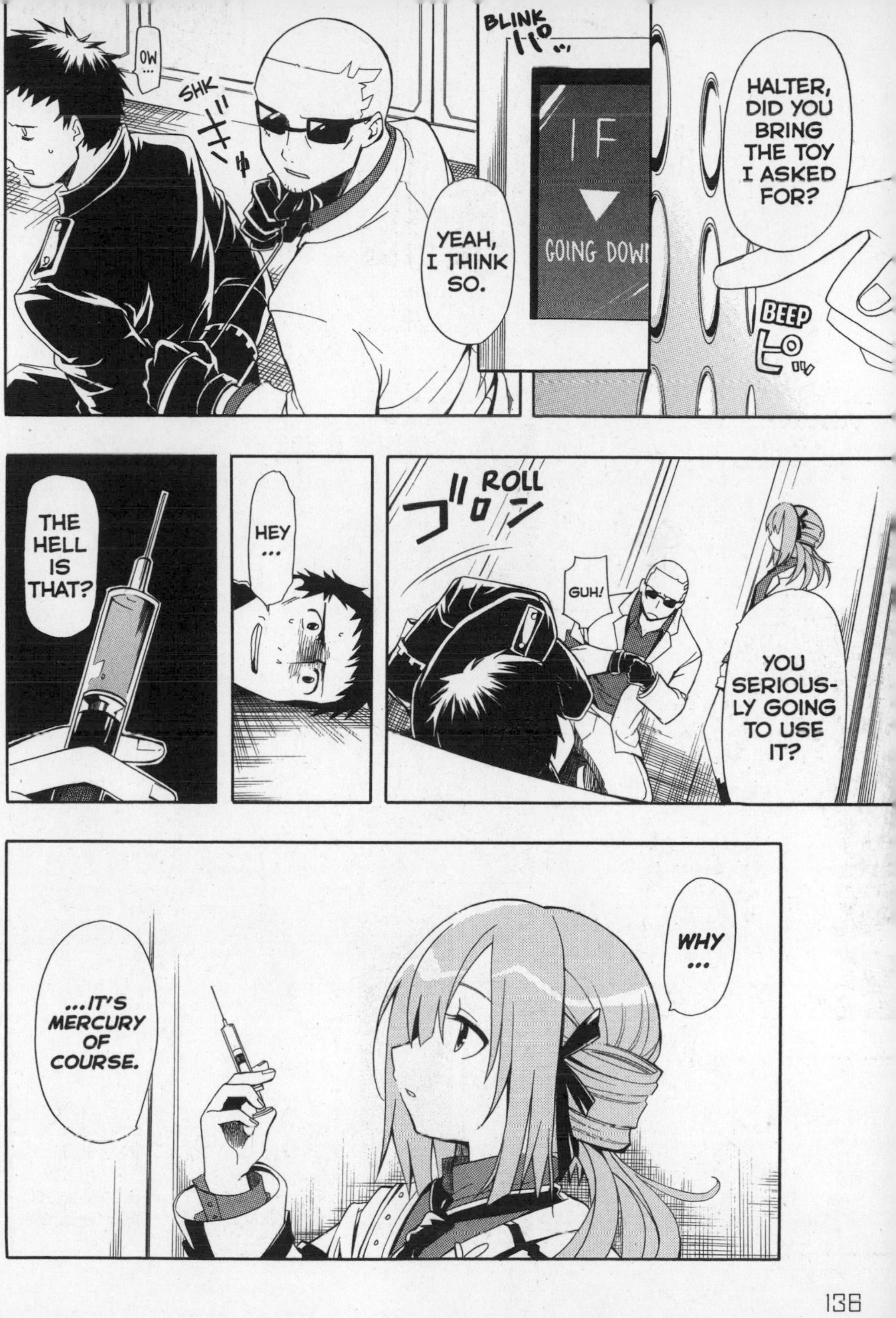
HALTER, DID YOU BRING THE TOY I ASKED FOR?
BEEP
BLINK
IF
GOING DOW
YEAH, I THINK SO.
SHK
OW...
ROLL
YOU SERIOUSLY GOING TO USE IT?
GUH!
HEY...
THE HELL IS THAT?
WHY...
...IT'S MERCURY OF COURSE.

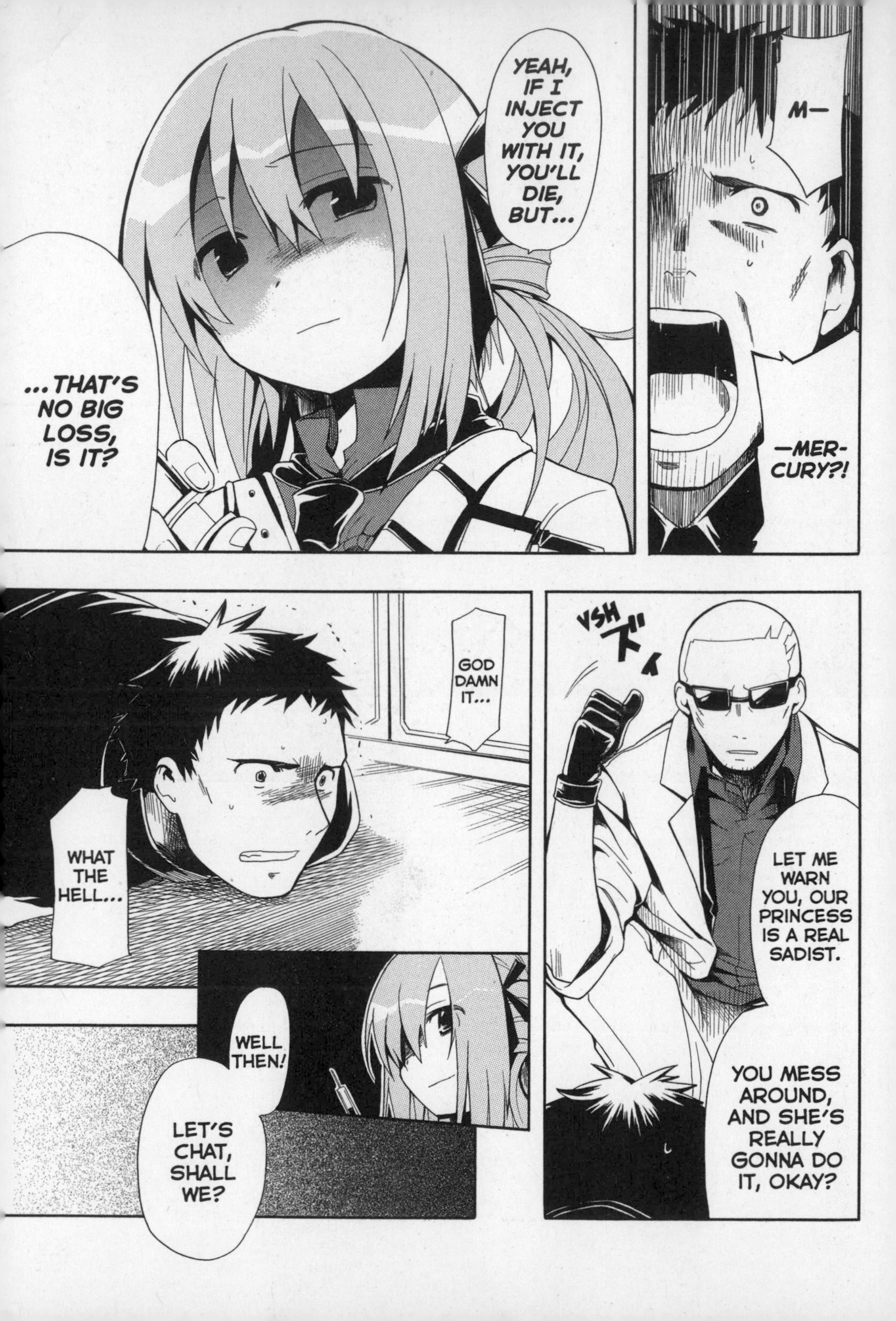
M—
—MER-CURY?!
YEAH, IF I INJECT YOU WITH IT, YOU'LL DIE, BUT...
...THAT'S NO BIG LOSS, IS IT?
VSH
LET ME WARN YOU, OUR PRINCESS IS A REAL SADIST.
YOU MESS AROUND, AND SHE'S REALLY GONNA DO IT, OKAY?
GOD DAMN IT...
WHAT THE HELL...
WELL THEN!
LET'S CHAT, SHALL WE?

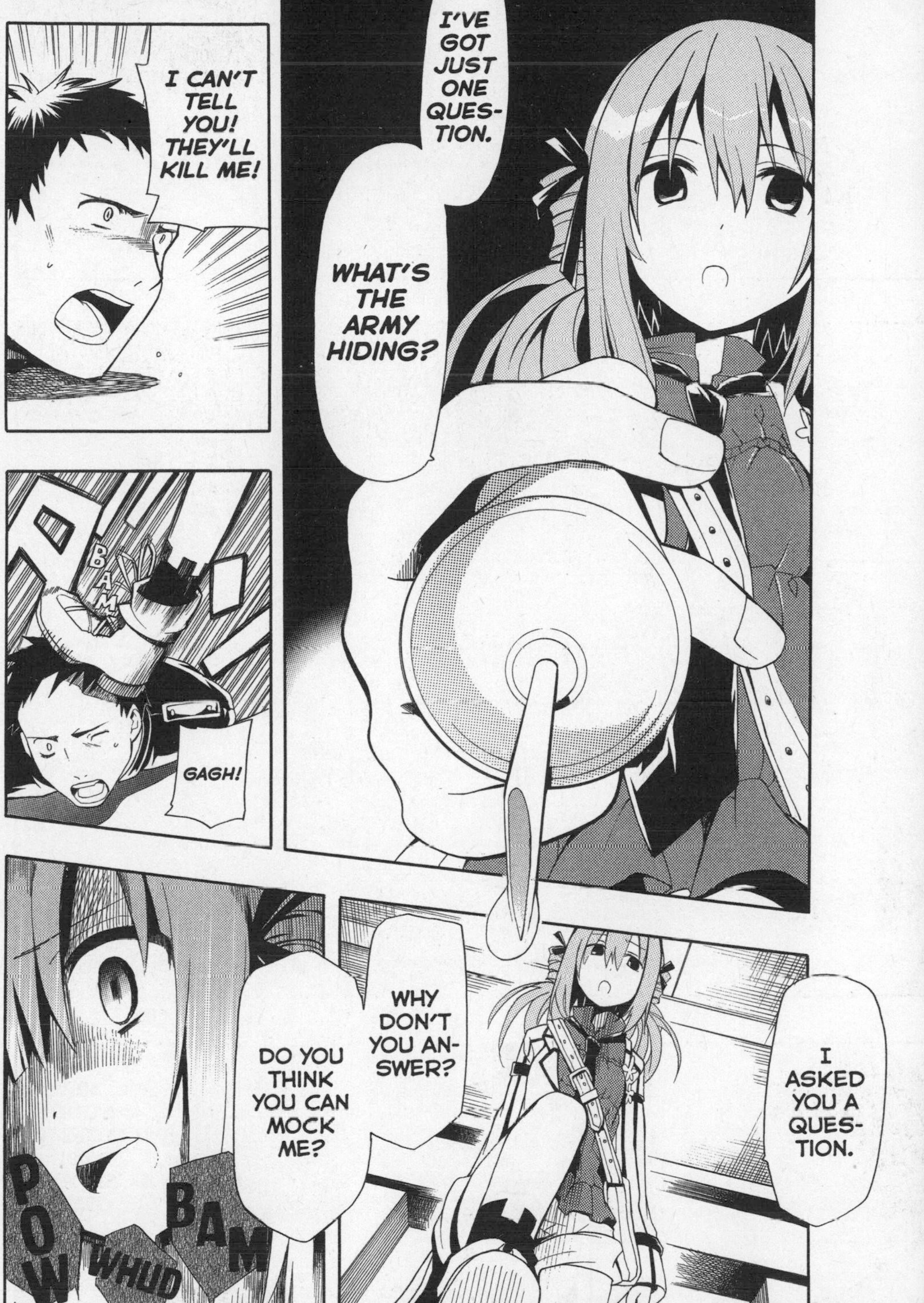
I'VE GOT JUST ONE QUES-TION.
WHAT'S THE ARMY HIDING?
I CAN'T TELL YOU! THEY'LL KILL ME!
BAM BAM
GAGH!
I ASKED YOU A QUES-TION.
WHY DON'T YOU AN-SWER?
DO YOU THINK YOU CAN MOCK ME?
BAM
WHUD
POW

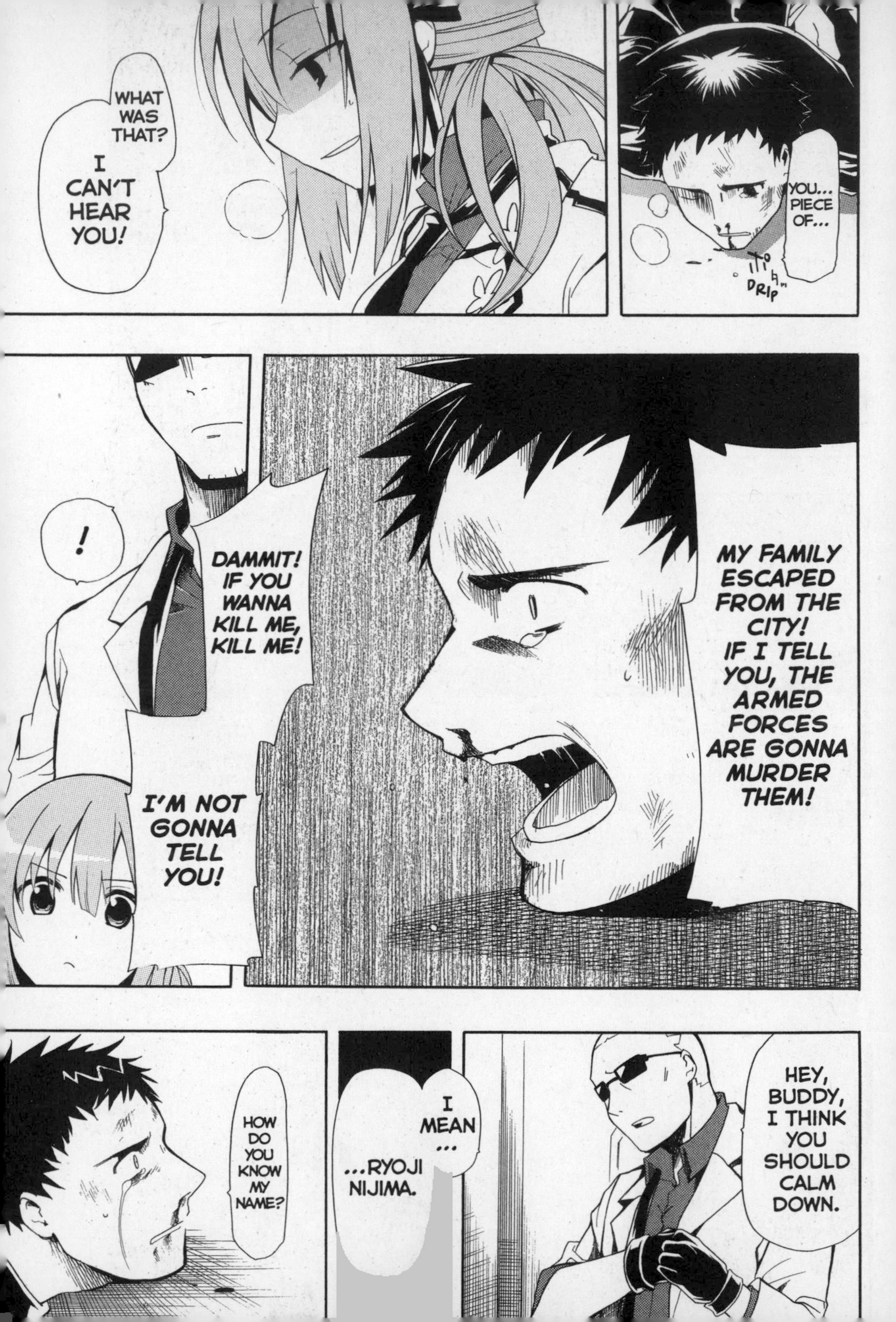
YOU... PIECE OF...
DRIP
WHAT WAS THAT?
I CAN'T HEAR YOU!
MY FAMILY ESCAPED FROM THE CITY! IF I TELL YOU, THE ARMED FORCES ARE GONNA MURDER THEM!
DAMMIT! IF YOU WANNA KILL ME, KILL ME!
I'M NOT GONNA TELL YOU!
!
HEY, BUDDY, I THINK YOU SHOULD CALM DOWN.
I MEAN ...
...RYOJI NIJIMA.
HOW DO YOU KNOW MY NAME?

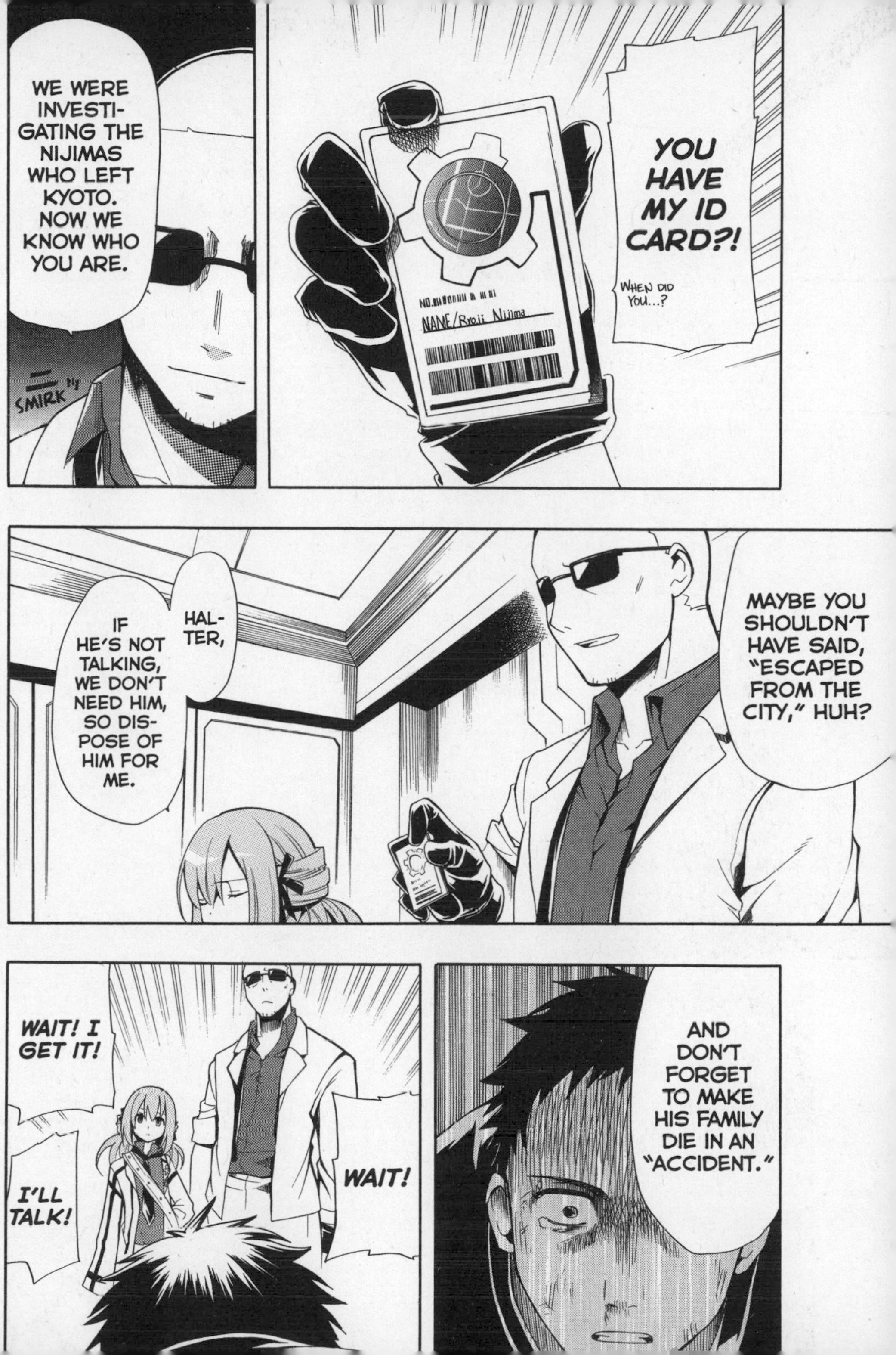
YOU HAVE MY ID CARD?!
WHEN DID YOU...?
NANE/Ryoji Nijima
WE WERE INVESTIGATING THE NIJIMAS WHO LEFT KYOTO. NOW WE KNOW WHO YOU ARE.
SMIRK
MAYBE YOU SHOULDN'T HAVE SAID, "ESCAPED FROM THE CITY," HUH?
HALTER,
IF HE'S NOT TALKING, WE DON'T NEED HIM, SO DISPOSE OF HIM FOR ME.
AND DON'T FORGET TO MAKE HIS FAMILY DIE IN AN "ACCIDENT."
WAIT!
WAIT! I GET IT!
I'LL TALK!

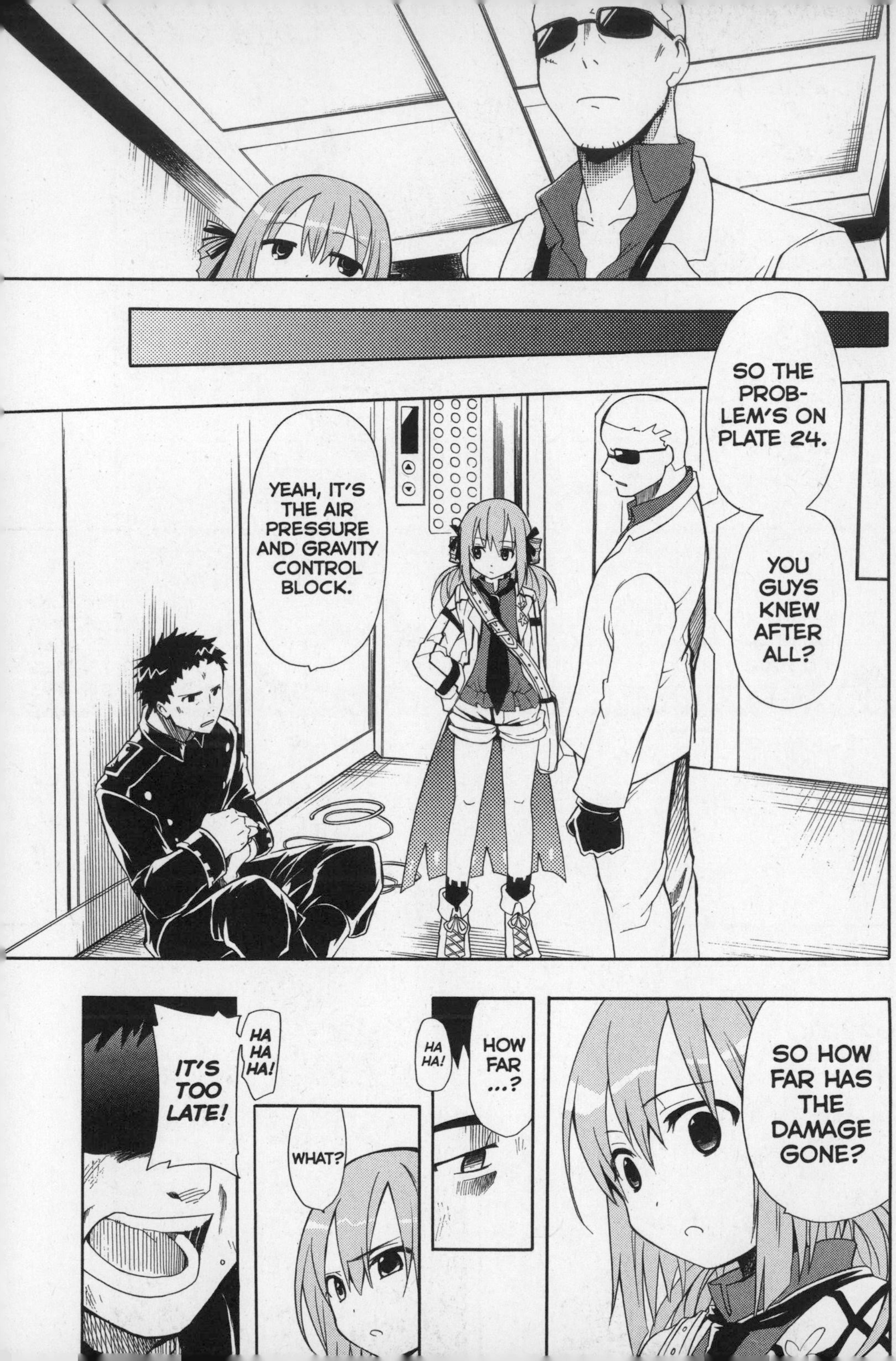
SO THE PROB-LEM'S ON PLATE 24.
YOU GUYS KNEW AFTER ALL?
YEAH, IT'S THE AIR PRESSURE AND GRAVITY CONTROL BLOCK.
SO HOW FAR HAS THE DAMAGE GONE?
HOW FAR ...?
HA HA!
WHAT?
HA HA HA!
IT'S TOO LATE!

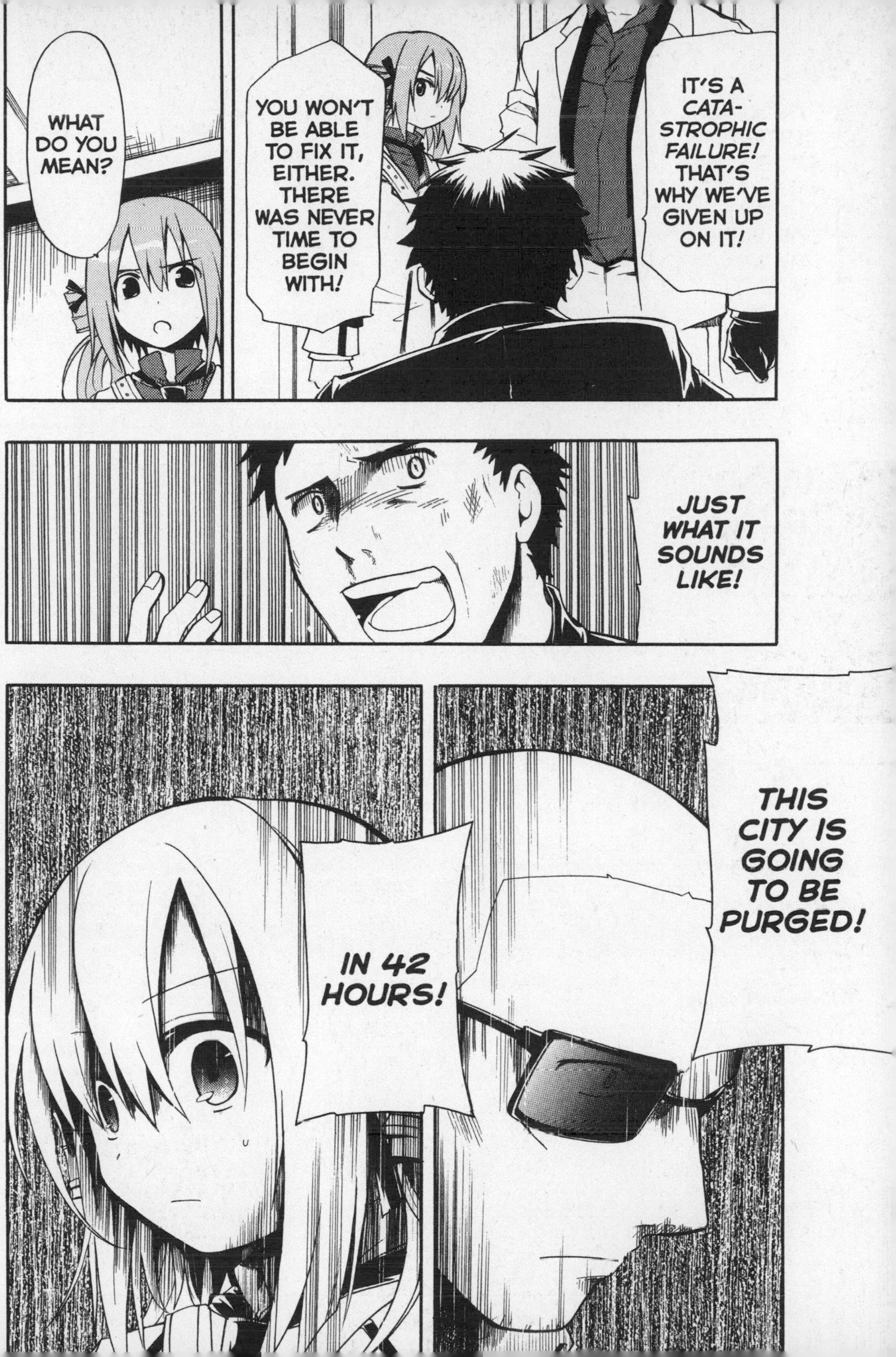
IT'S A CATA-STROPHIC FAILURE! THAT'S WHY WE'VE GIVEN UP ON IT!
YOU WON'T BE ABLE TO FIX IT, EITHER. THERE WAS NEVER TIME TO BEGIN WITH!
WHAT DO YOU MEAN?
JUST WHAT IT SOUNDS LIKE!
THIS CITY IS GOING TO BE PURGED!
IN 42 HOURS!

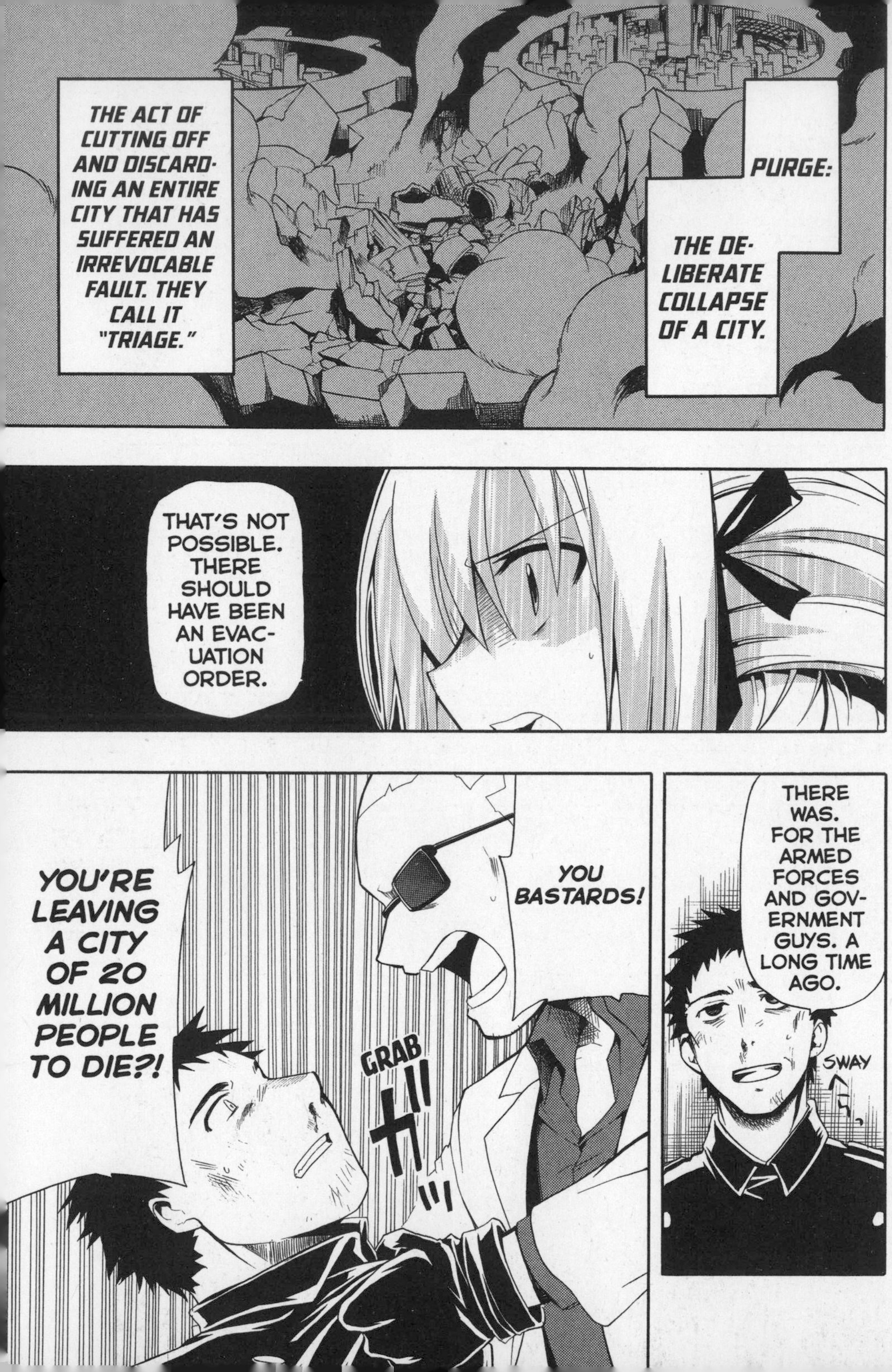
PURGE:
THE DE-LIBERATE COLLAPSE OF A CITY.
THE ACT OF CUTTING OFF AND DISCARD-ING AN ENTIRE CITY THAT HAS SUFFERED AN IRREVOCABLE FAULT. THEY CALL IT "TRIAGE."
THAT'S NOT POSSIBLE. THERE SHOULD HAVE BEEN AN EVAC-UATION ORDER.
THERE WAS. FOR THE ARMED FORCES AND GOV-ERNMENT GUYS. A LONG TIME AGO.
SWAY
YOU BASTARDS!
YOU'RE LEAVING A CITY OF 20 MILLION PEOPLE TO DIE?!
GRAB

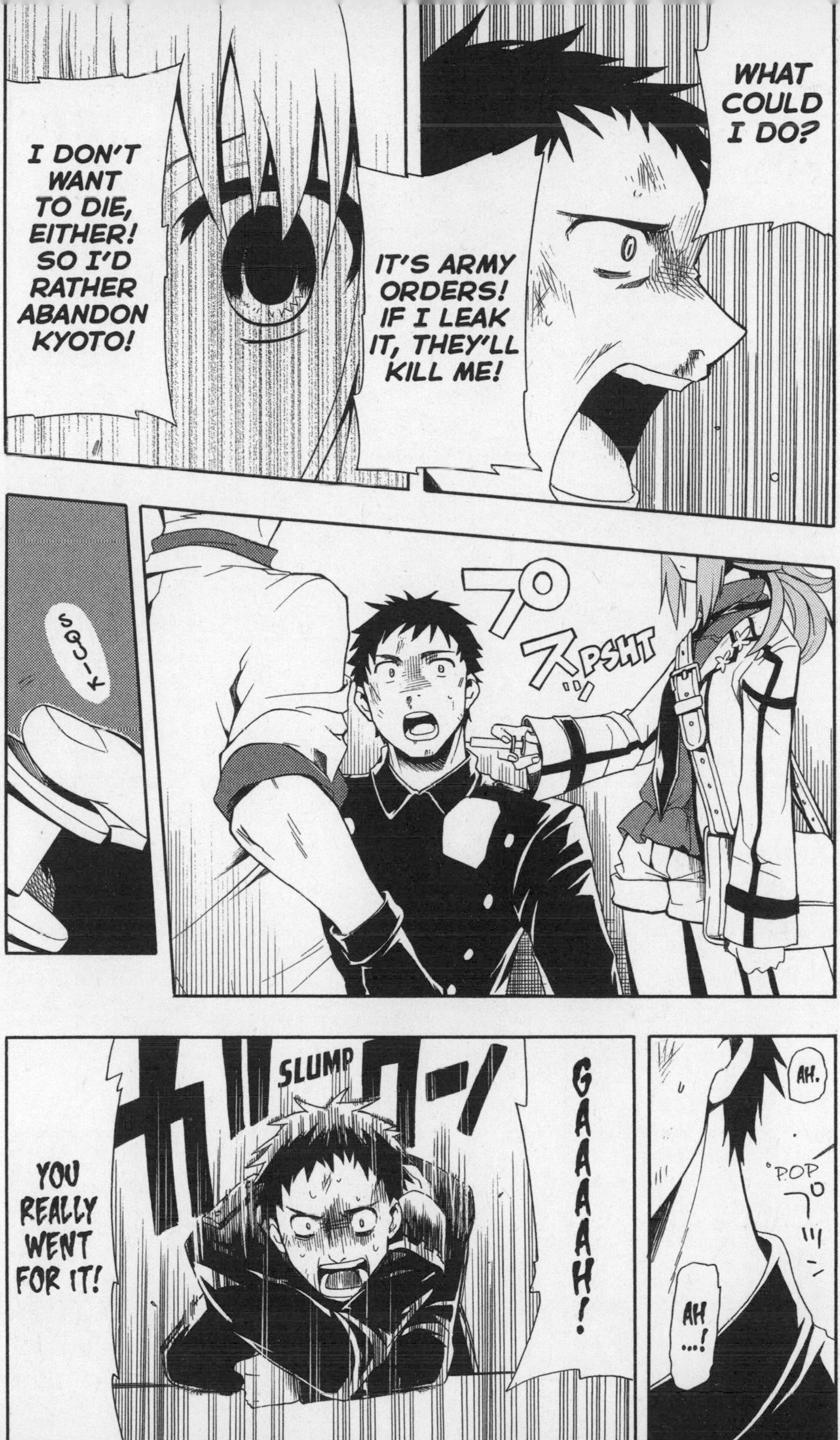
WHAT COULD I DO?
IT'S ARMY ORDERS! IF I LEAK IT, THEY'LL KILL ME!
I DON'T WANT TO DIE, EITHER! SO I'D RATHER ABANDON KYOTO!
PSHT
SQUIK
AH.
POP
AH...!
GAAAAAH!
SLUMP
YOU REALLY WENT FOR IT!

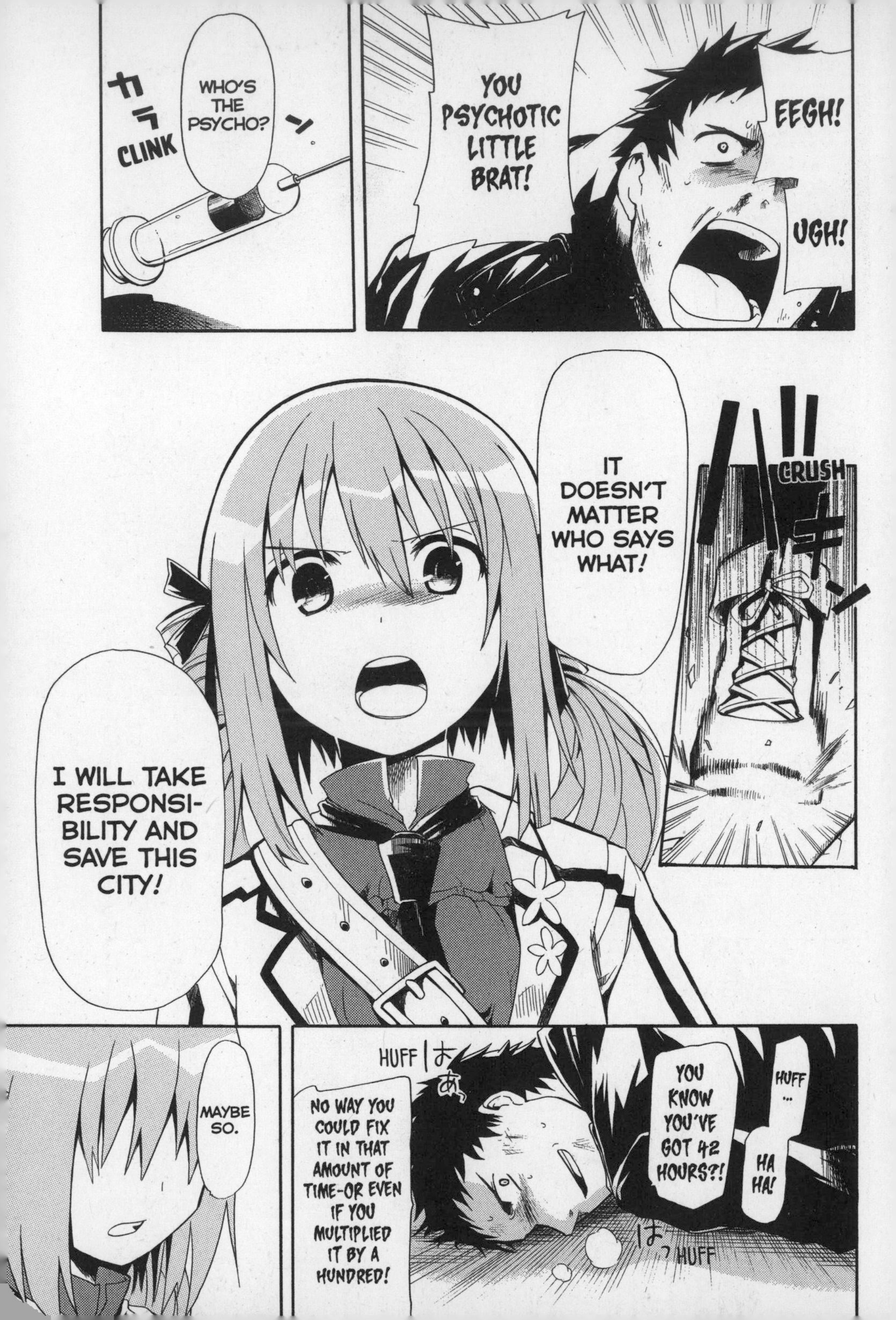
EEGH!
YOU PSYCHOTIC LITTLE BRAT!
UGH!
WHO'S THE PSYCHO?
カラン
CLINK
バキン
CRUSH
IT DOESN'T MATTER WHO SAYS WHAT!
I WILL TAKE RESPONSI-BILITY AND SAVE THIS CITY!
HUFF ...
HA HA!
YOU KNOW YOU'VE GOT 42 HOURS?!
はあ
HUFF
NO WAY YOU COULD FIX IT IN THAT AMOUNT OF TIME-OR EVEN IF YOU MULTIPLIED IT BY A HUNDRED!
はっ
HUFF
MAYBE SO.

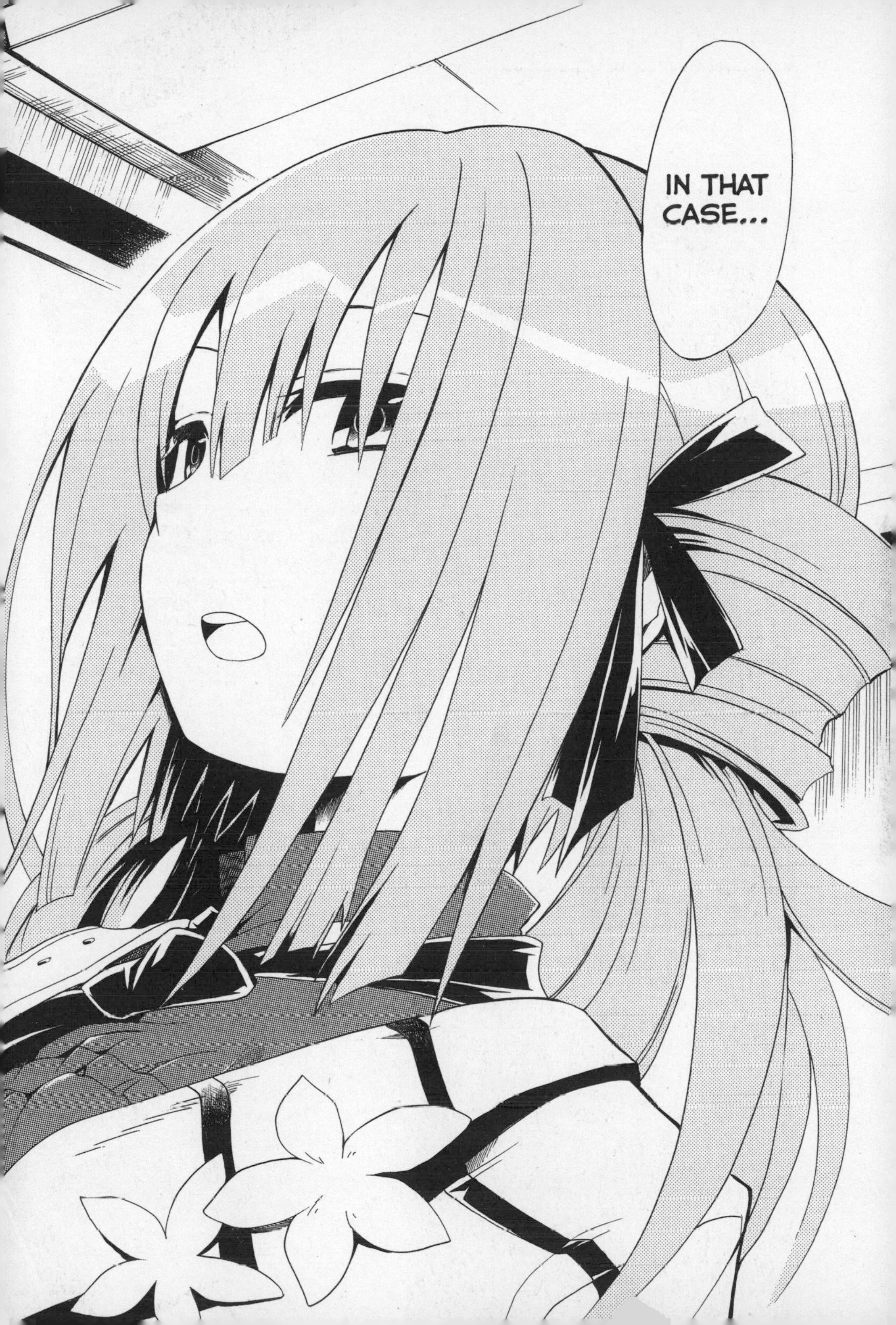
IN THAT CASE...

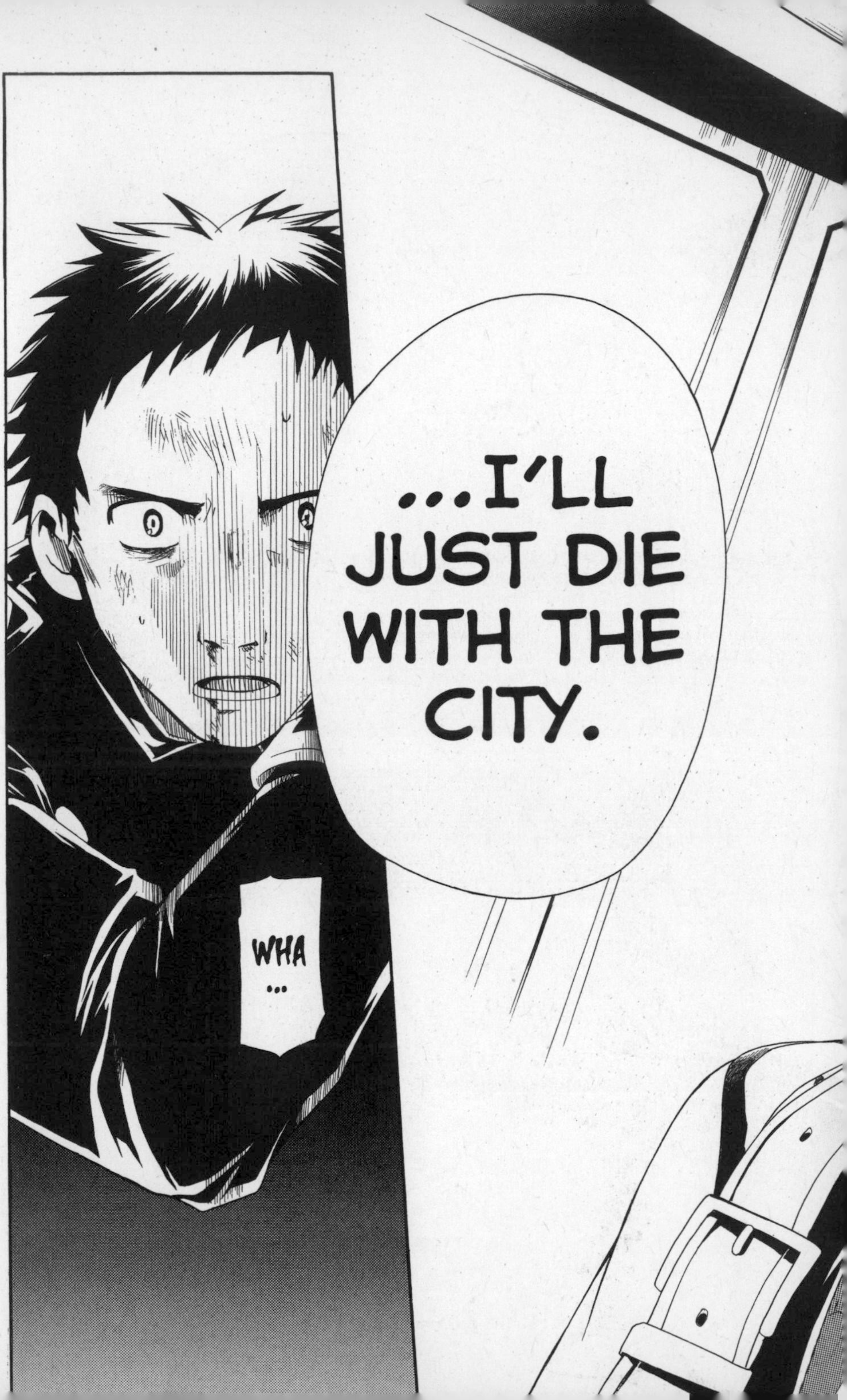
...I'LL JUST DIE WITH THE CITY.
WHA...

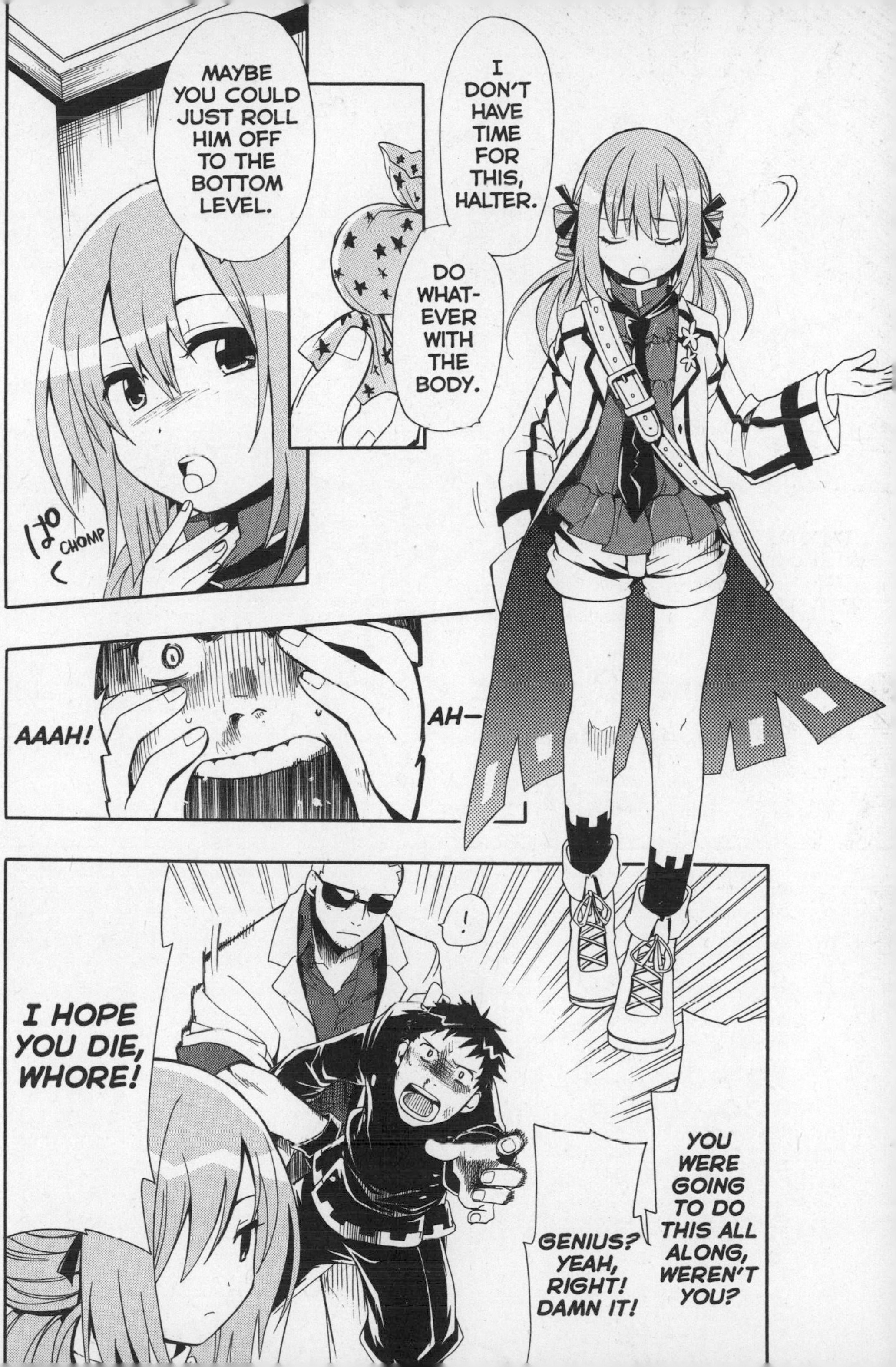

I DON'T HAVE TIME FOR THIS, HALTER.
DO WHATEVER WITH THE BODY.
MAYBE YOU COULD JUST ROLL HIM OFF TO THE BOTTOM LEVEL.
ぱく
CHOMP
AH—
AAAH!
!
YOU WERE GOING TO DO THIS ALL ALONG, WEREN'T YOU?
GENIUS? YEAH, RIGHT! DAMN IT!
I HOPE YOU DIE, WHORE!

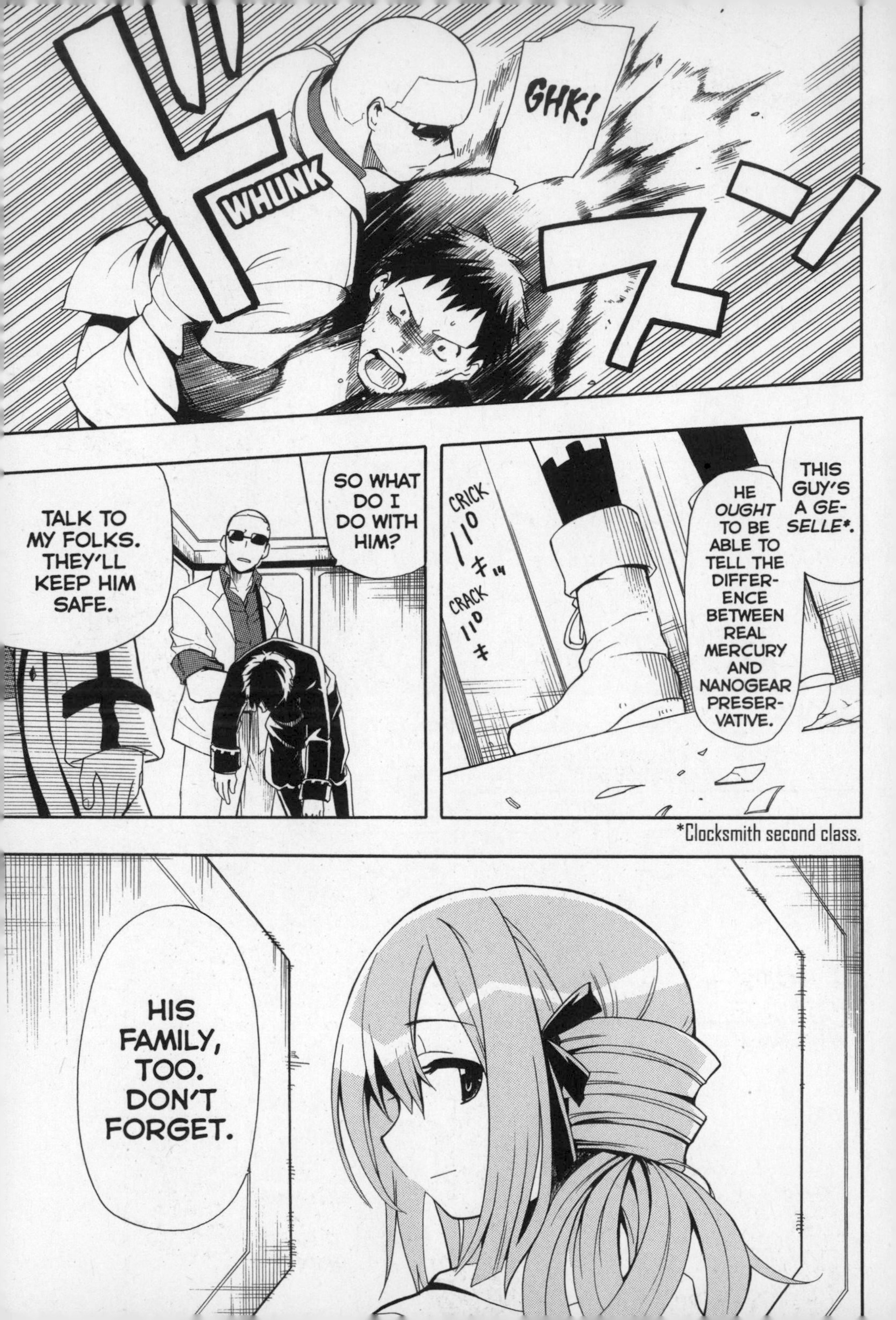
GHK!
WHUNK
THIS GUY'S A GESELLE*.
HE OUGHT TO BE ABLE TO TELL THE DIFFERENCE BETWEEN REAL MERCURY AND NANOGEAR PRESERVATIVE.
CRICK
CRACK
SO WHAT DO I DO WITH HIM?
TALK TO MY FOLKS. THEY'LL KEEP HIM SAFE.
HIS FAMILY, TOO. DON'T FORGET.
*Clocksmith second class.

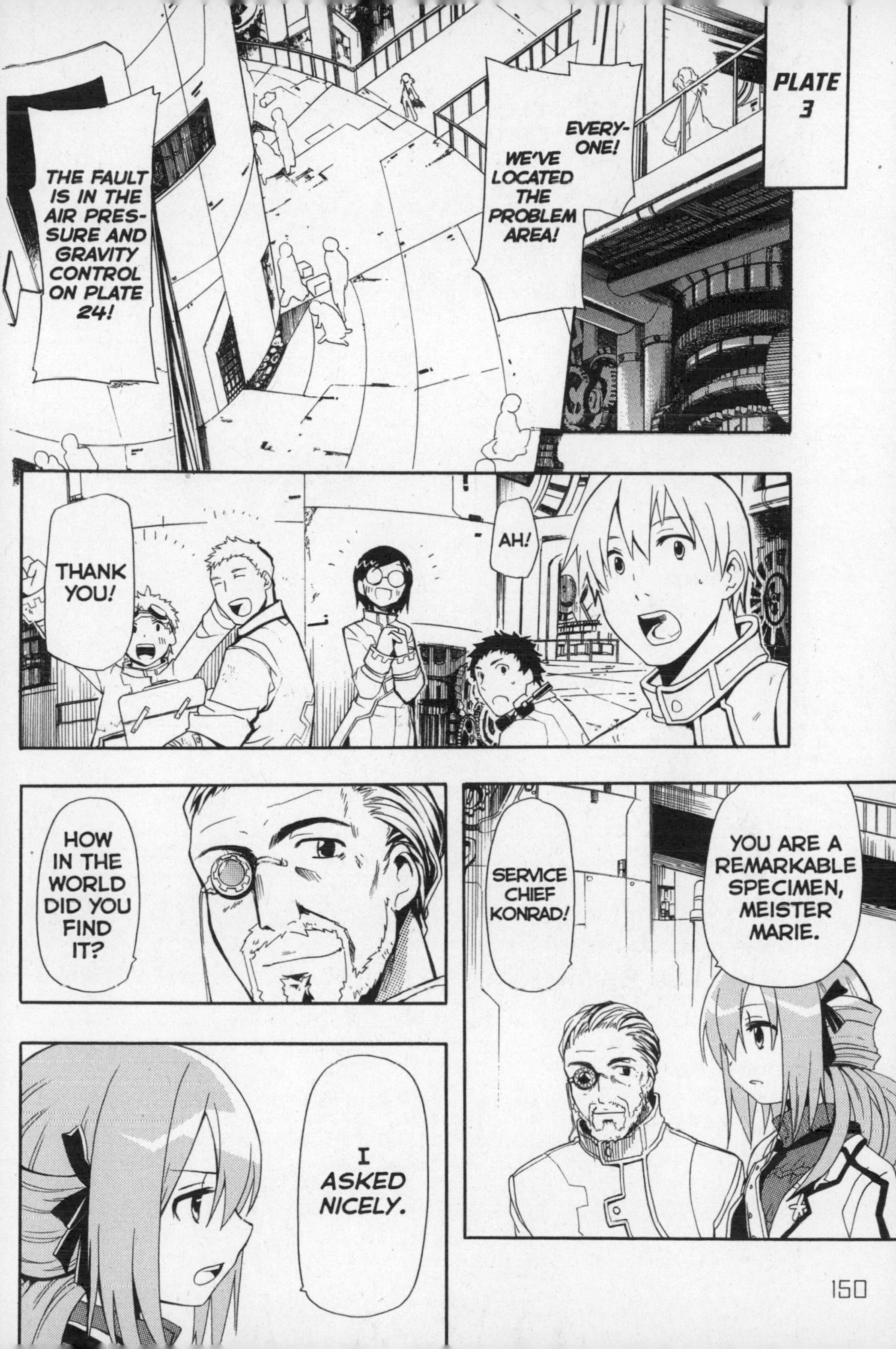
PLATE 3
EVERY-ONE!
WE'VE LOCATED THE PROBLEM AREA!
THE FAULT IS IN THE AIR PRESSURE AND GRAVITY CONTROL ON PLATE 24!
AH!
THANK YOU!
YOU ARE A REMARKABLE SPECIMEN, MEISTER MARIE.
SERVICE CHIEF KONRAD!
HOW IN THE WORLD DID YOU FIND IT?
I ASKED NICELY.

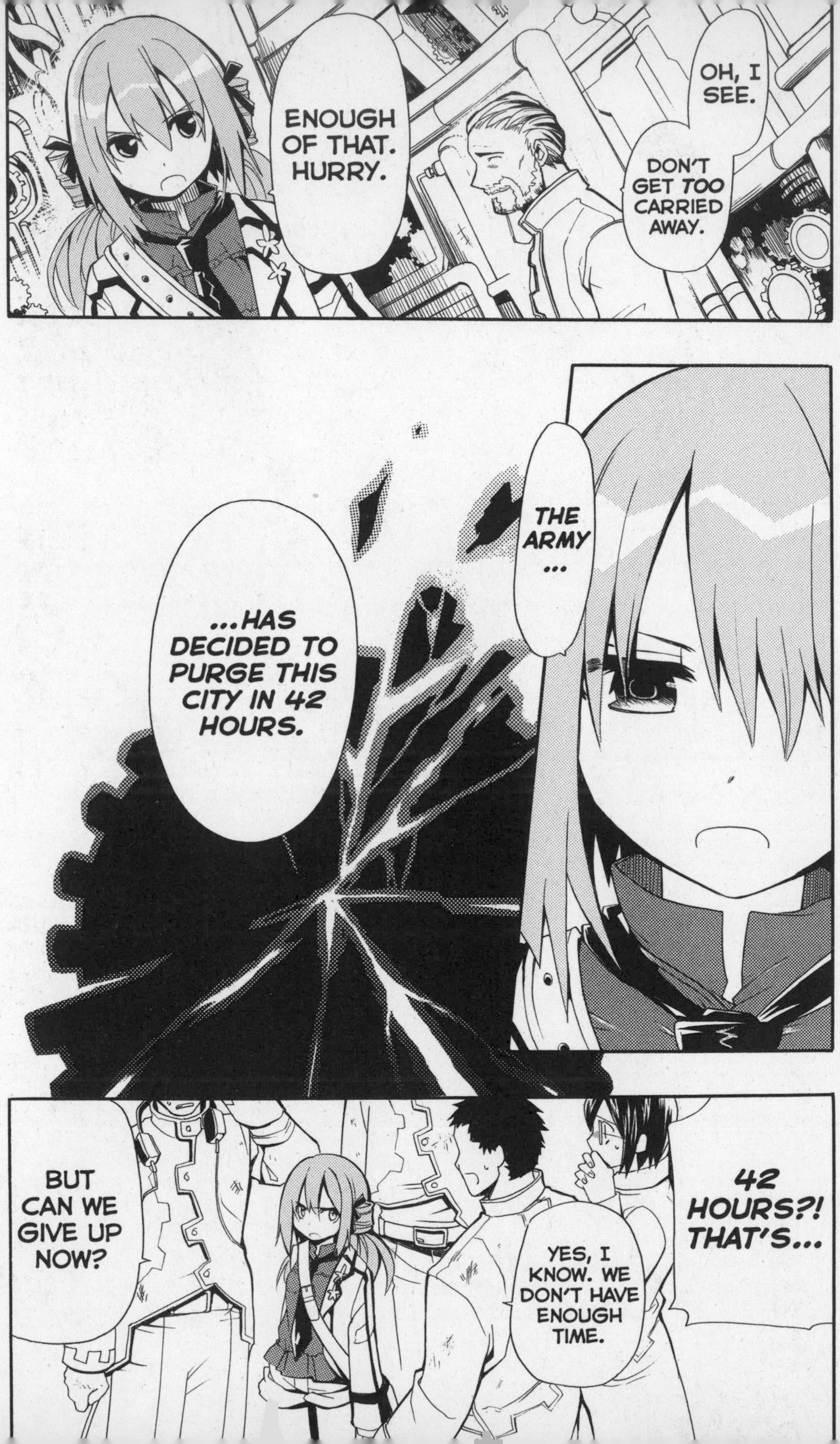
OH, I SEE.
DON'T GET TOO CARRIED AWAY.
ENOUGH OF THAT. HURRY.
THE ARMY...
...HAS DECIDED TO PURGE THIS CITY IN 42 HOURS.
42 HOURS?! THAT'S...
YES, I KNOW. WE DON'T HAVE ENOUGH TIME.
BUT CAN WE GIVE UP NOW?

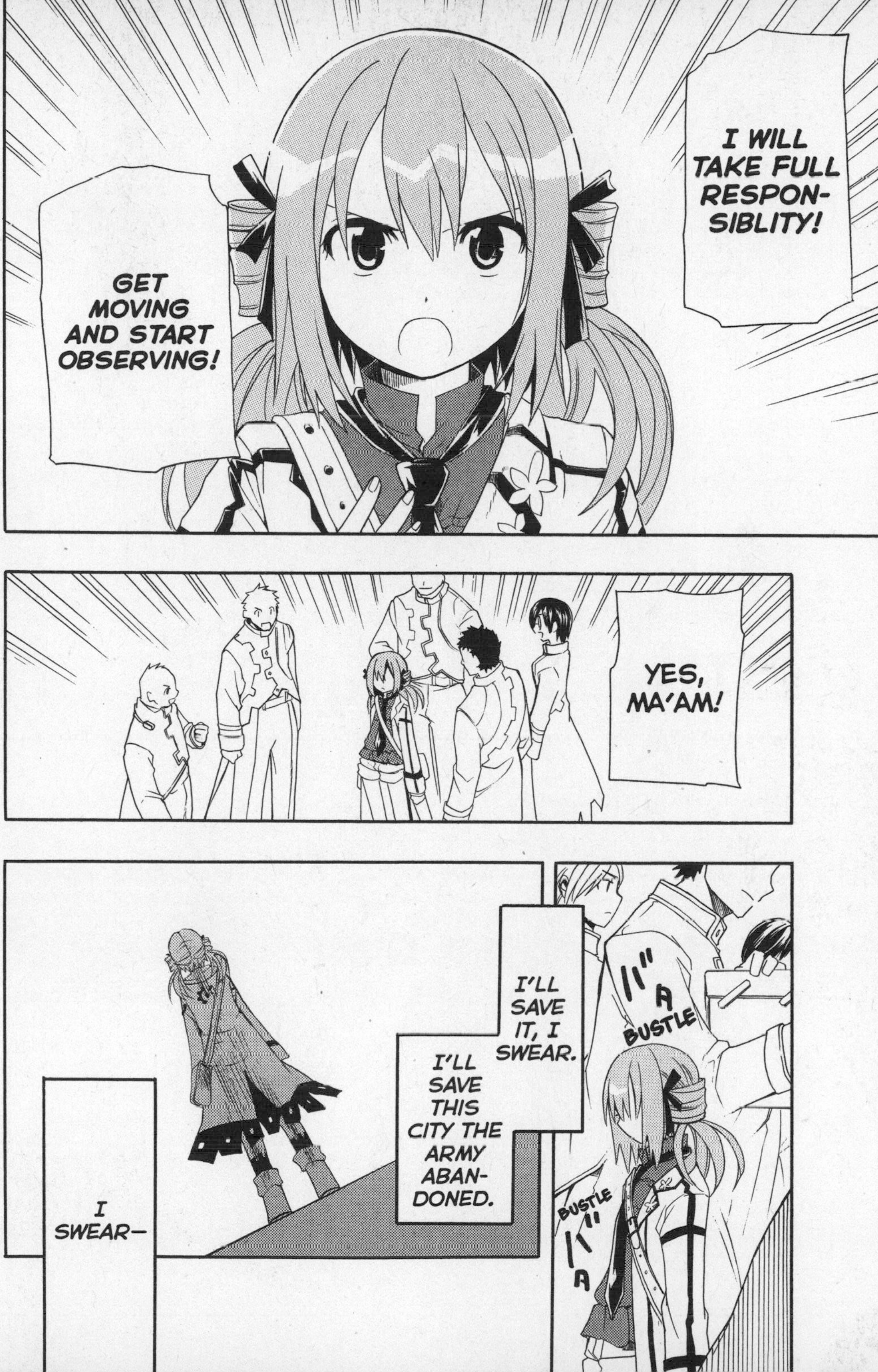
I WILL TAKE FULL RESPON-SIBLITY!
GET MOVING AND START OBSERVING!
YES, MA'AM!
BUSTLE
BUSTLE
I'LL SAVE IT, I SWEAR.
I'LL SAVE THIS CITY THE ARMY ABAN-DONED.
I SWEAR—

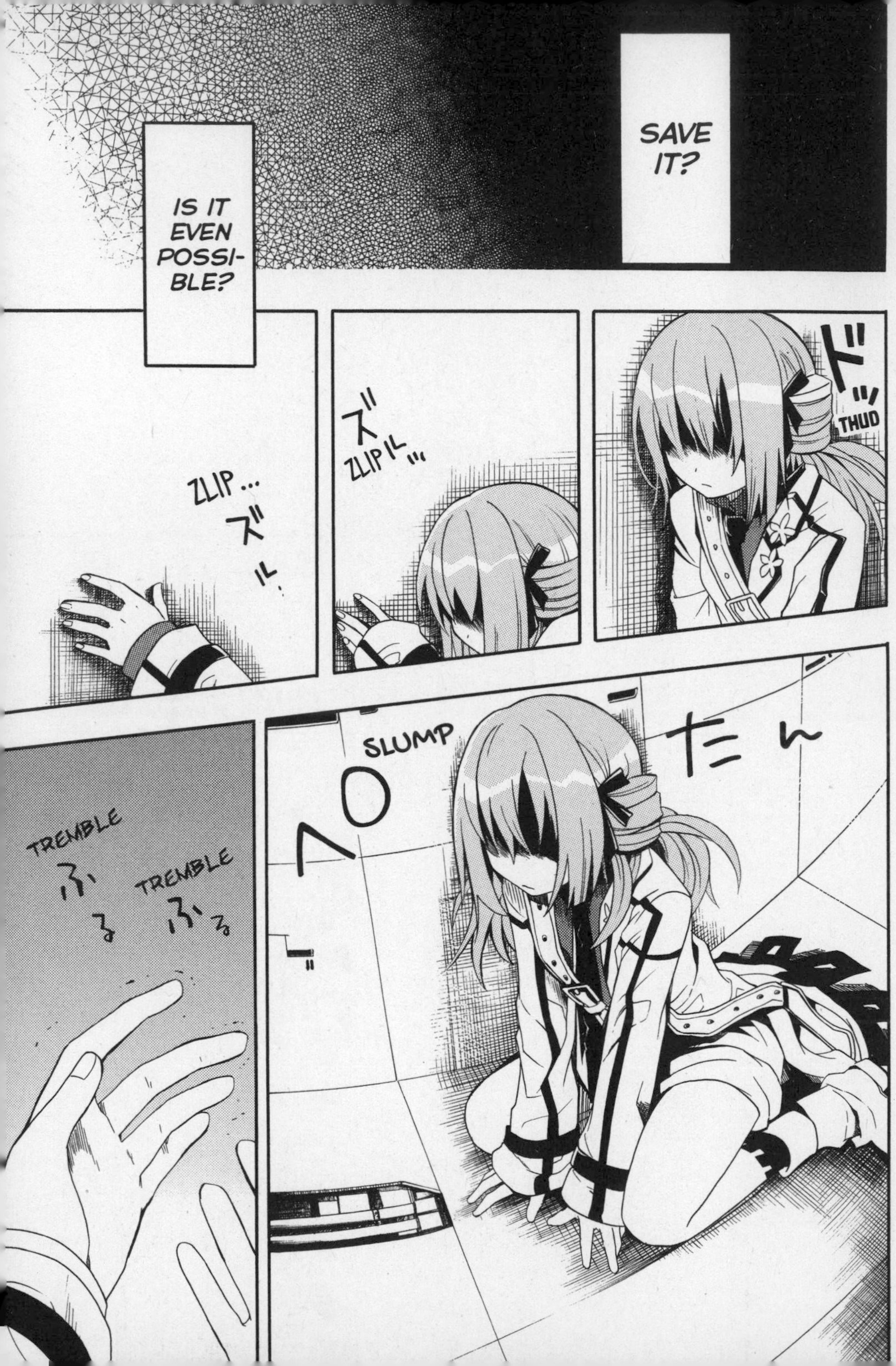
SAVE IT?
IS IT EVEN POSSI-BLE?
ドッ
THUD
ズルッ
ZLIP
ZLIP...
ズル
へたん
SLUMP
TREMBLE
ふる
TREMBLE
ふる

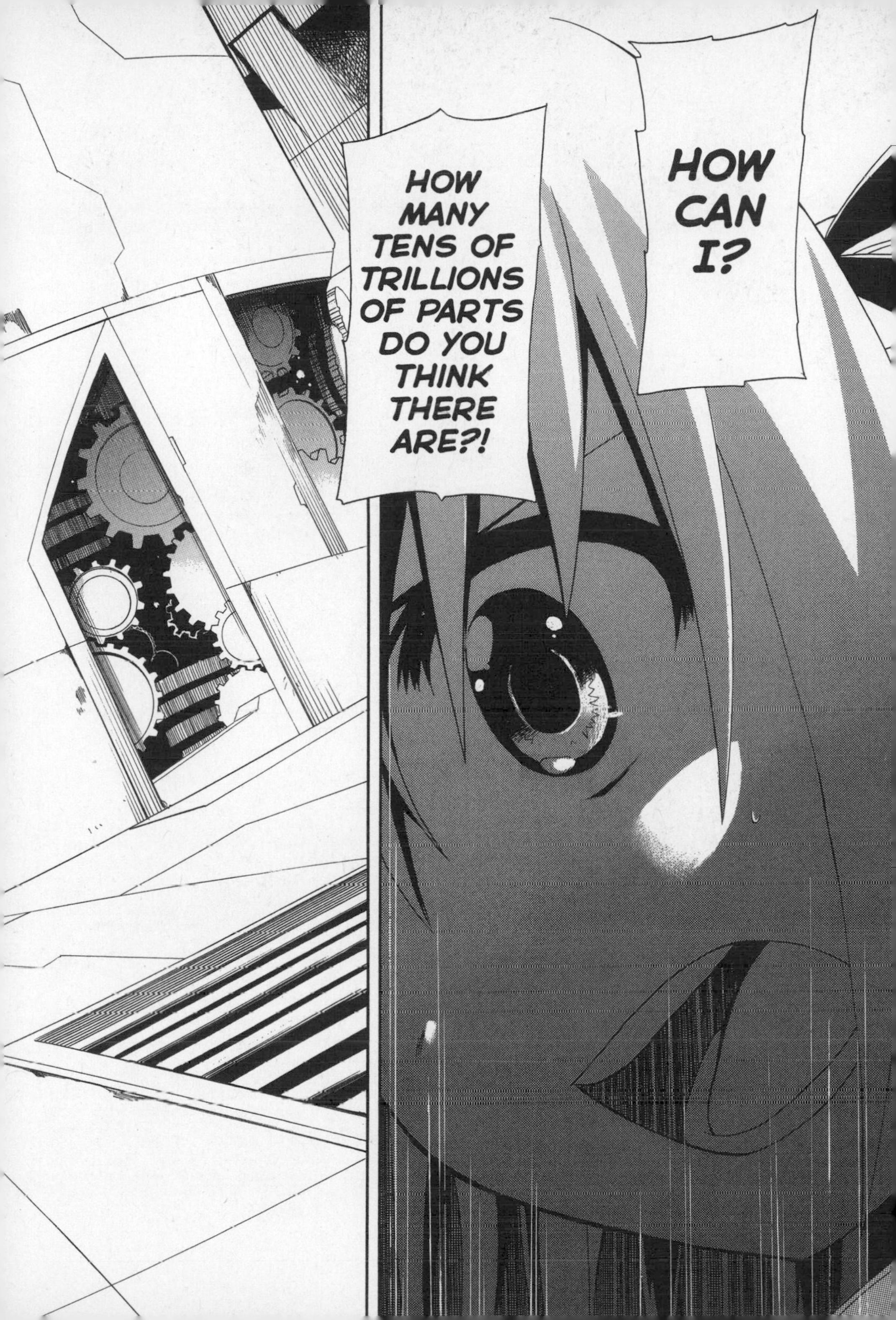
HOW CAN I?
HOW MANY TENS OF TRILLIONS OF PARTS DO YOU THINK THERE ARE?!

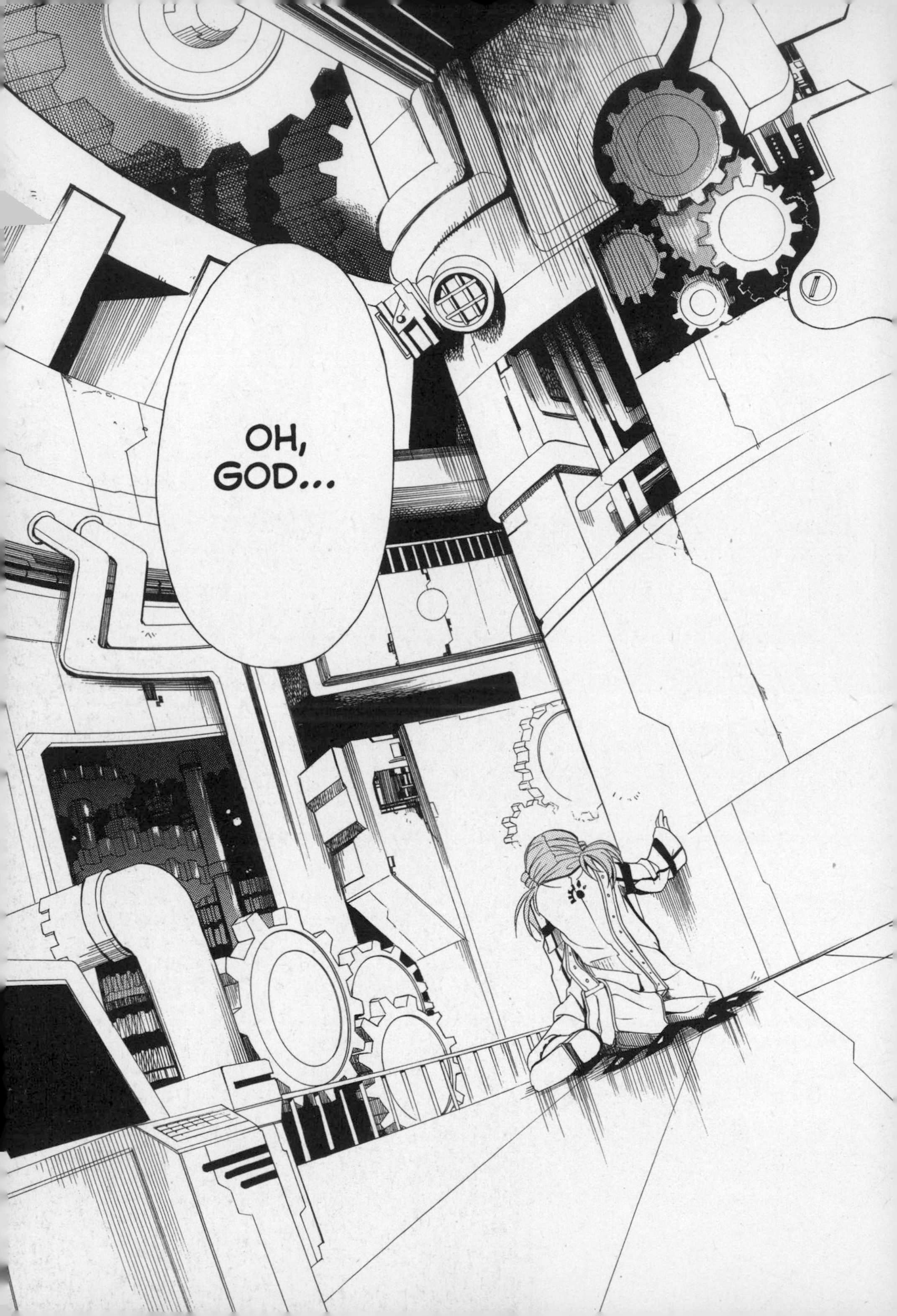
OH, GOD...

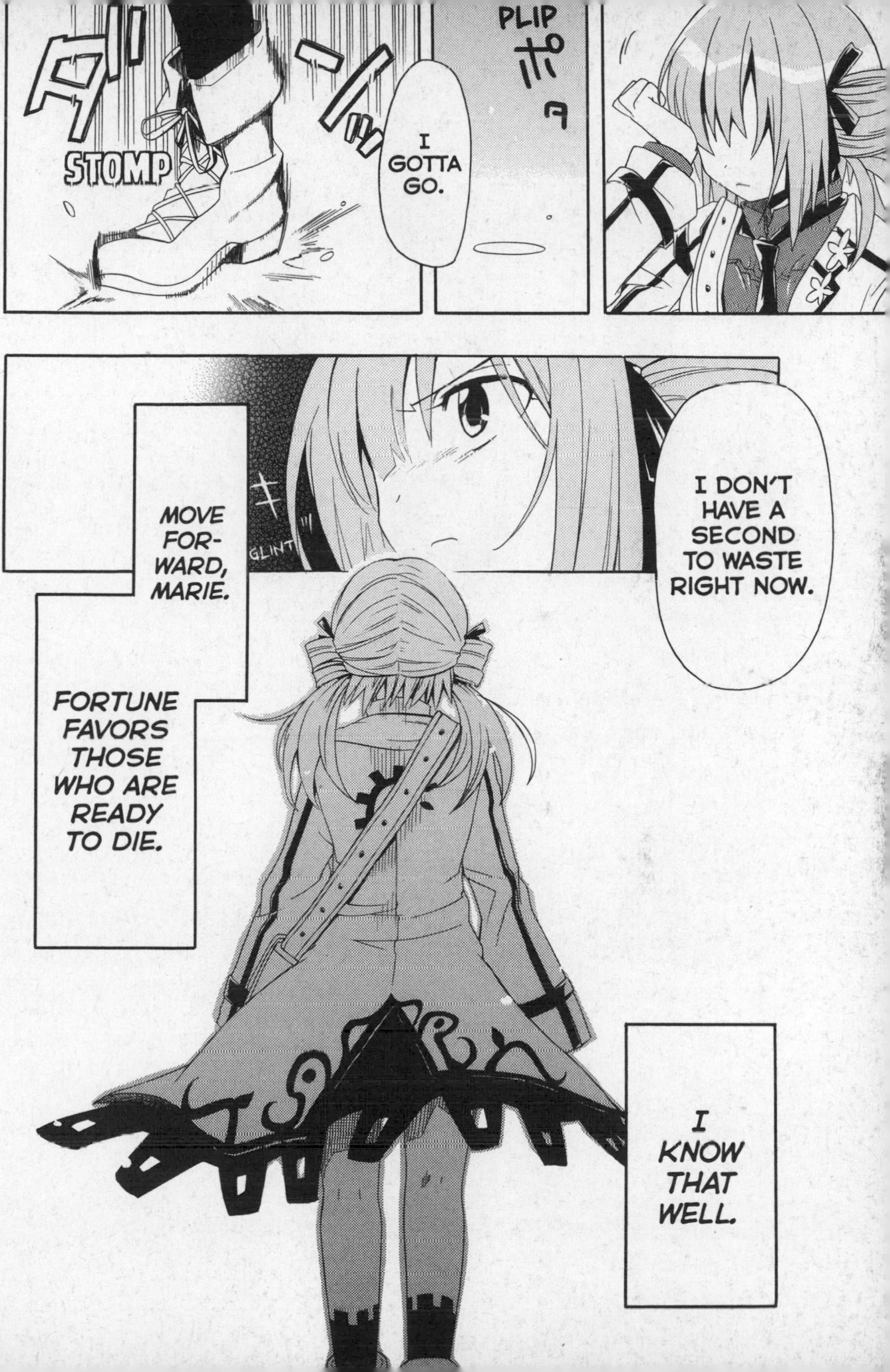
PLIP
ポタ
I GOTTA GO.
STOMP
I DON'T HAVE A SECOND TO WASTE RIGHT NOW.
GLINT
MOVE FOR-WARD, MARIE.
FORTUNE FAVORS THOSE WHO ARE READY TO DIE.
I KNOW THAT WELL.

Clockwork Planet

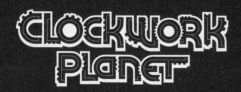

CLOCKWORK PLANET

Clock 4: Vainney Halter

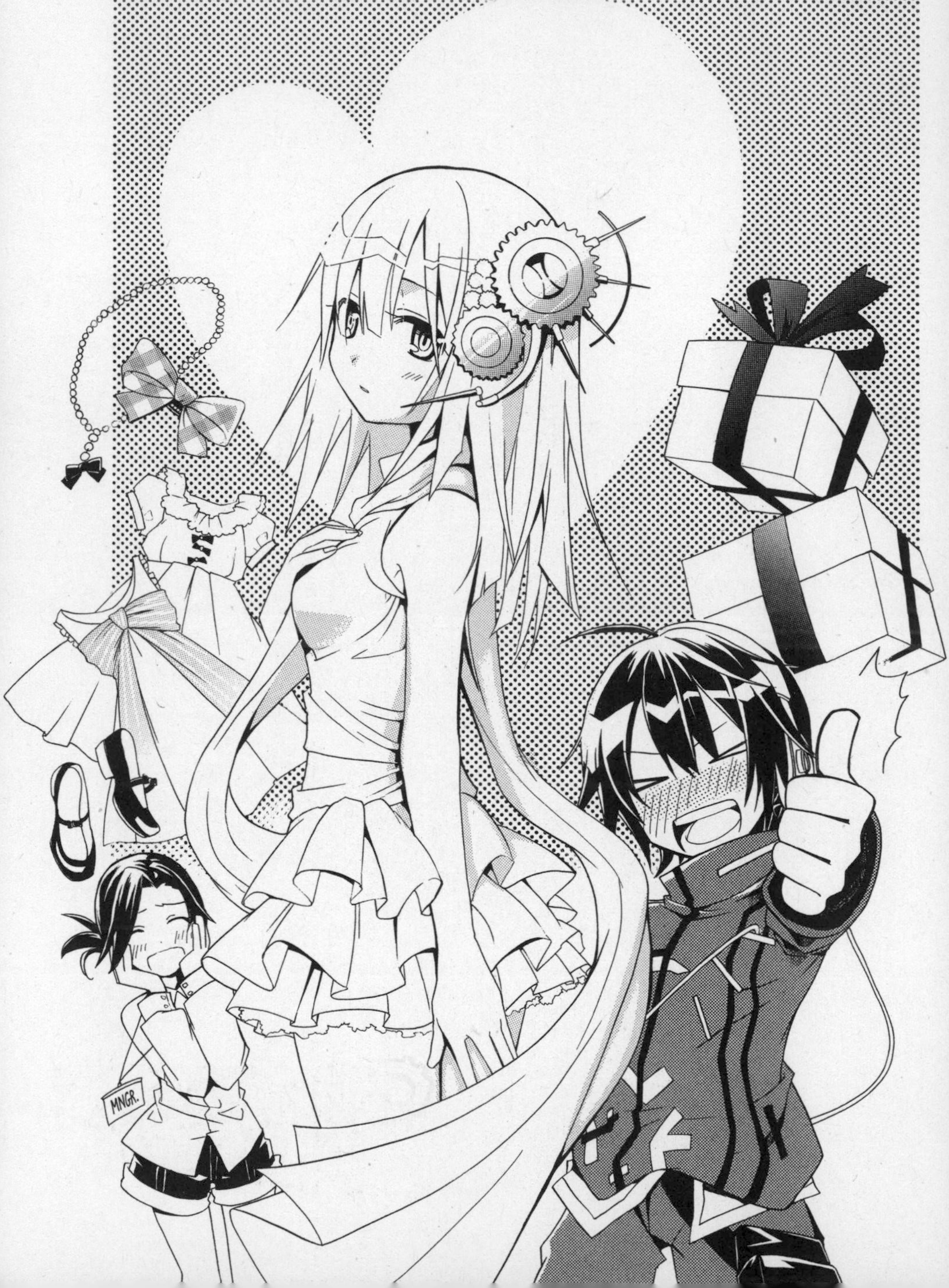
MNGR.

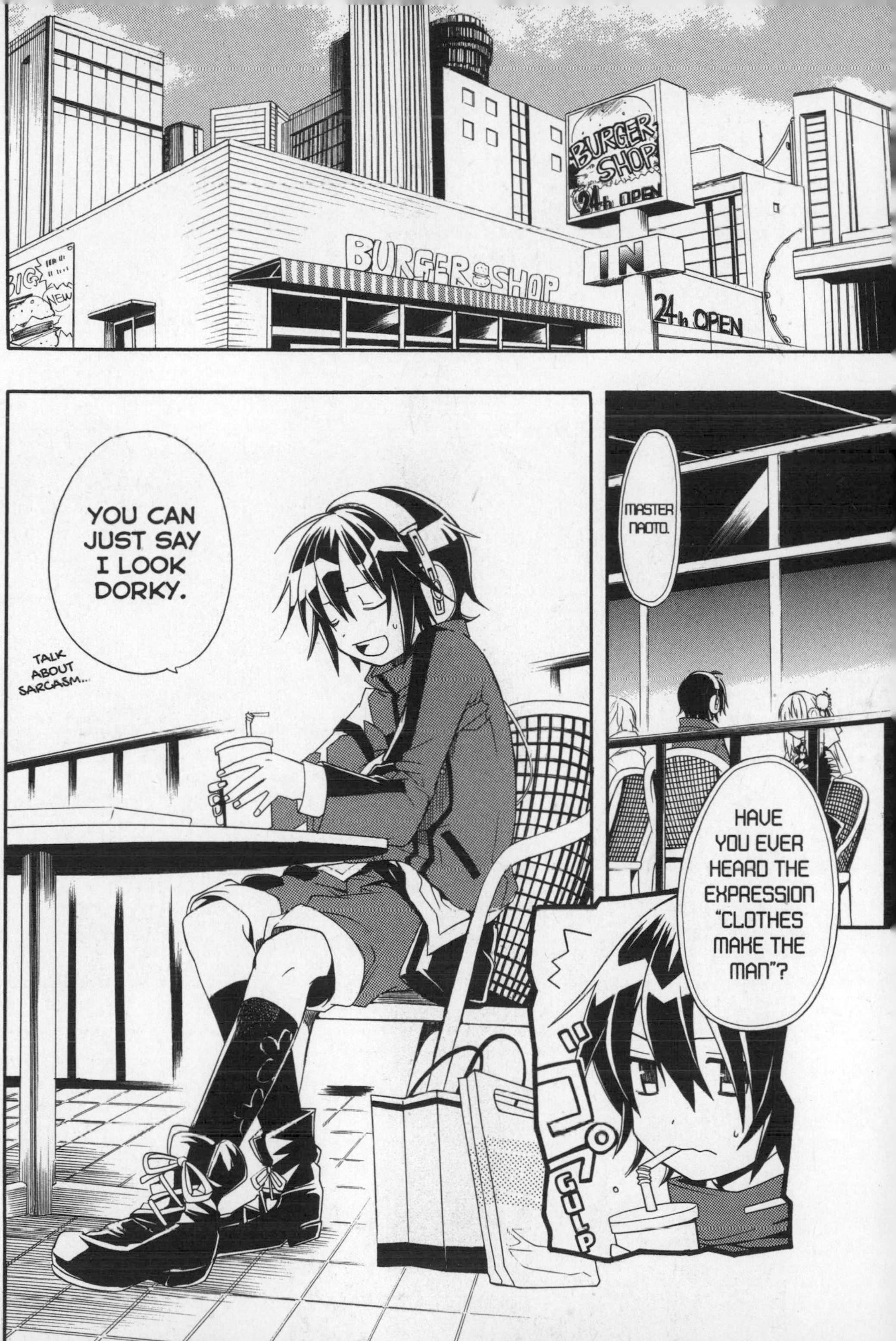
BURGER SHOP
24h OPEN
IN
24h OPEN
BURGER SHOP
BIG
NEW
MASTER NAOTO.
HAVE YOU EVER HEARD THE EXPRESSION "CLOTHES MAKE THE MAN"?
GULP
YOU CAN JUST SAY I LOOK DORKY.
TALK ABOUT SARCASM...

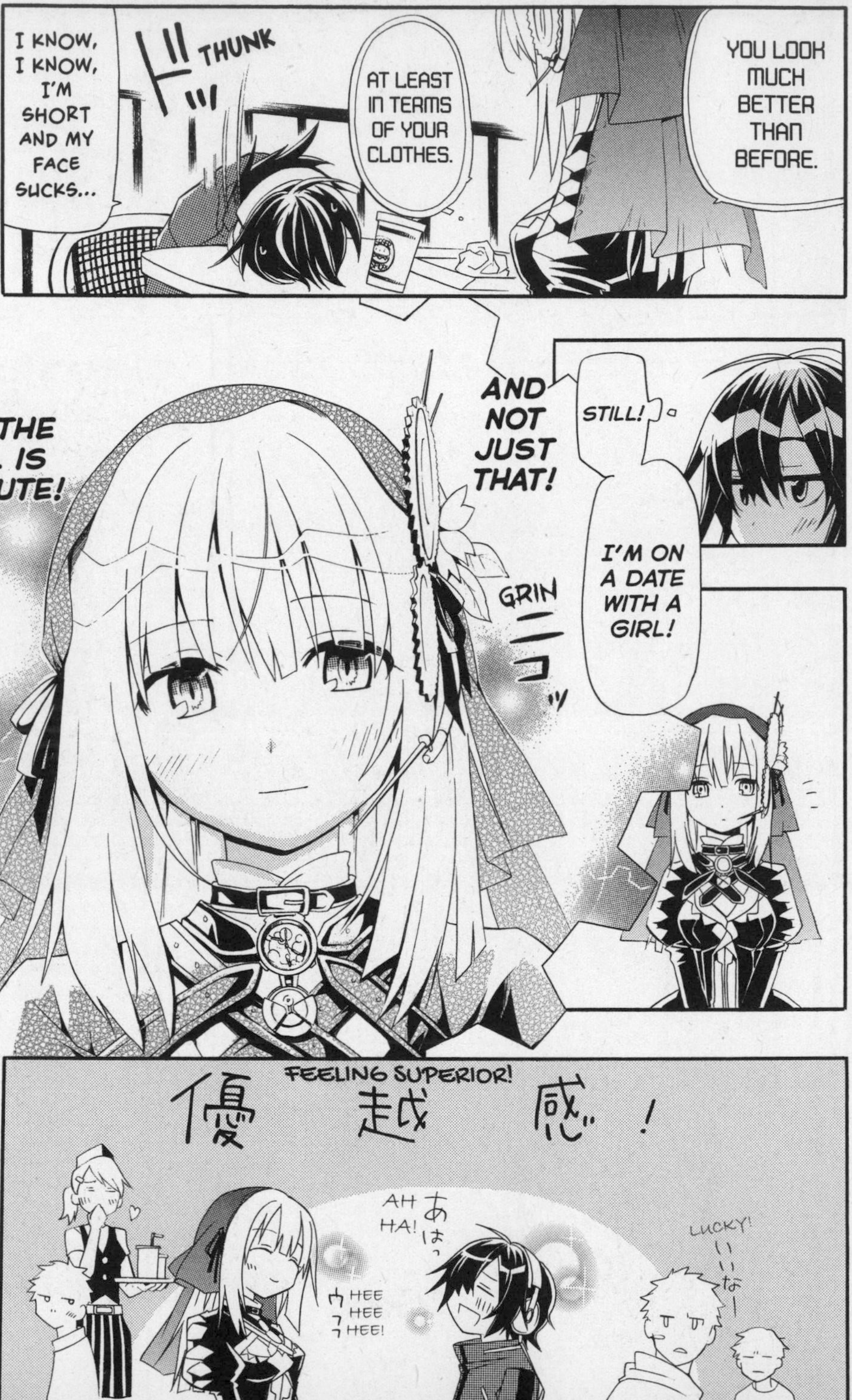
YOU LOOK MUCH BETTER THAN BEFORE.
AT LEAST IN TERMS OF YOUR CLOTHES.
ドッ
THUNK
I KNOW, I KNOW, I'M SHORT AND MY FACE SUCKS...
STILL!
AND NOT JUST THAT!
I'M ON A DATE WITH A GIRL!
BUT THE GIRL IS CUUUUTE!
GRIN
ニコッ
FEELING SUPERIOR!
優越感！
LUCKY!
いいな～
AH HA!
あはっ
HEE HEE HEE!
ウフフ

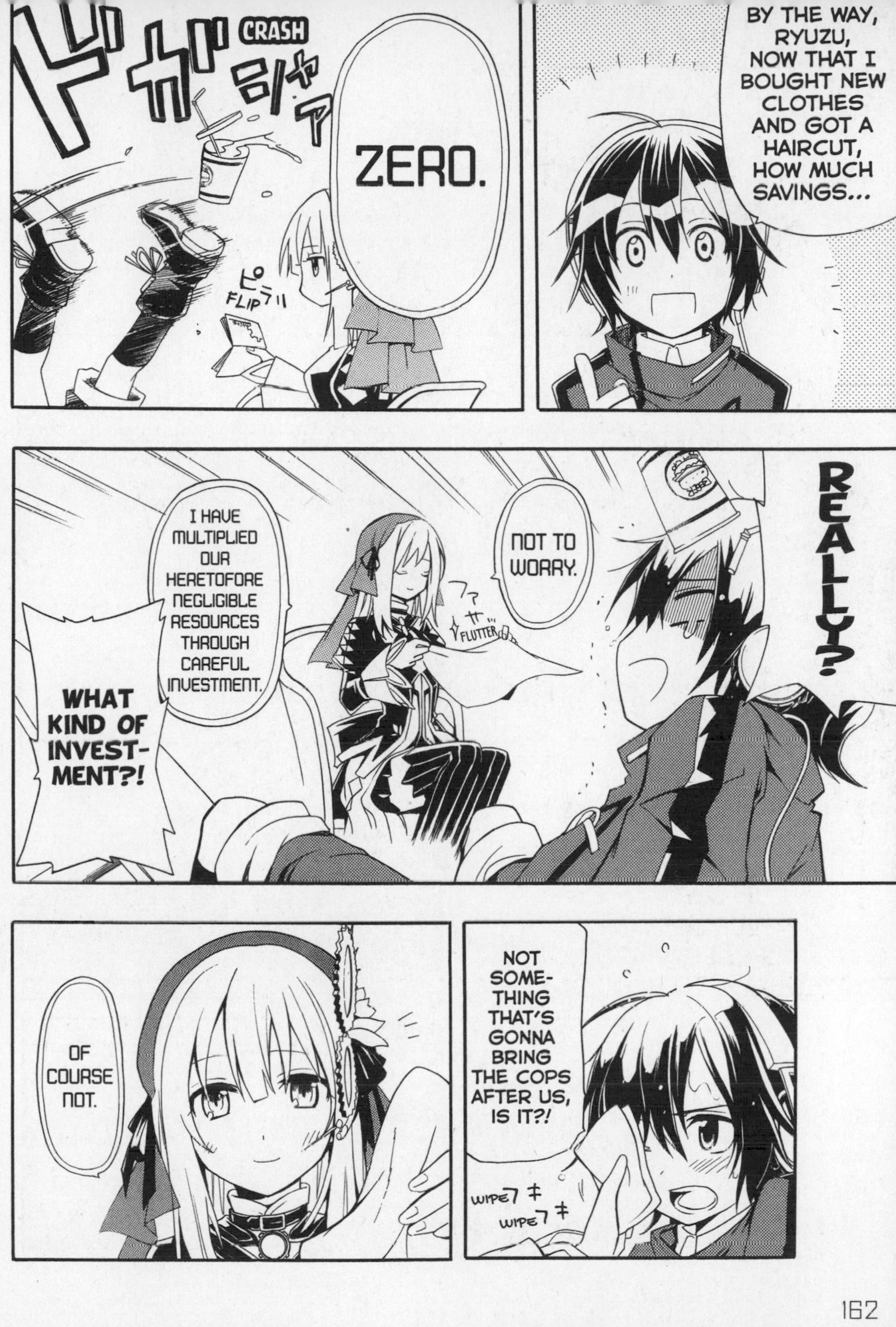
BY THE WAY, RYUZU, NOW THAT I BOUGHT NEW CLOTHES AND GOT A HAIRCUT, HOW MUCH SAVINGS...
CRASH
ZERO.
FLIP
REALLY?
NOT TO WORRY.
FLUTTER
I HAVE MULTIPLIED OUR HERETOFORE NEGLIGIBLE RESOURCES THROUGH CAREFUL INVESTMENT.
WHAT KIND OF INVEST-MENT?!
NOT SOME-THING THAT'S GONNA BRING THE COPS AFTER US, IS IT?!
WIPE
WIPE
OF COURSE NOT.

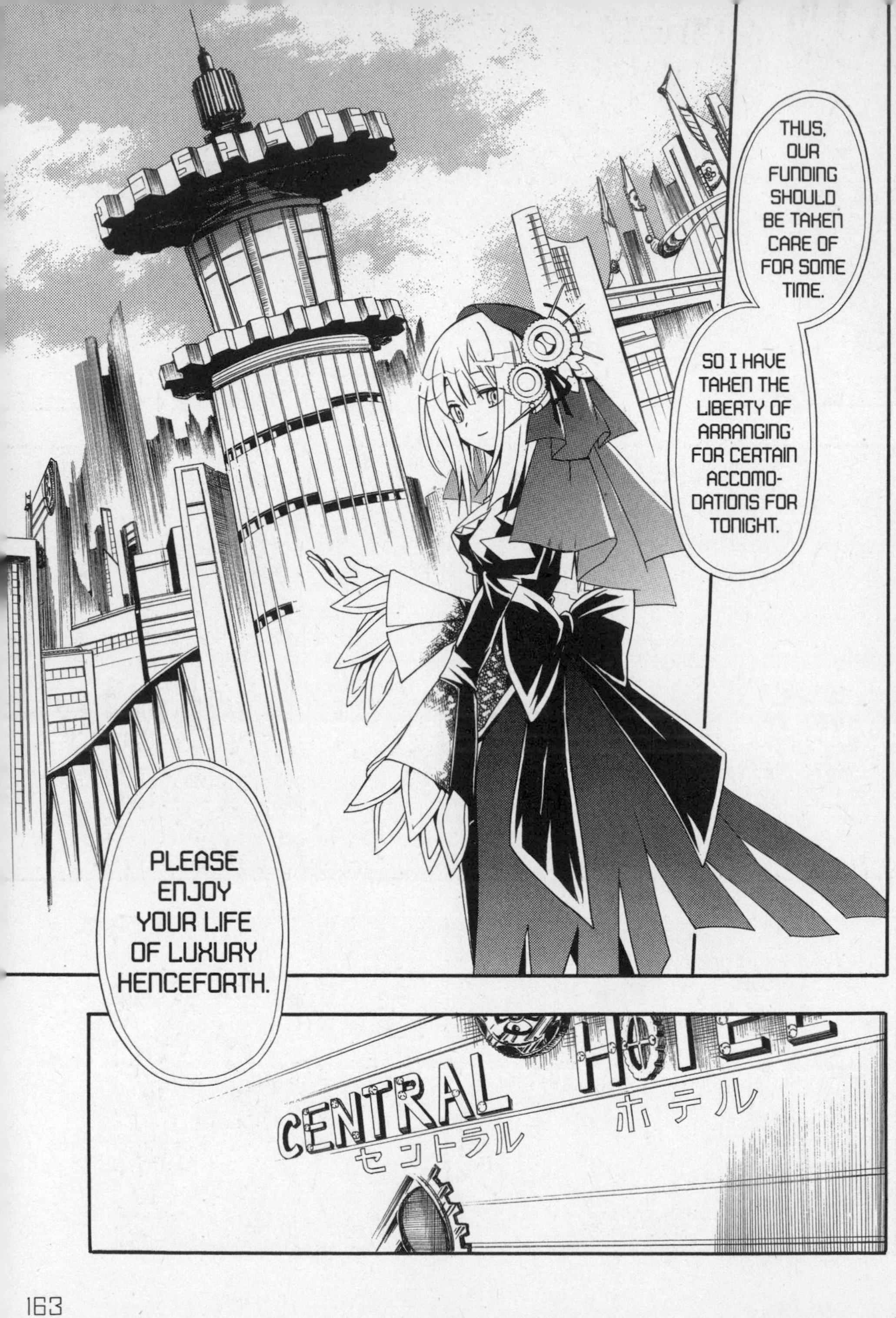
THUS, OUR FUNDING SHOULD BE TAKEN CARE OF FOR SOME TIME.
SO I HAVE TAKEN THE LIBERTY OF ARRANGING FOR CERTAIN ACCOMO-DATIONS FOR TONIGHT.
PLEASE ENJOY YOUR LIFE OF LUXURY HENCEFORTH.
CENTRAL HOTEL
セントラル ホテル

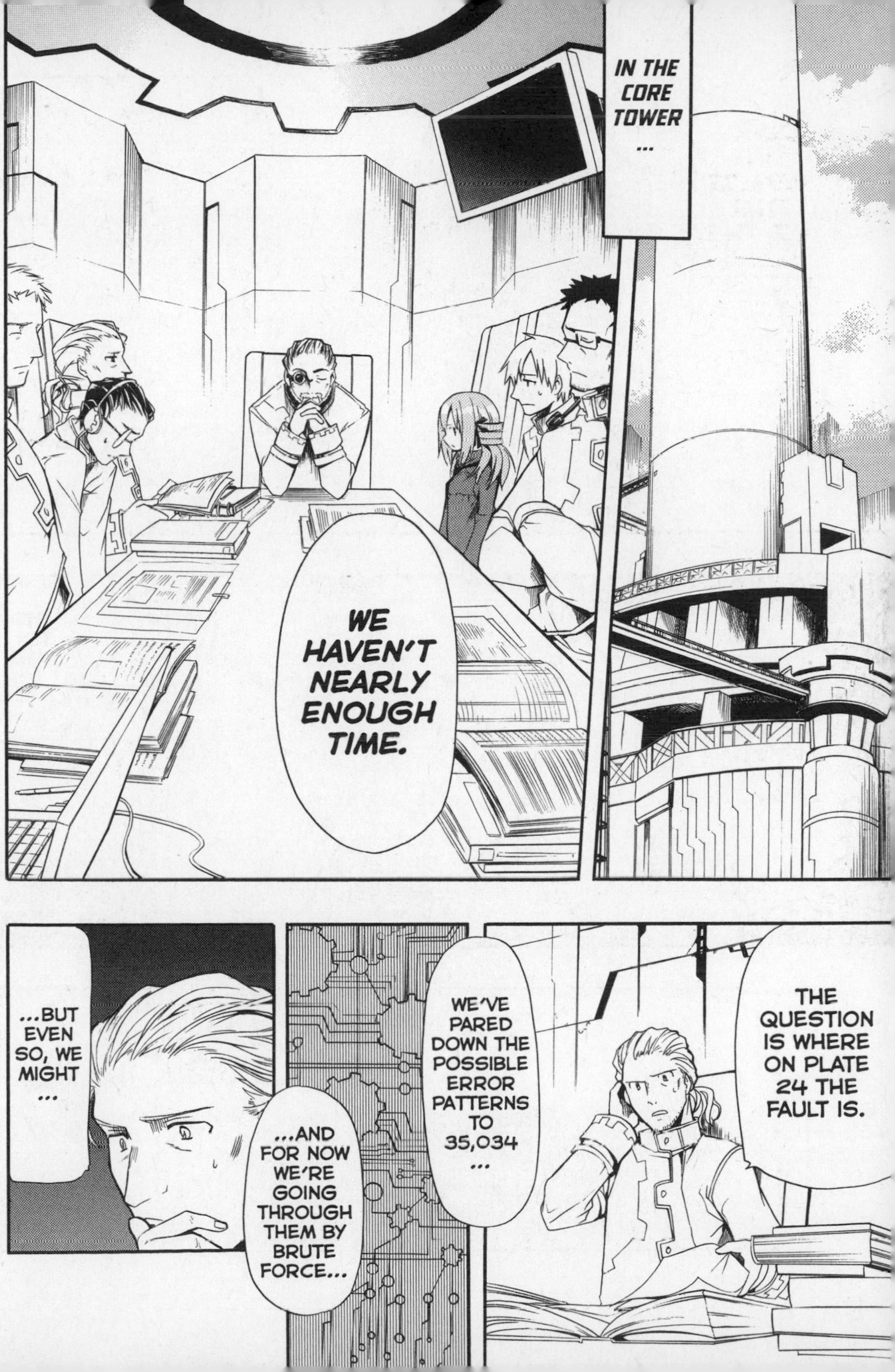
IN THE CORE TOWER ...
WE HAVEN'T NEARLY ENOUGH TIME.
THE QUESTION IS WHERE ON PLATE 24 THE FAULT IS.
WE'VE PARED DOWN THE POSSIBLE ERROR PATTERNS TO 35,034 ...
...AND FOR NOW WE'RE GOING THROUGH THEM BY BRUTE FORCE...
...BUT EVEN SO, WE MIGHT ...

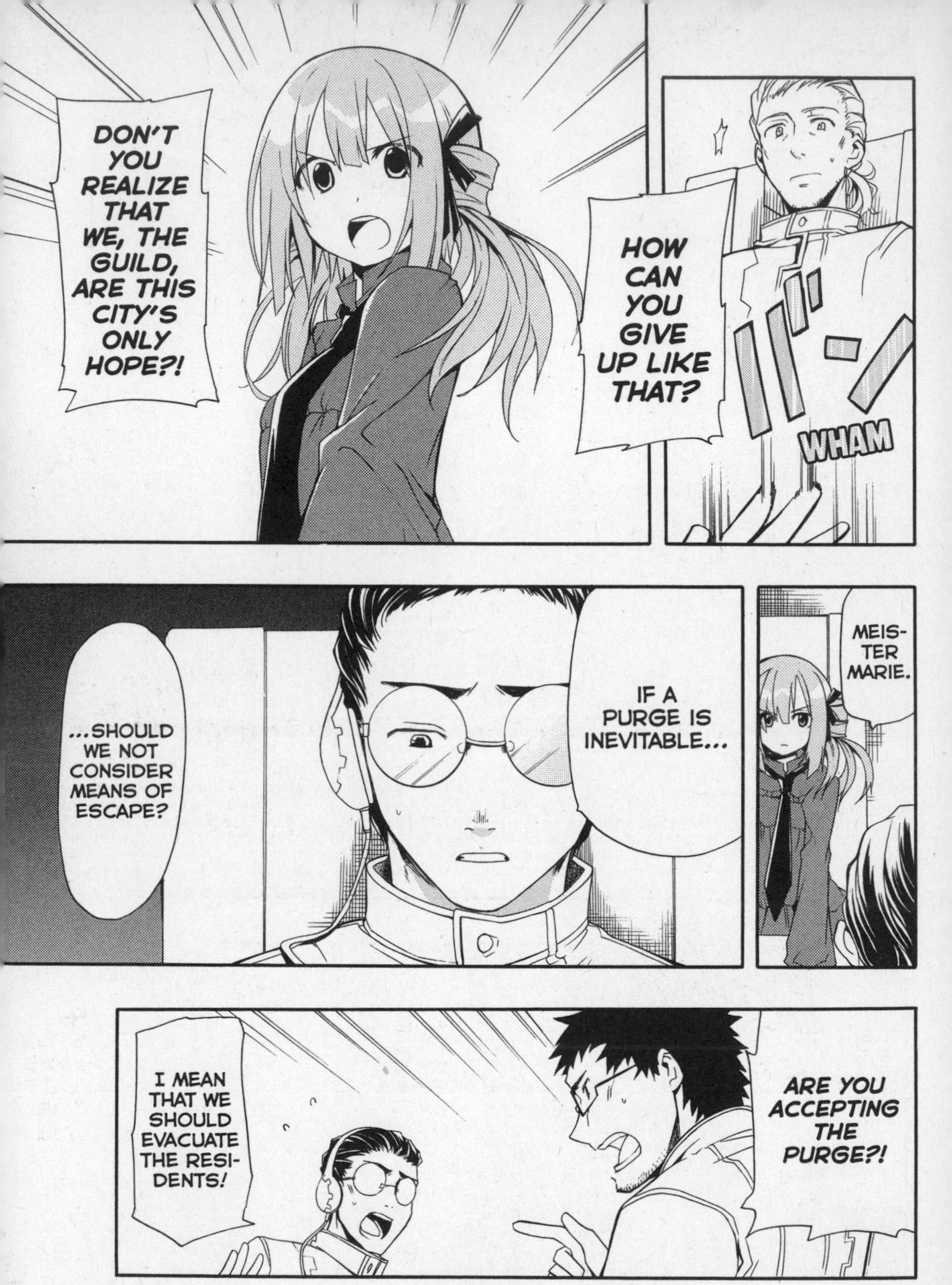
HOW CAN YOU GIVE UP LIKE THAT?
WHAM
DON'T YOU REALIZE THAT WE, THE GUILD, ARE THIS CITY'S ONLY HOPE?!
MEIS-TER MARIE.
IF A PURGE IS INEVITABLE...
...SHOULD WE NOT CONSIDER MEANS OF ESCAPE?
ARE YOU ACCEPTING THE PURGE?!
I MEAN THAT WE SHOULD EVACUATE THE RESI-DENTS!

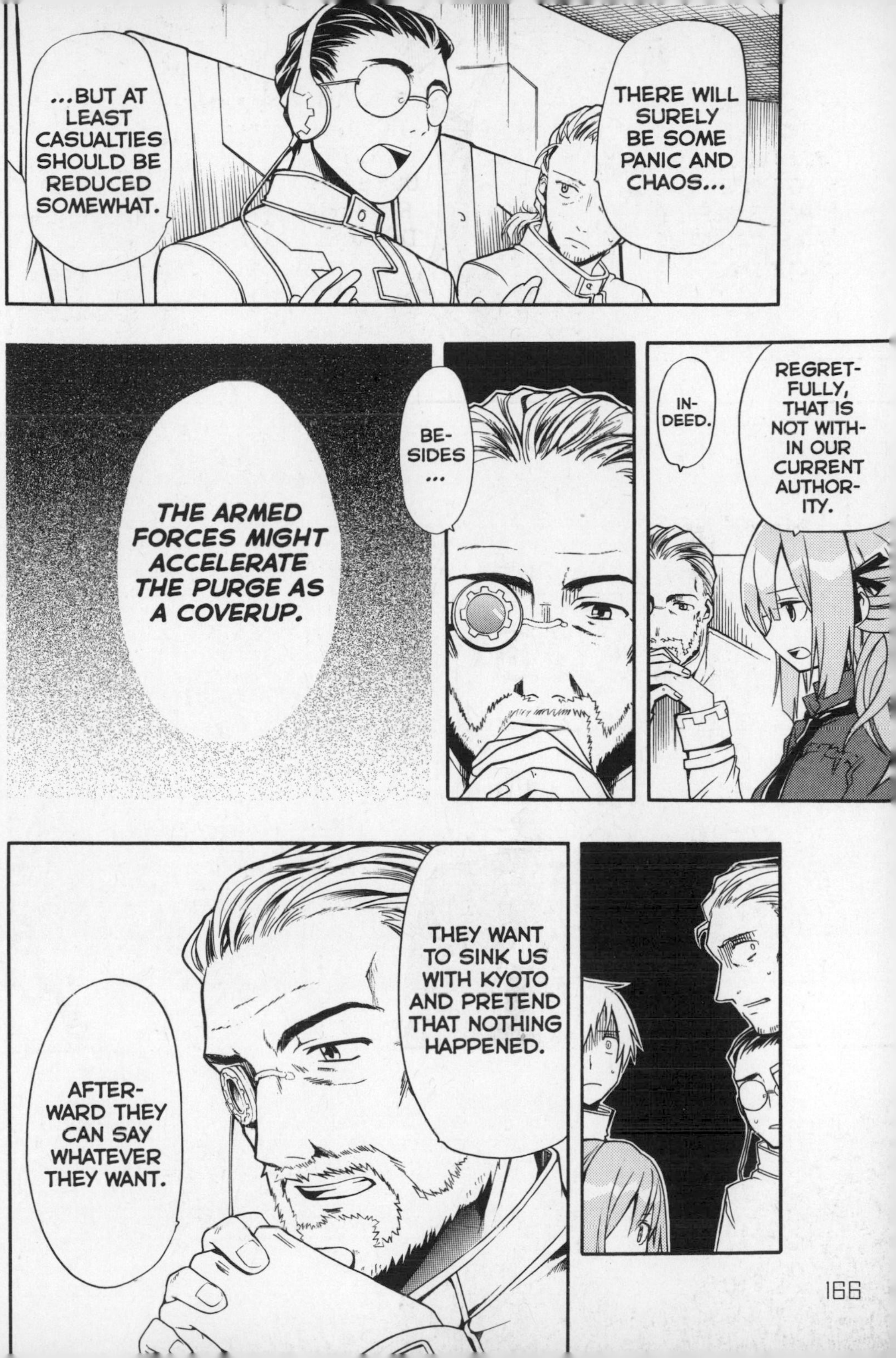
THERE WILL SURELY BE SOME PANIC AND CHAOS...
...BUT AT LEAST CASUALTIES SHOULD BE REDUCED SOMEWHAT.
REGRETFULLY, THAT IS NOT WITHIN OUR CURRENT AUTHORITY.
INDEED.
BESIDES...
THE ARMED FORCES MIGHT ACCELERATE THE PURGE AS A COVERUP.
THEY WANT TO SINK US WITH KYOTO AND PRETEND THAT NOTHING HAPPENED.
AFTERWARD THEY CAN SAY WHATEVER THEY WANT.

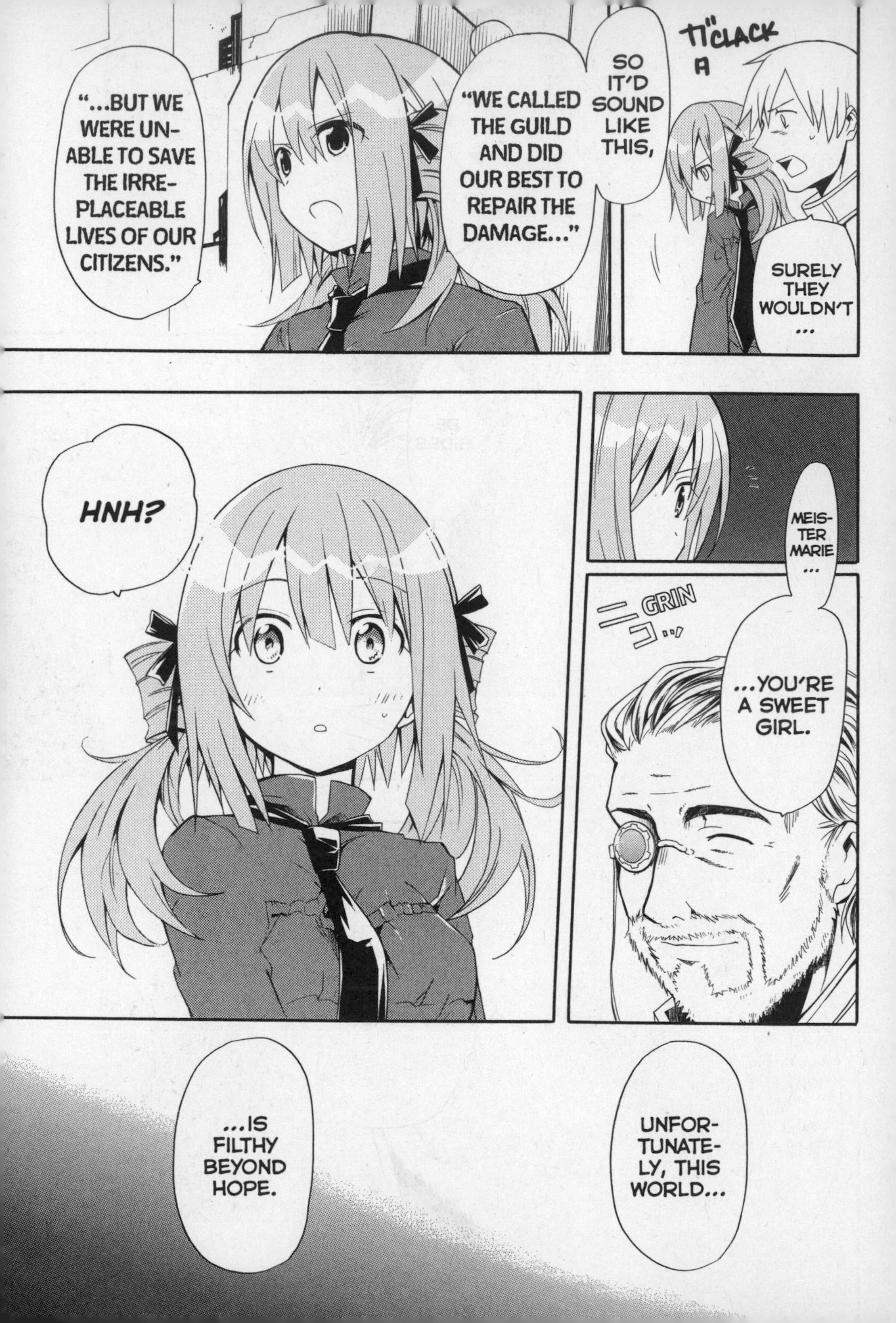
CLACK
SO IT'D SOUND LIKE THIS,
SURELY THEY WOULDN'T ...
"WE CALLED THE GUILD AND DID OUR BEST TO REPAIR THE DAMAGE..."
"...BUT WE WERE UN-ABLE TO SAVE THE IRRE-PLACEABLE LIVES OF OUR CITIZENS."
MEIS-TER MARIE ...
GRIN
...YOU'RE A SWEET GIRL.
HNH?
UNFOR-TUNATE-LY, THIS WORLD...
...IS FILTHY BEYOND HOPE.

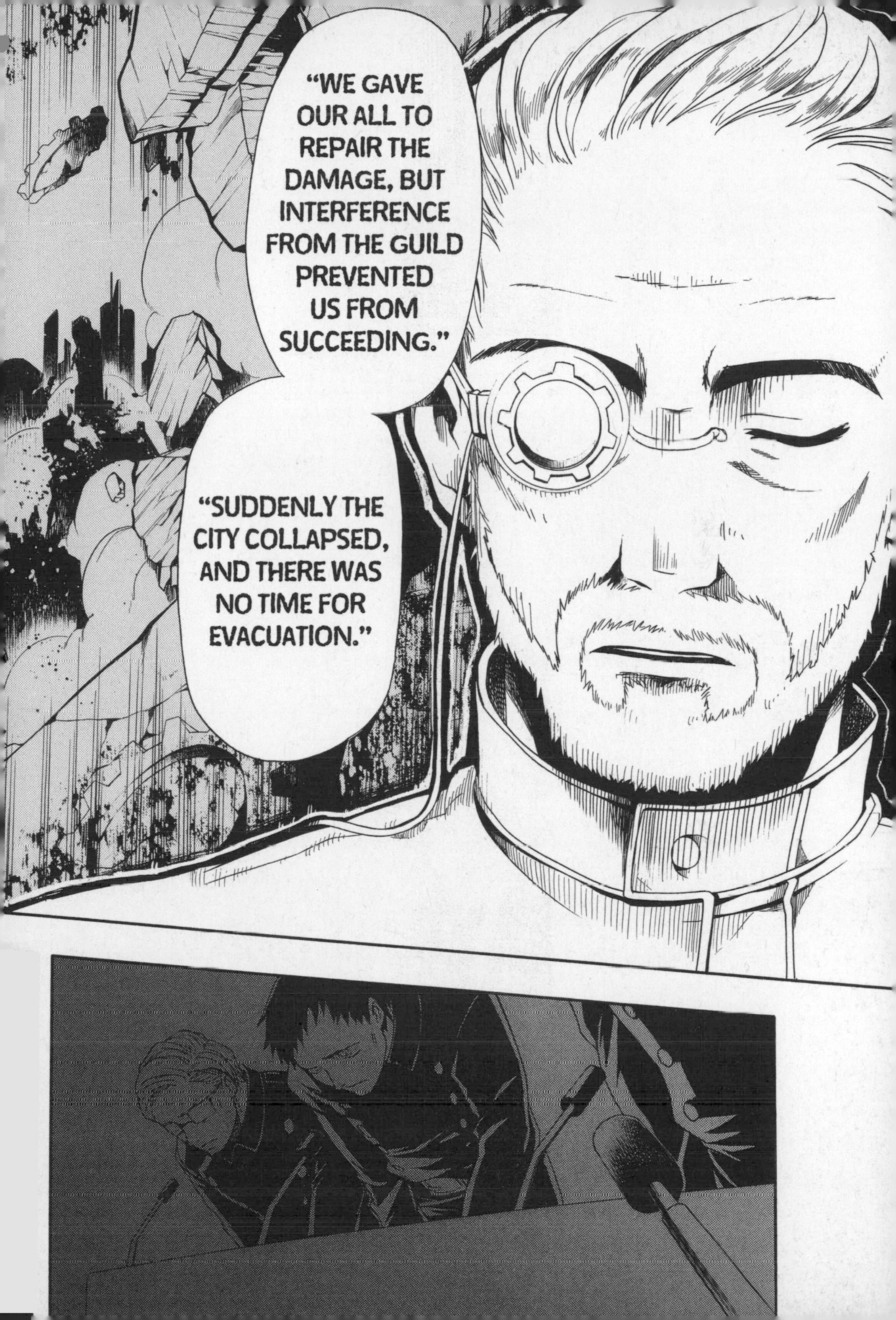
"WE GAVE OUR ALL TO REPAIR THE DAMAGE, BUT INTERFERENCE FROM THE GUILD PREVENTED US FROM SUCCEEDING."
"SUDDENLY THE CITY COLLAPSED, AND THERE WAS NO TIME FOR EVACUATION."

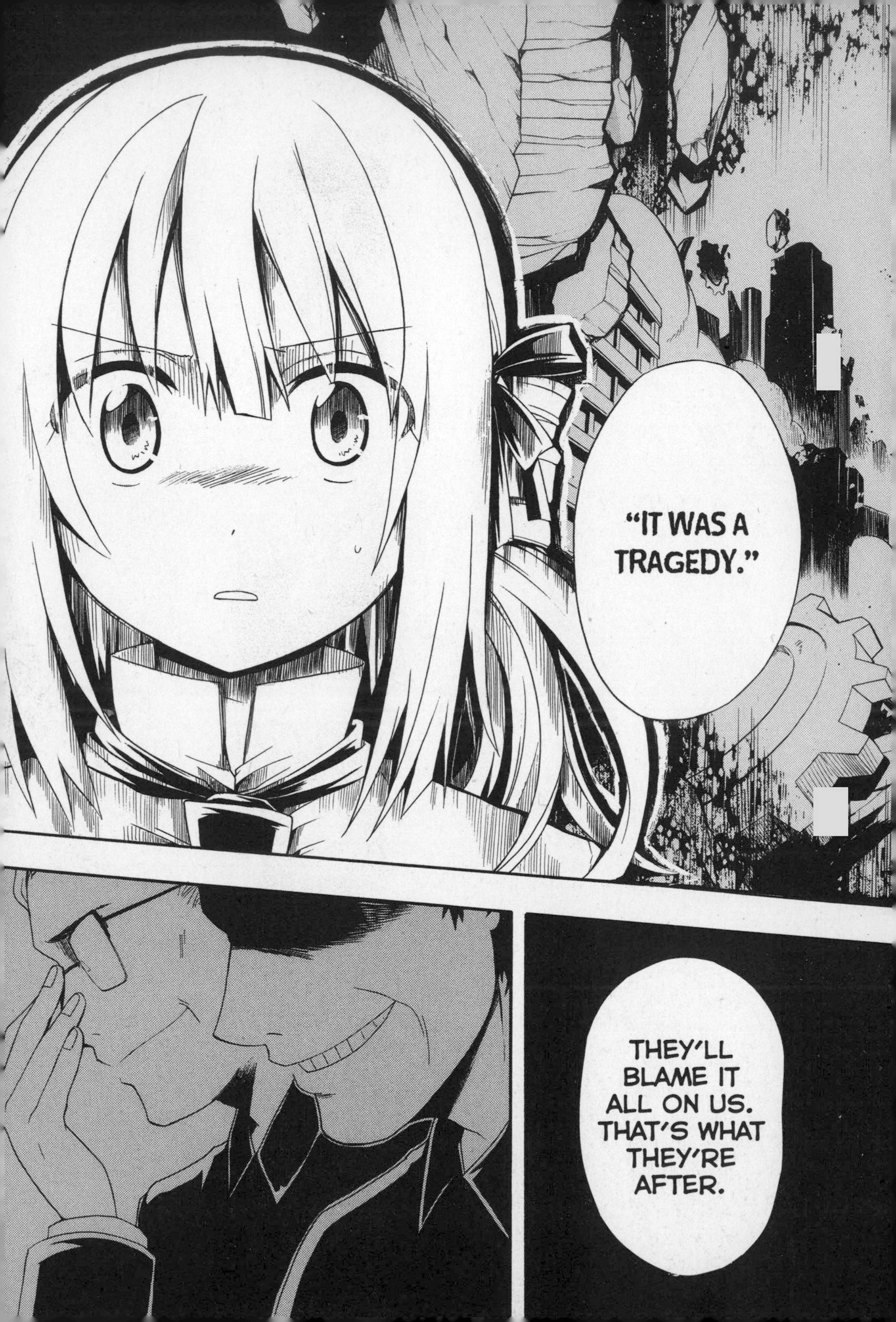
"IT WAS A TRAGEDY."
THEY'LL BLAME IT ALL ON US. THAT'S WHAT THEY'RE AFTER.

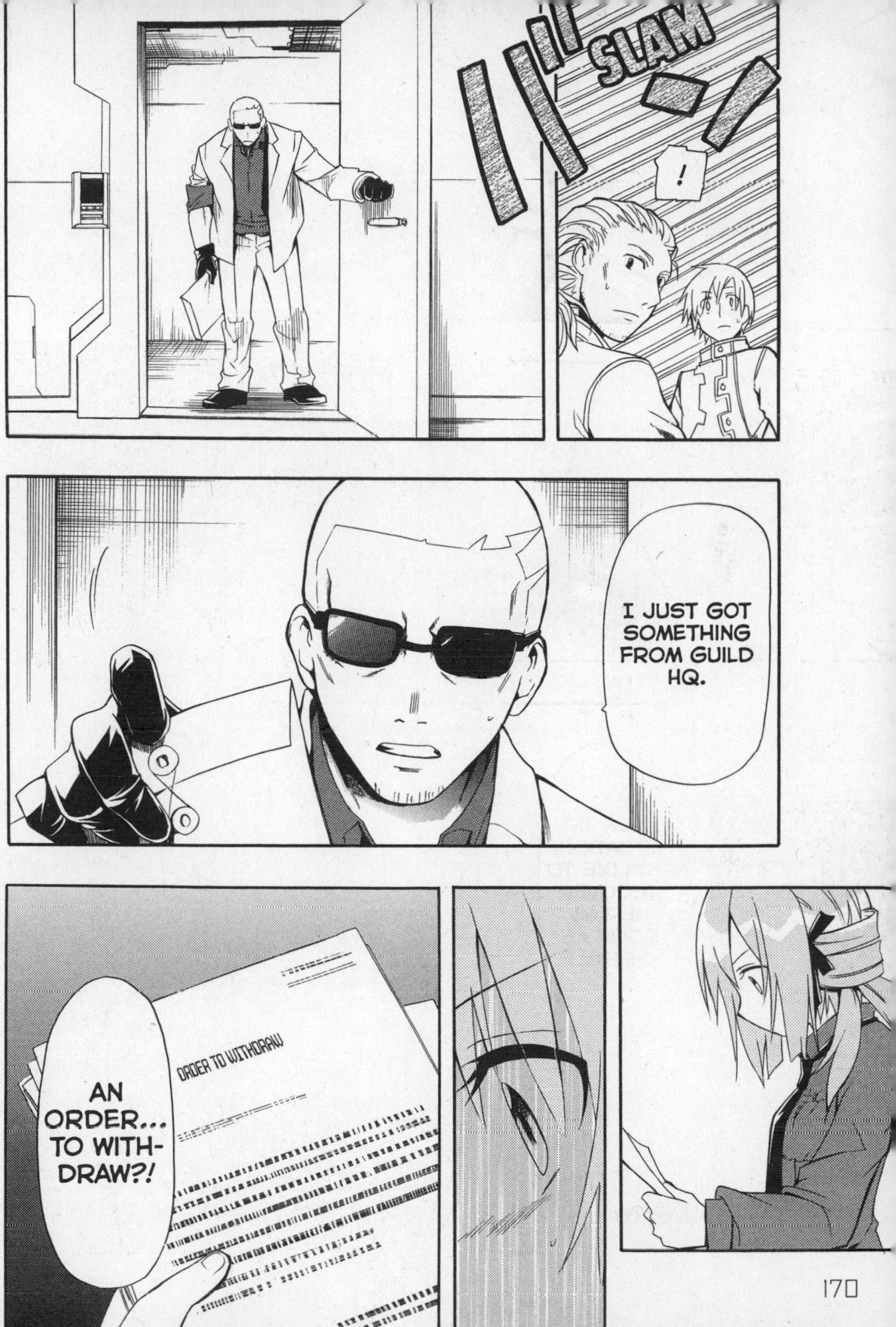
SLAM
!
I JUST GOT SOMETHING FROM GUILD HQ.
ORDER TO WITHDRAW
AN ORDER... TO WITH-DRAW?!

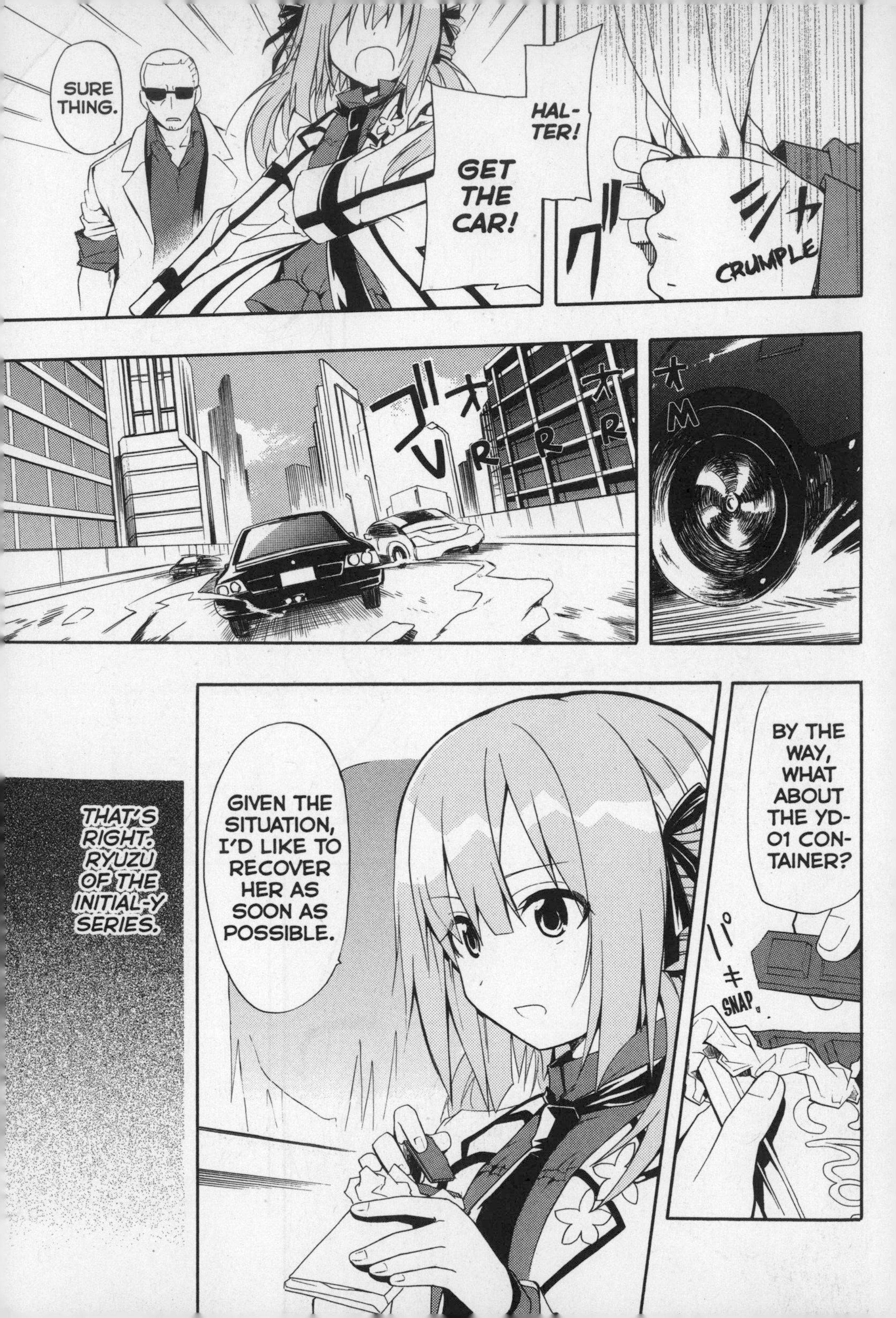
グシャ
CRUMPLE
HAL-
TER!
GET THE CAR!
SURE THING.
オ
M
ブオオ
VRRR
BY THE WAY, WHAT ABOUT THE YD-01 CON-TAINER?
パキ
SNAP.
GIVEN THE SITUATION, I'D LIKE TO RECOVER HER AS SOON AS POSSIBLE.
THAT'S RIGHT. RYUZU OF THE INITIAL-Y SERIES.

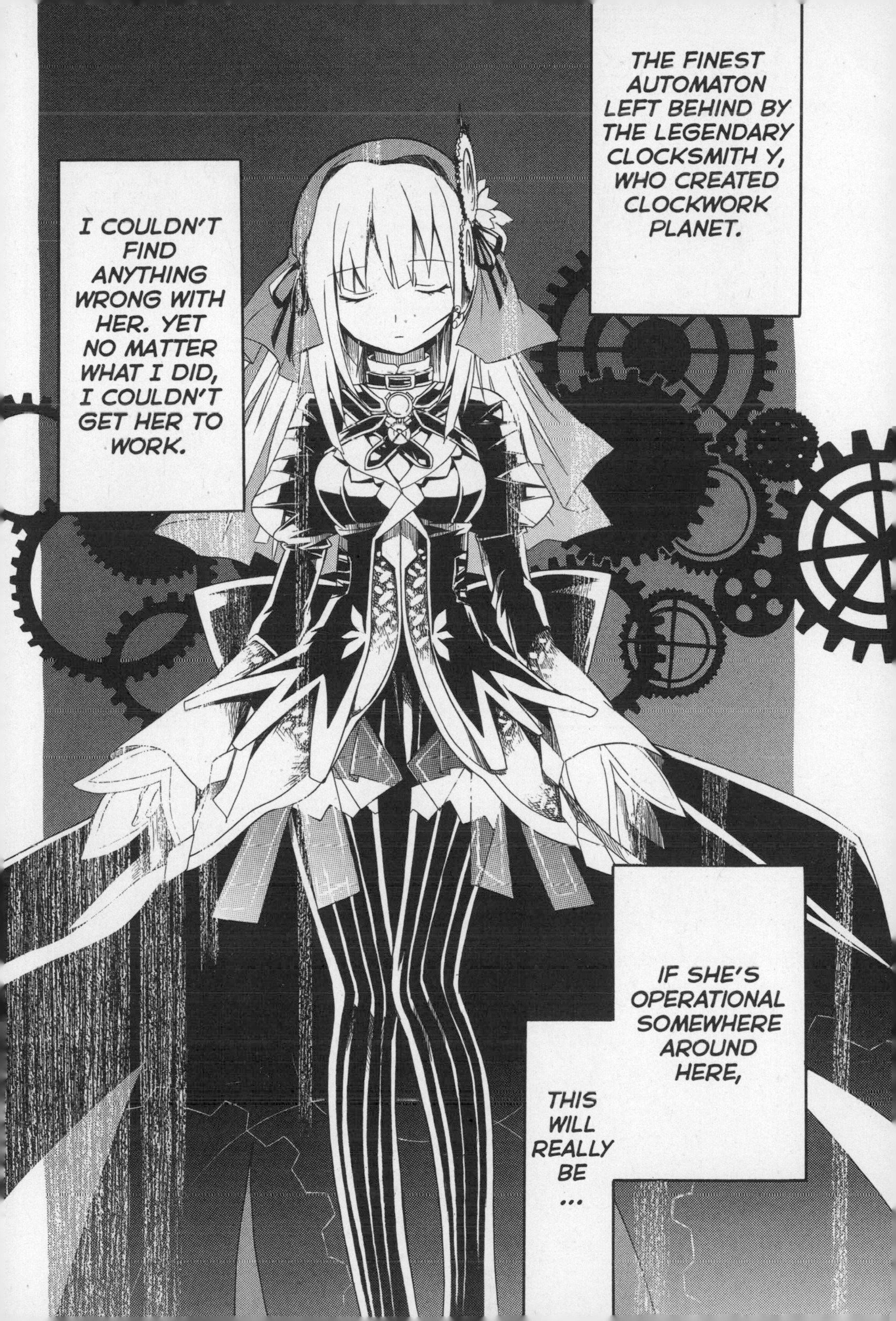
THE FINEST AUTOMATON LEFT BEHIND BY THE LEGENDARY CLOCKSMITH Y, WHO CREATED CLOCKWORK PLANET.
I COULDN'T FIND ANYTHING WRONG WITH HER. YET NO MATTER WHAT I DID, I COULDN'T GET HER TO WORK.
IF SHE'S OPERATIONAL SOMEWHERE AROUND HERE,
THIS WILL REALLY BE ...

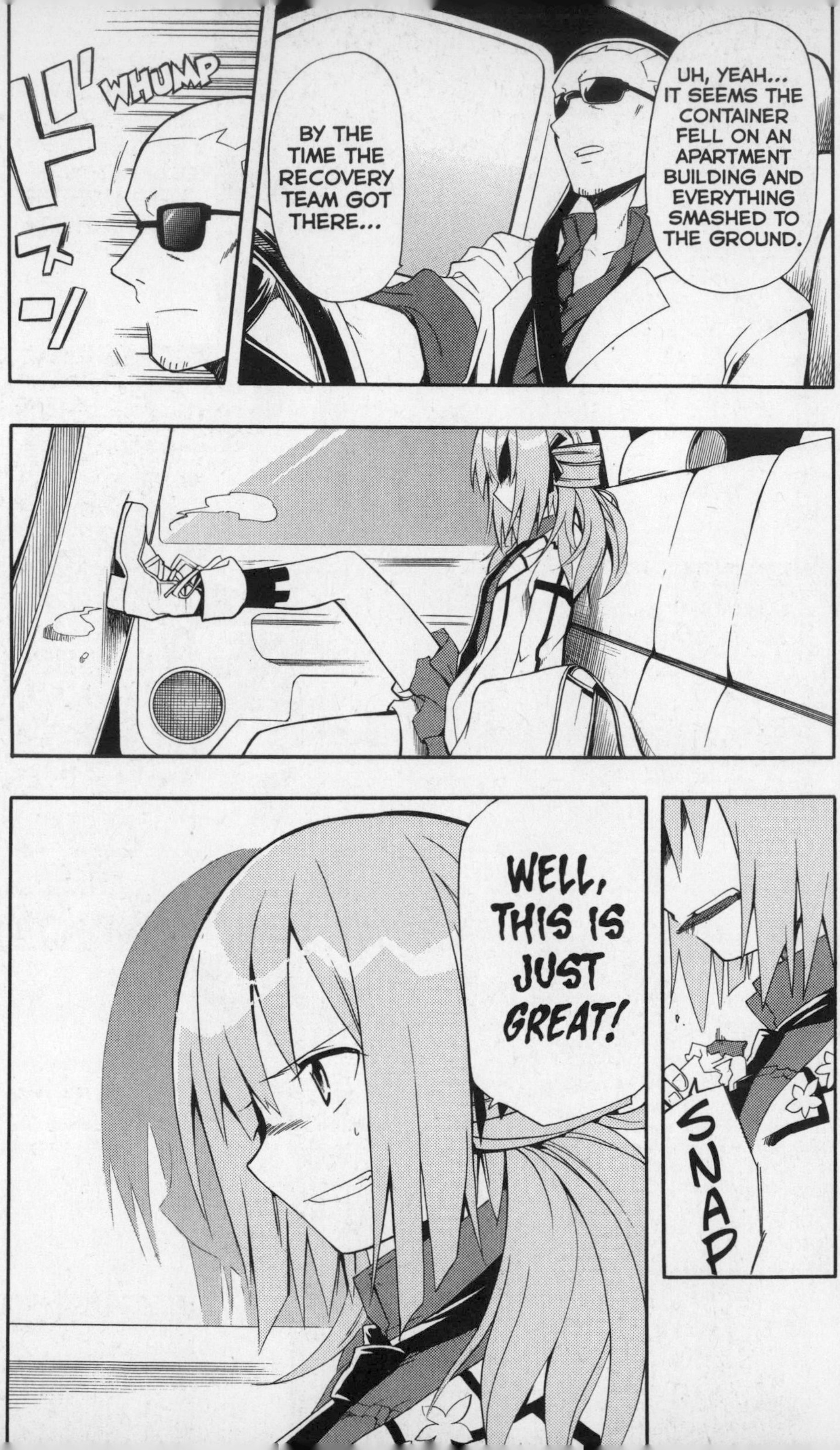
UH, YEAH... IT SEEMS THE CONTAINER FELL ON AN APARTMENT BUILDING AND EVERYTHING SMASHED TO THE GROUND.
BY THE TIME THE RECOVERY TEAM GOT THERE...
WHUMP
SNAP
WELL, THIS IS JUST GREAT!

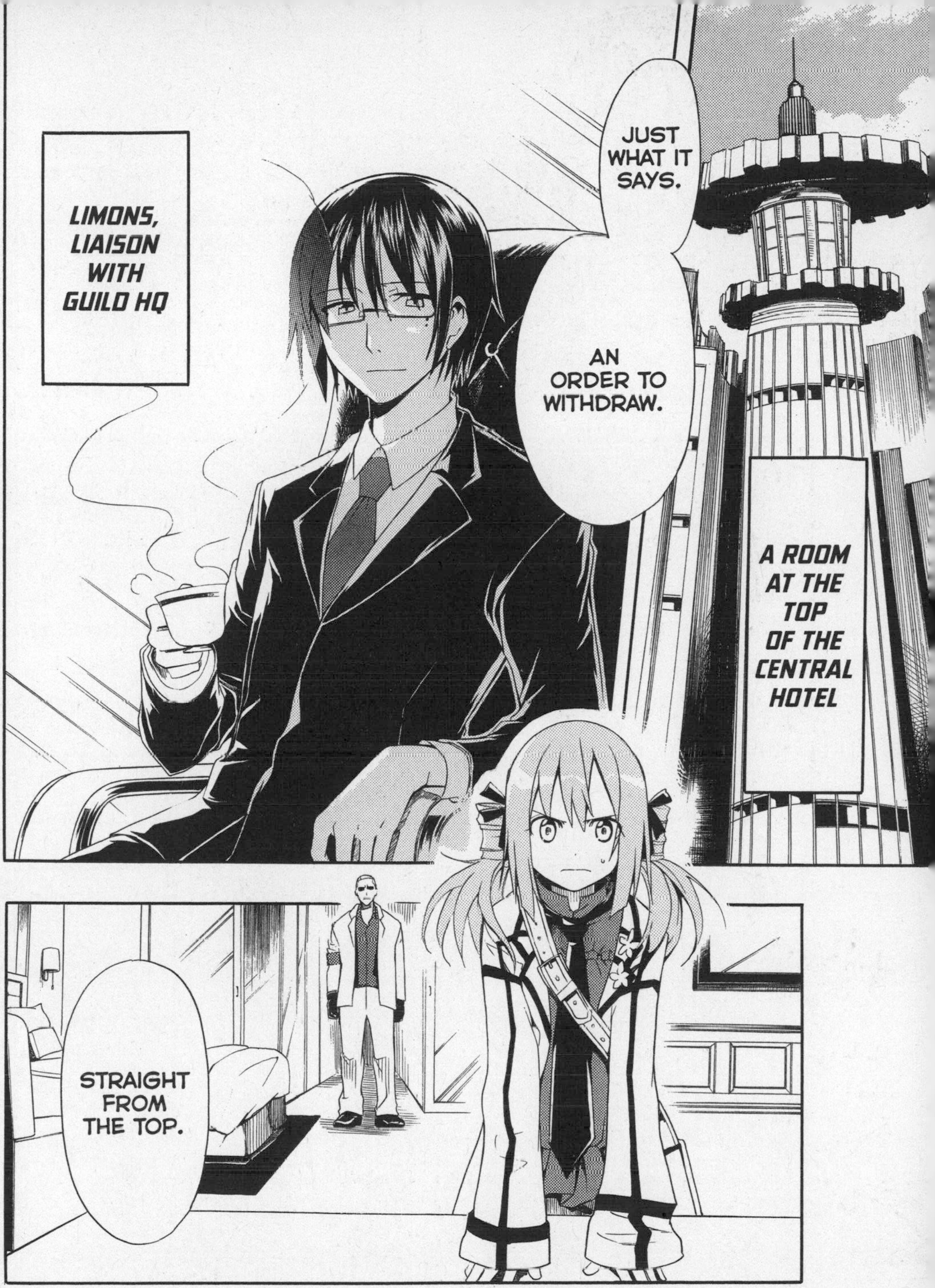
A ROOM AT THE TOP OF THE CENTRAL HOTEL
LIMONS, LIAISON WITH GUILD HQ
JUST WHAT IT SAYS.
AN ORDER TO WITHDRAW.
STRAIGHT FROM THE TOP.

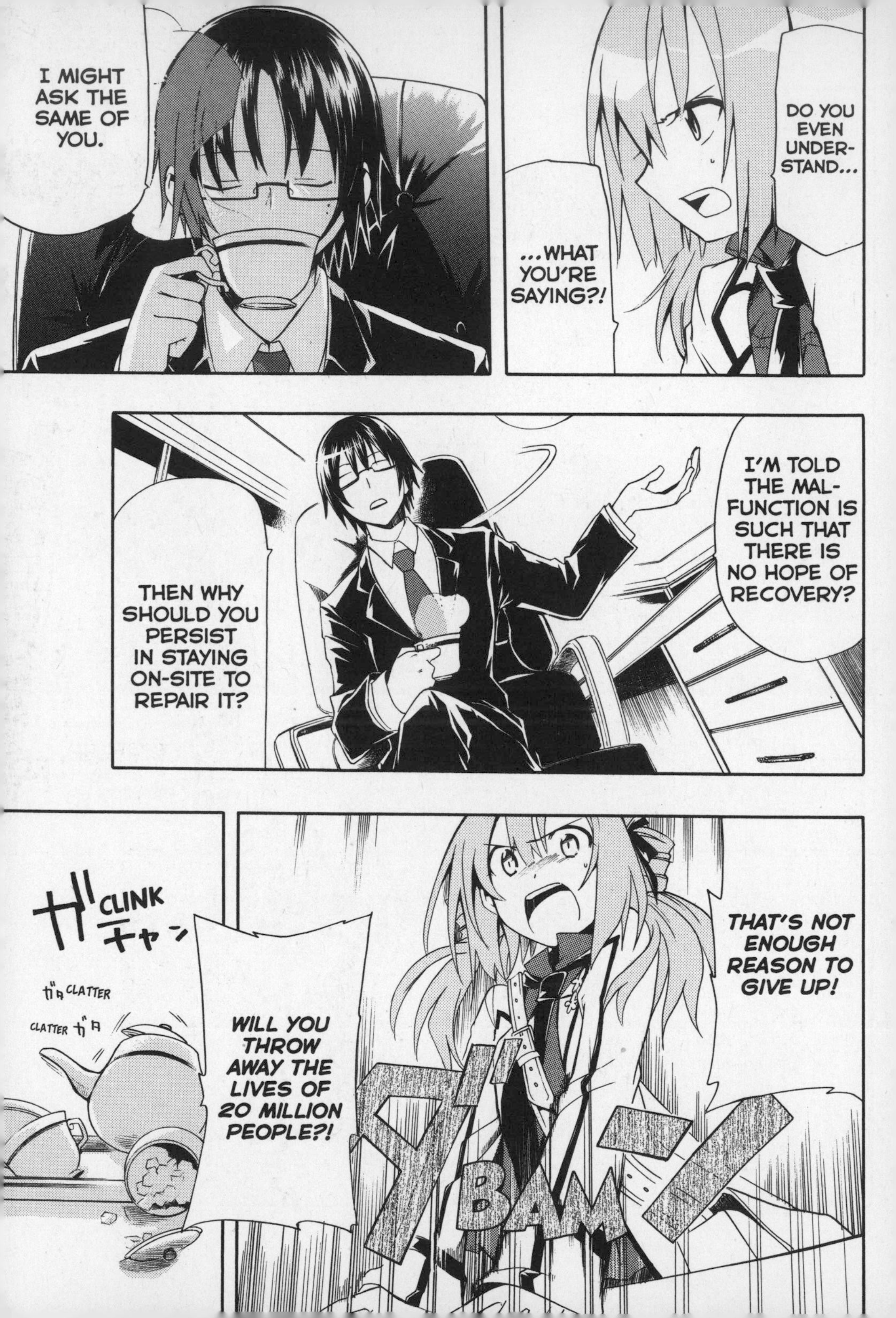
DO YOU EVEN UNDER-STAND...
...WHAT YOU'RE SAYING?!
I MIGHT ASK THE SAME OF YOU.
I'M TOLD THE MAL-FUNCTION IS SUCH THAT THERE IS NO HOPE OF RECOVERY?
THEN WHY SHOULD YOU PERSIST IN STAYING ON-SITE TO REPAIR IT?
THAT'S NOT ENOUGH REASON TO GIVE UP!
WILL YOU THROW AWAY THE LIVES OF 20 MILLION PEOPLE?!
BAM
CLINK
CLATTER
CLATTER

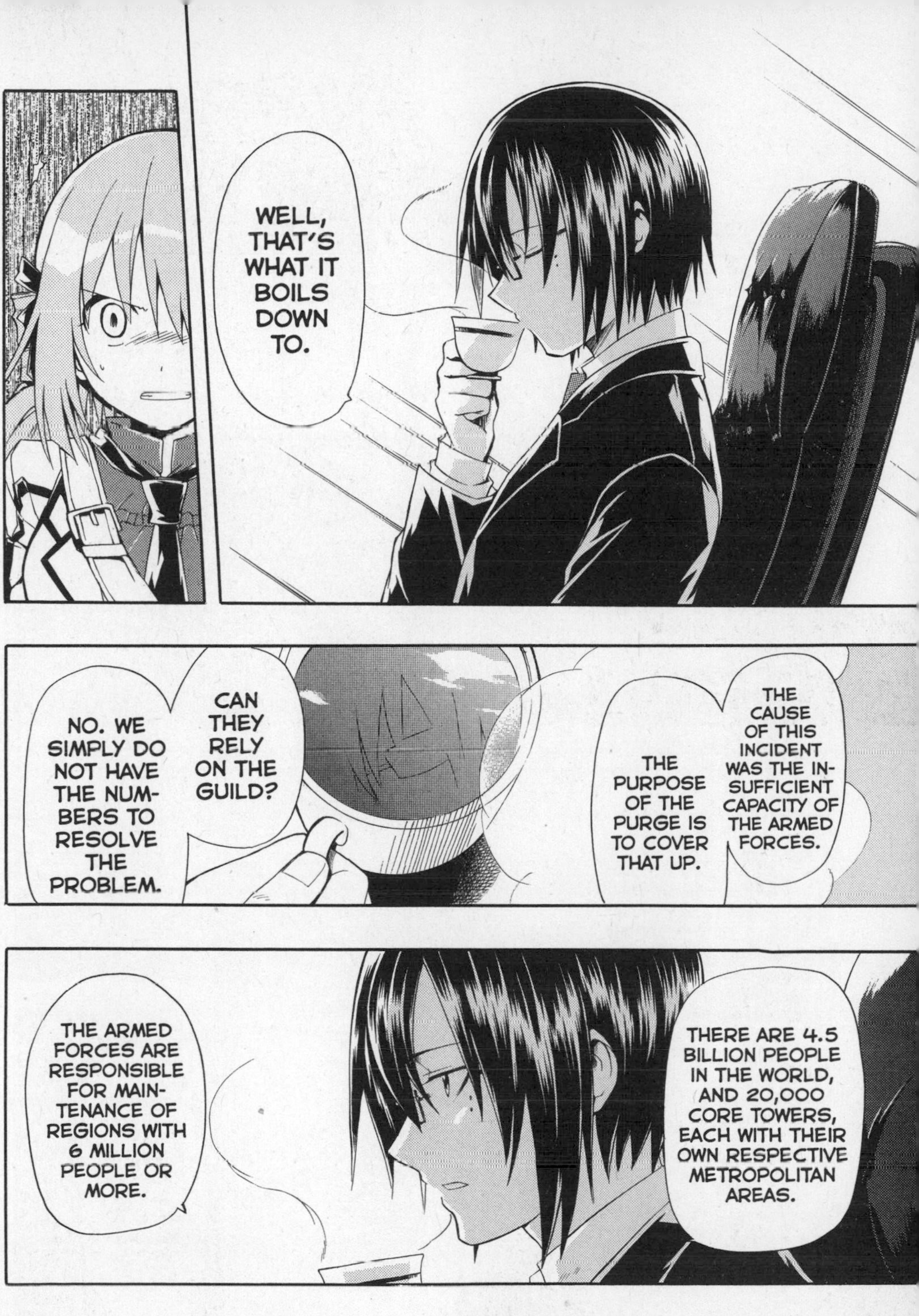
WELL, THAT'S WHAT IT BOILS DOWN TO.
THE CAUSE OF THIS INCIDENT WAS THE INSUFFICIENT CAPACITY OF THE ARMED FORCES.
THE PURPOSE OF THE PURGE IS TO COVER THAT UP.
CAN THEY RELY ON THE GUILD?
NO. WE SIMPLY DO NOT HAVE THE NUMBERS TO RESOLVE THE PROBLEM.
THERE ARE 4.5 BILLION PEOPLE IN THE WORLD, AND 20,000 CORE TOWERS, EACH WITH THEIR OWN RESPECTIVE METROPOLITAN AREAS.
THE ARMED FORCES ARE RESPONSIBLE FOR MAINTENANCE OF REGIONS WITH 6 MILLION PEOPLE OR MORE.

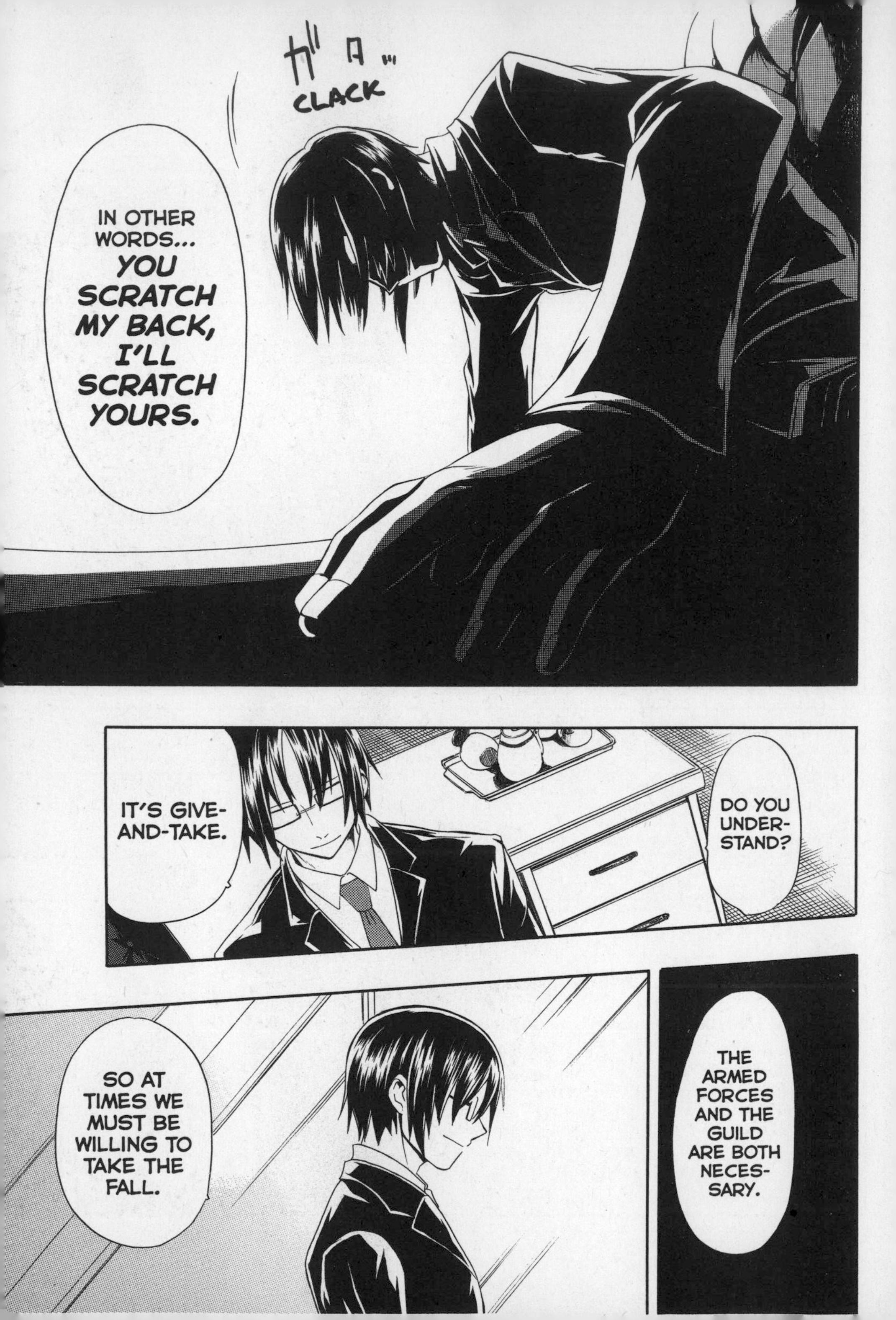
ガタ
CLACK
IN OTHER WORDS... YOU SCRATCH MY BACK, I'LL SCRATCH YOURS.
DO YOU UNDER-STAND?
IT'S GIVE-AND-TAKE.
THE ARMED FORCES AND THE GUILD ARE BOTH NECES-SARY.
SO AT TIMES WE MUST BE WILLING TO TAKE THE FALL.

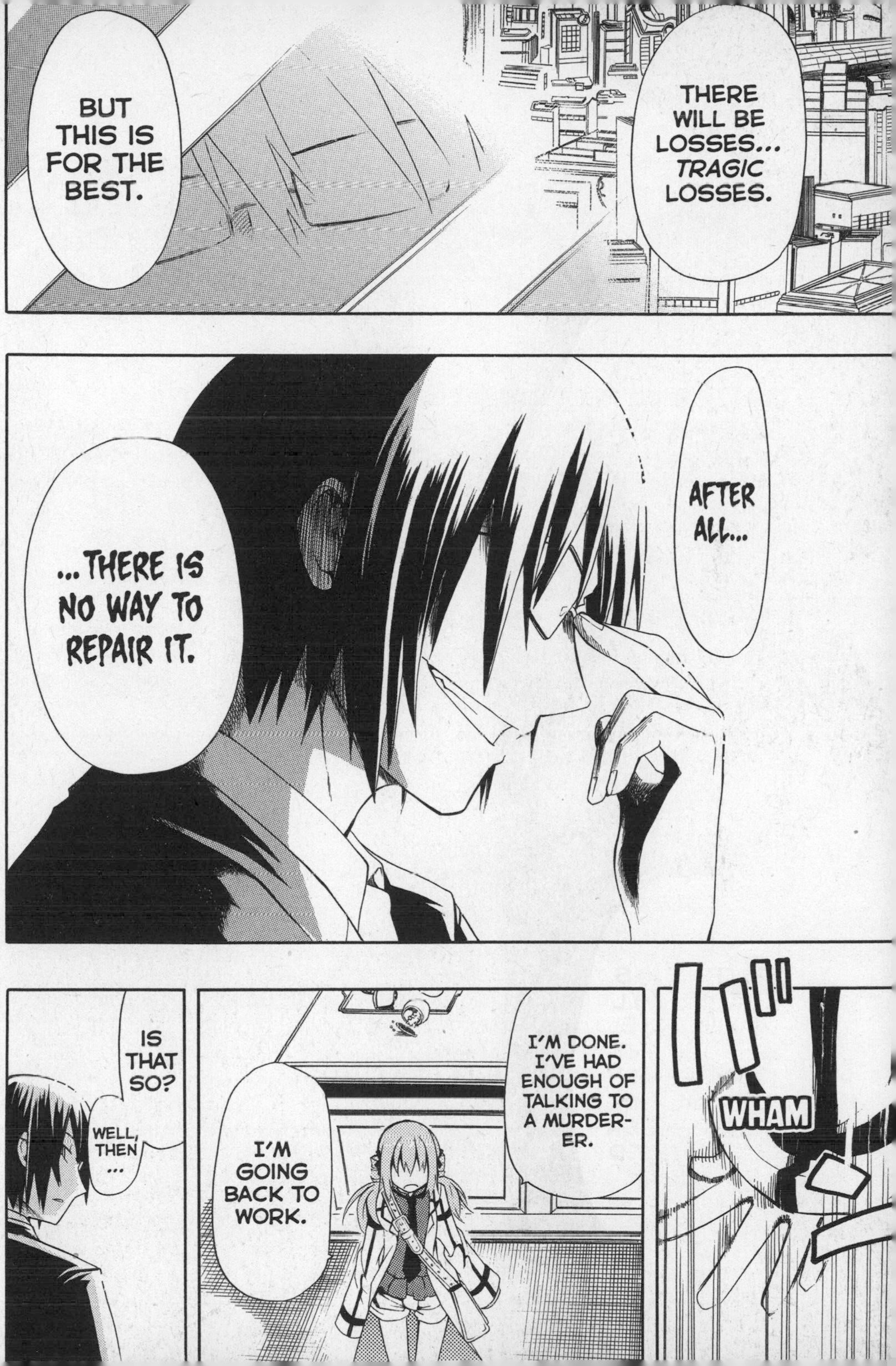
THERE WILL BE LOSSES... *TRAGIC* LOSSES.
BUT THIS IS FOR THE BEST.
AFTER ALL...
...THERE IS NO WAY TO REPAIR IT.
WHAM
I'M DONE. I'VE HAD ENOUGH OF TALKING TO A MURDER-ER.
I'M GOING BACK TO WORK.
IS THAT SO?
WELL, THEN ...

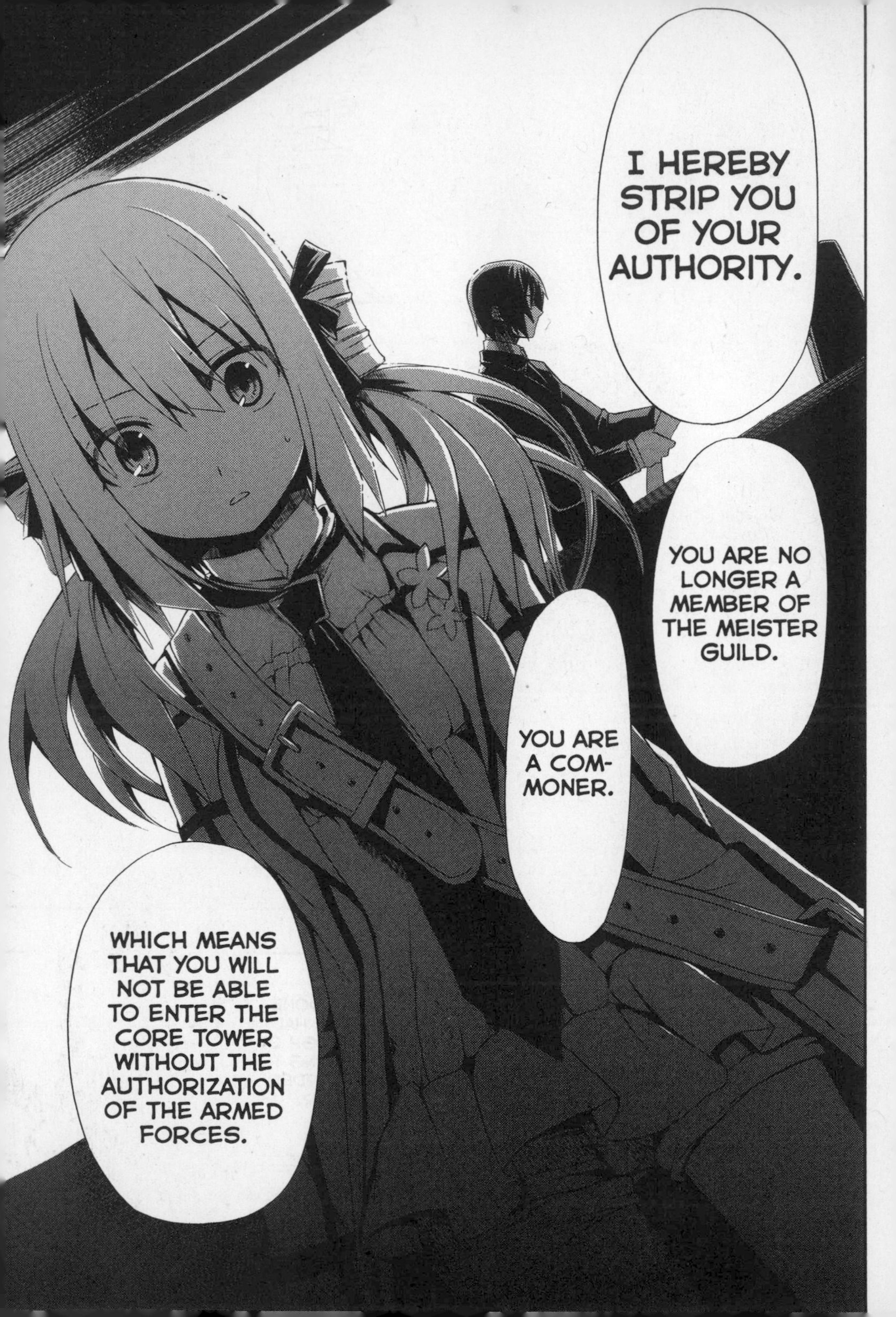
I HEREBY STRIP YOU OF YOUR AUTHORITY.
YOU ARE NO LONGER A MEMBER OF THE MEISTER GUILD.
YOU ARE A COM-MONER.
WHICH MEANS THAT YOU WILL NOT BE ABLE TO ENTER THE CORE TOWER WITHOUT THE AUTHORIZATION OF THE ARMED FORCES.

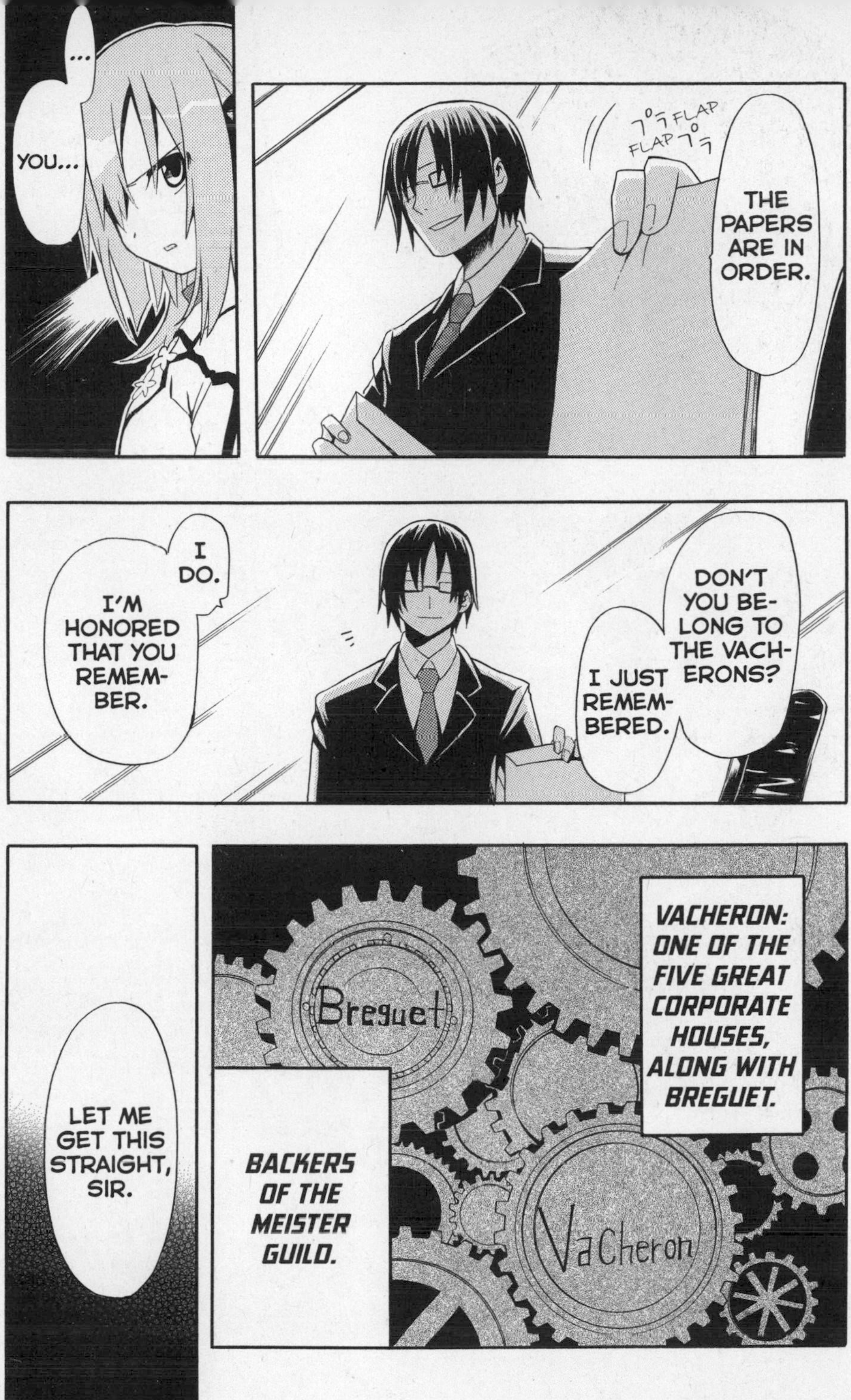
プラ FLAP FLAP プラ
THE PAPERS ARE IN ORDER.
...
YOU...
DON'T YOU BELONG TO THE VACHERONS?
I JUST REMEMBERED.
I DO.
I'M HONORED THAT YOU REMEMBER.
VACHERON: ONE OF THE FIVE GREAT CORPORATE HOUSES, ALONG WITH BREGUET.
Breguet
BACKERS OF THE MEISTER GUILD.
Vacheron
LET ME GET THIS STRAIGHT, SIR.

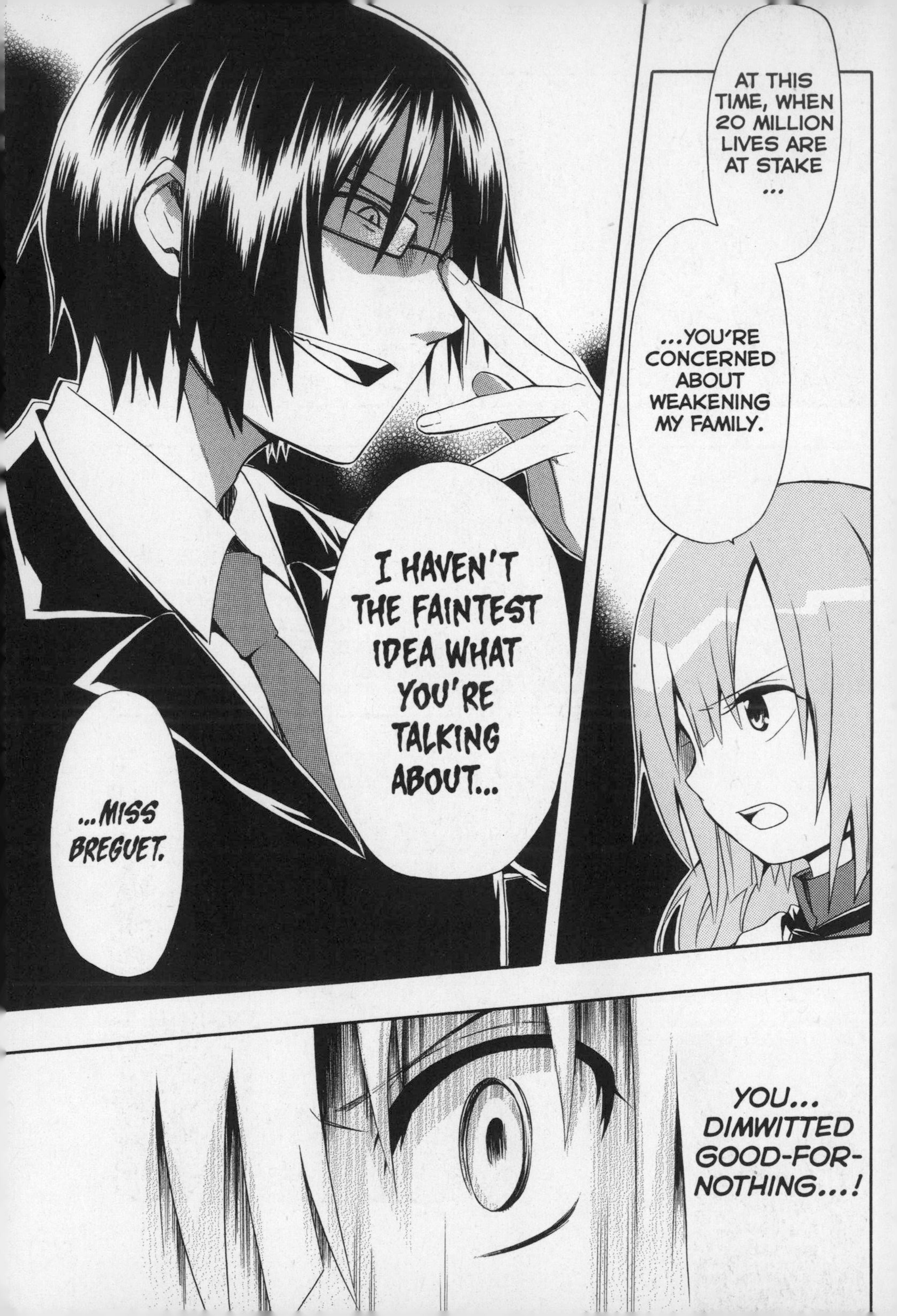
AT THIS TIME, WHEN 20 MILLION LIVES ARE AT STAKE ...
...YOU'RE CONCERNED ABOUT WEAKENING MY FAMILY.
I HAVEN'T THE FAINTEST IDEA WHAT YOU'RE TALKING ABOUT...
...MISS BREGUET.
YOU... DIMWITTED GOOD-FOR-NOTHING...!

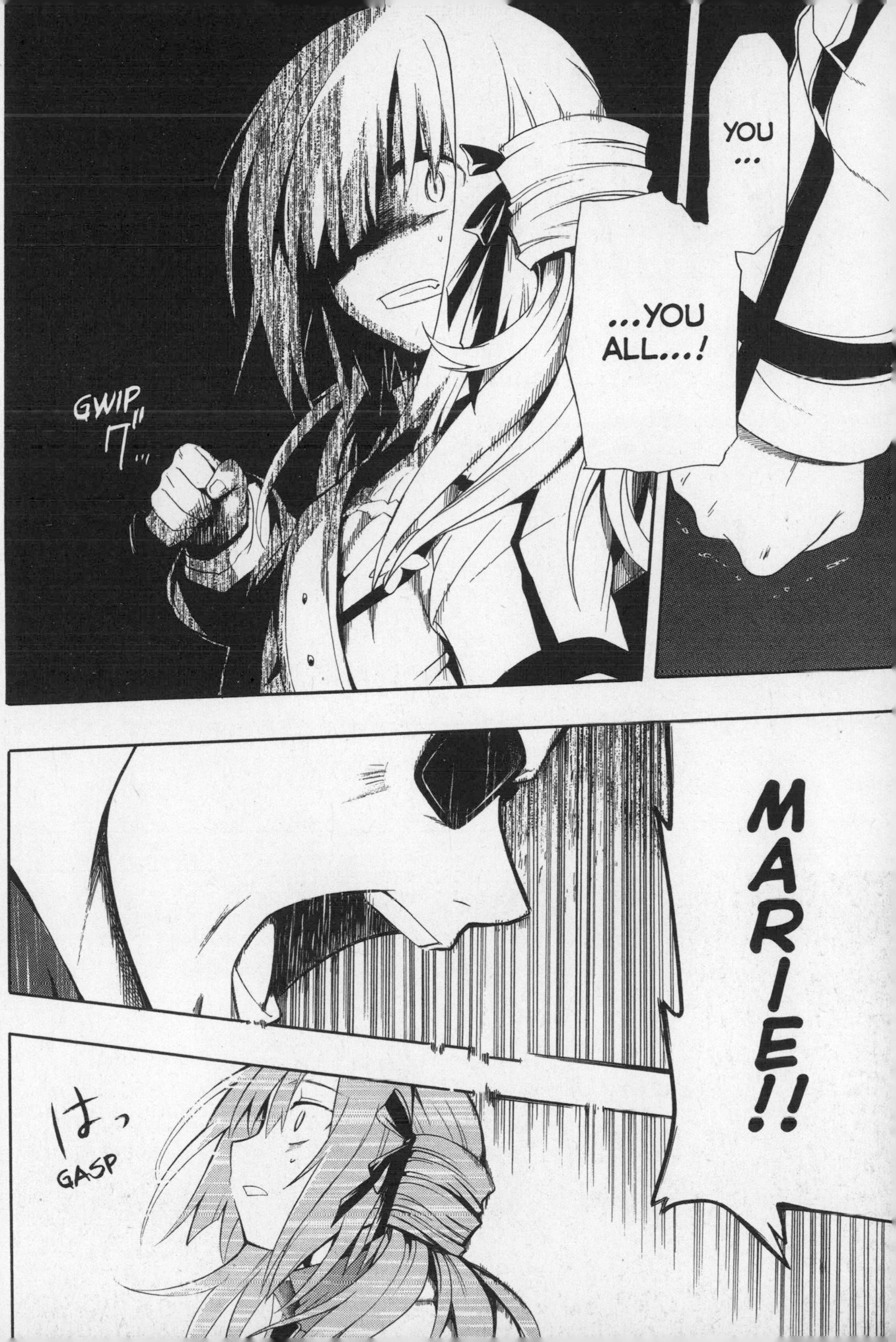
YOU ...
...YOU ALL...!
GWIP
ワ゛...
MARIE!!
はっ
GASP

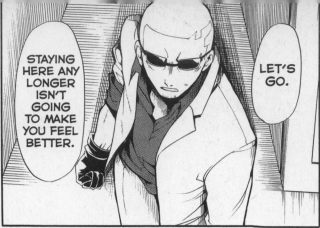

STAYING HERE ANY LONGER ISN'T GOING TO MAKE YOU FEEL BETTER.

LET'S GO.

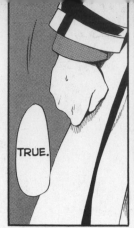

TRUE.

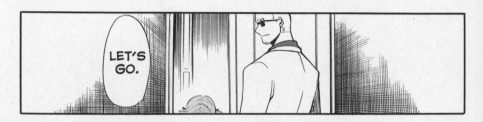

LET'S GO.

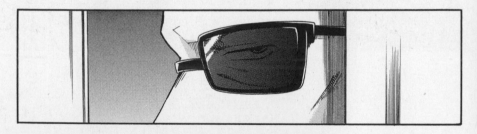

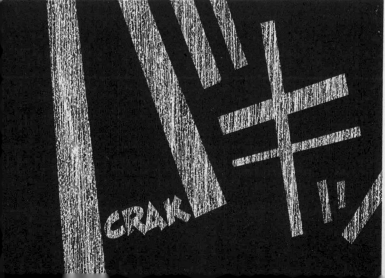

CRAK

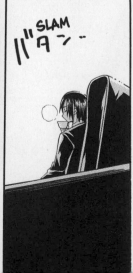

SLAM

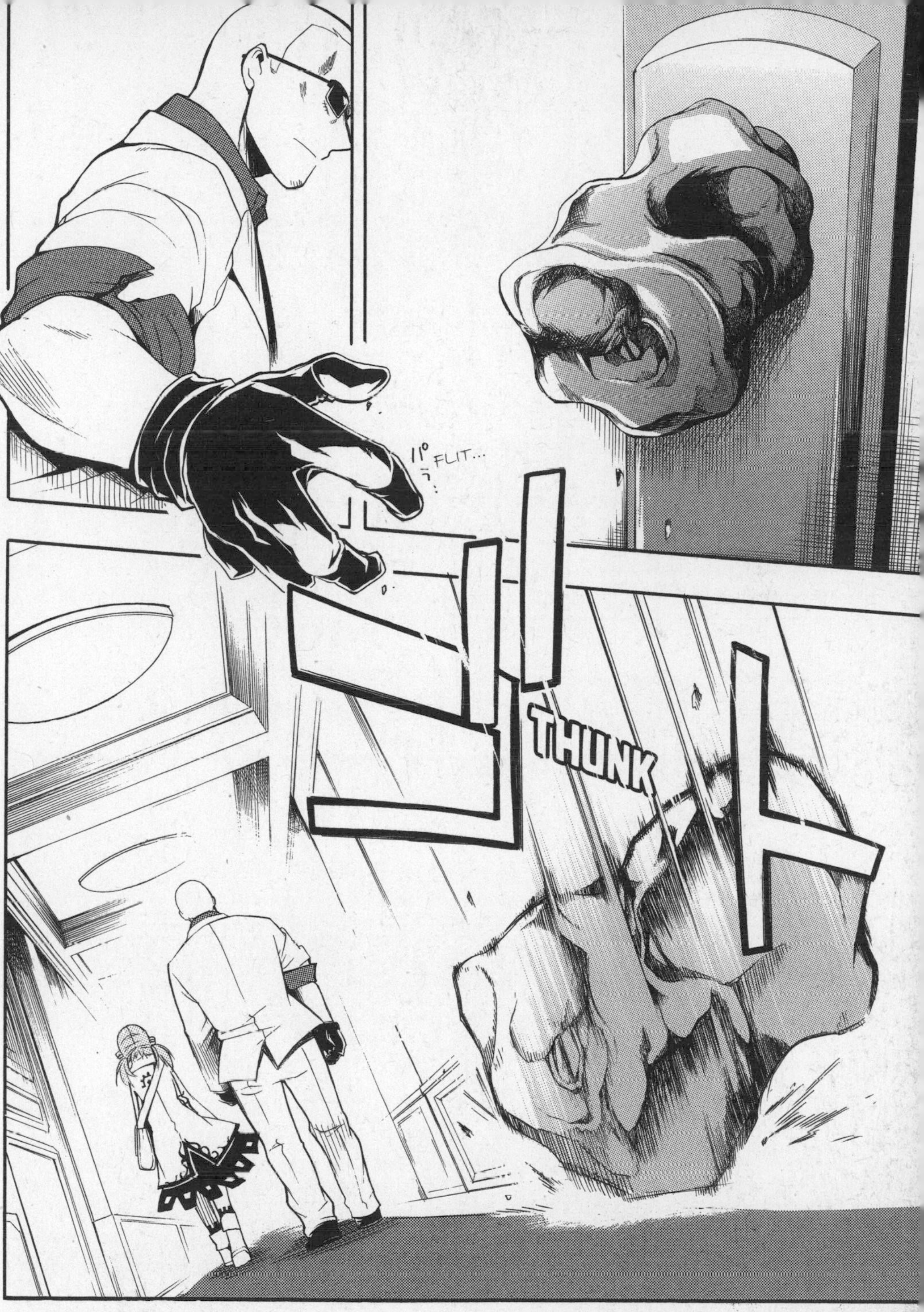

FLIT...
THUNK

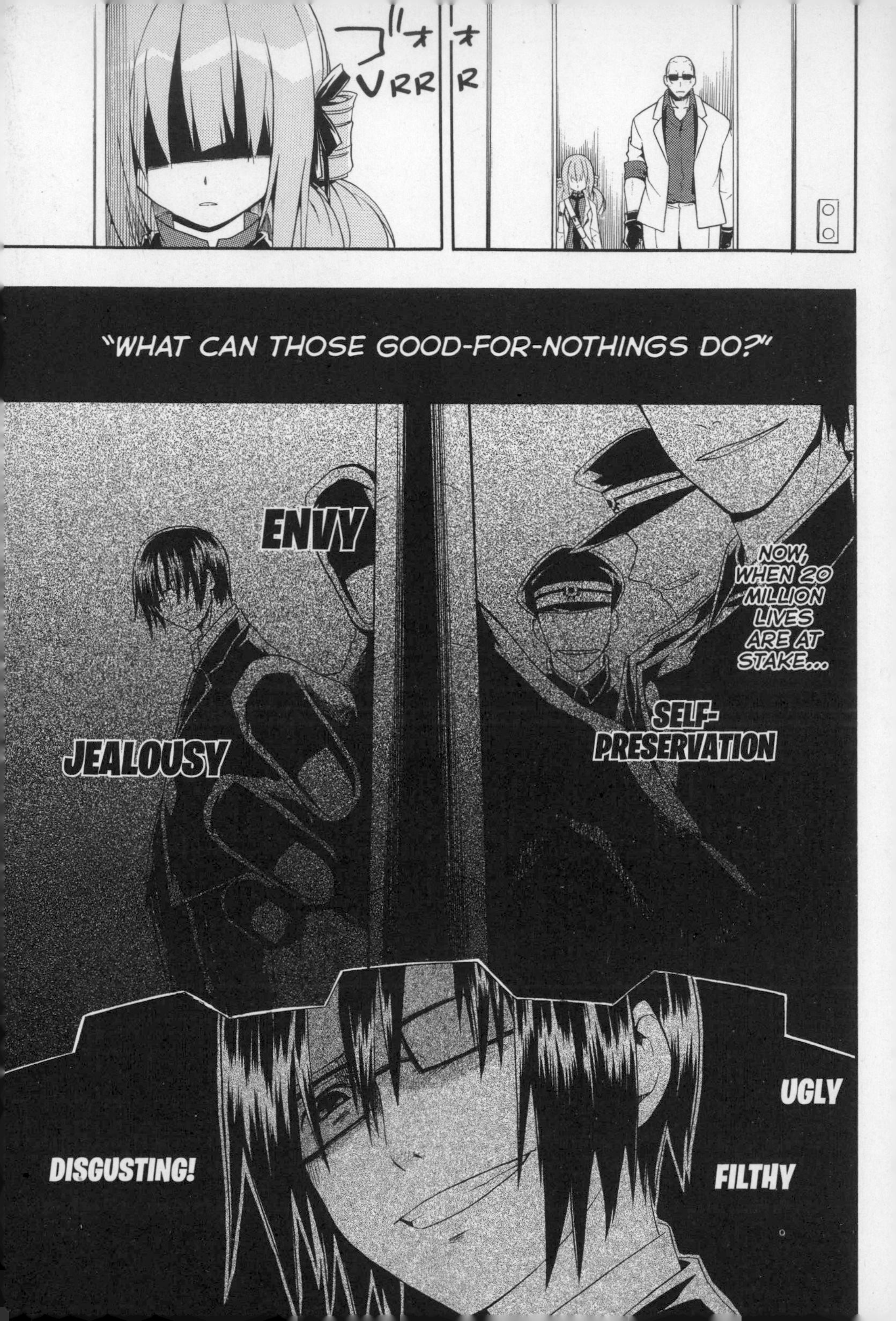

ゴォォ
VRRRR
"WHAT CAN THOSE GOOD-FOR-NOTHINGS DO?"
NOW, WHEN 20 MILLION LIVES ARE AT STAKE...
SELF-PRESERVATION
ENVY
JEALOUSY
UGLY
FILTHY
DISGUSTING!

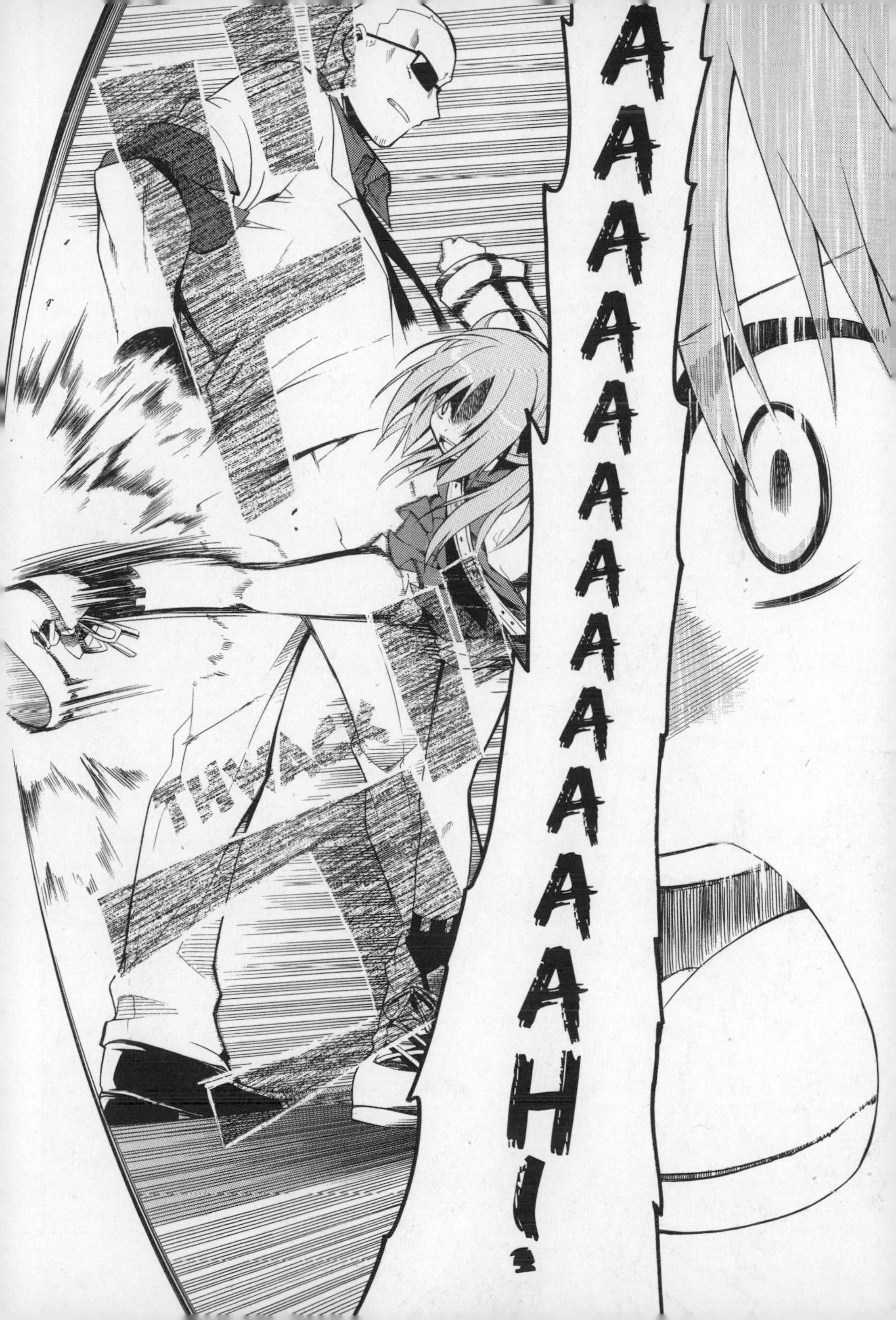
AAAAAAAAAAAAH!
THWACK

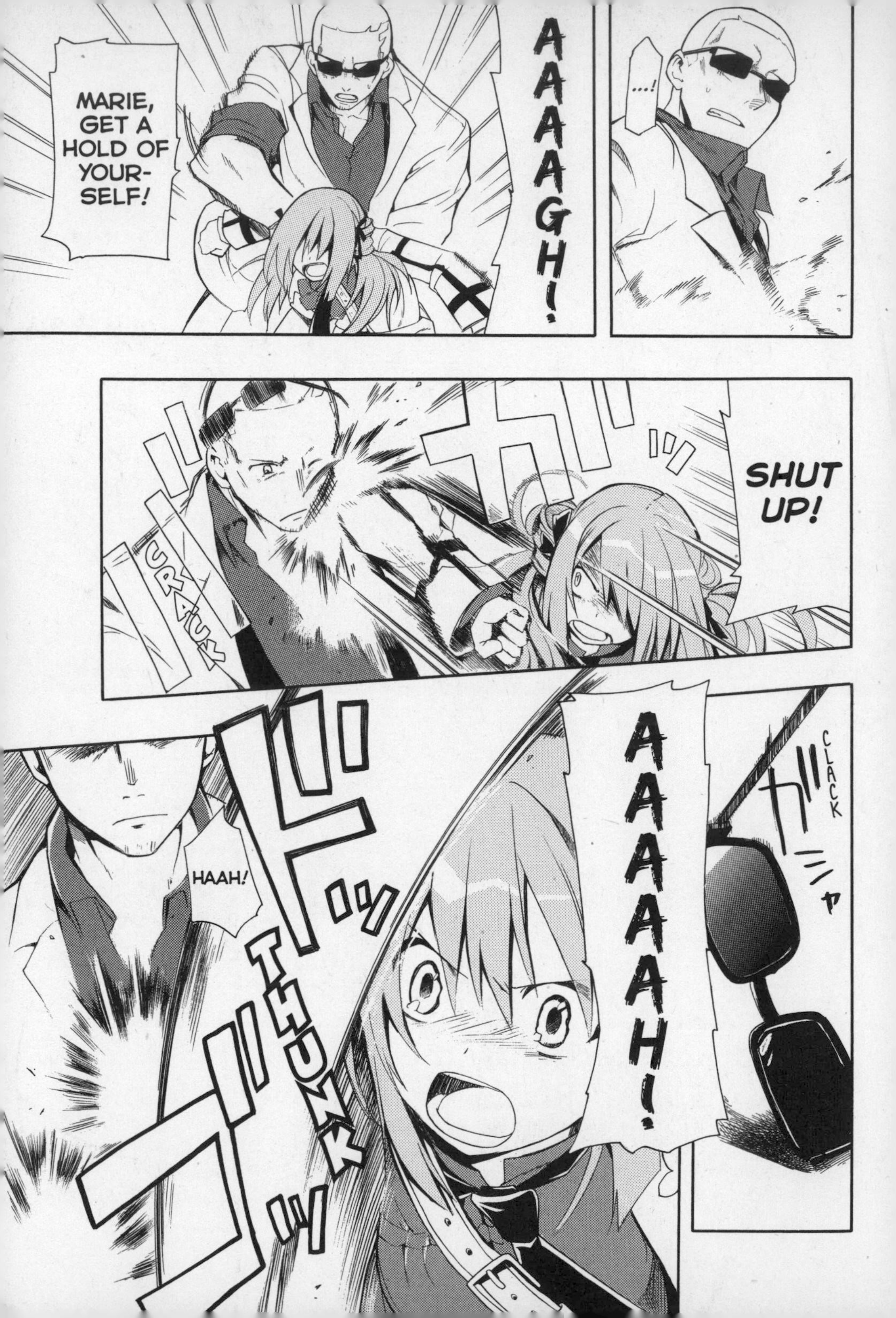
...!
AAAAGH!
MARIE, GET A HOLD OF YOUR-SELF!
SHUT UP!
CRAUK
CLACK
AAAAAH!
HAAH!
THUNK

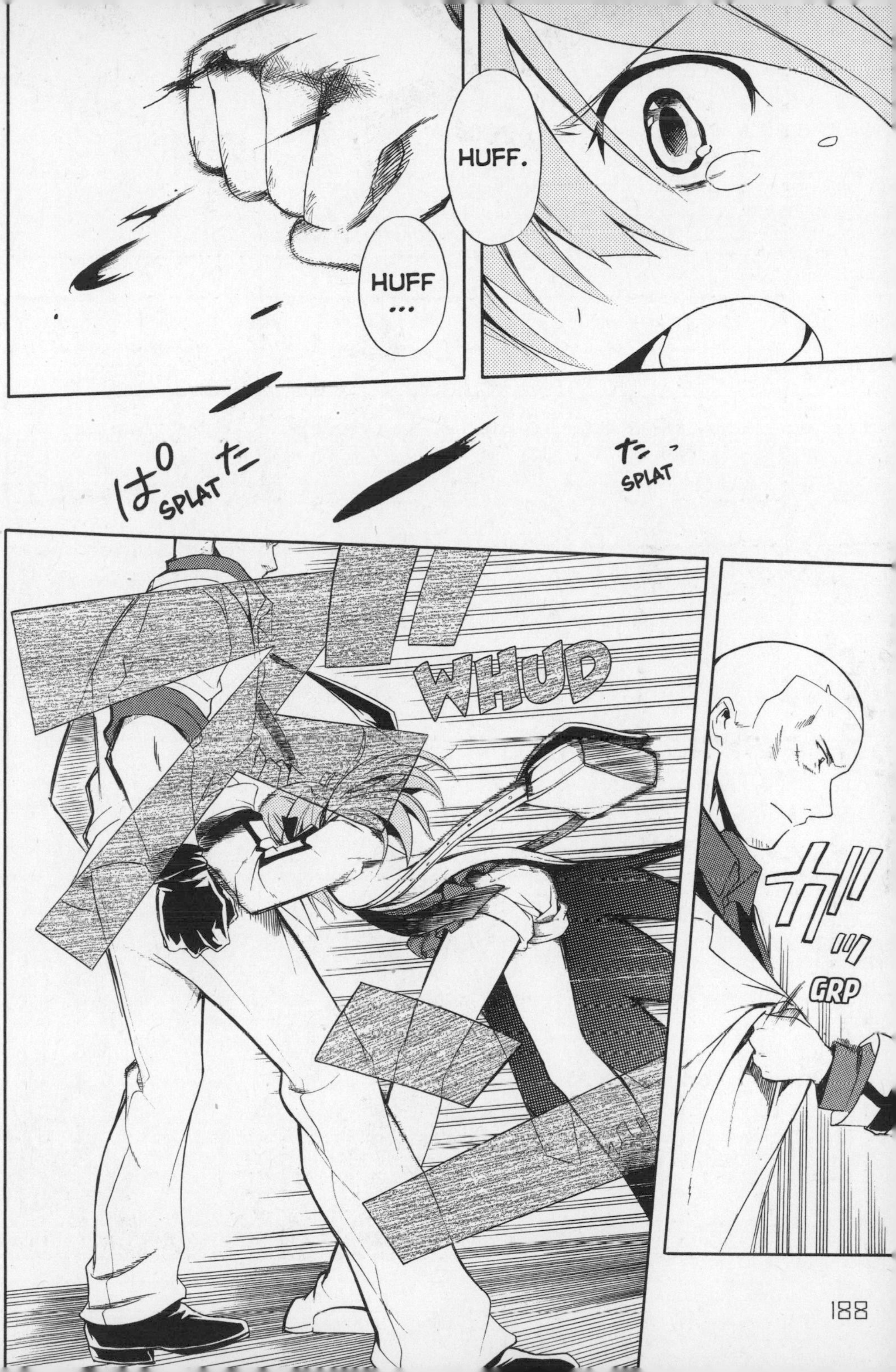
HUFF.
HUFF ...
たっ
SPLAT
ぱ
SPLAT
た
ガッ
GRP
WHUD

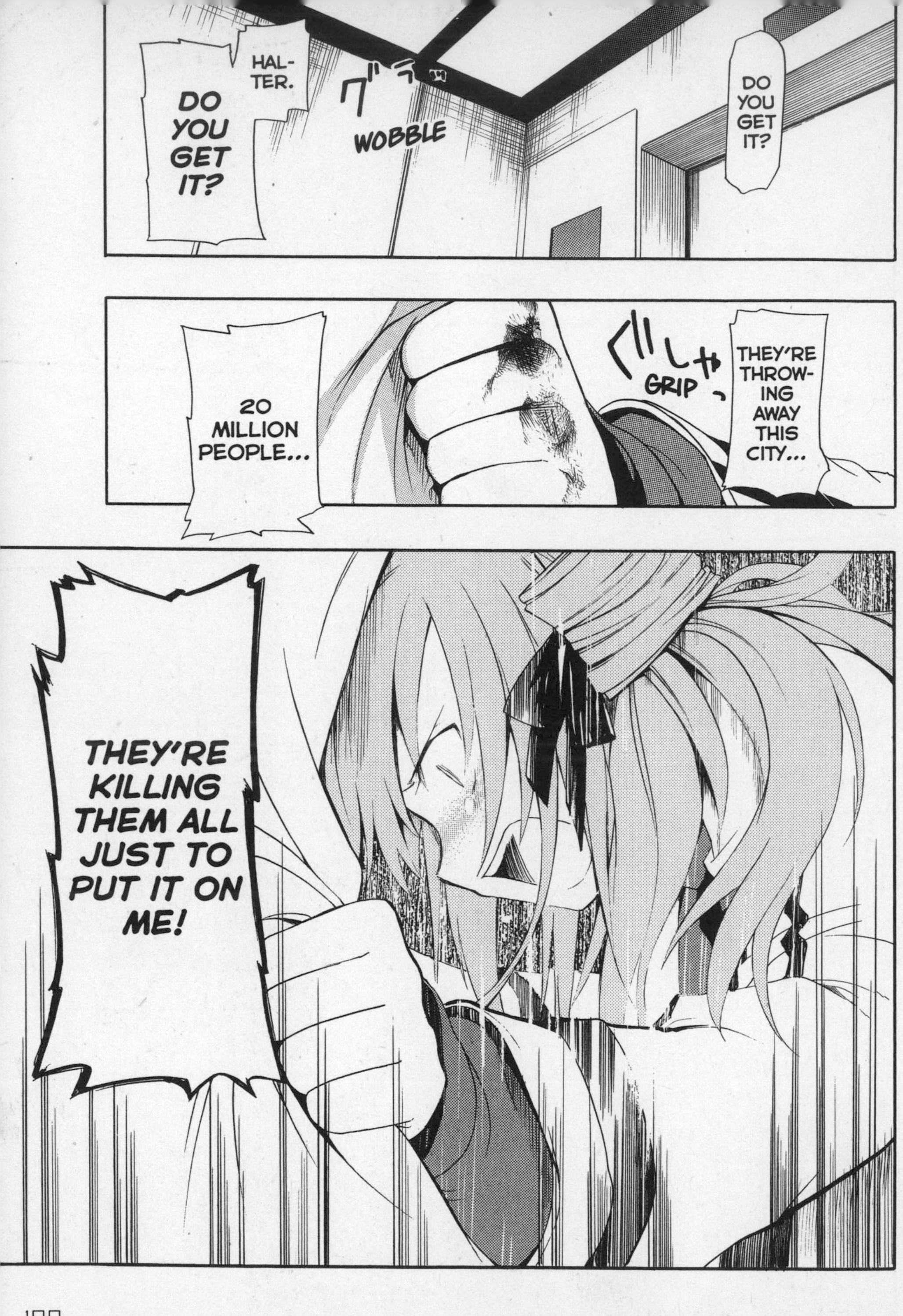
DO YOU GET IT?
WOBBLE
HAL-TER.
DO YOU GET IT?
THEY'RE THROWING AWAY THIS CITY...
GRIP
20 MILLION PEOPLE...
THEY'RE KILLING THEM ALL JUST TO PUT IT ON ME!

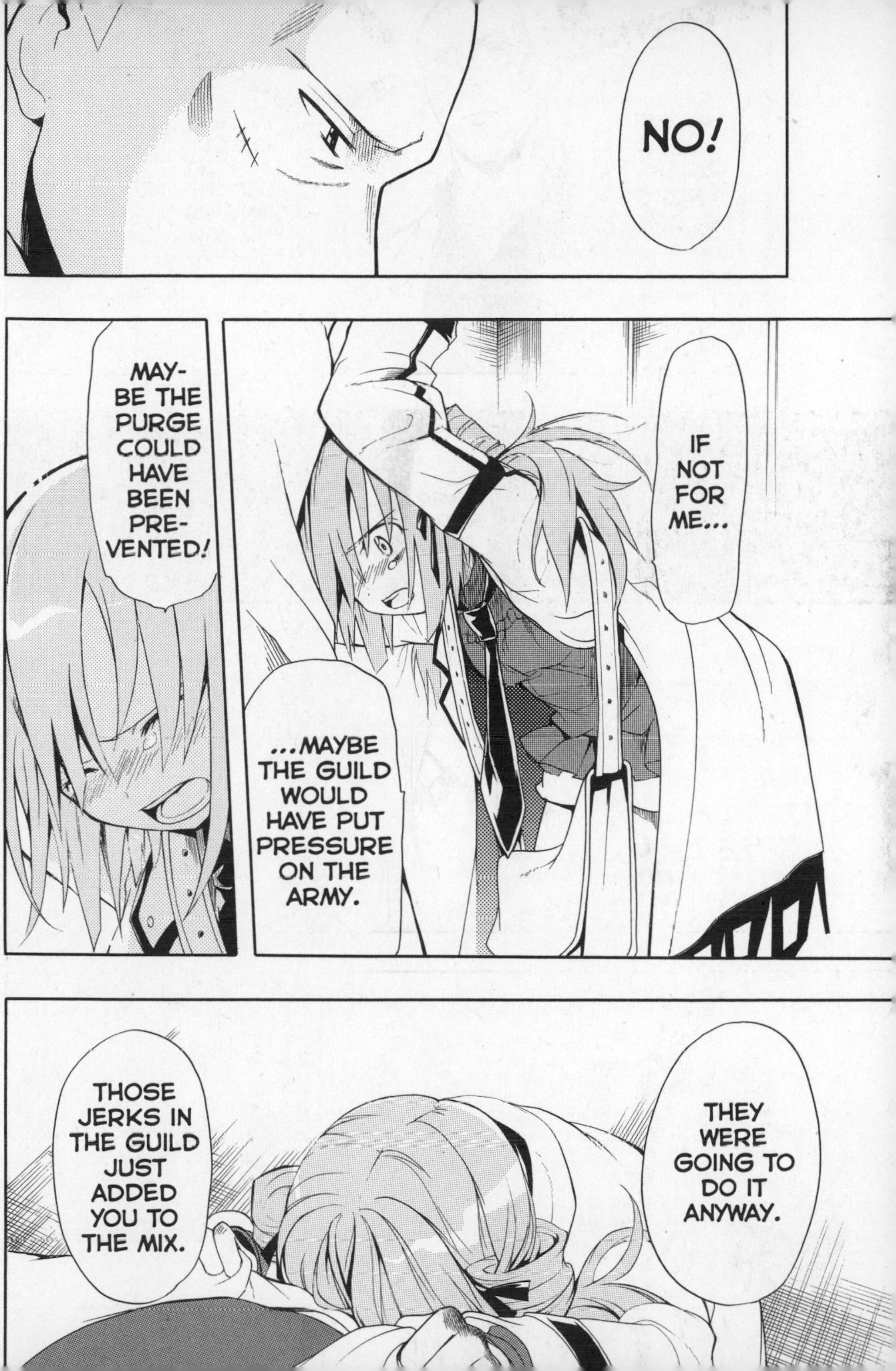
NO!
IF NOT FOR ME...
...MAYBE THE GUILD WOULD HAVE PUT PRESSURE ON THE ARMY.
MAY-BE THE PURGE COULD HAVE BEEN PRE-VENTED!
THEY WERE GOING TO DO IT ANYWAY.
THOSE JERKS IN THE GUILD JUST ADDED YOU TO THE MIX.

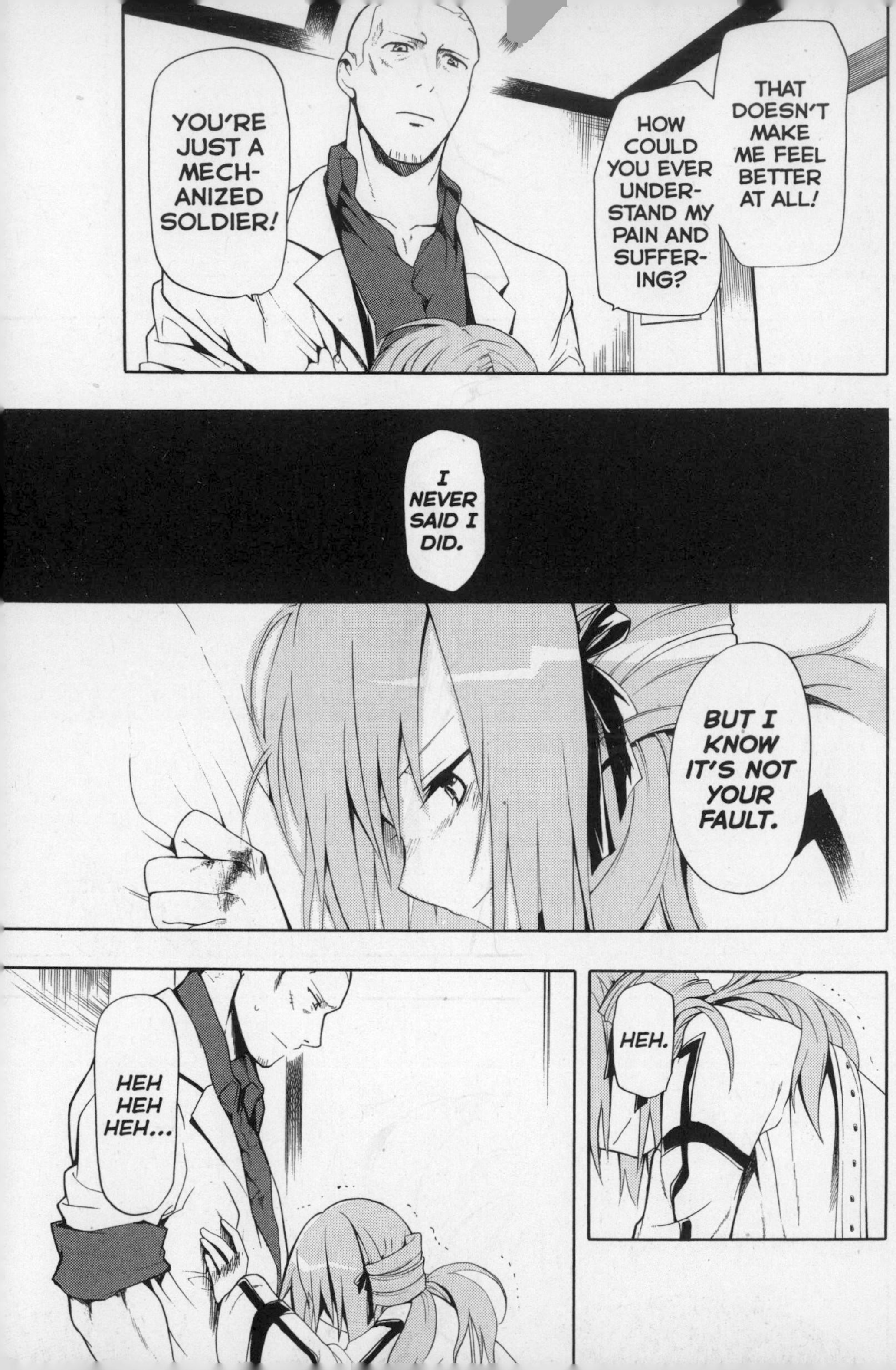
THAT DOESN'T MAKE ME FEEL BETTER AT ALL!
HOW COULD YOU EVER UNDERSTAND MY PAIN AND SUFFERING?
YOU'RE JUST A MECHANIZED SOLDIER!
I NEVER SAID I DID.
BUT I KNOW IT'S NOT YOUR FAULT.
HEH.
HEH HEH HEH...

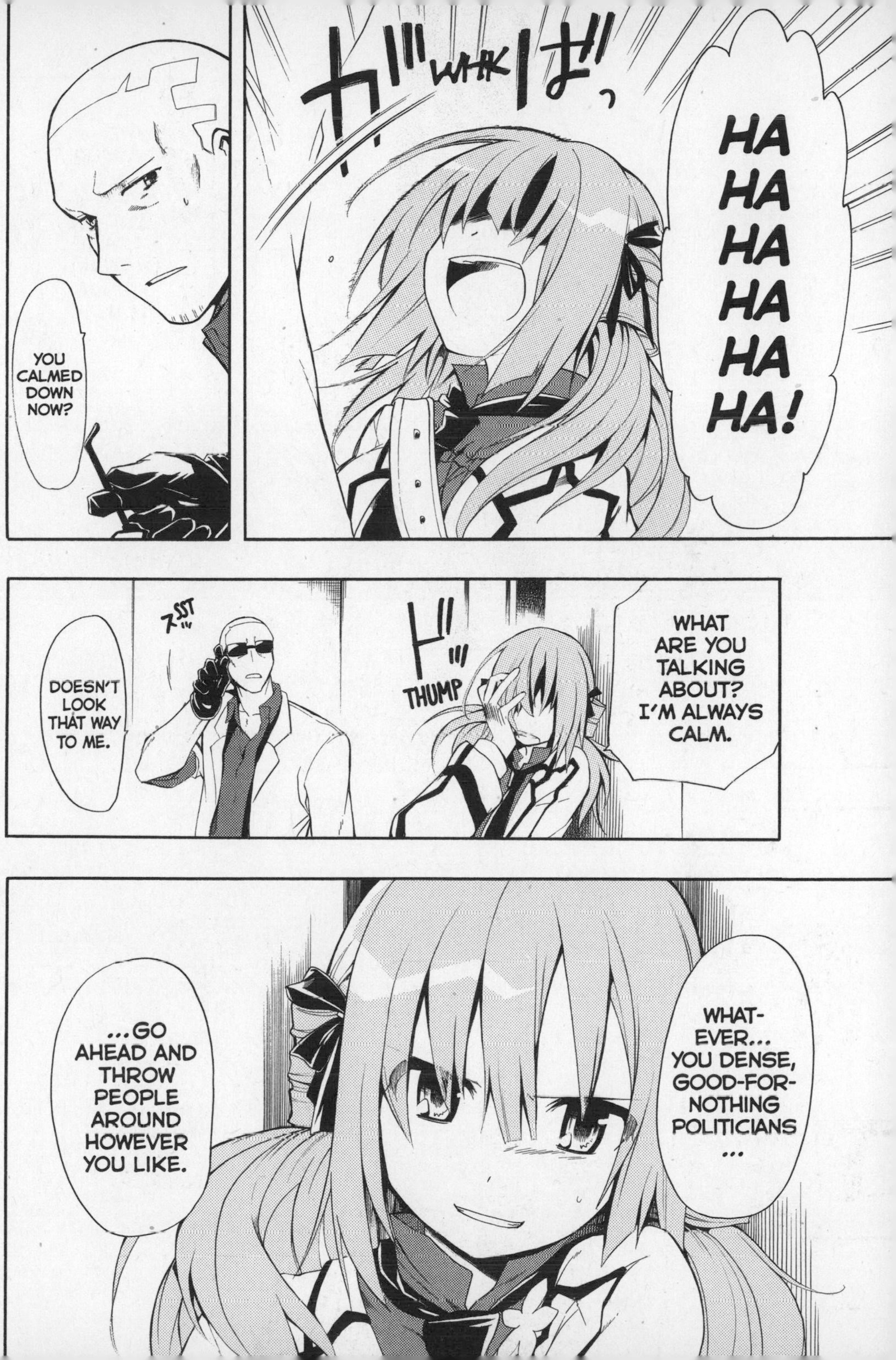
WHAK
HA HA HA HA HA HA HA!
YOU CALMED DOWN NOW?
WHAT ARE YOU TALKING ABOUT? I'M ALWAYS CALM.
THUMP
SST
DOESN'T LOOK THAT WAY TO ME.
WHAT-EVER... YOU DENSE, GOOD-FOR-NOTHING POLITICIANS...
...GO AHEAD AND THROW PEOPLE AROUND HOWEVER YOU LIKE.

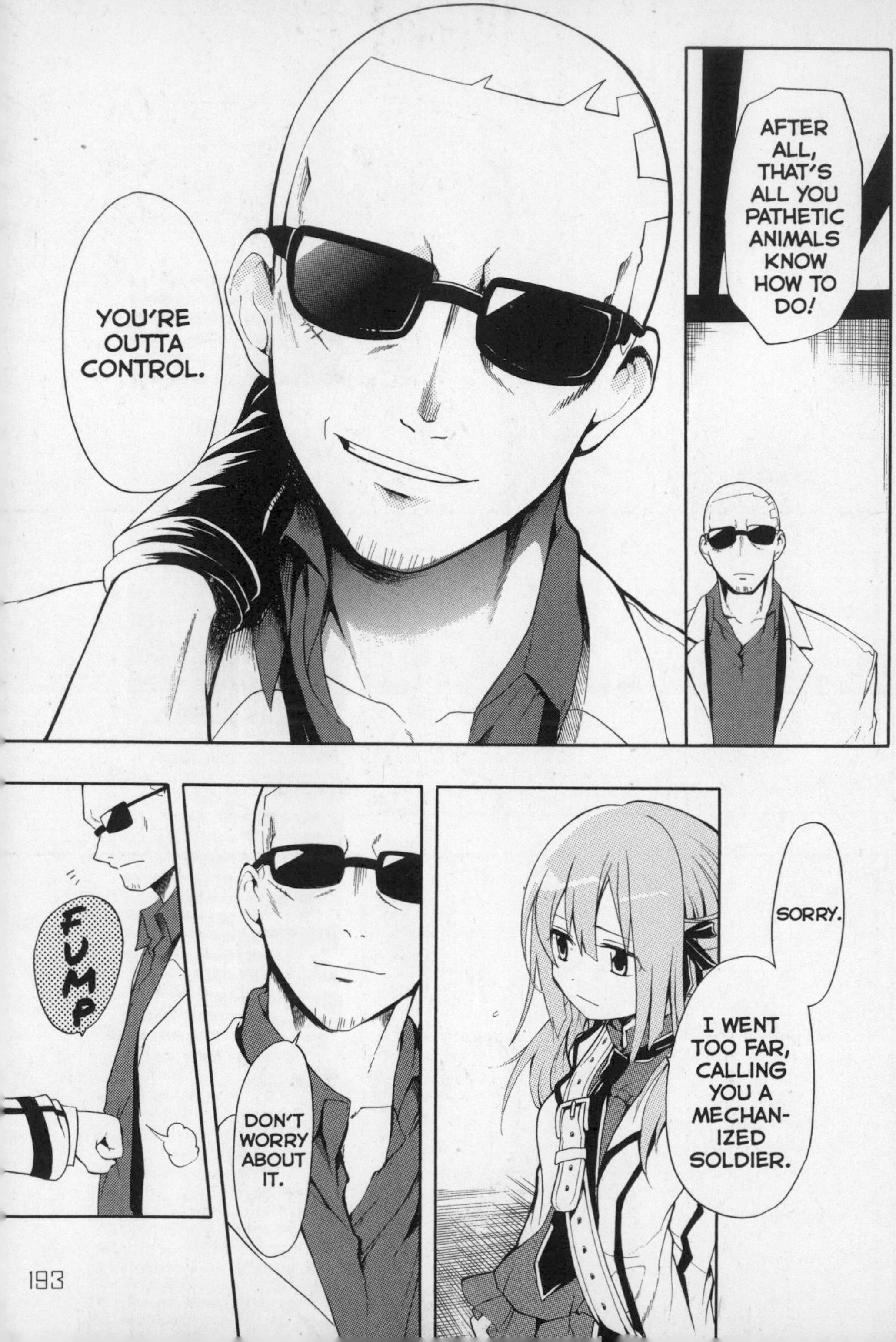
AFTER ALL, THAT'S ALL YOU PATHETIC ANIMALS KNOW HOW TO DO!
YOU'RE OUTTA CONTROL.
SORRY.
I WENT TOO FAR, CALLING YOU A MECHAN-IZED SOLDIER.
DON'T WORRY ABOUT IT.
FUMP

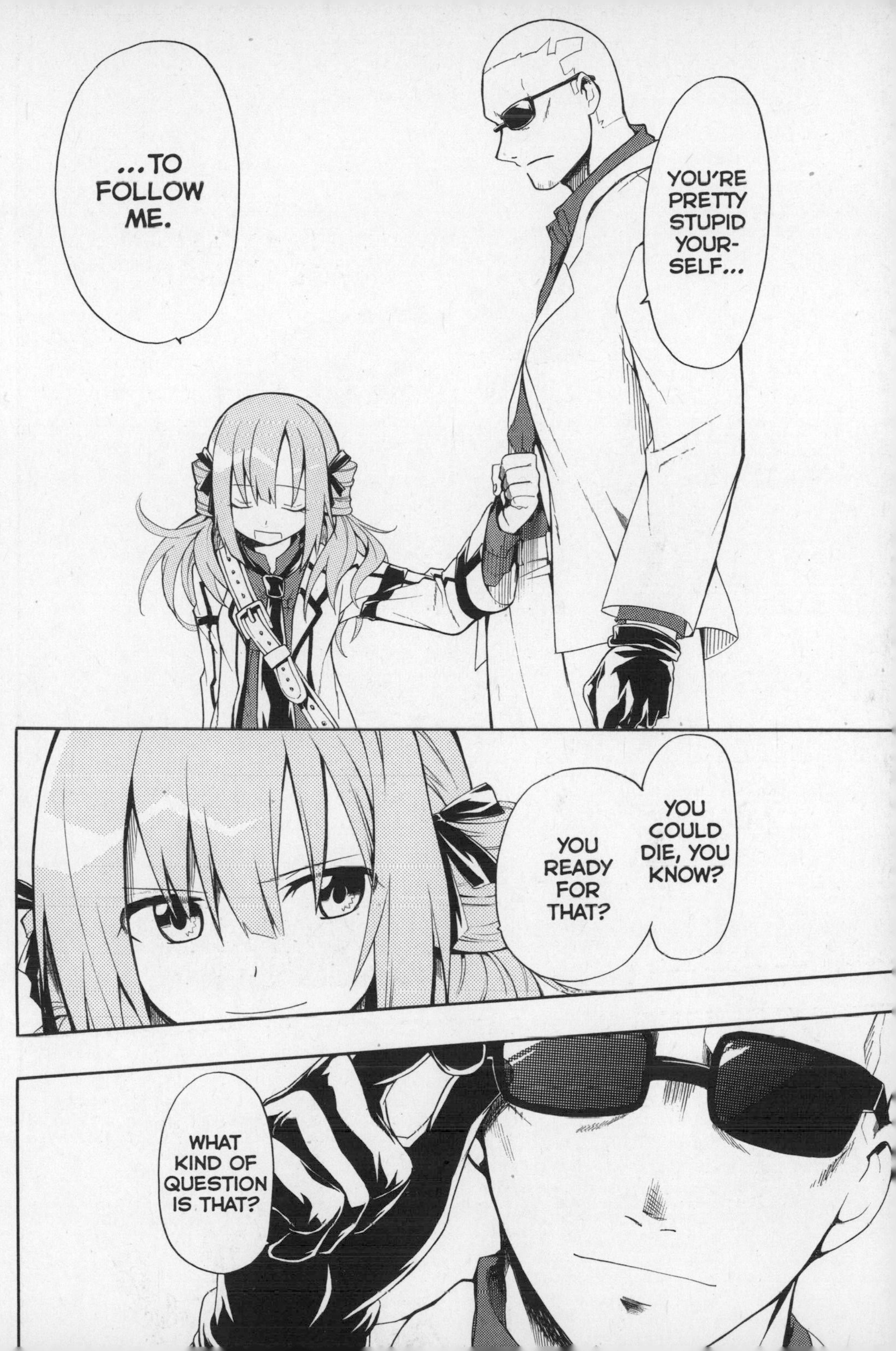
YOU'RE PRETTY STUPID YOURSELF...
...TO FOLLOW ME.
YOU COULD DIE, YOU KNOW?
YOU READY FOR THAT?
WHAT KIND OF QUESTION IS THAT?

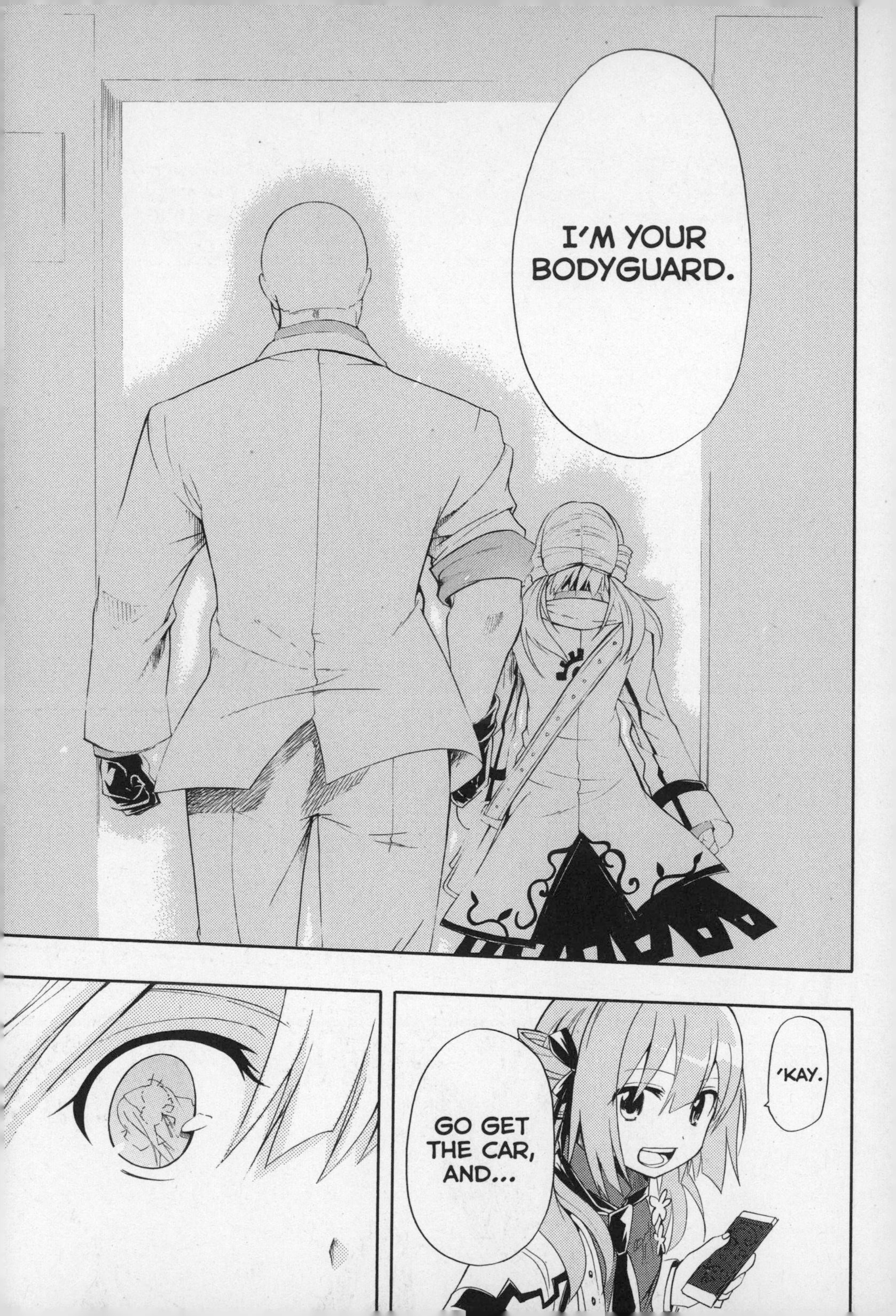
I'M YOUR BODYGUARD.
'KAY.
GO GET THE CAR, AND...

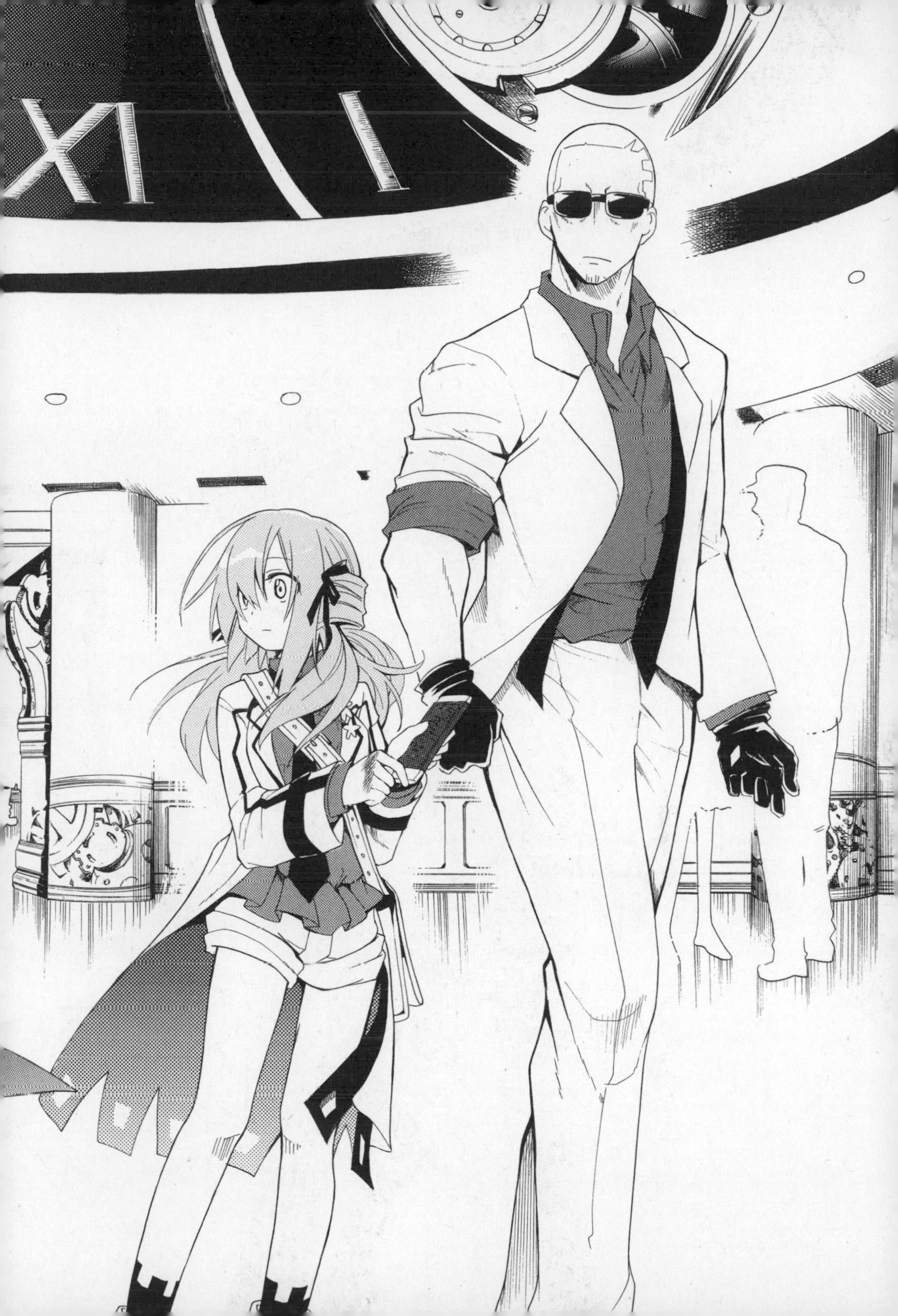

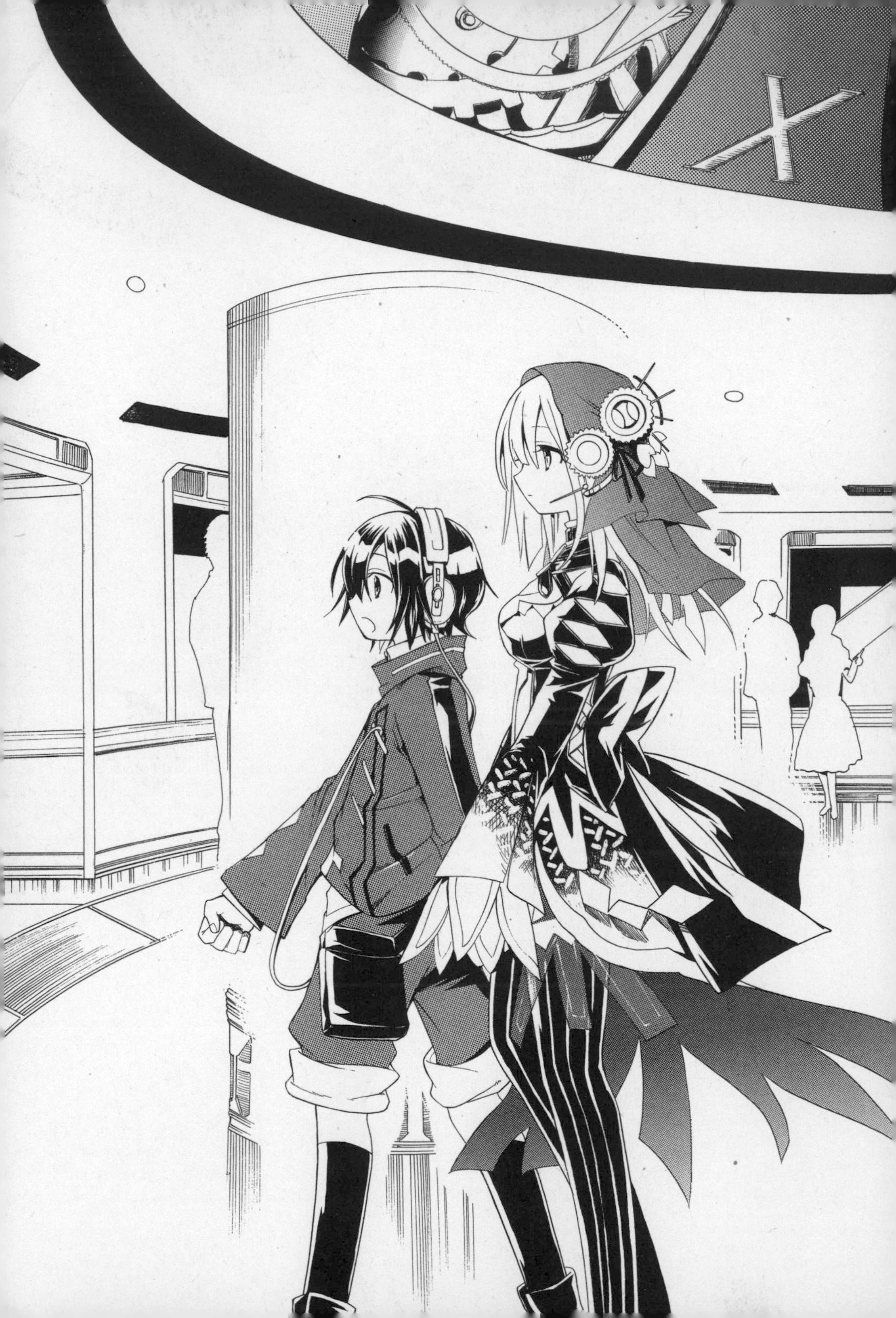

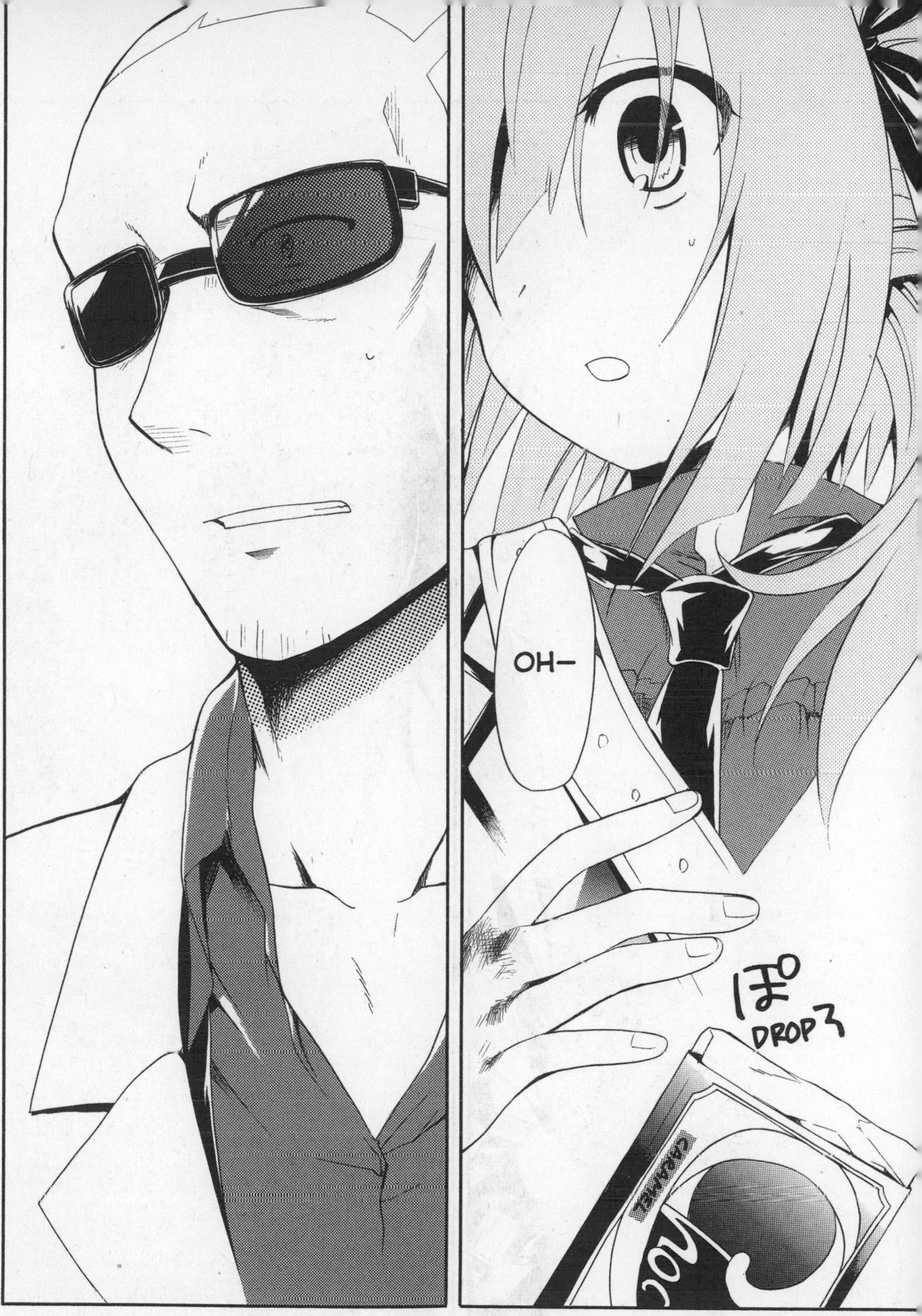
OH—
ぽ
DROP
CARAMEL

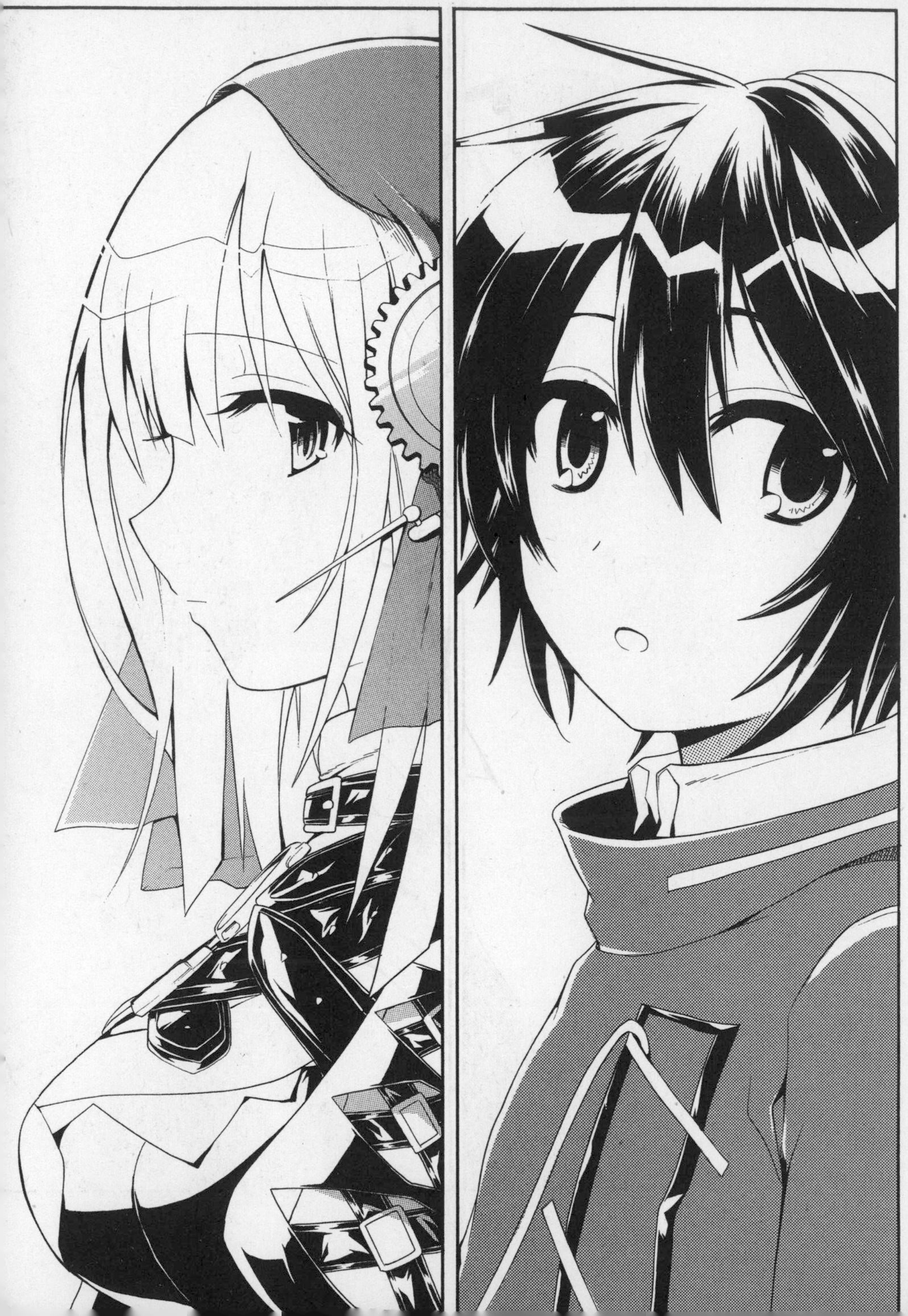

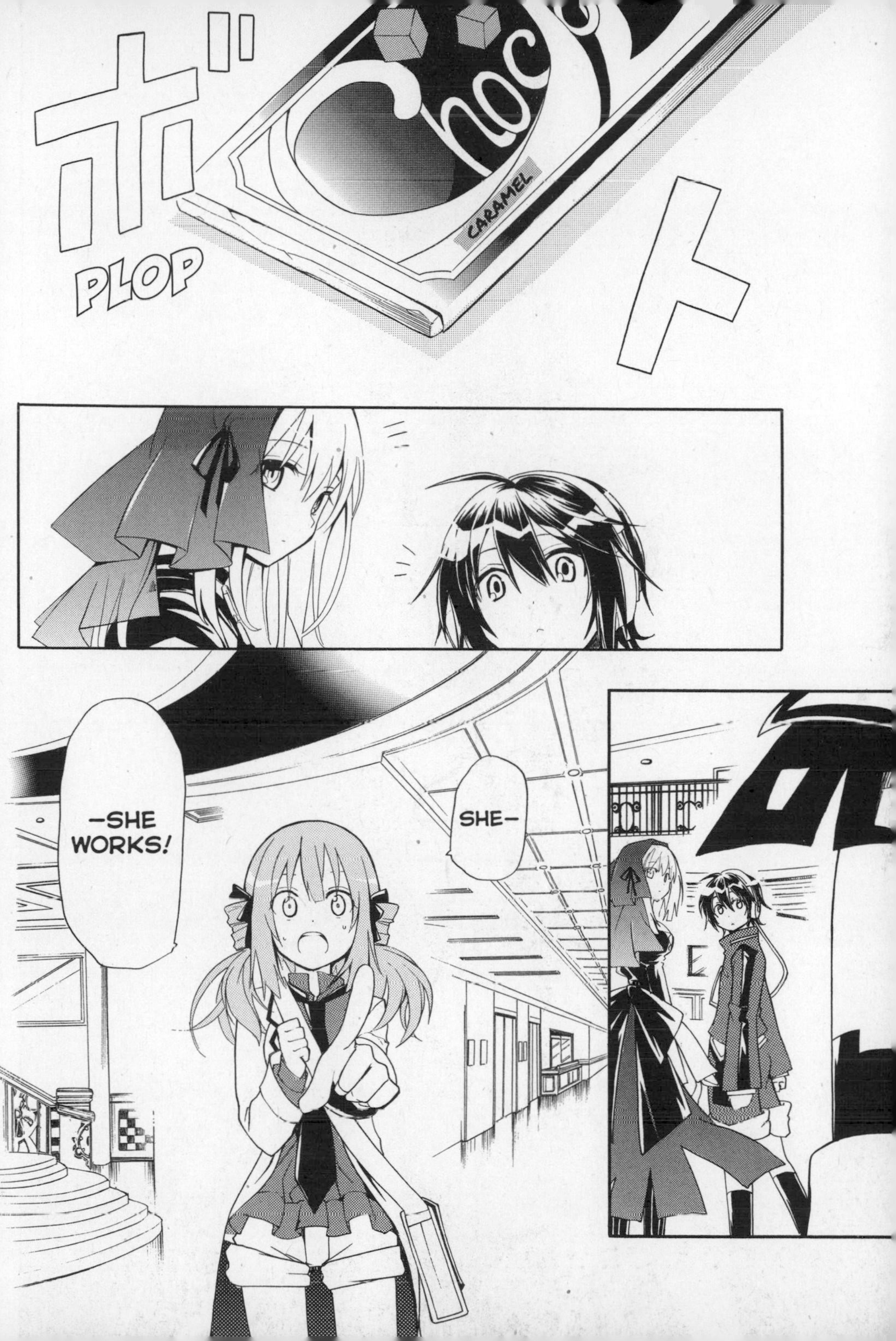
ボト
PLOP
CARAMEL
SHE—
—SHE WORKS!

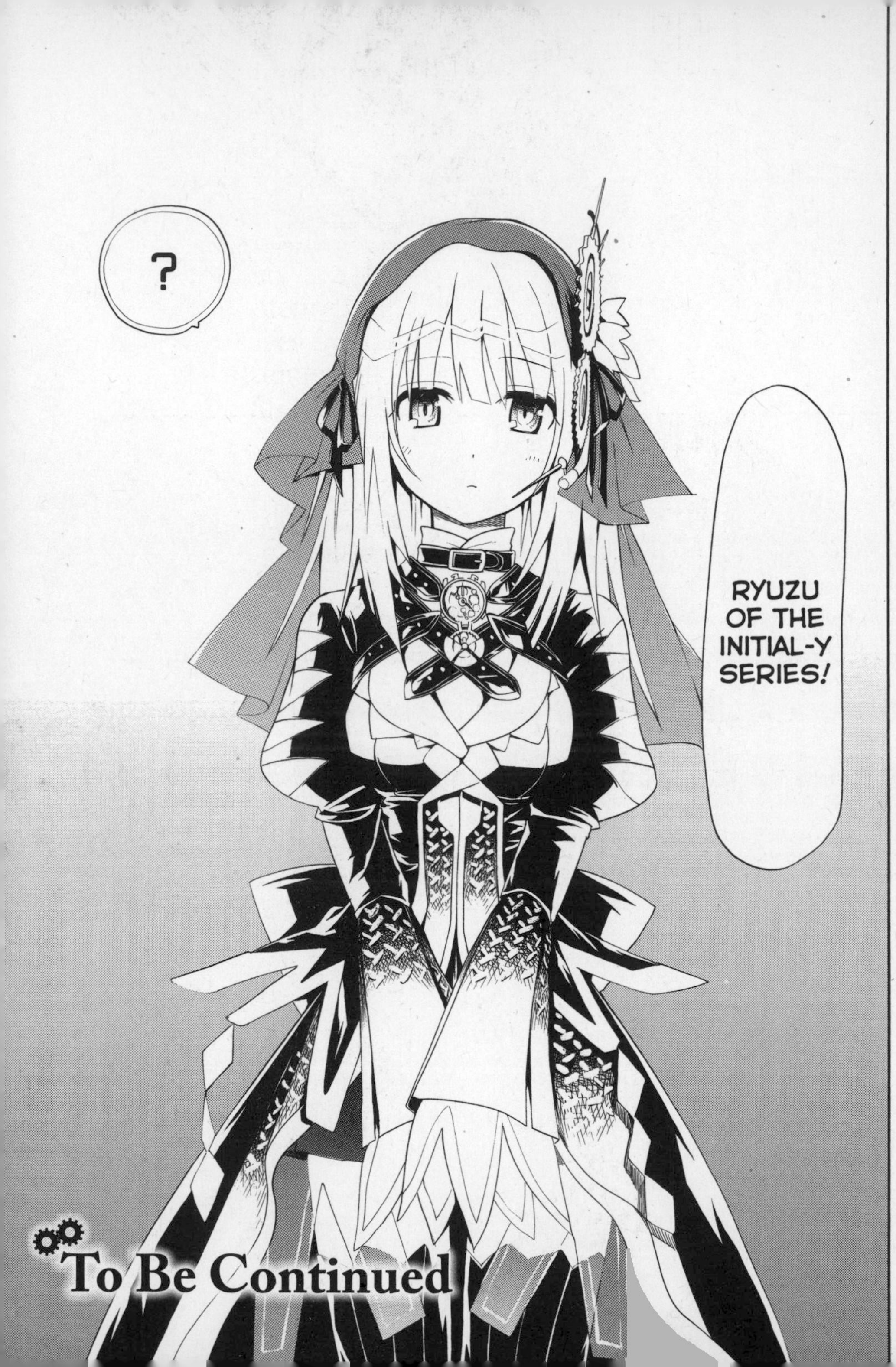

RYUZU OF THE INITIAL-Y SERIES!
?
To Be Continued

Yuu Kamiya & Tsubaki Himana Afterword

TH: Uhh, ahem. We hereby celebrate the first volume of the manga version of *Clockwork Planet*. A big thank you to everyone who's bought it! I hope you'll continue to read it, and also check out the original—

YK: What a square. Boring.

TH: Uh, well...but to go straight into jokes...you know?

YK: I guess. But, man, they really grilled us about the setting details for the manga, didn't they?

TH: Umm, yeah. I couldn't believe how you rolled out all that stuff I've never heard of. And it's not like we've got a bible for it or—

YK: What? Sure we do.

TH: Huh? **YK:** Huh?

TH: Huh? Wait, wait, we do?!

YK: Well, yeah. In my head.

TH: Are you trying to pick a fight with your co-author? Anyway, I remember when you saw the designs, you were like, "Oh, so this is what the world is like." I have to question whether you actually have it in your head in the first place.

YK: Come on, man. A wise man once told me, "Show, don't tell, if you want your readers to be surprised." That's why I've never made a bible.

TH: What's the point of surprising your co-author? Wait a sec, do you actually know what the rest of the Initial-Y series looks like already?

YK: What? Sure I do. All of them.

TH: All right! Let's get writing that out, shall we? You're really killing me here!

YK: Sure, whatever, but hey, isn't the manga going to catch up with us at this rate?

TH: Huh? **YK:** Huh?

YK: I mean, look, if volumes keep coming out every four months, that's like, way too fast. Dude, how many months did it take you to get from Volume 1 to Volume 2 of the novels?

TH: S-seven months, I guess...

YK: And how long are you planning to take on Volume 3, buddy?

TH: W-well... Hey! We're passing these books back and forth! Isn't it your responsibility, too?

YK: Sure, so you know what that means—

TH/YK: Kuro, please slow down the *(The rest of this afterword has been omitted at the discretion of the editor.)*
[Kuro-san]

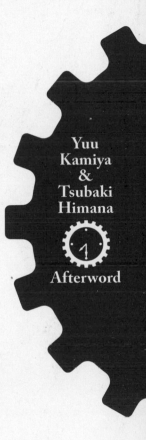

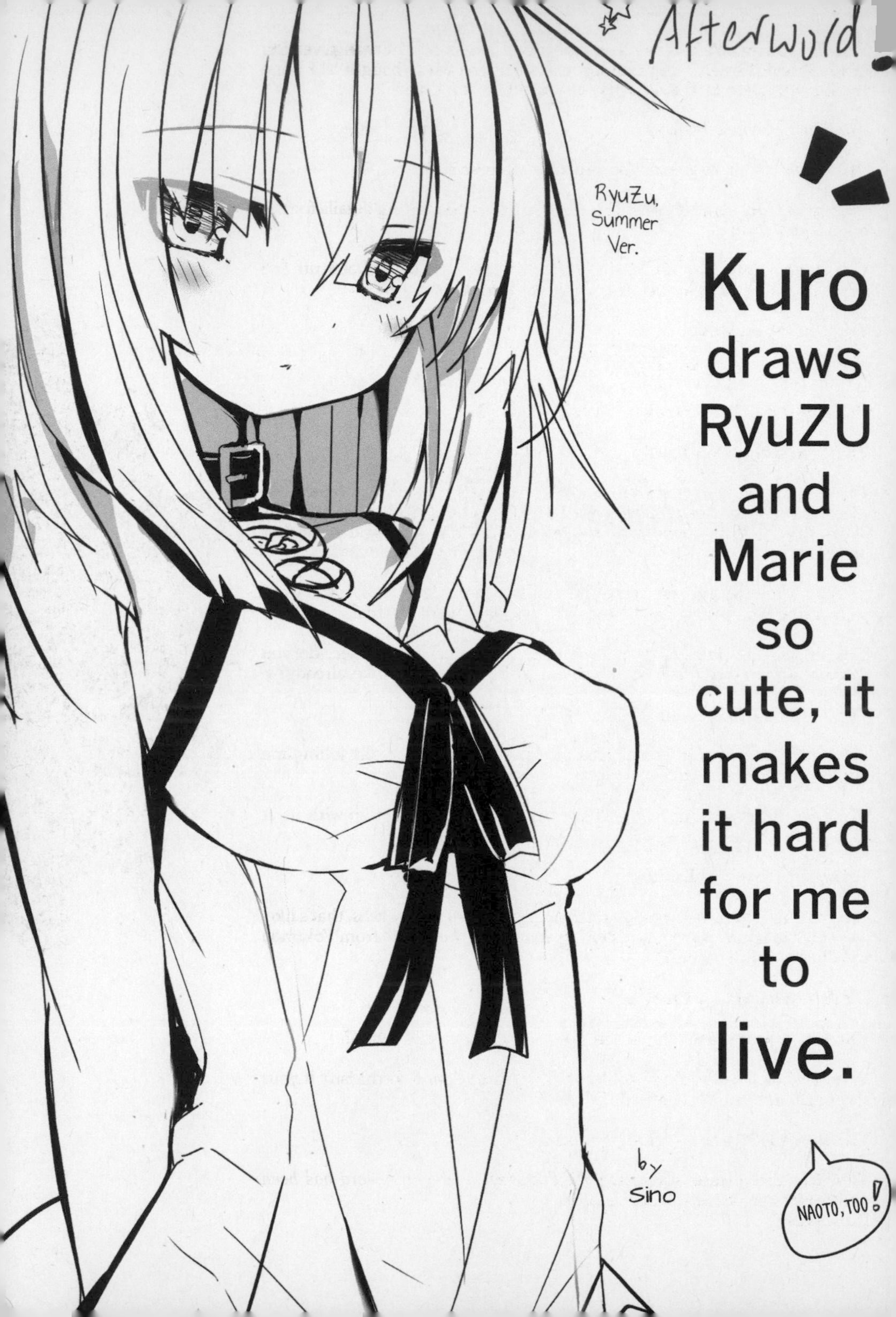
Afterword!
RyuZu, Summer Ver.
Kuro draws RyuZU and Marie so cute, it makes it hard for me to live.
by Sino
NAOTO, TOO!

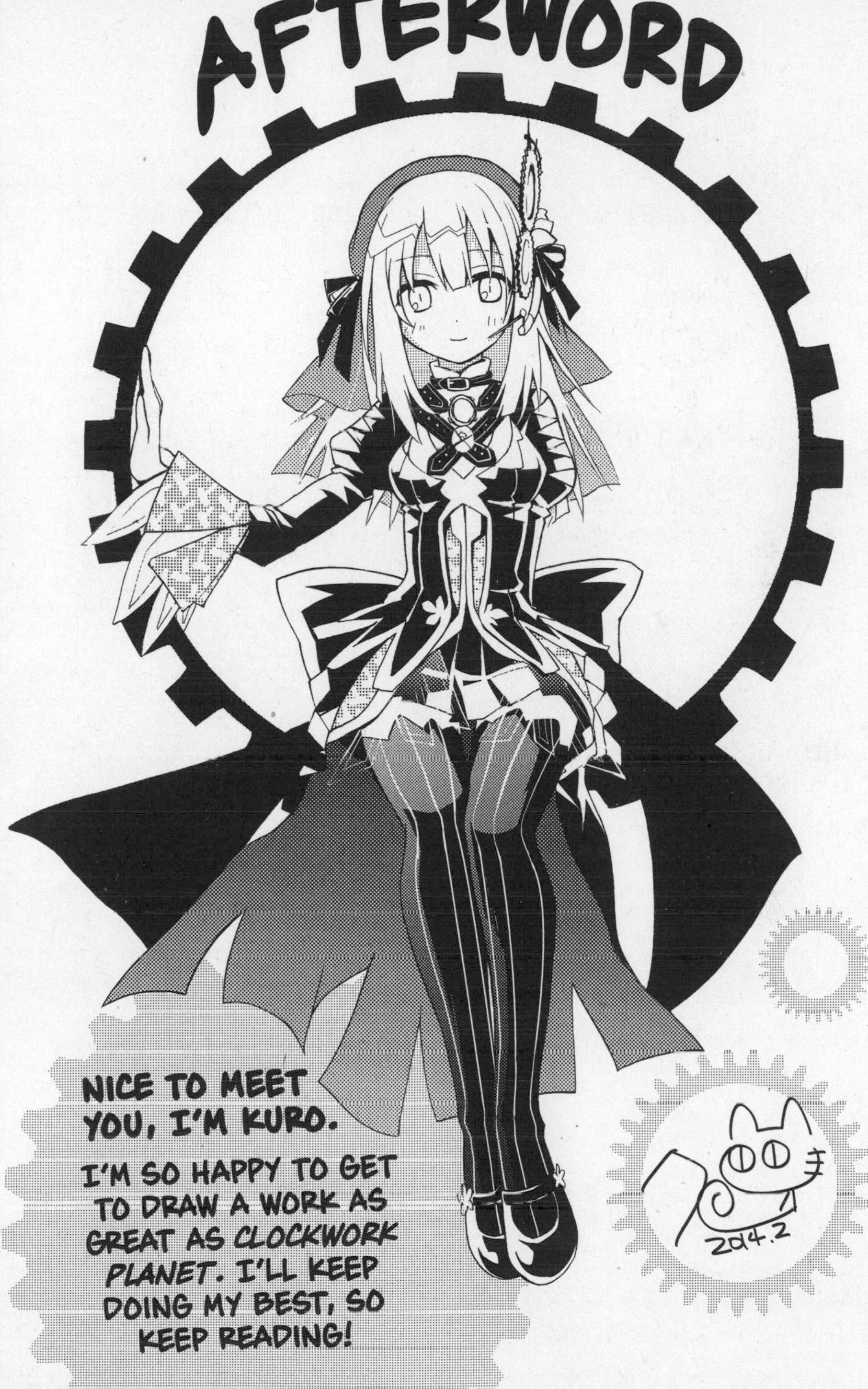
AFTERWORD
NICE TO MEET YOU, I'M KURO.
I'M SO HAPPY TO GET TO DRAW A WORK AS GREAT AS *CLOCKWORK PLANET*. I'LL KEEP DOING MY BEST, SO KEEP READING!
2014.2

⚙ About the Artist ⚙

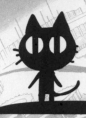

Kuro

From Okayama, lives in Okayama, born August 10, blood type A. Won the 22nd Sirius Rookie Award with the piece titled, "Turn Around." *Clockwork Planet* is her first serialized work.

Kuro's blog is called *elephant* and can be found at: http://elephant.hanagumori.com/

⚙ Original Creators ⚙

Yuu Kamiya

One of Brazil's hottest creators (according to the editor). Co-author of *Clockwork Planet*, author and illustrator of *No Game No Life*, illustrator of *Itsuka Tenma no Kuro-usagi* (*A Dark Rabbit Has seven Lives*), etc.

Tsubaki Himana

One of Japan's hottest writers (according to the editor). Co-author of *Clockwork Planet*.

Sino

One of Japan's hottest illustrators (according to the editor). Illustrator of *Clockwork Planet*, *Kamisama no Inai Nichiyōbi* (*Sunday without God*), *Lance N' Masques*, etc. Apologizes profusely in prostration to Kuro for making RyuZU's design so complicated.

Translation Notes

Machine Nerd, page 12

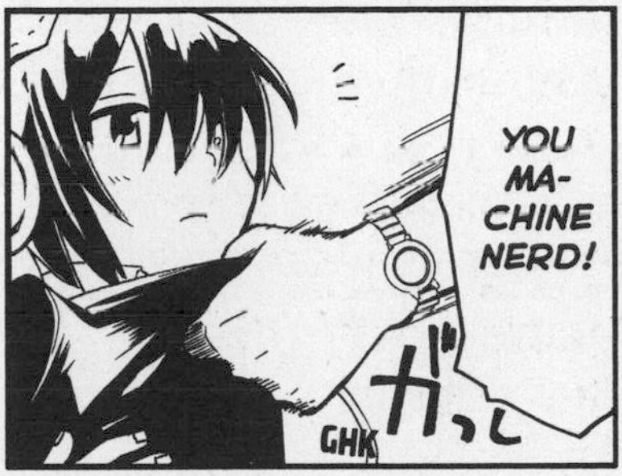
YOU MA-CHINE NERD!
ガっし
GHK

The Japanese phrase used here is *kikai otaku*. *Kikai* means machine and *otaku* describes a fan. There can be many types of *otaku*, from machine to anime, to trains, etc. Often mistakenly appropriated in English as “nerd/geek,” an otaku is an obsessive fan who hoards information and merchandise of their favorite things. The word “otaku” in Japanese is a formal and honorific pronoun that the speaker uses to address “you” or “your family,” reflecting an insider culture that respects each individual as an expert in their own obsession. In general, otaku connotes an inability to function “normally” in society, so Japanese otaku are shamed for it and might try to hide it in their public lives.

Achievements, page 15

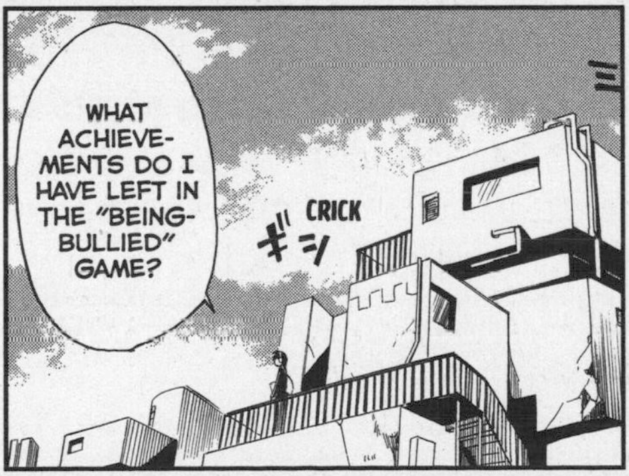
WHAT ACHIEVE-MENTS DO I HAVE LEFT IN THE "BEING-BULLIED" GAME?
ギッ
CRICK

Naoto asks what he has left until *ijime kompuriito*. *Ijime* means bullying; *kompuriito* comes from *complete* and means to complete a collection or “100-percent” a game (in contrast to *kuria*, from *clear*, which means merely beating it).

Automaton, page 16

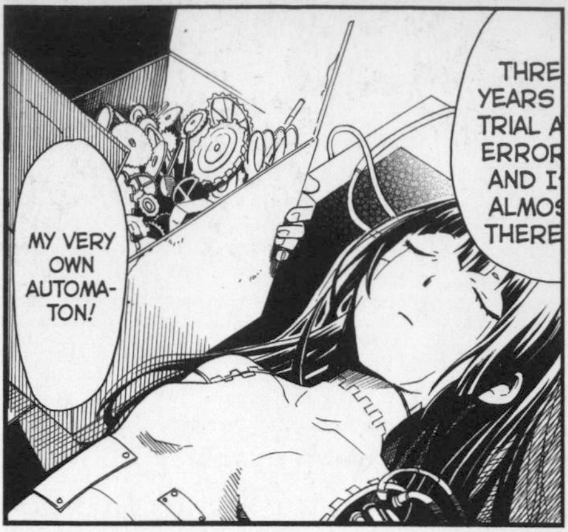
THRE
YEARS
TRIAL A
ERROR
AND I
ALMOS
THERE
MY VERY OWN AUTOMA-TON!

Otomata is Japanese for *automaton*, from the English plural *automata*. Japanese does not require inflection of nouns as singular or plural. Most loanwords from European languages assume their original singular forms regardless of number, but some loanwords assume their original plural forms regardless of number, such as *ōtomata* and *mitokondoria* (mitochondrion).

Master, page 48

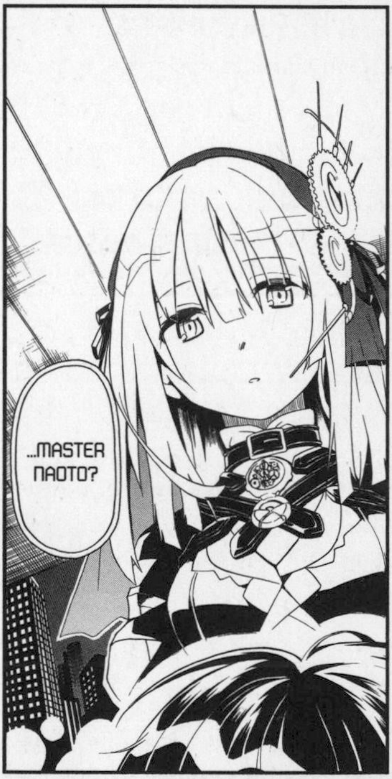
...MASTER NAOTO?

The Japanese original represents the dialogue of groups of various nationalities consistently as Japanese with Japanese honorifics, and so the English translation consistently uses English with English honorifics. For reference, RyuZU's "Master Naoto" and "Miss Marie" are originally "*Naoto-sama*" and "*Marie-sama*," and the Meisters' "Meister Marie" is originally "*Marie-sensei*." In German, normal usage is the masculine term *Meister* and the feminine term *Meisterin*, but English and Japanese both use *meister* for either gender. In the Japanese original, *Meister*, not *sensei*, is used for the free-standing noun.

RyuZU, page 49

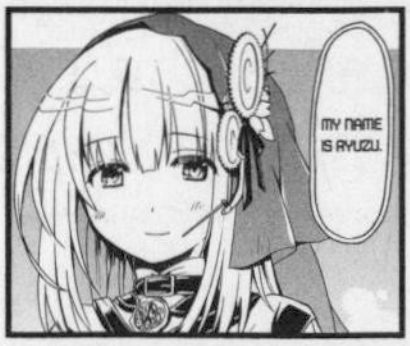
MY NAME IS RYUZU.

RyuZU means "crown," as in "watch crown." The literal meaning is "dragon head."

So sorry, page 51
The deeply serious form of apology seen here is called a *dogeza*, where one sits and bows one's head to the floor.

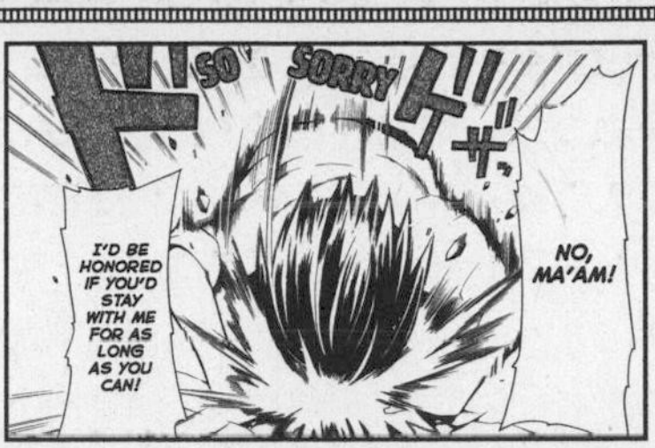
SO SORRY
NO, MA'AM!
I'D BE HONORED IF YOU'D STAY WITH ME FOR AS LONG AS YOU CAN!

One who follows, page 54
Japanese sometimes glosses characters with small ("ruby") characters adjacent to indicate how they should be pronounced. One common creative use of this mechanic is to write what a character means in the main text and what the character says in the gloss ("Who was that ~~girl~~ person you were talking to?"). *Clockwork Planet* introduces key terms with explanatory epithets in the main text and spoken names in the gloss. The English version annotates the epithets.

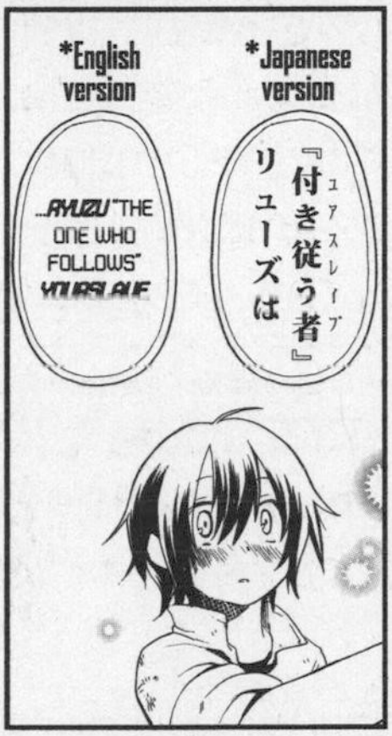
*English version
*Japanese version
...RYUZU "THE ONE WHO FOLLOWS"
『付き従う者』
ユアスレイブ
リューズは

Attendance Award, page 58
In Japan, when a student has perfect attendance in school, they get an award.

Akihabara, page 70
Akihabara is a district of Tokyo famous as a go-to location for otaku, particularly those interested in anime and manga.

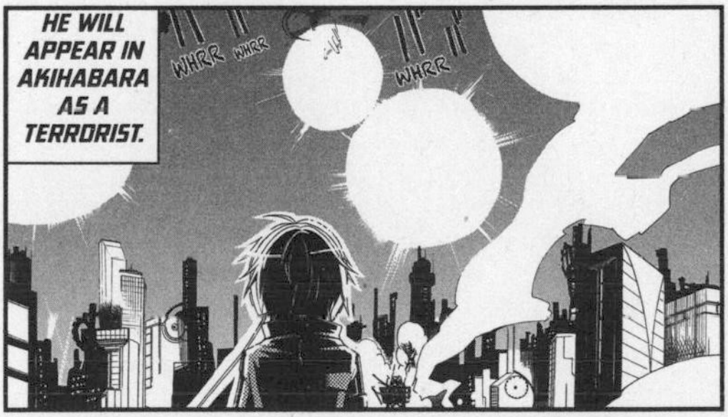
HE WILL APPEAR IN AKIHABARA AS A TERRORIST.
WHRR WHRR
WHRR

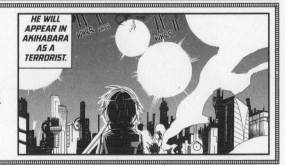

Second-years, page 81
Japanese school has kindergarten, six years of elementary school, three years of junior high, and three years of high school.

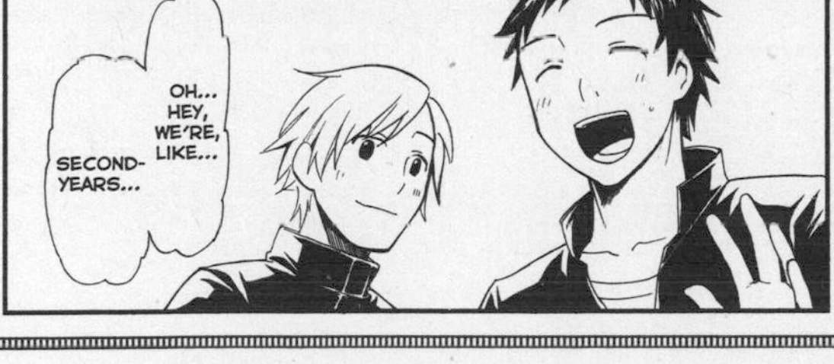
OH... HEY, WE'RE, LIKE...
SECOND-YEARS...

Manga café, page 87
Manga cafés charge patrons by the hour and are known as cheap places to crash.

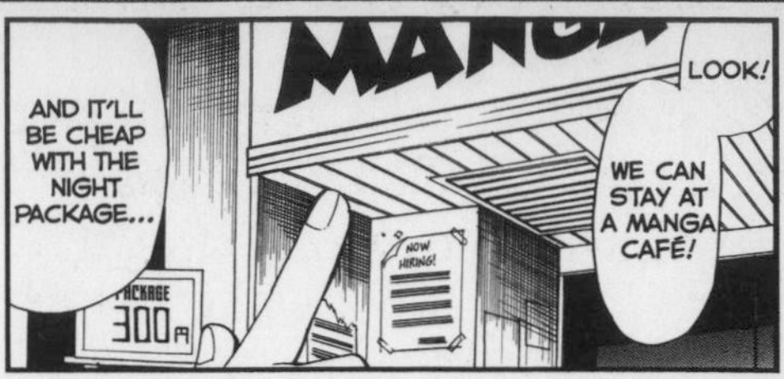
LOOK!
WE CAN STAY AT A MANGA CAFÉ!
AND IT'LL BE CHEAP WITH THE NIGHT PACKAGE...

Fragments, pages 113–114
Heavy use of sentence fragments is a signature of Kamiya's style. Japanese uses fragments slightly more freely than English in general, but Kamiya takes it to frenetic extremes, especially in the early volumes of his novel series *No Game No Life*.

GIVE, page 119
Japan in general doesn't have tipping, but it does have some philanthropy.

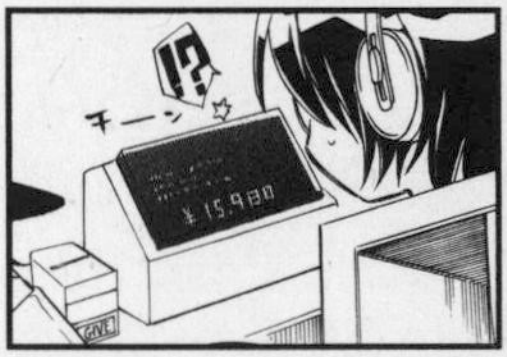
!?
チーン
¥15,980

KODANSHA COMICS

THE HEROIC LEGEND OF ARSLAN

READ THE NEW SERIES FROM THE CREATOR OF FULLMETAL ALCHEMIST, HIROMU ARAKAWA! NOW A HIT TV SERIES!

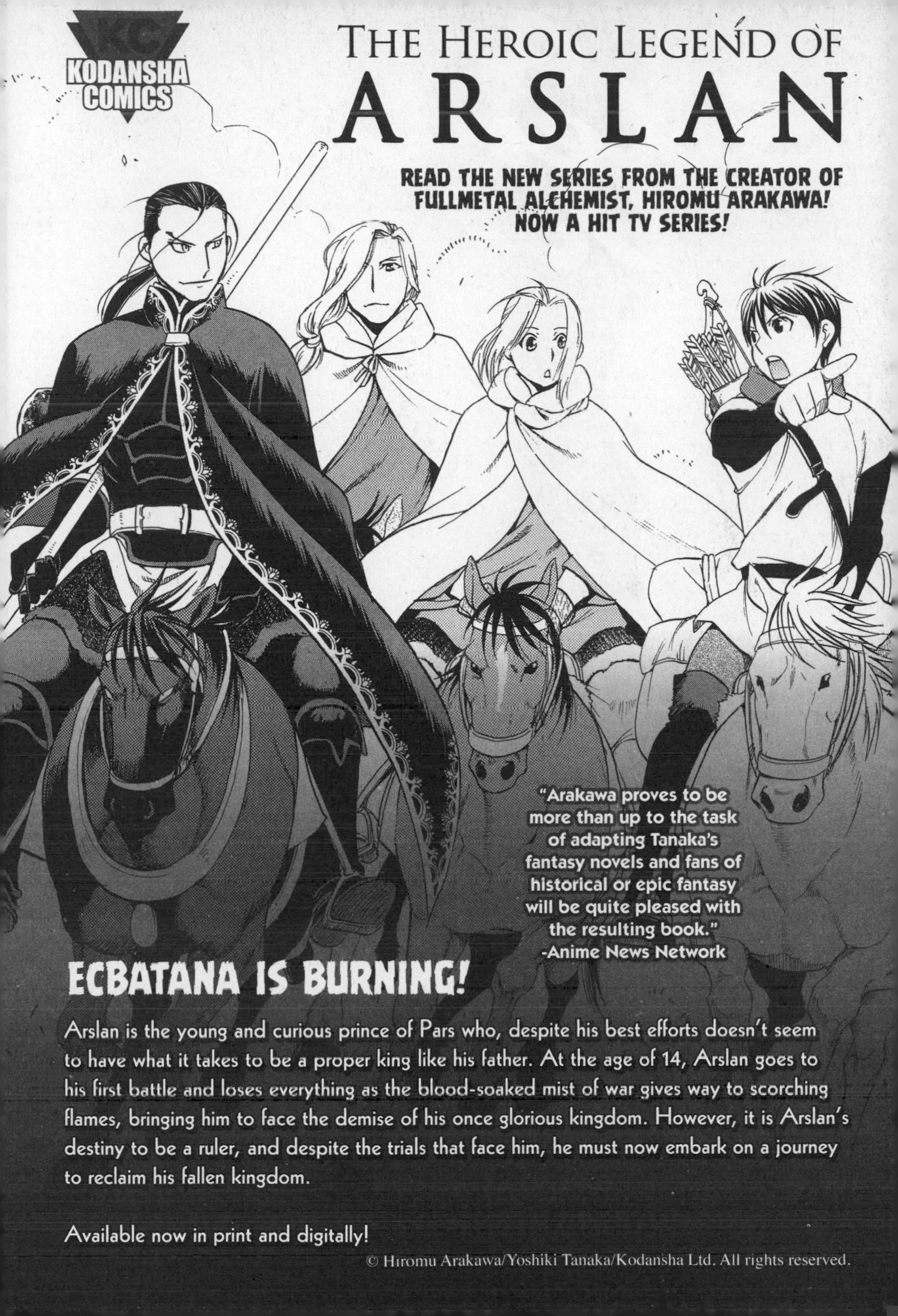

"Arakawa proves to be more than up to the task of adapting Tanaka's fantasy novels and fans of historical or epic fantasy will be quite pleased with the resulting book."
-Anime News Network

ECBATANA IS BURNING!

Arslan is the young and curious prince of Pars who, despite his best efforts doesn't seem to have what it takes to be a proper king like his father. At the age of 14, Arslan goes to his first battle and loses everything as the blood-soaked mist of war gives way to scorching flames, bringing him to face the demise of his once glorious kingdom. However, it is Arslan's destiny to be a ruler, and despite the trials that face him, he must now embark on a journey to reclaim his fallen kingdom.

Available now in print and digitally!

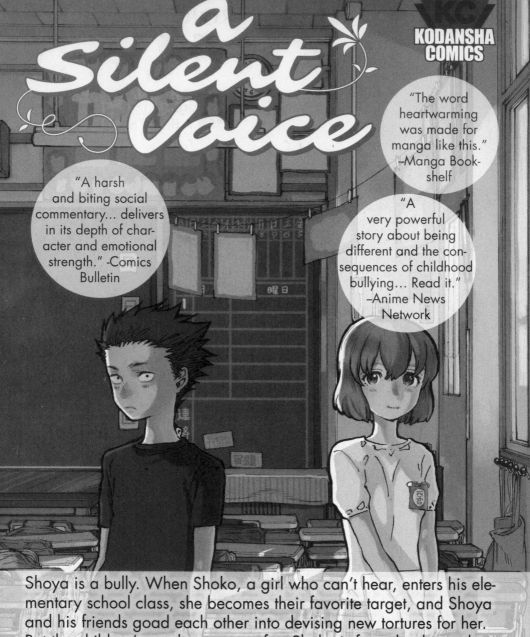

a Silent Voice

KODANSHA COMICS

"The word heartwarming was made for manga like this." –Manga Book-shelf

"A harsh and biting social commentary… delivers in its depth of char-acter and emotional strength." -Comics Bulletin

"A very powerful story about being different and the con-sequences of childhood bullying… Read it." –Anime News Network

Shoya is a bully. When Shoko, a girl who can't hear, enters his ele-mentary school class, she becomes their favorite target, and Shoya and his friends goad each other into devising new tortures for her. But the children's cruelty goes too far. Shoko is forced to leave the school, and Shoya ends up shouldering all the blame. Six years lat-er, the two meet again. Can Shoya make up for his past mistakes, or is it too late?

Available now in print and digitally!

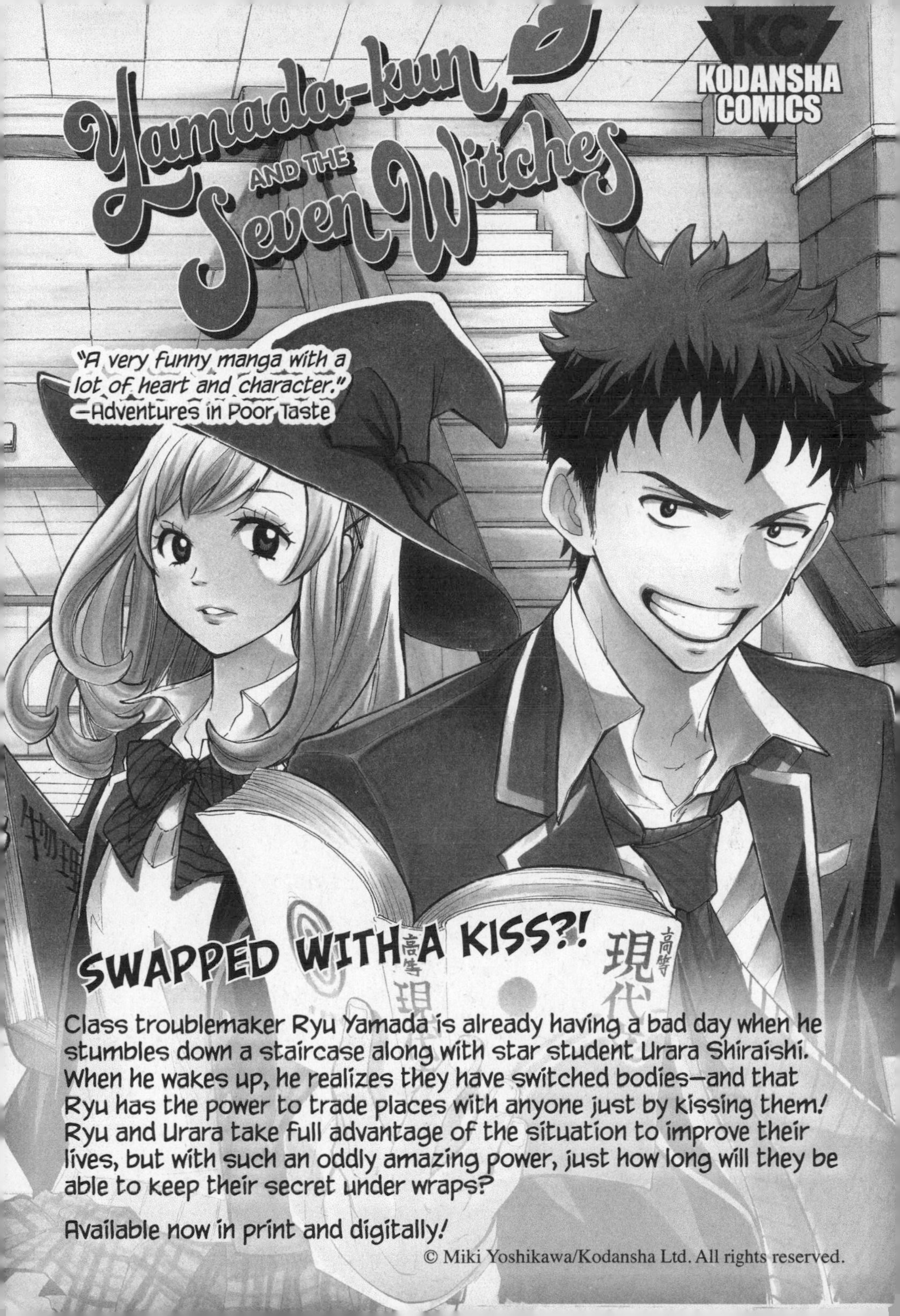
KC KODANSHA COMICS
Yamada-kun AND THE Seven Witches
"A very funny manga with a lot of heart and character."
—Adventures in Poor Taste
SWAPPED WITH A KISS?!
Class troublemaker Ryu Yamada is already having a bad day when he stumbles down a staircase along with star student Urara Shiraishi. When he wakes up, he realizes they have switched bodies—and that Ryu has the power to trade places with anyone just by kissing them! Ryu and Urara take full advantage of the situation to improve their lives, but with such an oddly amazing power, just how long will they be able to keep their secret under wraps?
Available now in print and digitally!
© Miki Yoshikawa/Kodansha Ltd. All rights reserved.

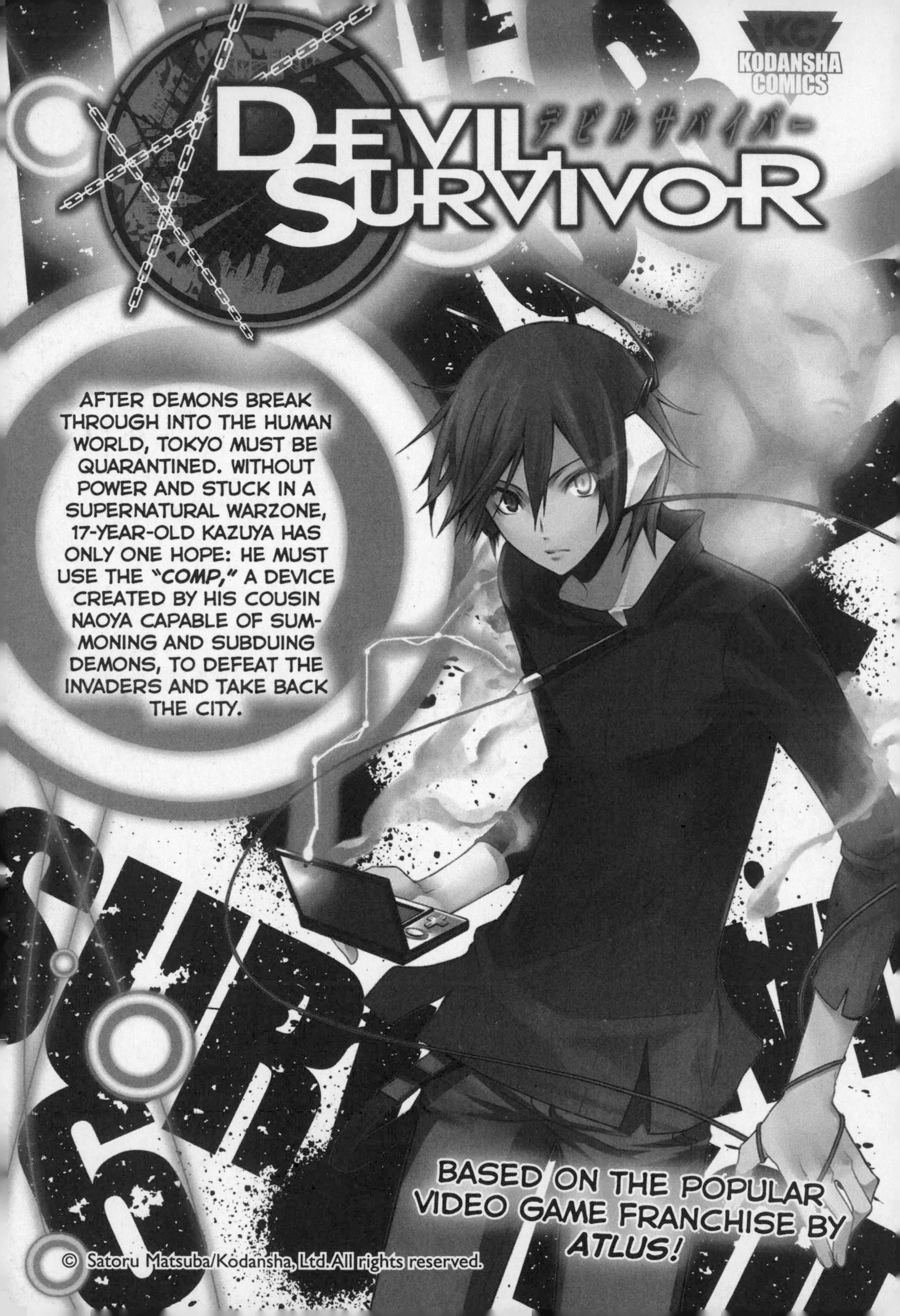
KODANSHA COMICS
DEVIL SURVIVOR
デビルサバイバー
AFTER DEMONS BREAK THROUGH INTO THE HUMAN WORLD, TOKYO MUST BE QUARANTINED. WITHOUT POWER AND STUCK IN A SUPERNATURAL WARZONE, 17-YEAR-OLD KAZUYA HAS ONLY ONE HOPE: HE MUST USE THE "COMP," A DEVICE CREATED BY HIS COUSIN NAOYA CAPABLE OF SUMMONING AND SUBDUING DEMONS, TO DEFEAT THE INVADERS AND TAKE BACK THE CITY.
BASED ON THE POPULAR VIDEO GAME FRANCHISE BY ATLUS!
© Satoru Matsuba/Kodansha, Ltd. All rights reserved.

A Kodansha Comics Trade Paperback Original
Clockwork Planet volume 1 copyright © 2014 Yuu Kamiya/Tsubaki Himana/Sino/Kuro
English translation copyright © 2017 Yuu Kamiya/Tsubaki Himana/Sino/Kuro
All rights reserved.

Published in the United States by Kodansha Comics, an imprint of
Kodansha USA Publishing, LLC, New York.

Publication rights for this English edition arranged through
Kodansha Ltd, Tokyo.

First published in Japan in 2014 by Kodansha Ltd., Tokyo

ISBN 978-1-63236-447-0

Printed in the United States of America.

www.kodanshacomics.com

9 8 7 6 5 4 3 2 1
Translation: Daniel Komen
Lettering: David Yoo
Editing: Haruko Hashimoto
Kodansha Comics edition cover design by Phil Balsman